Men, ideas and tanks

11-12-96

War, Armed Forces and Society

General Editor: Ian F.W. Beckett

Men, ideas and tanks

British military thought
and armoured forces,
1903–1939

J.P. Harris

Manchester University Press
Manchester and New York

distributed exclusively in the USA and Canada by St. Martin's Press

Copyright © J.P. Harris 1995

Published by Manchester University Press
Oxford Road, Manchester M13 9NR, UK
and Room 400, 175 Fifth Avenue, New York, NY 10010, USA

Distributed exclusively in the USA and Canada
by St. Martin's Press, Inc., 175 Fifth Avenue, New York,
NY 10010, USA

British Library Cataloguing-in-Publication Data
A catalogue record for this book is available from the British Library

Library of Congress Cataloging-in-Publication Data applied for
Harris, J.P.
    Men, ideas, and tanks : British military thought and armoured
forces, 1903–1939 / J.P. Harris.
        p. cm.
    Includes bibliographical references and index.
    1. Great Britain. Army—Armored troops—History. I. Title.
UE57.H37   1996
358'.18'094109041—dc20   95–21173
                                                          CIP

ISBN 0 7190 3762 X *hardback*
     0 7190 4814 1 *paperback*

First published 1995

99 98 97 96 95   10 9 8 7 6 5 4 3 2 1

Typeset in Hong Kong
by Graphicraft Typesetters Ltd., Hong Kong

Printed in Great Britain
by Biddles Ltd., Guildford and King's Lynn

Contents

Figures and maps

Figures

Maps

Acknowledgements

Many people have helped with the research for this book. Three principal archive centres were used: the Public Record Office at Kew, the Liddell Hart Centre for Military Archives at King's College London and the Tank Museum at Bovington. Archives at the National Maritime Museum at Greenwich, the National Army Museum at Chelsea, the Imperial War Museum, Churchill College Cambridge, the University of Birmingham and the Army Staff College at Camberley were also consulted, though to a much lesser extent. Thanks are due to the archivists at all these institutions for their assistance and courtesy, and especially to Mr David Fletcher of the Tank Museum and Patricia Methven and Kate O'Brien of the Liddell Hart Centre at King's. Mr A.J. Williams of the Public Record Office gave considerable assistance through his (as yet unpublished) guide to sources in the PRO relating to armoured warfare and the mechanization of the British Army. Mr Andrew Orgill and his staff at the Central Library of the Royal Military Academy Sandhurst were enormously helpful in procuring published sources.

The following people read substantial sections (in some cases virtually all) of the book in draft and made valuable comments: Dr Stephen Badsey, Professor Ian Beckett, Mr Lloyd Clark, Mr David Fletcher, Dr David French, Dr Paddy Griffith, Professor Richard Ogorkiewicz, Dr John Pimlott, Dr Gary Sheffield, Mr Peter Simkins and Mr Keith Simpson. Mr Mike Taylor also gave useful advice. Dr Christopher Duffy's encouragement and counsel helped the author through some difficult times. David Fletcher deserves particular gratitude. Throughout the project he gave unstintingly of his time and expertise. The book could scarcely have been written without his assistance.

Thanks are also due to Professor John Gooch for his willingness to recommend the project to Manchester University Press when it was first suggested and to Professor Ian Beckett for continuous support in his capacity as General Editor of the *War, Armed Forces and Society* series. Jane Thorniley-Walker, as History Editor of Manchester University Press, was unfailingly courteous and helpful.

All errors of fact and interpretation are, of course, the responsibility of the author alone.

To the memory of my mother,
Margaret Thelma Harris

Introduction

Armoured forces have played a crucial role in many of the wars of the twentieth century and their origins and early development thus form a subject of considerable historical importance. The British experience is of particular significance and interest. The British were the first to develop the tank, the first to use it in action and could reasonably claim to be world leaders, both theoretically and practically, in military mechanization, until the early 1930s. It cannot be said that the early evolution of British armoured forces is a neglected subject – vast numbers of books and articles have appeared. The present work, however, makes much use of some underexploited primary sources (especially for the period of the First World War) and presents some new interpretations.

The historiography of this subject has, of course, been massively influenced by the writings of Major-General J.F.C. Fuller and Sir Basil Liddell Hart, especially by those of the latter. Even before returning to the primary sources there are reasons to suspect that these dominating influences may not have been altogether healthy. Some unsavoury aspects of Fuller's life and thought have been well known for a long time. Fuller made no effort to conceal his involvement with occultism and (at one period) the "magician" Aleister Crowley on the one hand, or with Oswald Mosley, anti-Semitism and Fascism on the other. But despite the doubts which these might be thought to cast on his judgement, many of his views on British tank forces and the British high command in the First World War are still taken remarkably seriously by some scholars. The unreliability of Liddell Hart as a historian of his own times (especially with regard to issues in which he was personally involved) has been highlighted by John Mearsheimer. But there has been no general re-evaluation of the early history of British armoured forces since the publication of *Liddell Hart and the Weight of History*.[1]

The development of British armoured forces in the first half of the twentieth century was, perhaps, the aspect of British military history which Liddell Hart was most successful in making his own. For that reason alone a revisionist work might seem to be required. It must be recognized, however, that Liddell Hart's monumental *The Tanks*,[2] his history of the Royal Tank Regiment and its antecedents, is in most respects a very good book, possibly his best. The discipline of writing regimental history, which involved submitting his drafts for scrutiny by the regiment's representatives, seems to have forced him to stick to the facts more and ride his hobby-horses less than he did in many of his other writings. *The Tanks*, though undocumented, is a work of impressive scholarship and, while its interpretations are sometimes questionable, is generally accurate in matters of fact. No attempt is made here to replace it as a regimental history.

The present work is not the history of a regiment but primarily a history of ideas. British thought on the use of armour began before any organization existed to man tanks and was never confined to the Royal Tank Regiment or its antecedents. In that sense the focus of this book is somewhat wider than that of the first volume of *The Tanks* which could not escape viewing matters from the perspective of a particular institution. On the other hand no attempt is made in the present work to narrate battles or exercises in the sort of detail found in Liddell Hart's regimental history. Battles and exercises could not, of course, be altogether omitted. Military thought has to be judged to a great extent in terms of its influence on them and they in turn play a vital role in shaping military thought. But it is the evolution of military ideas which is the focus of this study, not the ebb and flow of battle or the development of any one military institution.

The focus of this book is on what might be described as the main stream of British military thought about armoured forces. This was concerned with their employment against first class European powers in the principal theatres of operations. Readers will have to look elsewhere for discussions of the use of armoured cars by the Duke of Westminster against the Senussi tribesmen or by T.E. Lawrence in support of the Arabian revolt or of the use of tanks at the Third Battle of Gaza. The extraordinary exploits of Locker Lampson and his armoured cars in eastern Europe have also been omitted on the grounds that they had no discernible influence on the evolution of British military thought. Nor will the reader find much here about the employment of armour in colonial policing situations, or on the North West Frontier of India, between the world wars. The development of ideas about the use of armoured forces in low intensity conflict is an interesting subject in itself and perhaps a particularly significant one for modern Western armour, the main employment of which in the immediate future may be in peacekeeping and "peace support" operations. It is, however, a rather different subject from that considered in the following pages.

Notes

1 J. Mearsheimer, *Liddell Hart and the Weight of History* (Cornell) 1988, passim.
2 B.H. Liddell Hart, *The Tanks, The History of the Tank Regiment and its Predecessors* (2 Vols) (Cassell) 1959.

1

Genesis

In December 1903 a remarkable science fiction story, "The Land Ironclads", appeared in the *Strand* magazine. It was by Herbert George Wells, then aged thirty-seven and, with tales like "The Time Machine" (1895) and "The Invisible Man" (1897), already establishing himself as a master of the genre. The child of increasingly impoverished lower middle class parents – his father a failed shopkeeper and his mother a household servant – Wells had been for some years apprenticed to a draper. He was largely self-educated until, by competitive examination, he obtained a free studentship to study science at Imperial College in Kensington in 1884. Mainly because his interests were diverted into literature and Socialist politics, he failed his third year examinations and did not complete his B.Sc. until 1890. In the meantime he became a teacher and branched out into journalism and popular writing, his output including novels like *Love and Mr. Lewisham* (1900) as well as science fiction stories. His central preoccupation was the future of mankind, particular interests including human sexual relations (of which he had extensive practical experience), the achievement of a more equitable social order, technology and war.[1]

"The Land Ironclads" is one of Wells's most prescient tales. Its subject is a war between two unnamed countries, one tradition-bound and agrarian, the other scientific, industrial and innovative. Though, from a modern perspective, the story seems prophetic of the tactical conditions of the Western Front 1914–18 it is not clear that the setting is European. When it was first published the South African War had been over for only about a year and a half and the agrarian economy, outdoor lifestyle and unreflective outlook of the defeated side are strongly suggestive of the Boers.[2]

The story opens with a conversation between a war correspondent and a lieutenant. The latter is peering out across No Man's Land from his own side's trenches to those of the enemy. Nothing is happening. Only one enemy soldier is visible and he is staring back at them with his own field glasses.

"And this is war!" exclaims the exasperated correspondent.
"No, it's Bloch," replies the subaltern.

The lieutenant's reply must have puzzled many of Wells's readers. The reference is to I.S. Bloch, the Polish banker who had written a six volume treatise on the future of war, a version of which appeared in an English edition entitled, *Is War Now Impossible?* in 1899.[3] On the basis of the advantage to the defender accruing from the firepower of modern weapons Bloch had predicted an entrenched miltary stalemate in the next European war. Protracted stalemate would result in prodigious strain on the belligerents and might result in economic and social collapse. In the middle of the First World War Wells was to return to Bloch's work, commenting:

> There has been no escaping Bloch after all and the deadlock, if no sudden peace occurs, can end now in only one thing, the exhaustion in varying degrees of all the combatants and the succumbing of the most exhausted. The idea of a conclusive end of the traditional pattern to this war, of a triumphal entry into London, Paris, Berlin or Moscow is to be dismissed altogether from our calculations. The end of this war will be a matter of negotiations between practically immobilized and extremely shattered antagonists.[4]

But, in "The Land Ironclads", written over a decade before the war, Wells *had* seen a means of escaping Bloch. In that story the deadlock has set in very shortly after the opening of hostilities: "To begin with they had had an almost scampering time; the invader had come across the frontier behind a cloud of cyclists and cavalry", but had been brought up short by "a line of prepared defences". The invader had also begun "grubbing trenches for himself as though he meant to sit down there to the end of time". Yet politically the invader cannot afford deadlock. As the lieutenant points out to the war correspondent: "They've got to win or else they lose. A draw's a win for our side."

During the night, after a mere month of stalemate, black and sinister shapes emerge from No Man's Land, shining searchlights before them. These are, of course, the "Land Ironclads" of the title. Science has found the answer and the "rowdy-dowdy cowpunchers and nigger-whackers" of the agrarian state are swiftly and decisively defeated by "the civilized men" of the other side.[5]

The ability of an industrial society to triumph over a rugged but unreflective culture of the outdoors seems to have been Wells's moral. There are distinct echoes here of the recently concluded South African War and fainter ones of the more distant American Civil War. Yet the story looks forward as well as back. There is a specific reference to Bloch and Bloch's prophecies were not primarily concerned with conflicts involving the "nigger-whacking" settlers of extra-European territories. They dealt with future war between developed states, especially with those between the European Great Powers. It was in Europe that such masses of men equipped with the latest weapons were likely to be assembled in such relatively confined spaces that continuous and virtually unbreakable fronts might be formed. That was the situation which in Wells's fiction and ultimately in historical reality produced "land ironclads".

How prophetic was Wells's vision of the technical side of armoured mobility? About eighty to a hundred feet long, the ironclads were, he explains, "essentially . . . narrow and very strong steel frameworks carrying the engines and borne upon eight pairs of big pedrail wheels, each about ten feet in diameter". These wheels were protected by an armoured "adjustable skirt" which appears to have been connected with an "iron top-cover".[6] The size appears with hindsight distinctly excessive and the structure somewhat bizarre. Wells's clear indication of steam as the power source appears curiously backward-looking when the internal combustion engine was already powering road vehicles, including experimental war cars.[7] To say that the Pedrail, a type of footed wheel, was a poor solution to the problem of cross-country mobility for a large armoured fighting vehicle would probably be an understatement. Yet its inventor, Mr B.J. Diplock, one of only two real people to be mentioned in the story (the other being I.S. Bloch), was eventually to become a manufacturer of caterpillar tracks. In this capacity he was, in 1915, to play a walk-on part in the drama of the evolution of the tank – a particularly curious example of Wells's fiction anticipating fact.[8]

Wells's treatment of weaponry and firepower also seems, with the benefit of hindsight, to have some odd aspects. The machine gun is mentioned but not given a very central role. In this respect Wells's vision accorded with rather than surpassed that of the European General Staffs of his day.[9] The stalemate in "The Land Ironclads" is to be produced mainly by the rifle. But this was probably also the case on the Western Front in 1914[10] when the scale of issue of machine guns was quite limited. Machine guns proliferated rapidly, however, and their importance had become so well established by 1915 that when tanks were being developed they were sometimes referred to as "machine gun destroyers".[11] The neutralizing of machine guns together with the crushing or removal of barbed wire (not mentioned at all by Wells) became their primary tactical roles.

The machine gun was also one of the main weapons installed in the first British tanks. Wells's ironclads, on the other hand, rely upon semi-automatic rifles protruding through port-holes in their sides. These rifles are operated from small cabins within the gigantic pedrail wheels by means of "the most remarkable sights imaginable which threw a bright little camera-obscura picture into the light tight box in which the riflemen sat below". Such technology seems over-elaborate and inappropriate for the task of shooting men densely packed in trenches to which Wells's ironclads move parallel and which they attack from fairly close range.[12]

Yet Wells did see with great clarity some of the main points about contemporary weaponry. He noted, of course, the paralysing effect on infantry tactics of the massed fire of magazine rifles – the whole story was founded on that. He correctly anticipated that artillery would be the main potential enemy of the "ironclad". Yet he also accurately predicted that there would be a tendency to move artillery back from the front line and an increasing emphasis on the counter-battery role. This would leave the guns badly positioned to deal with the new kind of threat which ironclads would pose:

> The defender had relied largely upon his rifles in the event of an assault. His guns he kept concealed at various points upon and beyond the ridge ready to bring them into action against any artillery preparation for an attack.

In Wells's story the gunners of the defending side make efforts to bring their pieces forward to engage the ironclads by direct fire and some ironclads sustain damage from this cause. But generally the artillery cannot change position quickly enough to prevent the defenders' trench system being overrun.[13]

Some of the tactics of Wells's ironclads are considerably in advance of anything which became possible in the First World War. They cross No Man's Land while it is still dark and use powerful searchlights both to see their way and to blind enemy infantry – a concept of the use of light as a weapon which was to engage some later British thinkers on armoured warfare.[14] They are so close to the defenders' first line of trenches by daylight that his use of artillery is seriously impaired.[15]

Wells did not see the need for his armoured fighting vehicles to co-operate very intimately with other arms. It is only when the ironclads have cleared the defenders' trenches that the attacker's cyclist infantry advance "in open order but unmolested to complete the work of the machines".[16] In stressing the independent action of armoured fighting vehicles and downplaying the need for inter-arm co-operation Wells was anticipating a trend in the thinking of British tank officers which was to emerge strongly after the First World War. It had results generally much less favourable than the outcome of the ironclads' operation in Wells's story.

Wells's "The Land Ironclads" was not of course the first the world had heard of fighting vehicles for use on land. Chariots had been a commonplace in the ancient world and war wagons of various kinds were known in the Middle Ages. The idea of an armoured fighting vehicle had been bandied about quite frequently since the Renaissance. In the early 1480s Leonardo da Vinci had written to Ludovico Sforza indicating that he was:

> building secure and covered chariots which are invulnerable and when they advance with their guns into the midst of the foe, even the largest enemy masses must retreat; and behind them infantry can follow in safety and without opposition.[17]

Nicolas-Joseph Cugnot, an officer serving with the Austrian Army in the Netherlands, was apparently attempting to develop a steam locomotive wagon from the early 1750s. His superiors were unimpressed.[18] Apparently having left the Austrian service after the Seven Years' War, between 1769 and 1771 he built two such vehicles as experimental gun tractors for General Gribeauval, the

French Army's head of artillery. They worked up to a point but were very slow and had to stop frequently to get up steam. The project was abandoned in 1771 after loss of ministerial patronage.[19]

The idea of a steam-powered, wheeled armoured vehicle had been patented in Great Britain as early as 1855. By the end of the nineteenth century Gottlieb Daimler's invention of the internal combustion engine had made the armoured car a practical military possibility. In 1902 Frederick Simms exhibited at the Crystal Palace a "motor war car" which was protected by bullet proof armour and which mounted Maxim guns in revolving turrets. Paul Daimler, Gottlieb's son, produced a similar vehicle in 1904 which he exhibited, without arousing real interest, to the Austrian and German military authorities. Armoured cars were thus a rather commonplace idea by 1914. But most European armies remained to be convinced of their utility and none were in service with the forces of belligerent powers.[20]

The technology necessary for an armoured cross-country vehicle also existed. The caterpillar track was already used in agriculture in the United States and several people had thought of the idea of using it for military purposes. A design for a caterpillar tracked military vehicle in most ways similar to and in some ways surpassing the 1916 tank had been offered to the British War Office in 1912. Its designer was Lancelot de Mole, an Australian who was to serve as a corporal in his country's infantry during the First World War. But de Mole's fairly satisfactory design submitted direct to the appropriate authority two years before the war had no influence at all on the development of British tanks during the First World War. His proposal was shelved and completely forgotten.[21] De Mole had considerable mechanical aptitude but what he had not supplied was a vision of the military circumstances which would create the need for his device.[22]

The initial, mobile phase of the First World War on the Western Front led to the rapid development of armoured cars by the Belgians and the British. To begin with civilian touring cars were fitted with machine guns. Later some armour was improvised. In the British forces armoured fighting vehicles were pioneered by perhaps the least probable branch of the armed services – the Royal Naval Air Service (RNAS) – the predecessor of the Fleet Air Arm.[23]

The impetus behind the British development of armoured cars

Figure 1 Churchill as First Lord of the Admiralty in the company of naval officers.

came from the First Lord of the Admiralty, Winston Churchill, in the sense that it was he who pitched the Royal Navy into military operations on the continent of Europe. Not yet forty, his life had already been crammed with action. Descendant of the first Duke of Marlborough, son of a Conservative politician and an American mother, educated at Harrow and Sandhurst, he was a former cavalry officer, former war correspondent, successful escapee from a Boer prison camp, ex-Tory MP and now a member of a Liberal Cabinet. His most obvious characteristics were demonic energy and a vivid imagination, though these were coupled with working methods which sometimes struck others as unbusinesslike and inconsiderate. He had driving ambition but this was not merely self-serving. Possessed of a strong sense of history, Churchill was devoted to the pursuit of the interests, as he saw them, of Great Britain and its Empire.[24]

On 27 August, as the Allied armies were being swept out of Belgium, a brigade of marines under Brigadier General G.G. Aston was, on Churchill's instructions, landed at Ostend. They were joined by a squadron of the Royal Naval Air Service (RNAS) which flew out from its base at Eastchurch. The Belgians were still holding out in Antwerp and Churchill had the idea of somehow assisting them and in the process tying down German forces and taking pressure off the British Expeditionary Force (BEF). The Eastchurch squadron of the RNAS was led by Commander C.R. Samson. On 28 August, the day after the arrival of British forces at Ostend, Samson was asked by General Aston to conduct a motor car reconnaissance in the direction of Bruges and this was duly carried out. The Royal Navy's forces remained only a few days at Ostend, receiving the order to evacuate on 30 August. But Samson, by nature a fire-eater, was reluctant to leave the Continent and the prospect of action for the quiet of Eastchurch. He used the excuse of a mist over the channel to land at Dunkirk and there, with the encouragement of the local British consul, he found justification for remaining.[25]

Samson's instincts accorded well with those of the First Lord. Churchill was keen to be in the thick of the action and the war at sea was not sufficiently intense to absorb his energies. There were rumours of the Germans preparing to mount Zeppelin (airship) raids on the British homeland. The War Office was desperately overworked and according to Churchill, "On the 3rd September 1914, Lord Kitchener asked me as First Lord of the Admiralty, to undertake responsibilty for the aerial defence of Great Britain against attacks by aircraft and particularly by Zeppelins, and this arrangement was subsequently confirmed by the Cabinet." Churchill was thus able to justify the maintenance of a naval detachment at Dunkirk on the grounds that it permitted air reconnaissance further inland from the Channel coast than was possible from aerodromes in Britain and that such reconnaissance would be useful in pinpointing the bases of German airships. According to Commodore Murray Sueter, the Director of the Air Department at the Admiralty, Churchill was encouraged to pursue this policy by the Foreign Office who, apparently prompted by the British consul, believed that the stationing of a Royal Navy force at Dunkirk would be good for local French morale.[26]

Replying to a memorandum from Churchill dated 1 September, Commodore Sueter recommended that the proposed base at Dunkirk be supplied with fifty armed motor cars to assist in forming temporary forward airfields "so as to enable aeroplanes to extend their flights to a greater distance". Characteristically Churchill authorized double the number of motor vehicles Sueter had

Figure 2 A relatively primitive Rolls-Royce armoured car of Samson's "Dunkirk Circus" with members of the Life Guards on the Menin Road.

proposed. Cars and lorries were actually used not only to assist in the establishment of temporary airfields but also to rescue crashed airmen and to run their own patrols. It seems that machine guns were fitted from the outset. Later armour began to be improvised using steel plate supplied by a local firm but it was not very effective.[27]

Sueter rose to the challenge. Forty-two years of age in 1914, the son of a fleet paymaster, he had been in the Royal Navy since he was fourteen. Technically minded and by nature innovative, he had worked with the first submarines to enter British service, took a strong interest in the development of airships for naval use, and, in 1912, was appointed Director of the Admiralty Air Department (which controlled the RNAS). The Air Department was directly answerable to the First Lord of the Admiralty rather than to any of the Sea Lords and Churchill tended to treat it as a personal fief. In the autumn of 1914, in support of what became unofficially known as "The Dunkirk Circus", Sueter established an RNAS Armoured Car centre at Wormwood Scrubs and initiated trials to discover the thickness of armour plate necessary to keep out German rifle bullets at various ranges. A variety of armoured cars

Figure 3   A 1914 Admiralty pattern Rolls-Royce armoured car mounting a Vickers gun in a revolving turret. By the time this excellent vehicle entered service the war of movement on the Western Front was over.

and lorries were produced. By December 1914 the classic Rolls-Royce armoured car which mounted a machine gun in a revolving turret had been developed from the Silver Ghost touring car. It, together with other varieties, was to serve in several theatres for the rest of the war. An Armoured Car Division of the RNAS had emerged.[28]

By early 1915 the force at Dunkirk had seventy armoured cars and lorries in addition to its aircraft.[29] But by the time its design had achieved some sophistication the armoured car had become virtually obsolete as far as the Western Front was concerned. The war had bogged down and the continuous lines of entrenchment prophesied by Bloch and Wells were being established. Though it was really no business of the Admiralty's, Churchill was soon asking Sueter to devise means of helping the infantry to cross No Man's Land and attack trench systems.[30]

Colonel Ernest Dunlop Swinton is, perhaps, the individual most commonly regarded as the father of the tank. (Whether this reputation is really justified will be explored below.) Born in Bangalore, India, in 1868, the son of a judge, he was commissioned into the

Figure 4
Ernest Swinton as a young officer.

Royal Engineers from Woolwich in 1888. After serving in the South African War he commenced, while still in the Army, a successful career as a writer of a sort of military fiction, producing *The Defence of Duffer's Drift* – an amusingly presented manual of minor tactics – in 1903. He followed this with a collection of stories entitled *The Green Curve* (1909). In 1910 he was brought into the historical section of the Committee of Imperial Defence (CID) to work on the history of the Russo-Japanese War and he became one of that organization's Assistant Secretaries in 1913. He was thus familiar with Whitehall and had some useful, highly placed contacts. His service on the CID coupled with his literary reputation led to his appointment, in 1914, as the official war correspondent. In this post he had a monopoly of the relaying of news from the front to the British press, ordinary newspaper men having been banned from the war zone.[31]

Swinton claims in his memoirs that he had been told before the war of the existence of a type of caterpillar tractor manufactured in the United States by the firm of Holt. His informant, Mr Hugh F. Marriot, a mining engineer he had met in South Africa, suggested that the vehicle's remarkable cross-country performance might allow it some military application. Observing developments on the Western Front during 1914, Swinton was reminded of Marriot's suggestion.[32]

On a visit to London on 20 October 1914 he had a conversation with his former chief, Colonel Maurice Hankey, previously secretary of the CID, now a factotum for the Prime Minister. They continued their discussions over lunch the following day. On the second occasion Captain Tulloch, an artillery officer who had conceived the idea of constructing a large fighting vehicle before the war, was also present. Precisely what was said on either occasion cannot now be known. But all three involved later gave evidence that the possible use of caterpillar tracks for a trench-crossing military vehicle had come up in the course of the second conversation.[33] There is also one critical piece of written evidence – a letter from Swinton to Hankey written from GHQ in France and dated 11 November 1914:

Re Caterpillar

I put your idea before Gen. Fowler the Chief Engineer on 22. 10. He wrote to the W.O. . . . . Whether it is the result of this or of the original information given by me (from Marriot) before the war, Marriot tells me that several have been ordered. This may be for purely tractive purposes, or for bursting in against positions as suggested by you.[34]

Taken at face value this letter suggests that it was Hankey rather than Swinton who proposed the use of an armoured assault vehicle mounted on caterpillar tracks. But it is possible that Swinton was employing the old trick of trying to get an influential person to take an interest in a project by persuading him that the project was really his own idea. Hankey never claimed to have been the first to suggest a caterpillar tracked assault vehicle. Indeed, he gave evidence after the war that he thought Swinton had first suggested the idea to him.[35]

Any claim that Hankey played a significant part in the genesis of the tank must be based on his paper dated 28 December 1914, sometimes known as the "Boxing Day Memorandum". Addressed to the Cabinet, this contained a general review of the strategic situation. Hankey argued that the war on the Western Front had reached a total impasse and that the government should consider making Great Britain's main military effort of 1915 elsewhere, possibly against Turkey – a dubious argument which was to have

dire consequences. But Hankey also discussed the tactical problems of trench warfare and made some suggestions for technical
means of overcoming these. One of these was to use:

> Numbers of large heavy rollers, themselves bullet proof, propelled
> from behind by motor-engines, geared very low, the driving wheel
> fitted with a caterpillar driving gear to grip the ground, the driver's
> seat armoured and a Maxim gun fitted. The object of this device
> would be to roll down the the barbed wire by sheer weight, to give
> some cover to men creeping up behind and to support the advance
> with machine gun fire.[36]

Hankey was thus suggesting land assault vehicles combining armour
plate, caterpillar tracks and machine-guns. In the new year of
1915, he circulated the suggestion to those ultimately responsible
for running the British war effort. It immediately struck a chord
with Churchill. On 5 January 1915 he wrote a letter to the Prime
Minister, Mr H.H. Asquith, commenting on Hankey's proposal.

> The present war has revolutionized all military theories about the
> field of fire. The power of the rifle is so great that 100 yards is held
> to be sufficient to stop any rush, and in order to avoid the severity
> of the artillery fire, trenches are often dug on the reverse slopes of
> positions, or a short distance in the rear of villages, woods or other
> obstacles. The consequence is that the war has become a short range
> instead of a long range war as was expected, and opposing trenches
> get ever closer together for mutual safety from each other's artillery
> fire. The question to be solved therefore is not the long attack over
> the carefully prepared glacis of former times, but the actual getting
> across of 100 or 200 yards of open space and wire entanglements . . . It
> would be quite easy in a short time to fit up a number of steam
> tractors with small armoured shelters in which men and machine
> guns could be placed which would be bullet-proof. Used at night they
> would not be affected by artillery fire to any extent. The caterpillar
> system would enable trenches to be crossed quite easily and the
> weight of the machine would destroy all wire entanglements.[37]

Swinton's claim to be the "originator" of the tank must rest largely
on his conversations with Hankey on 20 and 21 October 1914, on
these having been echoed in Hankey's "Boxing Day Memorandum"
and on that in turn having had a vital influence on Churchill.
Churchill certainly responded favourably to Hankey's memorandum. But in the area of armoured fighting vehicles it does not

seem that its influence was crucial or led to any definite result. Churchill was already looking at mechanical solutions to the problems of war on the Western Front and was being presented with ideas from more than one source.[38] Through Sueter he had his finger on some fairly advanced work on armoured car design and Sueter and the RNAS had already started developing machines to assist the infantry in crossing No Man's Land.[39] Giving evidence to a Royal Commission in 1919, moreover, Churchill stated that the proposal he put to Asquith on 5 January 1915 in response to Hankey's memorandum bore no fruit:

> I have ascertained that Mr. Asquith, two or three days after receiving this letter, laid it personally before Lord Kitchener and urged him to prosecute research into all these matters with vigour. I think he also sent Colonel Hankey's Memorandum of a few day's earlier. Lord Kitchener therefore remitted the matter to the Department of the Master General of the Ordnance.[40]

After some brief investigations and experiments the War Office had dropped the matter. In Churchill's words:

> It came to nothing: no action was taken ... I lost touch with this sequence of events after writing my letter to the Prime Minister. It begins with Colonel Swinton; it goes on to Sir Maurice Hankey['s memorandum] that was followed by my letter; then Mr. Asquith sent it to Lord Kitchener and then Lord Kitchener remitted it to the Master General of the Ordnance. Certain investigations were made but the matter came to a dead end.[41]

All the evidence confirms Churchill's version of events. Kitchener's War Office established a committee under the Director of Fortifications and Works, General Scott-Moncrieff. This committee looked at the proposals by Hankey, at a design for an automatic bridging device which had been produced at Churchill's request by Admiral Bacon, the general manager of the Coventry Ordnance Works, at a Holt caterpillar tractor and at a vivid memorandum by Captain Tulloch entitled "The Land Ship". Tulloch proposed employing an automotive engineer, providing him with all the necessary facilities and allowing him to design a "land ship" from scratch. But the majority opinion was that the war would be over before an entirely new kind of machine could be designed and produced. It was decided that only adaptations of existing machines could be considered. A Holt tractor was subjected to an extremely stringent test at Shoeburyness on 17 February 1915. Its performance was judged unsatisfactory and, though a few further trials were conducted, all War Office experiments of this type had fizzled out by June 1915. In fairness to the War Office it should be pointed out that the department was vastly overworked at the time and had more pressing problems.[42]

Meanwhile the RNAS was continuing its own experiments. A revealing passage in Commodore Sueter's memoirs clearly indicates whence came the impetus:

> It is quite true to say at this period of the War not only myself but most of my Staff were getting pretty fed up and exasperated at Mr. Churchill's policy of giving us all the hard nuts to crack as anything new he wanted done was always given to the Air Department, a compliment we did not, with so much air work on hand, always appreciate. His actions always recalled to my mind the title of one of Mr. Cochran's earliest revues – "One Dam [*sic*] Thing After Another". Nevertheless, I was making every endeavour to get out a useful weapon for trench warfare *to keep this forceful man quiet*. [Emphasis added][43]

At some point late in 1914 it occurred to Sueter that infantry might be able to advance across No Man's Land behind mobile armoured shields. He summoned an engineer from Vickers to design such a shield. A drawing was made and a wooden mock-up constructed. Originally this device was intended to be pushed forward on a single wheel to be positioned at the centre of the screen. But during trials, apparently conducted very early in 1915, it was discovered that on soft ground the wheel sank into the mud. Sueter began to look at the possibility of using a caterpillar track instead of a wheel. He had been familiar with caterpillars for many years and had advised Captain Scott to take a tracked sleigh on his Antarctic expedition. At the end of 1914 or perhaps the first few days of 1915 Sueter told a member of his staff to procure a caterpillar. In this way the Admiralty Air Department made contact with the only British company then manufacturing caterpillars – the Pedrail Transport Company of Fulham, a firm established, owned and managed by Bramah Joseph Diplock, whose name had been associated with "land ironclads" as long ago as 1903.[44]

On 13 January 1915 Diplock supplied a small truck which ran on a caterpillar track to the Air Department's station at Wormwood

Scrubs. Sueter organized a demonstration of this vehicle for Churchill on Horse Guards Parade on 16 February 1915. The vehicle was
not powered but Sueter was able to show that, even when very
heavily laden, it could easily be drawn by a single horse or pushed
by one man. Indeed Sueter encouraged Churchill to push Diplock's
vehicle around Horse Guards Parade.[45]

No one has ever disputed that the Horse Guards Parade demonstration took place. Sueter's intention was undoubtedly to show
Churchill that caterpillar tracks might be useful in solving the problems of trench warfare. But its precise significance is a matter of
some controversy. Sueter claimed in his memoirs that it was the
decisive step – Churchill's establishment of the Admiralty Landships
Committee (the agency which developed tanks) stemming directly
from it.[46] But Churchill himself did not remember it that way.

Sueter later claimed that, when demonstrating Diplock's machine, he pointed out to Churchill that it might be possible to
make an armoured car run on tracks instead of wheels, thus converting it into a cross-country vehicle. But it may be that Sueter's
recollection was influenced by hindsight and that at this stage he
was only recommending the Diplock track as a means of moving
armoured shields, the purpose for which he had originally acquired it. Anyway Churchill had been aware of the existence of
caterpillar tracks since at least 5 January, more than a month
before the Horse Guards Parade demonstration. We do not know
how he first heard of them or whether he had ever seen one in
operation, but he had mentioned them as the basis of a possible
powered armoured vehicle in his letter to Asquith.[47] There is thus
no reason to assume that he would have gained much additional
insight from seeing the Diplock truck.

One of the truly decisive events in the genesis of the tank may
have occurred the evening before the demonstration on Horse
Guards Parade. (Subsequent investigations were not able to pinpoint the date precisely, the evidence is conflicting.) Churchill
attended a dinner party given by the Duke of Westminster, who
commanded an armoured car squadron. The party was largely
composed of the Duke's fellow officers from the RNAS. During
discussions of the war Flight Commander T.G. Hetherington, chief
transport officer of the Armoured Car Division, mentioned his idea
of a gigantic land battleship with 40-foot wheels. He had put this
to Sueter late in 1914. Sueter had rightly considered it impractical

Figure 5
Eustace Tennyson D'Eyncourt.

and had not pursued it. But, now revived and put directly to the
First Lord in the congenial setting of a dinner party, this grandiose
and rather absurd idea had profound results. It led directly to
Churchill's establishment of the Director of Naval Construction's
Committee, also known as the Admiralty Landships Committee.[48]
As Churchill himself pointed out, there is a continuous "chain of
causation" from the formation of this committee to the first ap-
pearance of the tank on the battlefield of the Somme.[49]

Churchill sent for Mr Eustace Tennyson d'Eyncourt, the Director of Naval Construction (DNC), on 20 February. Their meeting
took place in Churchill's bedroom at the Admiralty, Churchill
being unwell at the time. Churchill was reluctant to lay further
burdens on Tennyson d'Eyncourt, who was already seriously overworked, but as he subsequently explained to the Royal Commission, "I was not altogether satisfied that the subject was being
handled by strong enough elements and strong enough personalities in the Armoured Car Division. I thought it was absolutely
necessary to break new ground and to have recourse to the greatest authority at my disposal in the Admiralty, the Director of
Naval Construction."[50]

Eustace Tennyson d'Eyncourt had been DNC since 1912. The
son of a metropolitan magistrate who was a cousin of the poet

Alfred Lord Tennyson, Eustace was educated at Charterhouse and was apprenticed at the age of eighteen to the Armstrong-Whitworth shipyard at Elswick. Two years later he took the naval architecture course at the Royal Naval College Greenwich as a private student. It was as one of the most talented naval architects of his day that he was picked as DNC by Churchill at the age of forty-four. His principal roles in the development of the tank seem to have been to reassure Churchill that the idea of constructing some sort of armoured trench-crossing vehicle was not a technical absurdity and to have helped keep the Landships Committee alive after Churchill left the Admiralty.[51]

The committee established for the development of landships initially consisted of:

Mr. Tennyson d'Eyncourt, Chairman
Colonel W.C. Dumble, (a former general manager of the London Omnibus Company)
Squadron Commander T.G. Hetherington (representing Sueter)
Mr. Dale Busell (representing the Admiralty Director of Contracts)[52]

This was later considerably expanded. Churchill, acting entirely on his own authority, without even consulting the Board of Admiralty, made available about £70,000 of public money for landship development. But the formation of a committee and the availability of large amounts of cash did not guarantee the production of a serviceable landship. The technical problems were great, the membership included no one with expertise in automotive engineering and the task was poorly defined. A further factor was that, though no one knew it when the committee was constituted, Churchill, its originator and patron, was to have only another three months at the Admiralty. As three out of the four Sea Lords were either uninterested in its activities or positively hostile there was a distinct risk of the committee being closed down before it had achieved any useful result.[53]

The first meeting took place on 22 February 1915. For knowledge of automotive engineering it was largely dependent upon two guests: Lieutenant R.F. Macfie, who was brought by Hetherington, and Colonel R.E.B. Crompton, invited by Colonel Dumble. Hetherington's suggestion, at the Duke of Westminster's dinner party, of a gigantic land battleship with 40-foot wheels had been instrumental in the creation of the committee. It is thus

hardly surprising that this was the first item to be discussed at the
first meeting. It seems to have been generally appreciated, however, that the machine Hetherington proposed was just too big
and heavy to achieve mobility. D'Eyncourt suggested building a
somewhat smaller wheeled landship based on the large howitzer
tractors then being manufactured by Foster's of Lincoln. But Macfie,
an RNAS officer who had worked at the RNAS Armoured Car
Centre at Wormwood Scrubs and had taken a strong interest in
caterpillar tracks, insisted that they were the solution to the problem of cross-country mobility. Crompton, an engineer of great
distinction, took the same line. Ultimately it was decided to construct two vehicles, one wheeled and the other tracked. Both were
to be very big machines capable of carrying fifty soldiers across
No Man's Land and into the enemy's trenches. Something of the
gigantism of Hetherington's original proposal had thus survived
the first meeting.[54]

Towards the end of the first meeting Colonel Crompton was
appointed as the committee's consulting engineer. This appeared
to be a sensible move. Crompton, though now in his seventies,
possessed great patriotism, enthusiasm, experience and expertise.
In India with the Rifle Brigade during the 1860s he had been
responsible for the adoption of long-distance steamers for road
haulage. After retiring from the Army he had established a profitable business for the supply of domestic electricity. But he returned to military service for the South African War of 1899–1902,
during which he commanded a specialist unit of electrical engineers who also ran steam traction engines. From the beginning of
the First World War Crompton had bombarded the War Office
with engineering ideas. In February 1915 he had submitted a
proposal for a "trench-straddling machine" – a giant armoured
tractor to transport infantry from their own into the enemy's
trenches. This proposal was immediately rejected by the War Office
but somehow came to the attention of the Landships Committee.[55]

Yet Crompton and his partner, L.A. Legros, for all their expertise and dedication, were not successful. Crompton's fixation on
the idea of a large vehicle capable of carrying a considerable
quantity of infantry was a contributory factor. That in turn may
have been symptomatic of a loss of mental flexibility accompanying advancing years.

In the next month some preliminary design work was done on

Figure 6 William Tritton.   *Figure 7* Walter Wilson.

the two types of landship (tracked and wheeled) and scale models were built and shown to the committee. At the end of March Churchill authorized the building of 18 landships, 12 based on the Diplock "pedrail" – the only type of caterpillar then manufactured in Great Britain – and 6 on wheels. The contract for the wheeled version was placed with the Lincoln firm of Foster's whose managing director, William Tritton, was ultimately to play a vital part in the tank's development. The contract for the tracked version was given to the firm of Foden's.[56]

At the Lincoln works Tritton was joined by Lieutenant Walter Wilson of the Royal Naval Volunteer Reserve. Tritton and Wilson became a dynamic and ultimately successful design partnership. Tritton was born in 1875, the son of an Islington stockbroker. After attending King's College London he had been apprenticed to a firm of engineers in Hammersmith. In 1905 he became the general manager of Foster's and was promoted to managing director in 1911. Wilson, a year older than Tritton, was the son of a Dublin barrister who, after a brief naval career, had taken a degree in mechanical sciences at King's College Cambridge, gaining a first on part one of the tripos. He became a very successful automobile engineer with a number of motor car and lorry designs to his credit. At the outbreak of war Wilson had rejoined the Navy and had become involved with the design of armoured lorries for the RNAS.[57]

One of the first tasks undertaken at Foster's was the construction of a full-size wooden mock-up of the wheeled landship. The wheels had already been scaled down from the 40-foot diameter of the original Hetherington conception to a mere 15 feet. But Tritton and Wilson appear quickly to have come to the conclusion that this conception was not practical. The main problems were its height, which would make the vehicle an easy target for the enemy's artillery, and its weight, which would make the wheels sink into soft ground. Tritton then tried to develop a smaller and lighter version powered by electricity from a generator stationed behind the lines. But this too was ultimately abandoned because a break in the cable, very likely under artillery fire, would have paralysed the vehicle.[58]

Meanwhile no serious work seems to have been done at Foden's on the tracked version of the landship. In April a labour dispute resulted in the contract being transferred to the Metropolitan Carriage and Wagon Company. That firm in turn made no obvious progress before asking to be relieved of the task in July because of pressure of other war work. The fact that five months was allowed to pass before serious work was done on caterpillar landships by any contractor is indicative of a lack of strong direction. It seems probable that Tennyson d'Eyncourt continued to regard work on the construction of conventional vessels as the most important call on his time and gave only a limited commitment to "landships".[59]

Also symptomatic of an unbusinesslike approach was the committee's failure formally to appoint a secretary for the first few months of its existence. The acting secretary until April was Mr D. Bussell of the Admiralty Contracts Branch. But he was then appointed to full membership of the committee and Lieutenant Albert Stern informally took over. Now aged thirty-six, Stern was of a merchant banking family, and had been educated at Eton and Christ Church before entering the family business, which he handled with great boldness. Because of a weak ankle he had experienced some difficulty in joining the armed forces at all and had offered to provide the Admiralty with an armoured car at his own expense. Stern was commissioned by the end of 1914 and found himself in the Armoured Car Division of the RNAS. Stern originally became involved with landships as an assistant to Hetherington. He was handicapped by lack of either military or technical knowledge, by his low rank and by the fact that until June he was not even given the formal position of secretary. Ultimately Stern was to demonstrate great self-confidence, acting with a decisiveness rather in excess of his formal authority. (His fearlessness of superiors may have stemmed partly from his large private fortune and his effectiveness in an executive role from habits acquired in business life.) But even he seems to have been floundering for the first few months of his attachment to the committee.[60]

Progress was not helped by the fact that (at least in theory) the committee was purely advisory and had no executive authority. It was heavily reliant on the RNAS Armoured Car Division to conduct experiments for it, No. 20 Squadron RNAS, of which Hetherington was given command, being assigned to this purpose. Orders to these naval personnel had to originate from Sueter as Director of the Admiralty Air Department or from Commander Boothby, the head of the Armoured Car Division. The personality of Boothby was a further complication. His extreme impatience with the lack of progress under Tennyson d'Eyncourt's direction is understandable and might be regarded as justifiable. But he also appears to have had an overriding concern with his own prerogatives and an addiction to red tape. He clashed not only with Tennyson d'Eyncourt but also with Crompton, Stern and Hetherington.[61]

Meanwhile Crompton, the committee's consulting engineer, in addition to trying to supervise work at the firms to which landship contracts had been allocated, was undertaking a great deal of design and experimental work in his own workshops with the help of his assistant, Legros. But before getting too absorbed in this work he wanted to see conditions at the front. On 20 March 1915 he, Hetherington and Stern (at this stage merely Hetherington's assistant) made a trip to France. The trip had not been planned adequately. They had no authority to be moving around in the zone of the armies and were turned back. Yet Crompton noticed that during their journey to the front they had to pass through many narrow village streets with sharp bends. He came to the conclusion that the long landships which he had hitherto visualized could never arrive at the front without sustaining serious damage. He thus decided to design an "articulated landship", i.e. a landship made in two sections, connected by a form of hinge. Crompton spent most of his time over the next several months trying to produce a workable machine of this nature. He failed and, probably at Stern's instigation, Tennyson d'Eyncourt sacked him on 5 August 1915.[62]

Despite his industry and enthusiasm it is arguable that the only really useful thing which Crompton achieved was to obtain from the United States two types of caterpillar tractor not generally available in Great Britain. These were the Killen-Strait, "a tiny agricultural tractor built in Wisconsin which ran on three sets of tracks like a tricycle" and the Bullock Creeping Grip tractor manufactured in Chicago. The Killen-Strait machine examined by Crompton at Wormwood Scrubs on 27 April 1915 proved to be of little use except for demonstrating the principle of the caterpillar track to politicians and soldiers. Crompton later discovered the sole Bullock tractor then working in Great Britain and went to inspect it on Greenhithe marshes near Dartford on 28 April. Being rather more impressed with the applicability of this latter type to landship development, Crompton got the Admiralty to order two from Chicago. Though the Holt type of caterpillar tractor was, by this stage, widely available in the British armed forces for the purpose of drawing artillery, for some reason which has never been adequately explained it played no part in the thinking of the Landships Committee or its engineers.[63]

In the middle of 1915 the life of the Landships Committee could easily have been extinguished before any result had been achieved. Winston Churchill, the committee's creator, was swept out of the Admiralty in May upon the formation of the first wartime coalition. Of the four Sea Lords only one (the Third, Admiral Tudor-Tudor) had any sympathy with the committee and its work. The committee itself was riven by internal dissensions. Commander F.L.M. Boothby, who commanded the RNAS Armoured Car Division, became exceedingly irritated at the lack of progress the committee was making under Tennyson d'Eyncourt. The irritation was mutual and on 1 July d'Eyncourt asked Sueter to remove Boothby from the committee. This Sueter duly (though it seems reluctantly) did.[64]

No useful military machine had yet been constructed. On 7 May the Committee had taken the decision to produce only two prototype machines: one of the "Big Wheel" type and one of Crompton's "Articulated Landships" based on tracks of the Bullock Creeping Grip variety. On 8 June the decision was taken (apparently on the basis of a letter of 5 June from Tritton and Wilson to Colonel Crompton explaining the difficulties they were having) to abandon the "Big Wheel" type.[65] Given that Crompton could not get his articulated machine to work, it increasingly looked as though a dead end had been reached.

Salvation came from two unexpected quarters: the new First Lord, Arthur Balfour and the War Office. At Churchill's request, Balfour decided to allow this special project of the previous First Lord to be continued and encouraged Churchill to play an active part in the committee. An increase in War Office interest in this Admiralty project from June 1915 onwards may, indirectly, have been due to Ernest Swinton. Until June 1915 Swinton put virtually nothing on paper about fighting vehicles. In that month, however, he produced a strongly worded memorandum on "The Necessity of Machine Gun Destroyers" for GHQ in France.[66] The Commander-in-Chief, Sir John French, liked Swinton's conception of an armoured assault vehicle and took the matter up with the War Office.[67] By that stage the War Office was already aware of the existence of the Landships Committee and the Director of Fortifications and Works, General Scott-Moncrieff, was already making his views known to it.[68] A knowledge that Sir John French was personally interested in the development of an armoured fighting machine was, however, bound to increase the War Office's attention.

The Sea Lords wanted everything to do with landships turned over to the War Office forthwith. But Balfour was not in such a hurry. He allowed some Admiralty personnel to continue to serve on the committee and encouraged Tennyson d'Eyncourt to remain as its chairman. He also permitted the Committee, against the opposition of the Fourth Sea Lord, to retain the services of No. 20 Squadron RNAS, commanded by Hetherington, for experimental work. The Landships Committee became a joint Admiralty–War Office committee that June[69] and continued to be so until its work was done.

It has already been mentioned that the Metropolitan Carriage and Wagon Company, having apparently made no progress with the design or construction of a tracked landship, asked to be relieved of this work early in July. At the same time Stern was

becoming increasingly disenchanted with Crompton. While lacking the competence to assess engineering matters, Stern was prepared to back his judgement about people. He seems to have
regarded the younger team of Tritton and Wilson as more likely
to produce a useful result than Crompton and Legros. When, in
August 1915, Crompton was sacked, Tritton's Lincoln firm was
given the contract to produce a tracked landship. There was a
certain irony about this. Tritton was the last engineer involved in
the project to accept that tracks were the solution to the problem
of cross-country mobility, being long convinced that they would
be jammed by barbed wire.[70]

Early in August some specially lengthened sets of Bullock Creeping Grip tracks had been obtained at Crompton's request from the
United States. On inspection of these tracks Tritton and Wilson
did not think that they were likely to prove strong enough. Nevertheless, because it was politically imperative to have something to
show for the time and money which the Landship Committee had
so far spent, they went ahead and produced a vehicle to run on
them. This vehicle, known as the Lincoln No. 1 Machine, was (if
the initial weakness of its tracks is ignored) far more of a practical
proposition than anything hitherto constructed. Tritton and Wilson
had abandoned the gigantism which had bedevilled earlier efforts.
They had dropped all thoughts of articulation or of tractor-and-
trailer arrangements and had built a unitary machine. They were
no longer proposing to produce a troop-carrier to transport a
trench storming party. They were engaged upon the design of a
true fighting vehicle.[71]

The regimental history of the Royal Tank Regiment attributes
the simpler and more practical concepts behind the work carried
out on behalf of the Landships Committee in mid-summer 1915
to the influence (direct and indirect) of Ernest Swinton. This may
be doubted. Swinton returned to London to act as one of the
secretaries for the Dardanelles Committee of the Cabinet in mid-
July but does not appear to have established contact with the
Landships Committee until late July or perhaps even August 1915.[72]
By that time the Lincoln No. 1 Machine was already being developed, Tritton and Wilson having stated their preference for a
smaller unitary machine as early as 5 June 1915.[73] War Office
involvement with the Landships Committee, which Swinton's
memorandum to French encouraged but did not originate, was

not necessarily a help in defining the type of vehicle required anyway. In a letter he sent to the Landship Committee in June, Scott-Moncrieff argued that landships must be provided with loopholes for rifles all along their sides in addition to having cannon and machine guns. So at that stage he must have been thinking of a very large vehicle and probably regarded troop-carrying as one of its main roles.[74]

The Lincoln No. 1 Machine was tested on Cross-o'-Cliffe Hill in Lincoln in September 1915. It failed because of the inadequacy of its Bullock tracks. During trench-crossing attempts the tracks sagged away from the rollers and came off their frames, totally disabling the vehicle. No tracks yet manufactured had been designed to stand the weight and general wear and tear to which landship tracks would be exposed and Tritton and Wilson were forced, as they had suspected they would be, to design and build a completely new type. Developing the new tracks took until 30 November. Yet a specification which Stern received from the War Office and presented to Tritton and Wilson on 26 August indicated that no performance of which the Lincoln No. 1 machine would be capable would meet the Army's requirements. The War Office specified that the landship should be capable of lifting itself over a parapet 4 feet 6 inches tall and crossing an 8-foot trench – more than double the figures on which Tritton and Wilson had been working up to this point.[75] Tritton and Wilson, and particularly the latter, seem to have been less than satisfied with the Lincoln No. 1 machine anyway. Earlier in August they had already started work on the design of a "Quasi-Rhomboidal" machine.

Yet for the time being Tritton and Wilson persisted with the Lincoln No. 1 Machine in order to test the new tracks. If they could produce tracks which really worked, a serviceable landship, which would meet War Office requirements, would only be a matter of time. The track problem was recognized as crucial not only by the Lincoln team but by Tennyson d'Eyncourt and Stern too. Thus when, on 22 September 1915, the Lincoln team were convinced that they at last had a satisfactory track (designed by Tritton) they sent what amounted to a victory telegram to the Landship Committee's small secretariat at Stern's office in Pall Mall. When tested on the Lincoln No. 1 Machine, on 30 November 1915, the new tracks worked perfectly. A reasonably serviceable landship was now very close.[76]

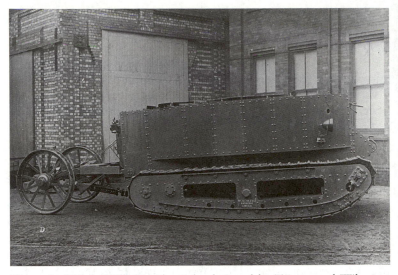

Figure 8 "Little Willie" with tracks designed by Tritton and Wilson at Foster's works in Lincoln.

The next step was to increase the trench-crossing capacity and somehow to give the machine greater climbing power. The method of doing this had already been worked out in theory by the end of August 1915 and a model constructed. In that month Wilson had suggested to Tritton a machine which he described as "Quasi-Rhomboidal" in shape.[77] This was to have tracks running right round the hull rather than just underneath it. The armament was to be carried in detachable sponsons (semi-turrets) on either side rather than in a revolving turret on top as was originally intended for the Lincoln No. 1 Machine. A rhomboidal machine would require very long tracks (which was a disadvantage unless they were also very robust) but the sharp angle at the front would give it much greater ability to climb. The design work was carried out in the White Hart Hotel, Lincoln, where both Tritton and Wilson had rooms during August. In effect "Little Willie" (as the Lincoln No. 1 Machine became known when fitted with Tritton's new tracks) was transformed into the quasi-rhomboidal tank (known as "The Wilson", "The Centipede" or "Big Willie" and later as "Mother") by enlarging the track frames until they were actually bigger than the hull they supported. The hull itself retained the

Figure 9 "Mother" at Hatfield Park early in 1916.

basic box shape of "Little Willie" but gained a raised cab at the front.[78]

On 16 January 1916 Mother made her first move in the works yard at Foster's. On 29 January she was tried out over a mock battlefield on Lord Salisbury's estate at Hatfield Park. There she performed well enough to be exhibited, on 2 February at the same location, to an illustrious audience which included David Lloyd George, the Minister of Munitions, and Lord Kitchener. Of those who saw her on this occasion almost all were impressed. Kitchener, who is said to have described Mother as "a pretty mechanical toy", appears to have been the only significant sceptic.[79] Kitchener's scepticism could have been dangerous were it not for the increasing and quite enthusiastic interest of GHQ in France.[80] In fact landships had arrived and would remain. Within eight months they would see action on the Somme.

The Mark I tank, derived from the Mother prototype, was produced in two versions, "male" and "female". The idea of the female tank was introduced by Swinton, who was worried that, unless there were lots of machine guns to shoot them down, hordes of German infantry might swamp the tanks. Female tanks, armed exclusively with machine guns, were therefore intended always to

Figure 10   Mark I (male) tank C19 moving towards the front, September 1916.

accompany males in battle. The male version was 26 feet 5 inches long, not including a tail consisting of 2 heavy wheels at the rear which was fitted as an aid to steering. (The tail did not prove to be of much use and was discarded in subsequent Marks.) The male Mark I was 13 feet 9 inches broad, 7 feet $4\frac{1}{2}$ inches high and weighed 28 tons when fully equipped. It carried a crew of 1 officer and 7 other ranks and was armed with 2 naval 6-pdr guns and 4 Hotchkiss machine guns. The female version was armed with 5 Vickers and 4 Hotchkiss machine guns and, at 27 tons, was a bit lighter. Manoeuvrability was severely limited in both versions. It is difficult to be precise about speed as this was so dependent on ground. Downhill over good ground Mark Is could overtake heavily laden infantry but in most conditions infantry would outpace them. The driver and commander in the cab at the front were equipped with periscopes and glass vision blocks. Gunners had telescopes. But vision was imperfect for everyone. Both male and female versions were appalling ergonomically, as indeed were all British tanks of this war. Major problems included the interior temperature which could easily rise to 100 degrees Fahrenheit and an atmosphere laden with petrol fumes and carbon monoxide.

The unsprung tracks gave a boneshaking ride and tended to pitch crew members against the hot engine. It involved great physical effort on the part of most of the crew to change gear. The interior noise level was in itself stressful and made communication between crew members difficult.[81]

Until their battlefield debut on 15 September 1916 no one could publicly claim credit for "tanks" (as landships became known) without incurring the penalty appropriate for a gross breach of military secrecy. Their use on that date, albeit on a very small scale and with mixed results, attracted great media interest and occasioned considerable inquisitiveness about their origins. Serving officers and civil servants involved in their development still did not, of course, have the right to make personal statements to the press. Competing unofficial claims were nevertheless soon circulating and these were bound to gain considerable attention in the absence of any official account of the tanks' genesis.[82]

On 21 September 1916 the *Morning Post* stated "other people have no doubt rendered great assistance, but to Colonel Swinton and to Colonel Swinton alone is the credit due as the originator and the persistent elaborator of the idea of the Tanks."[83] This was a sweeping claim. It seems very unlikely that it could have originated with anyone other than Swinton himself. In the final analysis who else would have had an interest in making it? We must assume that Swinton was exploiting the unrivalled connections with the press which he had been able to build up as official war correspondent.

Having laid the groundwork during the war, Swinton pressed his claim in 1919 at the Royal Commission set up to give awards to inventors. Tritton and Wilson, undeniably the people who had solved the technical problems and made tanks a reality, were the main financial beneficiaries from the Royal Commission.[84] There was justice in that. The Commissioners were also very perceptive in their analysis of Churchill's role. On the first page of their report they stated their

> desire to record their view that it was primarily due to the receptivity, courage and driving force of the R. Hon. Winston Spencer Churchill that the general idea of the use of such a machine as the "Tank" was converted into practical shape. Mr. Winston Churchill has very properly taken the view that all his thought and time belonged to the State and that he was not entitled to make any claim for an award,

even had he wished to do so. But it seems proper that the above view should be recorded by way of tribute to Mr. Winston Churchill.[85]

But the Commission's treatment of Swinton's claim was distinctly generous:

> This officer, acting outside the scope of his general duties, made an important contribution to the invention and adoption of the Tank. This contribution included First the conception in October 1914 of a Machine Gun destroyer of the general character of the Tank, Secondly the persistent, energetic and successful advocacy from then onwards of the value and feasiblity of the employment of such an instrument of warfare, and Thirdly the specific definition in June 1915 of the necessary characteristics of the weapon, the conditions of its use and the tests which it must be made to satisfy.[86]

Swinton had indeed been thinking of the use of a caterpillar tracked assault vehicle since autumn 1914. We have Hankey's evidence coupled with one brief note from Swinton to Hankey to establish that point. But what had he actually done about it? He claims in his memoirs to have had two conversations with Lord Kitchener though we have only his word for that. He had committed nothing to paper in his dealings with any institution (or any individual other than Hankey) until June 1915. By that time the Landships Committee had been in existence for over three months without Swinton's having become aware of the fact. For a man of Swinton's literary gifts his efforts up to June 1915 can hardly be said to have constituted tireless advocacy. It seems likely that nothing he did up to that date played any part in what Churchill called the "chain of causation" which produced the tank. Swinton's June memorandum on "The Necessity of Machine Gun Destroyers" certainly did awaken the interest of GHQ[87] and that in turn may have played a part in increasing the War Office's interest in and representation on the Landships Committee. Given the Admiralty's general lack of interest in landships after the fall of Churchill, War Office support was certainly of some importance. But Swinton had nothing to do with the establishment of the Landships Committee and played no part in the solution of any of the technical difficulties involved in the design of the successful tank.

During the inter-war period and well into the Second World War Swinton devoted considerable effort to impressing upon the British public that the development of the tank was principally due to him. A large part of his private papers at King's College London consists of newspaper cuttings extolling the part he had played. (Indeed he seems to have devoted far more effort to this kind of belated self-advertisement than he had to advocacy of the tank in the critical period between October 1914 and June 1915 when he first fully expounded his ideas on paper.) Doubtless Swinton's Fellowship of All Souls and Chichele Chair of the History of War at the University of Oxford[88] contributed to the seriousness with which his claims were taken.

These claims were pushed to their furthest limit in his war memoir *Eyewitness* (1932). This is skilfully written. It is generally not bombastic, and in the body of the book few, if any, statements are made to which it is possible to give the lie. Swinton's most grandiose and misleading claim is slipped in, almost in passing, on the second page of his Foreword.

> Many pages are given up to two outstanding features of the military operations on land – the devastating employment of the machine gun by the Germans and the British reply in the creation of the Tank. I devote much space to the latter without apology because as *its originator* [emphasis added] I was intimately concerned with it from the beginning; because that beginning, at first deliberately surrounded in secrecy, has never been fully disclosed; and because this weapon played a part in the War far greater than has been generally realised, or at all events admitted by our leaders.[89]

Much of the above is questionable and Swinton goes on to make claims for the significance of the tank during the First World War which most modern historians of that conflict would regard as exaggerated to the point of absurdity. Swinton's claim to be the "originator" (singular) of the tank is an outrageous piece of conceit. Coming from a man of Swinton's knowledge and intelligence it smacks of intellectual dishonesty. He must have known that no one individual could legitimately claim that title. Yet his desire for it is not difficult to understand. He possessed a very strong historical sense and appears to have had at least as much vanity as most people. He probably felt that if he could establish himself in the public mind as the prime mover behind the development of the tank he would have assured himself a more important place in military history than any of his other achievements could guarantee him.

A more interesting question (and one much more significant for understanding military innovation and the obstacles to it) is why, from October 1914 to June 1915, Swinton did so little to advocate the tank concept. Part of the answer certainly lies in the personality of Swinton's boss at this critical period – the Secretary of State for War, Lord Kitchener. Kitchener's style of leadership was in some respects very authoritarian and in this context he demonstrated the reluctance to experiment which is sometimes reckoned a classic feature of the authoritarian mentality. Swinton indicates that after putting the idea to Kitchener without getting any support he hesitated to press too hard because he dreaded a direct order to drop it.[90] But probably of equal importance was Swinton's career officer's mentality. He was keen to be thought an innovator if it would benefit his career and reputation and was most assertive after the war in pressing his claim to be so. But at the critical period he seems not to have been prepared to take serious career risks in innovation's pursuit.

Swinton's exaggerated claims in the media for his own part in the tank's development inevitably caused anger and resentment. The BBC's *The Listener* magazine received (but did not publish) a letter of protest from Sueter after a radio broadcast Swinton made on 15 February 1940. Sueter was extremely sensitive on the issue of tank origins. He had felt since 1916 that he and the RNAS were being cheated of their share of the credit. So strongly did he feel on the issue that in 1917 he wrote to the King. The letter was passed to the Admiralty and incurred their lordships' severe displeasure. Sueter was relieved of his command (of RNAS units in Italy) and never again employed. Though he was promoted to Rear-Admiral on his retirement in 1920 he was granted very little official recognition for the work he had done on the development of armoured fighting vehicles. The expression used in Swinton's broadcast (presumably in relation to his caterpillar proposal of October 1914) which caused Sueter so much annoyance was, "I put this idea forward and so the tank was conceived."[91] Sueter's letter was immoderate in tone and tended somewhat to overstate his own role but he rightly pointed out that the tank owed its genesis to the Admiralty.[92]

H.G. Wells was most offended by what had been reported to him of the claims Swinton had made on radio. He responded with a letter (which *The Listener* foolishly published) so abusive in tone as to make Sueter's look moderate. Coming from a professional writer of Wells's stature the ineptitude of the attack would seem scarcely credible except that Wells was always known for excitability and petulance and age may have further impaired his judgement. Swinton's broadcast *was* misleading about his part in the development of the tank. But Wells launched his attack on the basis of hearsay without having heard it. Wells's letter stated that he had been told "that Sir Ernest Swinton had been describing himself on the air as the 'inventor' of the tank". He went on to allege that "for all practical purposes the tank was invented and described in 1903, and that Sir Ernest lifted – without fully understanding the possibilities of the idea he was lifting – that quite clear and explicit description".[93]

Wells was putting his head in a legal noose. Swinton had not in fact described himself as the tank's "inventor". Moreover Wells's claim that the 1915 tank was simply "lifted" from a "clear and explicit description" in his 1903 story was nonsense. Wells's description of the ironclads in his story is not particularly clear and their technology does not, with the benefit of hindsight, appear at all practical. Wells's claim that Swinton did not understand how to use tanks was certainly defamatory. Though one can make criticisms of the papers Swinton wrote on this subject (see the next chapter) he was at least as perceptive about it as anyone else. In short Wells made a fool of himself. He paid the price. A legal action brought by Swinton (settled out of court) obliged Wells to retract and to pay substantial damages.[94]

But it would be wrong to let Wells's ineptitude in this matter prejudice our judgement about his actual contribution to the genesis of the tank. His story certainly contained no technical ideas which were both original and immediately useful. The real question is whether his vision of armoured cross-country vehicles overturning an entrenched military stalemate had any effect on the minds of those responsible for the development of the first tank. It is not possible to answer this definitively but there is some (inconclusive) evidence for Wells's influence and this is reviewed below.

A draft history of the tank's evolution prepared by the CID in 1916 contains in its first paragraph the statement that, "It is certain that for some time a military engine of this nature had been outlined in the brains of several people among who were *at least some who had never heard of H.G. Wells' thrilling and anticipa-tory story written some years back*" (emphasis added).[95] Though this does not constitute proof, the clear implication is that most of the people referred to had heard of it and that it was regarded as one source of inspiration. Stern, the secretary of the Landships Committee, certainly seems to have believed that Wells had had some influence on the development of landships, perhaps through Hetherington's land battleship idea which had led to the establish-ment of the committee. In October 1916 Stern took Wells to see tanks "to show him how his idea had at last been realised".[96]

The *Strand* magazine, in which Wells's story had appeared, was a popular publication, frequently found in gentlemen's clubs and officers' messes. Even Swinton admitted to having read "The Land Ironclads" though he claimed to have "entirely forgotten it" by 1914.[97] Swinton himself became a writer of military fiction about the time "The Land Ironclads" was published[98] and, given that the latter was such a successful military story by a man establishing himself as one of the country's foremost authors, it might be suspected that Swinton's claim to have forgotten it was less than entirely honest. But that is not a very important point. Swinton's role in the tank's development was relatively minor.

Despite his almost complete lack of technical knowledge Church-ill's role, however, was central. Mother was designed by Tritton and Wilson but they did not conceive the idea of a trench-crossing armoured vehicle. They were given the task by the Landships Committee. This committee was established by Churchill who gave it its purpose and supplied funds for its initial work on his sole authority. Churchill's influence on Balfour also played a major part in keeping the committee and its work going after he left the Admiralty. Churchill is reported by Colonel Repington, the mili-tary correspondent of *The Times*, to have acknowledged during an interview on 21 September 1916 that the Wells story was an influence upon his thinking. In formal statements he made about the origins of the tank in 1919, and later in his memoirs, he gave it a similar, admittedly rather vague, acknowledgement.[99]

The tank was conceived in France at roughly the same time as in Great Britain and the first orders were placed only slightly later. The British, however, were about seven months ahead in getting tanks into action and the first two types of French tank, the Schneider and the St Chamond, were distinctly inferior to the

British Mark I in terms of obstacle-crossing ability. What accounts for the British lead over the Continental belligerents in this field? The involvement of the Admiralty seems to have been crucial. The military administrations of all the belligerents were under great stress in the first months of war and it was difficult to find time and resources for complex technical innovation. The French showed remarkable initiative and resourcefulness in producing tanks as rapidly as they did. The two most radical German departures of 1915, strategic bombing and chemical warfare, initially involved no new technology, chlorine and airship production being well established before the war. The British War Office faced the problem of a vast, improvised expansion of the Army and was even more overstretched administratively than its Continental counterparts.[100] The Admiralty, however, had immense resources which were not quite at full stretch and these proved critical. But it is doubtful whether any of them would have been used for "landship" development had it not been for the awesome (though in other cases often misdirected) dynamism of Winston Churchill.

Notes

1   N. and J. Wells, *The Time Traveller, the Life of H.G. Wells* (Weidenfeld and Nicolson) 1973, pp. 3–184. D. Smith, *H.G. Wells: Desperately Mortal* (Yale) 1986, pp. 3–116. W.W. Wagar, *H.G. Wells: Journalism and Prophecy 1893–1940* (Bodley Head) 1964, *passim*. R. Calder in *Dictionary of National Biography* (henceforth DNB) 1941–50, pp. 944–949.

2   H.G. Wells, *The Complete Short Stories of H.G. Wells* (Ernest Benn) 1966, pp. 117–118.

3   I.S. Bloch, *Is War Now Impossible?, Being an Abridgement of the War of the Future in Its Technical, Economic and Political Relations* (Gregg Revivals) 1991, esp. pp. 3–62.

4   Wagar, *op. cit.*, p. 71.

5   Wells, *op. cit.*, pp. 115–138.

6   *ibid.*, p. 131.

7   R.M. Ogorkiewicz, *The Technology of Tanks*, Vol. I (Jane's) 1991, p. 2.

8   On Diplock's involvement with tank development in 1914–15 see *Minutes of Proceedings of the Royal Commission on Awards to Inventors* p. 36, 8 October 1919, p. 3, 623.438 (41) TANK DESIGN AND DEVELOPMENT/56 (henceforth *Minutes Of Proceedings*),

library of the Tank Museum, Bovington (henceforth Tank Museum). On Diplock's career generally see D. Fletcher, "'A New System of Heavy Goods Transport', the Extraordinary Story of B.J. Diplock", *The Vintage Commercial Vehicle Magazine*, Vol. 5, No. 23, Nov.–Dec. 1989.

9   H. Strachan, *European Armies and the Conduct of War* (Allen and Unwin) 1983, pp. 113–114.

10   Certainly Churchill attributed it to the rifle rather than the machine gun. Churchill to Asquith, 5 January 1915, quoted in *Minutes of Proceedings*, 7 October 1919, p. 3, Tank Museum.

11   Swinton to GHQ, "The Necessity for Machine Gun Destroyers", 1 June 1915, Swinton Papers, Tank Museum and Cabinet Minutes, 10 October 1916, PRO CAB 42/21.

12   Wells, *op. cit.*, pp. 131–135.

13   *ibid.*, pp. 129–131.

14   For a discussion of a later development of this theme, the "Canal Defence Light" (CDL) concept see B.H. Reid, *J.F.C. Fuller: Military Thinker* (Macmillan) 1987, pp. 205–208. For a technical discusion of CDLs and the use of searchlights on conventional tanks see Ogorkiewicz, *op. cit.*, Vol. II, pp. 149–151.

15   Wells, *op. cit.*, pp. 122–124.

16   *ibid.*, p. 128.

17   Quoted in J.F.C. Fuller, *Tanks in the Great War* (John Murray) 1920, p. 5

18   The information on Cugnot's early experiments during his Austrian service is from the yet unpublished research of the present writer's colleague, Dr Christopher Duffy, the leading expert on Maria Theresa's Army.

19   Conservatoire National des Arts et Métiers, *La Voiture à Vapeur de Cugnot 1770* (Paris) 1956, *passim.*

20   Ogorkiewicz, *op. cit.*, Vol. I, p. 2 and D. Fletcher, *Landships* (HMSO) 1984, p. 1.

21   On tracked armoured vehicle proposals other than de Mole's see Ogorkiewicz, *op. cit.*, pp. 2–3. On the lack of influence of de Mole's proposal see *Report of the Royal Commission on Awards to Inventors*, 17 November 1919, p. 5, 623.438 (41) TANK DESIGN AND DEVELOPMENT/48, Tank Museum.

22   The writer owes this point to Mr David Fletcher, the librarian of the Tank Museum.

23   M. Sueter, *The Evolution of the Tank* (Hutchinson) 1937, 27–51.

24   R. Churchill, *Winston S. Churchill, Youth, 1874–1900* (Heinemann) 1966, *passim* and A.J.P. Taylor, *English History, 1914–1945* (Oxford) 1965, p. 4.

25   "Royal Naval Air Service Reports of Reconnaissances carried out

by Naval Aeroplanes and Armed Motor Support, 1st September to 31st October, 1914", Air Department, 6 November 1914, Tank Museum. C.R. Samson, *Fights and Flights* (Ernest Benn) 1930, pp. 3–19. B.H. Liddell Hart, *The Tanks*, Vol. I (Cassell) 1959, pp. 18–20.

26 Churchill's evidence, *Minutes of Proceedings*, 7 October 1919, p. 6, para. 6, Tank Museum and Sueter, *op. cit.*, p. 28.

27 "History of Armoured Cars, Juggernauts, Land Battleships, Tanks", 20 September 1916, memorandum by M. Sueter, p. 1, TUDOR 3, Tudor Papers, Liddell Hart Centre for Military Archives (henceforth LHCMA), King's College London.

28 For Sueter's own account of his experimental work with armoured cars see Sueter, *op. cit.*, pp. 27–51. For Churchill's views on the RNAS contribution see his account of tank origins dated 1 September 1919, pp. 2–5, paras 5–11, PRO T 173/164. P.K. Kemp on Sueter in DNB 1951–60.

29 Fletcher, *op. cit.*, p. 1.

30 Sueter, *op. cit.*, pp. 64–65.

31 On the general acceptance of Swinton's claim to be the father of the tank see for example K. Macksey, *The Tank Pioneers* (Jane's) 1981, pp. 12–15; S. Bidwell and D. Graham, *Fire-Power: British Army Weapons and Theories of War 1904–1945* (Allen and Unwin) 1982, p. 137; H. Winton, *To Change an Army: General Sir John Burnett-Stuart and British Armoured Doctrine, 1927–1938* (Brassey's) 1988, p. 14. On Swinton's career before 1914 see Liddell Hart on Swinton, DNB 1951–60, pp. 946–948.

32 E. Swinton, *Eyewitness* (Hodder and Stoughton) 1932, pp. 31–32.

33 *Minutes of Proceedings*, 7 October 1919, Statement by the Attorney-General, Sir Gordon Hewart, p. 2, and evidence given by Major-General E.D. Swinton, p. 15, Tank Museum.

34 Swinton to Hankey, 11 November 1914, HNKY 4/6/21, Hankey Papers, Archive Centre, Churchill College Cambridge. Quoted in Liddell Hart, *op. cit.*, pp. 23–24.

35 Liddell Hart, *op. cit.*, p. 24.

36 Hankey's memorandum of 28 December 1914 and Churchill to Asquith, 5 January 1915, quoted in the Attorney-General's opening statement to the Royal Commission, *Minutes of Proceedings*, 7 October 1919, p. 3, Tank Museum.

37 W. Churchill, *The World Crisis, 1915* (Thornton Butterworth) 1923, pp. 72–73 and Albert Stern, *Tanks 1914–18, the Logbook of a Pioneer* (Hodder and Stoughton) 1919, p. 17.

38 *Minutes of Proceedings*, 7 October 1919, p. 11, paras 85–100, Tank Museum. Sueter, *op. cit.*, p. 45.

39 *Minutes of Proceedings*, 7 October 1919, p. 7, Tank Museum.

40 *ibid.*, p. 8.

41   W. Churchill, *op. cit.*, pp. 72–73.

42   *Minutes of Proceedings*, 7 October 1919, pp. 3–4, Liddell Hart, *op. cit.*, pp. 27–29, and, on overstretch at the War Office, Hankey to Swinton, 5 May 1932, Swinton Papers, LHCMA.

43   Sueter, *op. cit.*, pp. 64–65.

44   Fletcher, *op. cit.*, p. 4.

45   *Minutes of Proceedings*, 8 October 1919, p. 38. Sueter, *op. cit.*, pp. 65–66.

46   Sueter, *op. cit.*, p. 66.

47   Churchill to Asquith, 5 January 1915, quoted on p. 3, *Minutes of Proceedings*, 7 October 1919, Tank Museum.

48   *Minutes of Proceedings*, 7 October 1919, paras 32–43, pp. 8–9, Tank Museum. On the Duke of Westminster's relationship with Churchill, involvement with the RNAS and armoured car development and on the critical dinner party see G. Ridley, *Bend'Or, Duke of Westminster* (Robin Clark) 1985, pp. 49–50, 80–87.

49   Churchill's account of tank origins, 1 September 1919, para. 20, p. 15, PRO T 173/164. W. Churchill, *The World Crisis, 1915*, p. 79. In both accounts Churchill slightly spoils his point by getting wrong the month in which tanks first went into action. It was September not August 1916.

50   Sueter, *op. cit.*, p. 47. *Minutes of Proceedings*, 7 October, pp. 8–9, Tank Museum.

51   E. Tennyson d'Eyncourt, *A Shipbuilder's Yarn* (Hutchinson) 1948, *passim* and K.C. Barnaby in DNB 1951–60, pp. 961–962. On d'Eyncourt's tank work see DEY/41, 42 and 43, Tennyson d'Eyncourt Papers, National Maritime Museum Greenwich. On d'Eyncourt's reassurance of Churchill and contribution to keeping the landship project going on under Balfour see Churchill's account of tank origins, 1 September 1919, paras 23 and 24, pp. 18–19, PRO T 173/1764.

52   "History of Armoured Cars, Juggernauts, Land Battleships, Tanks", 20 September 1916, memorandum by M. Sueter, TUDOR 3, Tudor Papers, LHCMA. How Colonel W.C. Dumble came to be on the committee is not completely clear. He was apparently a Canadian by origin and had attended the Royal Military College at Kingston but continued his military education in Britain where he was apparently commissioned into the Royal Engineers before taking up civilian employment as a motor bus manager, work in which he seems to have been engaged up to 1914. It is possible that his involvement with the Admiralty began with the provision of motor transport for Royal Marines sent by Churchill to the Continent in 1914. Obituary, *Cobourg Sentinel-Star*, Wednesday 27 February 1963, Tank Museum.

53 Churchill's account of tank origins, 1 September 1919, pp. 14–17, paras 19–23, PRO T 173/164. Liddell Hart, *op. cit.*, pp. 31–35.

54 *Minutes of Proceedings*, 7 October 1919, para. 40, and *History of the Ministry of Munitions, Vol. XII, The Supply of Munitions, Part III: Tanks*, 1920 (henceforth *The Supply of Munitions*), pp. 8–9, SWINTON B2, Swinton Papers, LHCMA.

55 Fletcher, *op. cit.*, pp. 4–5. Crompton to War Office, 22 February 1915, "A Self-Moving Armoured Fort for the Attack and Destruction of the Enemy's Trenches", Crompton Papers, Tank Museum.

56 *The Supply of Munitions*, p. 12, SWINTON B2, Swinton Papers, LHCMA.

57 On Tritton see W. Rigby, "The Man Who Made Tanks", *Lincolnshire Life*, March 1968 and J.W. Hill in DNB 1941–50, pp. 888–889. On Walter Wilson Obituary Notice, 069.02(41) WILSON A14, Wilson Papers, Tank Museum, article by A.A. Miller in DNB 1951–60, pp. 1062–1063 and A.G. Wilson, *Walter Wilson: Portrait of an Inventor* (Duckworth) 1986, *passim*.

58 On early work conducted at the Lincoln works of Foster's by Tritton and Wilson see Foster's to Crompton, 5 June 1915, Stern Papers, LHCMA.

59 Tennyson d'Eyncourt, *op. cit.*, p. 113.

60 K. Macksey on Stern in DNB 1961–1970, pp. 980–982. A. Stern, *Tanks 1914–18, The Log Book of a Pioneer* (Hodder and Stoughton) 1919, pp. 17–39.

61 Boothby to Hetherington, Stern and Wilson, 29 June 1915, Stern Papers, LHCMA. Crompton to Tennyson d'Eyncourt, 6 August 1915, Crompton Papers, Tank Museum.

62 Crompton to Tennyson d'Eyncourt, 20 April 1915, Crompton's Progress Report, 24 April 1915 and Crompton to d'Eyncourt, 6 August 1915, Crompton Papers, Tank Museum.

63 Fletcher, *op. cit.*, pp. 5, 9 and 10.

64 *Minutes of Proceedings*, 8 October 1919, evidence of Sueter, p. 40, para. 475, Tank Museum. Sueter, *op. cit.*, p. 79.

65 Foster's to Crompton, 5 June 1915, Stern Papers, LHCMA.

66 On Balfour's attitude to landships see W. Churchill, *op. cit.*, p. 81. Swinton to GHQ, "The Necessity for Machine Gun Destroyers", 1 June 1915, Swinton Papers, Tank Museum.

67 French to War Office, 22 June 1915, Swinton Papers, Tank Museum.

68 On 16 June 1915 Scott-Moncrieff sent a letter to the Landships Committee stating "the view of the General Staff" on armaments for the proposed landships and this was read out at a meeting on 22 June 1915. Landships Committee Progress Report, 23 June 1915, Stern Papers, LHCMA.

69 War Office to Admiralty, 121/Stores/2531 (DFW), 21 June 1915

and Admiralty to War Office, S.0786/15/3199, 30 June 1915, PRO ADM 116/1339.

70 On the abandonment of landship work by the Metropolitan Carriage and Wagon Company see Stern, *op. cit.*, p. 29. On the sacking of Crompton and Legros see Tennyson d'Eyncourt's minute of 6 August 1915, and Crompton to Admiralty, 12 August 1915, PRO ADM 116/1339. See also Admiralty to Crompton, 5 August 1915 and Crompton to Stern, 9 August 1915, Stern Papers, LHCMA. On relations between Stern and Crompton see Fletcher, *op. cit.*, p. 10. On Tritton's slowness to abandon the big wheel concept see Foster's to Crompton, 5 June 1915, Stern Papers, LHCMA. Tritton remarks: "The first condition laid down was that the engine should be able to traverse . . . ground badly broken up by heavy shell-fire and that it should pass over ground covered with the usual wire entanglements. In our opinion large diameter wheels are the only method of meeting these two requirements."

71 *The Supply of Munitions*, pp. 24–27, SWINTON B2, Swinton Papers, LHCMA. Fletcher, *op. cit.*, pp. 11–12.

72 Liddell Hart, *op. cit.*, p. 41. Even in Swinton's evidence to the Royal Commission and in his memoirs there is no indication of his having had direct contact with the Landships Committee before late summer 1915. *Minutes of Proceedings*, 7 October 1919, pp. 17–18 and Swinton, *op. cit.*, pp. 169–170.

73 Foster recommended that "the propelling mechanism and fighting part of the machine [should be] incorporated in one vehicle". Foster's to Crompton, 5 June 1915, Stern Papers, LHCMA.

74 Scott-Moncrieff's letter of 16 June 1915, quoted in Landships Committee Progress Report, 23 June 1915, Stern Papers, LHCMA.

75 Stern, *op. cit.*, p. 31, and Fletcher, *op. cit.*, p. 11.

76 *Minutes of Proceedings*, 20 October 1919, p. 139.

77 *ibid.*, p. 139. The expression "Quasi-Rhomboidal" to describe the shape of the successful tank design known as "Big Willie" or "Mother" is used in detailed notes inserted into several copies of Stern, *op. cit.*, pp. 30–31, including the copy in the library of the Royal Military Academy Sandhurst. These notes are obviously by someone who was intimately involved in the design of tanks. It is believed by the librarian of the Tank Museum, Mr David Fletcher, that they are by Walter Wilson. We know that Wilson regarded Stern's book as generally accurate but in need of some correction in matters of technical detail. See Wilson to Williams, para. 3, 22 January 1954, Wilson Papers, Tank Museum.

78 Tritton to Captain G.M. Williams, 18 July 1918, 623.438(41) TANK DESIGN AND DEV/53, Tank Museum. Fletcher, *op. cit.*, pp. 12–13.

79 Tennyson d'Eyncourt to Lord Kitchener, 30 January 1916, inviting

Kitchener to attend the Hatfield Park trial the following Wednesday afternoon, DEY/42, Tennyson d'Eyncourt Papers, National Maritime Museum. Liddell Hart, *op. cit.*, p. 50.

80 On the interest of GHQ in France see Haig to War Office, 9 October 1916, PRO WO 32/5754.

81 W. Miles, *Military Operations France and Belgium, 1916, 2nd July 1916 to the End of the Battles of the Somme* (Macmillan) 1938, p. 249, Swinton, *op. cit.*, pp. 226–227 and Fletcher, *op. cit.*, p. 16.

82 "History of Armoured Cars, Juggernauts, Land Battleships and Tanks", 20 September 1916, memorandum by M. Sueter, para. 1, TUDOR 3, Tudor Papers, LHCMA.

83 Quoted in Sueter, *op. cit.*, p. 180.

84 Ministry of Munitions to Walter Wilson, 12 December 1919, notifying him that £15,000 had been awarded to him and Tritton jointly, 068.02 (41) WILSON A12, Wilson Papers, Tank Museum.

85 *Report of the Royal Commission on Awards to Inventors*, p. 1, 17 June 1919, 623.438 (41) TANK DESIGN AND DEVELOPMENT/ 48, Tank Museum.

86 *ibid.*, pp. 1 and 2.

87 French to War Office, 22 June 1915, Swinton Papers, Tank Museum.

88 Swinton held this Oxford chair from 1925 to 1939. DNB 1951–60, p. 948.

89 Swinton, *op. cit.*, p. 10.

90 *ibid.*, p. 121.

91 Sir Murray Monachie (Director of Talks, BBC) to Swinton, 3 May 1940, SWINTON C, Swinton Papers, LHCMA.

92 Sueter to Sir Cecil Graves, BBC, 30 April 1940, SWINTON C, Swinton Papers, LHCMA.

93 Wells letter in *The Listener*, 15 May 1941. Quoted in "Statement of Claim in the King's Bench Division, High Court of Justice", 1941 S. No. 1152, Swinton Papers, LHCMA.

94 For Swinton's ideas on the employment of tanks see Swinton to GHQ, "The Necessity for Machine Gun Destroyers", 1 June 1915, Swinton Papers, Tank Museum, and "Notes on the Employment of 'Tanks'", February 1916, Stern Papers, LHCMA. On the legal settlement see Wells to Swinton, 22 July 1941, Swinton Papers, LHCMA.

95 "The Tank Machine Gun Destroyer", PRO ADM 116/1339.

96 Stern, *op. cit.*, pp. 11, 99 and 107.

97 Swinton, *op. cit.*, pp. 177–178.

98 Swinton, *Over My Shoulder* (George Ronald) 1951, p. 144.

99 Colonel Repington's diary, 21 September 1916, quoted in Liddell Hart, *op. cit.*, p. 22. Churchill's account of the origins of the tank dated 1 September 1919, para. 1, p. 1, PRO T 173/1764: "There was no novelty about the idea of an armoured vehicle to travel

across country and over trenches and other natural obstacles while carrying guns and fighting men. Mr. H.G. Wells, in an article written some years ago, practically exhausted the possibility of imagination in that sphere." Churchill also associated Hetherington's proposal for gigantic land battleships with Wells, thinking them (*ibid.*, para. 18, p. 14) "rather on the lines suggested in Mr. H.G. Well's [*sic*] article". Churchill's evidence in *Minutes of Proceedings*, 7 October 1919, para. 2, p. 6, and para. 32, p. 8, was essentially the same. See also W. Churchill, *The World Crisis, 1915*, p. 79.

100 On the development of the tank in France see Stern, *op. cit.*, pp. 103–104 and Ogorkiewicz, *op. cit.*, pp. 6–7. On airship production in Germany see J. Terraine, *White Heat* (Sidgwick and Jackson) 1982, pp. 27–28 and on administrative overstretch at the War Office in 1914–15 see Hankey to Swinton, 5 May 1932, SWINTON C, Swinton Papers, LHCMA.

2

Tanks, visionaries and officialdom: June 1915–November 1916

Swinton's claim to be the prime mover in the British genesis of the tank was dismissed in the last chapter but it is necessary to figure him early and prominently in any account of the development of British thought on tank use. Months before the appearance of "Mother" Swinton had become the first British officer to set down in writing a definite concept of what tanks were needed for and how they ought to be employed.[1] On 1 June 1915 he addressed a memorandum on this subject to GHQ, expressing himself with all the energy and lucidity which might be expected of a successful writer of popular fiction.

Swinton was deeply impressed with the apparent ease with which the Germans were maintaining their position in the west while taking the offensive on other fronts. He believed they were holding their front in France and Belgium with "a minimum of men". They had "grasped the principle that on the defensive numbers of men can be replaced to a very large extent by skilfully and scientifically arranged defences and armament and by machinery". The key feature of the German defensive system was, he thought, the employment of machine guns on an unprecedented scale.[2] Swinton did not provide an estimate of either the number of German machine guns or of the number of German soldiers per mile of front and he may well have been giving the Germans rather too much credit for both tactical ingenuity and machine gun production at this stage in the war. Yet he was obviously right to indicate that the combination of an effective German defence in the west and successful offensives elsewhere was potentially fatal to the Allied cause. Seeking technical means of improving Allied offensive performance in the west was a perfectly logical response.

Swinton could envisage only two methods of overcoming a machine gun based defence. The first was to acquire sufficient artillery and high explosive ammunition to blast a way through. This was not currently within Great Britain's capacity, though it might eventually become so. The second method involved the use of "Armoured Machine Gun Destroyers". These would be "petrol tractors on the caterpillar principle of a type which can travel up to 4 miles an hour on the flat, can cross a ditch up to 4 foot in width without climbing, climb in and out of a cavity and can scramble over a breastwork". The machines were to be armoured against the most penetrative type of German bullet and to be armed with a couple of heavy machine guns and a 2-pdr gun.[3]

Swinton thought it essential to take the Germans by surprise with the first use of these machines. In order to achieve this Swinton recommended that they "should be built at home secretly and their existence should not be disclosed until all are ready. There should be no preliminary efforts with a few machines." The "Destroyers" should be brought up to the railheads only the day before the attack and then "distributed at night along the front of action". They should then be "placed in deep pits, with ramps leading from the rear and out to the front over the parapet, dug as required along our front line".[4]

Despite his warning about wasting the element of surprise by operations "with a few machines" Swinton himself visualized the employment of only about 50. He imagined an attack on a front of only about 5,000 yards (about 3 miles) with the Destroyers about 100 yards apart. At this stage Swinton did not emphasize the need for Destroyers to crush wire, still less did he identify this as their most important role, which in fact it became. He advocated a short preliminary bombardment to break the German wire the night before the operation and "occasional bursts of rifle fire" to discourage the Germans from repairing their entanglements before first light.

Swinton recommended that wherever possible individual Destroyers should be targeted on specific, previously identified machine gun emplacements. They could eliminate the machine guns by driving straight at them and crushing them or by the fire of their 2-pdr guns. The Destroyers might not be able to physically annihilate the enemy's infantry but they could probably succeed in "attracting to themselves the attention of the enemy and most of his fire". Thus the British infantry, who would leave their own trenches and commence the assault just as the Destroyers reached the hostile parapet, would be able to cross the fire-swept zone between the lines "practically unscathed". Swinton recognized, as Wells had in "The Land Ironclads", that artillery was the main potential enemy of armoured fighting vehicles. He therefore recommended that during the assault the British artillery should be concentrated on the German artillery "in order to keep down its fire". There would be no need to bombard the German trenches which would be reduced by the action of the Destroyers and the infantry alone.[5]

Some criticisms can certainly be made of Swinton's paper. Wire cutting by artillery the night before the attack would have significantly reduced the degree of surprise achievable. Exactly how Destroyers and infantry were to co-operate was not explained in any detail. While warning against "preliminary efforts with a few machines" the result of which would be "to give the scheme away", Swinton was suggesting an initial attack with only fifty Destroyers and on a fairly narrow front. It is inconceivable that such an offensive could have gained any decisive result. Even if all the Destroyers performed adequately in mechanical terms, it seems unlikely that more could have been attained than a shallow and fairly narrow break-in of the type actually achieved using a hurricane artillery bombardment at Neuve Chapelle the previous March.[6] Was it worth all the trouble and expense of developing an entirely new weapons system just for that? Swinton had given no indication of how a breach in the enemy's front could be exploited. A break-in on such a narrow front could be sealed off and would be counter-attacked (experience had already shown) by troops drawn from other sectors.[7] Yet Swinton had achieved some tactical insights and must be given full credit for being the first to raise the tank idea with GHQ.

GHQ's initial response to Swinton's memorandum came from his fellow sapper, the Engineer-in-Chief, Major-General G.H. Fowke. It was utterly negative. (Fowke's and Kitchener's seem to have been the only official responses to the tank idea which can be dismissed as simply Blimpish.[8] Even in these cases a degree of impatience with the idea may be partially excused on the grounds of over-work.) In a note to French, Fowke cast doubt on the practicability of constructing such a machine as Swinton suggested, proposing that "we should descend from the realm of imagination to solid facts",[9] a phrase which, as Swinton later pointed out, could be used to pour cold water on any new technical idea. Swinton sent a rejoiner on 15 June insisting the type of machine which he visualized probably could be constructed and that the idea should not be dismissed without trial.[10]

Despite the pronounced scepticism of his principal engineer, Field-Marshal Sir John French gave the proposal favourable attention. A cavalry officer by original training, French was not a particularly deep thinker and was unsuited to high command on the Western Front. His temperament was somewhat mercurial and his nerve insufficiently steady. But he did not have a closed mind. He was, for example, unusually at home in Liberal Party circles for an Army officer of his time and somewhat "advanced" in his views on sex and marriage.[11] His involvement with the development of the tank was slight but important. He communicated his interest to the War Office on 22 June:

> I have the honour to forward herewith the suggestions put forward by Lieut-Colonel E.D. Swinton, DSO, RE ...
> There appears to be considerable tactical value in this proposal, which adapts the peculiar qualifications of the caterpillar mode of traction to the transport of a species of armoured turret across ... uneven ground, especially in connection with the trench warfare which is the feature of the present operations; and particularly if the production of these machines can be a surprise to the enemy.[12]

From 22 June 1915 to the tanks' baptism of fire on 15 September 1916 there was not the slightest opposition from GHQ to the machine gun destroyer/landship idea. Indeed positive expressions of support from two successive Commanders-in-Chief[13] overcame what appears to have been profound scepticism on the part of Kitchener, the Secretary of State for War. In the first nine months of 1916 the main problem Swinton and other tank advocates had with GHQ was trying to contain its impatience to employ tanks in the field.

After June 1915 Swinton was, for several weeks, quiescent on the subject of tanks. He had no idea whether any action was being taken. Some time after returning to London to serve as an assistant secretary to the Cabinet's Dardanelles Committee in July, however, he stumbled across the Landships Committee.[14] Having discovered that work on armoured fighting vehicles of the sort which he had advocated was already in progress he sent a note, dated 26 August, to the Prime Minister, suggesting an inter-departmental conference on the subject.[15] A conference under the aegis of the CID involving the Admiralty, the War Office and the Ministry of Munitions duly took place on 28 August, though it is not clear that it achieved much. The Admiralty and the War Office had been in communication about landships for months and the involvement of the Ministry of Munitions was arguably somewhat premature as no vehicle was yet approaching readiness for production. The conference merely agreed that the War Office should keep the Landships Committee up to date on conditions on the Western Front and that the Ministry of Munitions would take charge of manufacture when the time came.[16]

After Tritton and Wilson had solved the main technical prob-lems and the emergence of a satisfactory landship prototype appeared imminent, Swinton arranged a further conference on Christmas Eve 1915. Because of the pressure of its existing work the Ministry of Munitions was reluctant, at this stage, to take responsibility for landship production. In the short run it was decided to create a special executive supply committee which would take instructions from the War Office. The executive committee would have authority to place an initial order for 50 machines and to begin raising troops to man them – 75 officers and 750 men being specified initially.[17] According to Swinton it was immedi-ately after the Christmas Eve conference that the term "tanks" was first applied to landships. Swinton, as part of his work for the CID had been ordered to find a cover-name for them and, after "water-carriers" had been considered and rejected, "tanks" was finally decided upon.[18] By 9 February Haig was using the term in official communication with the War Office.[19]

Meanwhile, in November 1915, having resigned from the gov-ernment over the decision to withdraw from Gallipoli, Winston Churchill had arrived on the Western Front and was learning the basics of trench warfare with the Grenadier Guards. But while still a pupil he thought he had much to teach. He regarded himself as bearing the Army "a good gift . . . the conception of a battle and of victory".[20] On 3 December he sent GHQ an ambitious memor-andum, "The Variants of the Offensive".[21] It offered a series of unorthodox approaches to the problems of trench warfare. Only the first of these, "The Attack by Armour", is of relevance here. By December Churchill had evidently lost touch with landship development. He believed that about seventy caterpillar landships were nearing completion[22] when not even Mother was yet built.

Churchill's vision of an armoured assault combined the use of caterpillar tracked landships with infantry shields. He envisaged the use of shields of two types: an individual shield which would be a curved oblong steel plate and would hang on the left shoulder "giving protection from just below the rim of the steel helmet to the hip". These would be discarded when the enemy's trenches were reached. He also recommended that:

> Composite shields covering from five to fifteen men and pushed along on either a wheel or, still better, a caterpillar, should also be used. These structures, about four foot high and fifteen broad should be used to mask machine guns which have been located and to give shelter to any wire cutting that may remain to be done.[23]

Churchill believed that the German machine guns were normally fired from ground level and thought it should be possible to "blanket off" their fire by planting composite shields forty or fifty yards in front of their positions. He recommended that while the shields were thus being used "the work of cutting the enemy's wire and the general domination of his firing line" could be effected by caterpillar machines. In describing their action Churchill came much closer to the practicable than he did with shields. He recommended that they be placed secretly along the whole front of an attack and launched into action ten or fifteen minutes before the infantry assault commenced. He described with a fair degree of prescience the cross-country performance of the emerging tanks but was overly optimistic in supposing that, "Nothing but a direct hit from a field gun [would] stop them."[24]

The caterpillar machines would move parallel to the enemy's trenches "sweeping his parapet with their fire and crushing and cutting his barbed wire". Through the gaps thus created the shield-bearing infantry would advance. Churchill made the perfectly valid point that:

> If artillery is used to cut wire the direction and imminence of the attack is proclaimed days beforehand. But by this method the assault follows the wire cutting almost immediately i.e. before any

reinforcements can be brought up by the enemy or any special defensive measures taken.[25]

Churchill had seen a demonstration, laid on by the RNAS a few months previously, of a Killen-Strait tractor fitted with a naval torpedo net cutter[26] and obviously envisaged the same technique being used on the battlefield. But it turned out to be impractical for tanks. The crews' field of vision was too restricted to have enabled them to cut accurately and the tank's weight made crushing the obvious (though an imperfect) solution to the problem of enemy wire.

Like Swinton the previous June, Churchill was not prepared to say much about what should be done after No Man's Land was crossed and the enemy's front broken into. At this stage he had no ideas to offer on exploitation and pursuit. He was not even clear whether caterpillar tracked vehicles would be able to tackle successive lines of entrenchments. "Until these machines are actually in France it is not possible to measure the full limit of their powers." The point needs to be reiterated that a modest break-in had already been proved possible (at Neuve Chapelle) if a preliminary bombardment of sufficient intensity were employed.[27] As with Swinton's so with Churchill's memorandum the case which had been made out for the development of an entirely new weapons system was not overwhelming. This was especially true given that both doubted whether it could be used successfully more than once.

Again like Swinton, Churchill did not see tracked armoured vehicles as instruments which were going to revolutionize war on the Western Front. He considered them useful only for one surprise attack for which they would make the crossing of No Man's Land and the seizure of the enemy's front-line trenches relatively easy. He was well aware that the enemy could take countermeasures against them and saw land mines and field artillery deployed in forward positions as obvious responses. "But if this trick worked once a new one could be devised for next time."[28]

One point of difference between Churchill and Swinton was that the former envisaged the armoured assault being mounted by night. In a passage which seems almost to plagiarize Wells's "Land Ironclads", Churchill indicated that "as they move forward into the enemy's positions his artillery would be increasingly hampered in firing at them and, with deepening confusion, estimating the location of and laying guns upon these moving structures would become almost impossible". Daybreak, Churchill thought, might leave the caterpillars "easy prey" for the enemy's artillery but "if daylight witnessed an entirely new situation they would have done their part even if they could not be withdrawn".[29] Night attacks were to prove virtually impossible for First World War tanks. Their crews could not see in the dark and they were thus likely to get stuck in ditches and bogs or on tree stumps. But Churchill was more perceptive than Swinton in seeing that dealing with wire and thus helping to achieve surprise was going to be one of the main tank roles. The tank's capacity to penetrate wire entanglements did mean that a preliminary bombardment could be dispensed with. A surprise attack could only be effective, however, if reasonably accurate supporting barrage and counter-battery fire could be generated from the moment the assault started without ranging shots (which would tend to warn the enemy) having been fired. Artillery techniques did not advance enough to make this possible until late 1917.[30]

Churchill's memorandum seems to have arrived on Sir Douglas Haig's desk shortly after the latter took over as Commander-in-Chief of the BEF on 19 December 1915. It proved useful, bringing the idea of tracked fighting vehicles to Haig's attention for the first time. Haig was to play a major role in the development and use of British armoured forces up to 1918, but, like virtually everything else about his conduct from December 1915 to November 1918, his attitude to tanks has been a matter of controversy. In order to help us make sense of it some account of his character and background is necessary. Fifty-four in 1915, he was a Scot, the son of a wealthy distiller. He had been educated at Clifton school, the University of Oxford (where he did not take his degree examinations) and the Royal Military College Sandhurst. Up to the point at which he had entered Sandhurst in 1884, at the relatively late age of twenty-two, there was nothing to distinguish him. But his dedication to a military career had become absolute there. He had passed out top from Sandhurst, winning the Anson Memorial Sword, and had joined the 7th Hussars in India.[31]

Haig was ambitious and studious. In 1896 he had entered Staff College and fallen under the influence of the distinguished military historian, Colonel G.F.R. Henderson, who had predicted a bright future for him. He had distinguished himself in the Sudan campaign of 1898 and in the South African War of 1899–1902. At the age of forty-three Haig was already a major-general. As a General Staff director in the War Office in 1906–09 he had worked closely with R.B. Haldane, the reforming Liberal Secretary of State for War. Much of Haig's work, at this period, particularly the drafting of the Field Service Regulations, had been designed very largely to help prepare the Army for a Continental war. In 1914 he had commanded the BEF's I Corps, an organization which evolved into First Army. He was widely regarded as primarily responsible for the British defensive victory at the First Battle of Ypres in the autumn of that year. There was growing dissatisfaction during 1915 with French's leadership and Haig was the obvious choice to succeed him.[32]

As Commander-in-Chief Haig was a remote figure. Though clear and forceful on paper he had always been somewhat reticent in manner and slow of speech. (It may be relevant here that he married only in his mid-forties.) He had, however, an iron will which was reinforced by a strong religious sense. His firm belief in ultimate victory was, in the final analysis, a great asset to the Allied cause. But his perpetual and usually excessive optimism was often dangerous to the forces under his command. Most subordinates found him intimidating. They were afraid to disagree with him or give him bad news. In some ways his outlook was conservative. He was, for example, most reluctant to accept how drastically diminished was the role of the cavalry under the circumstances of the Western Front. On the other hand he was diligent, knowledgeable (within limits) about his profession and wide open to technical innovation. During his command the supply of aircraft was practically always at the top of the BEF's list of munitions priorities and he accepted, apparently with alacrity, Eric Geddes' proposal to revolutionize its logistics with light railways.[33]

Haig apparently read Churchill's "Variants of the Offensive" on Christmas Day 1915. French had been familiarized with the tank concept by Swinton and had contacted the War Office about it. But it is not clear whether the War Office had kept French up-to-date and certainly no one had informed Haig. In a pencilled note on Churchill's paper he asked, "Is anything known about the caterpillar referred to in para 4, page 3?"[34]

Had Haig been as blinkered as he has sometimes been portrayed he would have simply dismissed "Variants". Churchill was a fallen political star, widely regarded as culpable for an unnecessary and unsuccessful campaign which had diverted resources from the vital Western Front. "Variants" could easily have been derided as another example of the amateurism which had led to the Dardanelles fiasco. Such an attitude on Haig's part would have been almost excusable in view of the size of the responsibility which he had just assumed and the pressure of work which presumably went with it. Haig had faults but opposition to new technology was certainly not one of them. Having read the memorandum and identified the caterpillar proposal as possibly significant, he had the matter investigated further. Major Hugh Elles, a sapper then working as a staff officer in GHQ's operations branch, was sent to London for this purpose and reported favourably to Haig on the Hatfield Park trial.[35]

Apart from his brief query on Churchill's paper Haig's first comment on tanks came on 9 February 1916. In a letter written in his own hand he informed the War Office that "the officers who represented me at the trials [of Mother] lead me to the conclusion that these 'Tanks' can be usefully employed in offensive operations by the force under my command". Haig had been given to understand that "thirty or forty at least could be supplied by next May without interfering with the supply of any war material". He wanted that number and if possible more. In order to preserve secrecy he suggested that:

> an official notification be made to all concerned that it is not proposed to proceed further with this invention and that knowledge that an order is being given for any "Tanks" to be made should be limited to as few people as possible.[36]

David Lloyd George, the Minister of Munitions, had also been impressed by the Hatfield Park demonstration of 2 February 1916 when Mother had first been shown to the great. He took the initiative in sending for Albert Stern and proposing that Stern's provisional Tank Supply Committee (later to become the Mechanical Warfare Supply Department) should be incorporated in his Ministry, reversing the Ministry's earlier reluctance to become involved with the new weapon. With Lloyd George's approval Stern placed an initial order for 100 machines.[37]

Meanwhile the War Office, with Haig's encouragement, was setting up an organization to man the tanks. A conference held on

14 February, and attended by both Swinton and Stern, decided that the "Tank Detachment" should form part of the Motor Machine Gun Service of the Machine Gun Corps and that it should be trained at Bisley.[38] Later the same month it was decided to put Swinton in charge of the detachment, the initial establishment of which was 15 companies, each comprising 2 sections of 6 tanks each. The title of the organization was changed in May to "Heavy Section Machine Gun Corps" and this eventually gave way to "Heavy Branch Machine Gun Corps". It did not long remain at Bisley, being transferred during the summer to a more remote and therefore secure location at Elveden, near Thetford, in Norfolk.[39]

On 5 April 1916 Haig requested that a further 50 tanks be added to the 100 which had already been ordered. GHQ considered that the proportion of female tanks (armed solely with machine guns) to male tanks (whose main armament was the naval 6-pdr gun) should be 2 to 1.[40] Haig informed Swinton on 14 April that he wanted some tanks in France by the middle of June. Swinton said he would try but doubted that it was possible. In a letter to GHQ of 26 April 1916, however, he agreed to deliver to France 75 tanks, together with the requisite trained crew, by 1 August.[41]

Having seen Mother at work Swinton elaborated his ideas on the correct employment of the new weapon and incorporated these in "Notes on the Employment of Tanks", completed in February 1916. He contemplated the use of about 90 tanks in an extended line with no more than 150 yards between them. He anticipated a frontage of 9,000 yards or about 5 miles for the attack. He did not envisage the use of more than one line of tanks or keeping any in reserve for the exploitation of initial success.[42]

Since his last essay on the subject 8 months previously Swinton had given more thought to the timing of the attack. He concluded that "the most favourable time for the tanks to advance so as to avoid the principal danger to which they will be exposed i.e. the hostile artillery fire, would be at night". But, having seen Mother, he realized, unlike Churchill, that the difficulty of navigating tanks at night virtually ruled this out. He therefore concluded that "the best moment for the start will be just before dawn, so soon as there is sufficient light in the sky to distinguish objects to some extent. A start at such a time will give the greatest number of hours of daylight for pressing on with the offensive".[43]

Swinton noted that in attacks launched up to this point in the

war the British infantry had usually found it possible to storm the
German front line trenches after a thorough bombardment. He
realized that it could be argued on that basis that tanks should be
held in reserve during the initial assault "and only sent forward to
help the infantry when the latter are held up by uncut wire and
machine gun fire". But Swinton recommended against this. The
infantry would suffer unnecessary casualties if the tanks were held
back. And once the infantry had gone over the top communication
with the tanks might prove difficult and they might not be able to
take any real part in the battle until all impetus had been lost.
Even more serious would be the effect of the "curtain of fire"
which the German artillery always brought down on No Man's
Land and the British front line trenches immediately after an assault had begun. If the commitment of the tanks were delayed
there would be considerable chance of their being caught in it.

The tanks, in Swinton's view, would be best employed leading
the assault, firing their machine guns at the parapet of the enemy
front-line trench as they did so. Once they had got about three-
quarters of the way across No Man's Land "the assaulting infantry should charge forward so as to reach the German defences
soon after the tanks have climbed the parapet and begun to enfi-
lade the trenches". In one critical respect his thinking had not
advanced since May 1915. Because he still envisaged the use of
only a small number of tanks he did not emphasize their wire-
crushing role and did not believe that an attack could be launched
without a preliminary, wire cutting bombardment:

> Each tank will clear only its own width through the entanglements,
> and though some of the assaulting infantry may make use of these
> gaps, the fact that an attack by tanks is to be made will not preclude
> the normal wire cutting fire of our guns and trench mortars across
> the section over which they operate.[44]

Swinton anticipated that when the tanks had reached the German
front line trenches they would pause briefly, sweeping the trenches
with fire and allowing the infantry to catch up before proceeding
at full speed (if possible along the lines of communication trenches
which would also be machine gunned) to the German second line.
Though he realized that tanks could be used as part of a step-by-
step advance geared to a pre-arranged artillery barrage, he was
inclined to deprecate this as a failure to exploit their full potential.

A step-by-step advance had the drawback of giving the enemy time to reinforce the sector threatened and should be avoided if possible. He believed by February 1916 that tanks had the power to force successive comparatively unbattered defensive lines and might stand a better chance of surviving if they kept moving rather than stopped part-way through the enemy's defensive system. "It is possible", he concluded, "that an effort to break through the enemy's defensive zone in one day may now be contemplated as a feasible proposition." Even if the tanks were reduced to 1 mile per hour during the actual attack, he supposed that an advance of 12 miles might be carried out in the daylight hours of a single day. "A movement on this scale will take our troops past the enemy's main artillery positions and would, if successfully effected, imply the capture or withdrawal of their guns." Thus while couching his memorandum in moderate terms, emphasizing that tanks could not win battles by themselves and were purely auxiliary to the infantry, Swinton was in fact making quite substantial claims, much more so than in his paper of June 1915.[45]

Swinton was convinced that if tanks were to achieve their full potential there would have to be a high degree of all-arms co-ordination. In particular the maximum possible suppression of the enemy's artillery was vital to success. To this end Swinton advocated not only counter-battery work by the British artillery but also (presumably to deal with the more rearward enemy heavy artillery) air attack. What was needed was not necessarily the total destruction of enemy guns but their suppression – "spoiling the enemy's shooting for the period of the advance". He considered, most perceptively, that gas shelling might serve very well for this purpose. As another means of protecting the tanks from enemy artillery, he advocated the emission of "clouds of smoke" – apparently he was thinking of employing smoke generators rather than smoke shell from artillery. With precisely the sort of tactical subtlety which had made *The Defence of Duffer's Drift* a success he advocated that "the release of smoke only on the sector where tanks are used might be accompanied by the release of gas and smoke elsewhere, so that the enemy would not know what was poisonous and what was not".[46]

There is much in Swinton's "Notes" to commend. In particular his recommendations for the co-ordination of tanks, infantry, artillery and aircraft, combined with the use of gas and smoke, may strike even the modern reader as fairly sophisticated. Yet even at the tactical level there are obvious weaknesses. The very high degree of surprise later achieved at Cambrai would not have been possible with the scheme which Swinton advocated because he did not believe it possible to dispense with artillery wire-cutting and thus regarded a preliminary bombardment as essential. He still did not place sufficient emphasis on the wire crushing role of tanks – actually the greatest contribution they could make to an infantry assault. Swinton, moreover, was not recommending the use of any kind of artillery barrage ahead of the tanks.[47] Yet without a barrage 90 to 100 tanks would have been nowhere near enough, in relation to the 5-mile stretch of front which Swinton proposed attacking, to have overwhelmed successive lines of defence. This would have been true even if all had managed to cross their start lines, and mechanical failures, "ditching" and other problems always precluded this in practice.

The degree of sophistication of military thought which Swinton had here achieved was, moreover, minor tactical rather than grand tactical or (in modern military parlance) "operational". Swinton gave some useful pointers to how a breakthrough might be accomplished though, in the complete absence of a supporting barrage, the specific type of operation he recommended would certainly have failed to achieve this and would probably have ended in a bloody repulse. But he had failed to indicate how such a breakthrough could be exploited. To have penetrated right through the enemy's system of field fortification on a 5-mile front would, of course, have been worth doing in itself for the losses it would have inflicted. But these would have been minor in relation to the total strength of the German Army on the Western Front. Swinton himself did not suggest that such an operation could decide the course of the war. This point is particularly significant in view of the fact that he very much doubted that a tank attack could succeed more than once. Under the heading "The Impossibility of Repeated Employment", he wrote:

> Since the chance of success of an attack by tanks lies almost entirely in its novelty and in the element of surprise, it is obvious that no repetition of it will have the same opportunity of succeeding as the first unexpected effort.[48]

He must have wondered whether all the energy being expended on this new instrument of war was really going to prove worthwhile.

In his memoirs Swinton was to indulge in bitter recrimination against GHQ about the allegedly premature employment of tanks in insufficient numbers on 15 September 1916.[49] Churchill and Lloyd George adopted the same tone of indignation and even the Official History, while treating the matter in an altogether more balanced way, seemed to some to degree to endorse the criticism.[50] But two points need to be borne in mind. First, despite having some good tactical ideas, Swinton, as we have already indicated, had not come up with anything like a formula for a substantial victory. Indeed it is very doubtful whether his prescription could have achieved a significant break-in to a German position. Secondly, Haig assured Swinton, at a meeting in April 1916, that he agreed with the latter's views on the employment of tanks[51] and a GHQ conference held as late as 26 June concluded that:

> in the attack carried out by Tanks, the Tanks should move forward so as to reach the German front line position by dawn followed up by our infantry which is to start forward from our line as soon as the Tanks reach the first line of the enemy; that in the further operations which will ensue by day light, Tanks should precede the infantry from place to place as quickly as possible; that the ultimate objectives of the tanks during this period should be:-
> 1. The German artillery positions
> 2. The German second or third lines;
> that the German artillery position might be assumed at an approximation to be at a distance of 2,000 to 3,000 yards from the German front line.[52]

The above is virtually a paraphrase of Swinton's "Notes" except that GHQ was having to take into account that the depth of German defensive positions had increased since February and that there would be further trench lines beyond the main gun-line. The GHQ scheme implies a continuous line of tanks across the whole frontage of the attack, just as Swinton had suggested. Nothing was said about the precise numbers to be employed – that would presumably have depended on how many Swinton could deliver – but in other respects Swinton's views were endorsed. Haig's decision to employ a relatively small number of tanks on 15 September 1916 was born of his concern with the progress of the Somme battle, which had begun on 1 July, coupled with the slow delivery of tanks and trained crews.[53] The advisability of some delay in the first use of tanks was proposed to the Prime Minister in July by

Swinton, Stern or both. Lloyd George took the matter up with the
Chief of the Imperial General Staff (CIGS), General Sir William
"Wully" Robertson, and he with Haig. Haig continued to favour
their employment in September, however, and Swinton made no
objection when Haig told him this at Advanced GHQ on 19 August.[54] Haig's position was spelt out to Robertson in a letter of 22
August:

> As soon as a satisfactory base of departure has been secured I hope,
> in combination with the French, to be able to make a further general
> advance on a considerable scale. This, for many reasons, cannot well
> be deferred beyond the middle of September or thereabouts, and I am
> counting on having at least 50 tanks available for it. If I get them I
> hope and think they will add very greatly to the prospects of success
> and to the extent of it. If I do not get as many as I hope I shall use
> what I have got, as I cannot wait any longer for them and it would
> be folly not to use every means at my disposal in what is likely to
> be the crowning effort of this year.
>
> I trust you will do your utmost to hasten the despatch of all the
> tanks that can possibly be sent in time.[55]

Robertson replied that he was giving the matter of tanks "every
attention".[56] One further attempt was made to persuade Haig to
delay the employment of tanks, however. This was by Lloyd
George's successor as Minister of Munitions, E.S. Montagu, who
was prompted by Stern and by the French Ministry of Munitions.
Stern had been in contact with those responsible for tank design
and production in France and they wanted to delay British tank
use until spring 1917 when France's own tanks would be ready.
Montagu went to see Haig early in September and found the latter
sympathetic but unwilling to change his plans.[57]

Given Haig's determination to use tanks in mid-September, GHQ
produced revised proposals for their employment entitled, "Preliminary Notes on Tactical Employment of Tanks". GHQ appears
to have despaired of having more than a handful of tanks to use
on the Somme and to have concluded that it must make some use
of whatever number became available in the next few weeks. At
this stage GHQ did evince some (not unreasonable) doubts about
Swinton's original conception of a tank attack, even assuming the
availability of the 90–100 tanks which Swinton had thought necessary. GHQ pointed out that Swinton's scheme implied "an approach march and deployment under cover, a surprise start, accurate

keeping of alignment and direction and a suitable objective such
as parallel lines of trenches in open country; these considerations,
combined with the extent and regularity of the target offered to
the enemy's artillery, render this a difficult operation". But
Swinton's approach was not dismissed. Rather, given Haig's determination to use whatever means were available to support the
renewal of the offensive on the Somme programmed for mid-
September and given the very small numbers of tanks likely to be
available by that time, GHQ was introducing an additional, more
modest conception of their use. The idea of a continuous attacking
wave was shelved. Tanks were to add weight to the attack at
points on the attack frontage where particular difficulty could be
expected.[58]

> The chief obstacles to any infantry advance are the villages, woods,
> strong points and hidden machine gun positions. No bombardment
> seems to succeed in obliterating all these places so completely as to
> prevent the reappearance of machine guns there as soon as the artil-
> lery lifts. The result is that the assault is checked in front of these
> points, and that those elements who continue to advance through the
> intervals are taken in the flank by machine gun fire.

GHQ thought it possible to pick out within the area selected for
an attack the points from which the greatest resistance was to be
expected. Tanks were to assist at these locations "so that they may
be overcome simultaneously with the parts where resistance is
less". That resistance should be overcome simultaneously right
along the front was extremely important to British tactics at this
period. Infantry advances were closely geared to an artillery fire
plan which could not be altered once the attack had started. The
barrage (whether creeping or jumping) moved ahead at a pre-
arranged rate and everything depended on the infantry keeping
close behind it. Thus in action

> numbers of tanks should be tasked to deal with each of these pivots
> of defence. They should be loosely supported by bodies of infantry
> told off for the purpose, who [would] advance under cover of the
> tanks, clear up behind them, and eventually consolidate the locality
> when taken . . . Each tank attack will be a definite operation against
> a limited objective allotted to a selected number of tanks and a
> selected body of infantry, all under one Commander. In certain cases
> a pair of tanks supported by a platoon might suffice.[59]

Adding weight to the assault at selected points was not, in principle, a stupid way of using a small number of tanks. But unless they had very intimate infantry support tanks were later found to be vulnerable in villages. They could not shoot into windows above the ground floor and their top armour was relatively weak so that grenades could be a problem. They were, as Swinton had already warned, of very little use in woods[60] where they tended to get stuck on tree stumps.

GHQ seems at this stage to have rejected Swinton's view of the impossibility of the repeated employment of tanks. To Haig's staff the tank became merely one new instrument amongst many which the conflict had produced. As with the others the best method of using tanks could only be worked out by practical experiment, an attitude which was more dispassionate and realistic than Swinton's.

The first detachment of tanks left Elveden for France on 13 August. By 6 September two companies were assembled at Yrench, nine miles north-east of Abbeville, and a small training centre was established there. Swinton was ordered by the War Office to remain in charge of the Heavy Branch at home. He selected Lieutenant-Colonel John Brough, a Staff College graduate, to take command of all tanks in France. Brough, however, quickly created a poor impression at GHQ and was relieved by the Heavy Section's only other Lieutenant-Colonel, R.W. Bradley. All the Heavy Section personnel were inadequately trained and there were also numerous mechanical problems. Despite the trouble which Tritton and Wilson had been to with the tracks, for example, these were still not robust enough and tended to break. To make matters worse, though GHQ theoretically regarded secrecy as of paramount importance, the tanks found that they were obliged to perform in public before fairly large audiences. This not only wasted time which could have been used for training but, according to some of their crew, resulted in excessive wear and tear which reduced the number available for action.[61]

On 6 September the tanks began to be moved forward by rail to an area known as the "Loop", between Bray and Fricourt, for training over cratered ground. Two nights before the attack tanks were moved to corps assembly positions between one and two miles behind the front and thence, on the next night, to their points of departure. Routes had been reconnoitred for them and tapes laid. The tanks moved during the hours of moonlight and

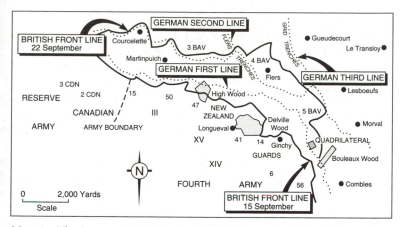

Map 1 The Somme, 1916: Battle of Flers-Courcelette, 15–22 September.

attempts were made to drown their noise with aircraft flying low over German positions during these periods. According to the Official History: "Simple flag and lamp codes were arranged from tanks to infantry and aircraft in order to signal 'out of action' and 'am on objective'. A proportion of the tanks were to carry pigeons."[62]

This is not the place to narrate in detail the actions of the tanks at their debut at the Battle of Flers-Courcelette on 15 September and on subsequent occasions during that month. There are several reasonably reliable accounts in print and an overview will here suffice (see also Map 1). Fifty tanks had been sent to France with the two companies actually employed on 15 September and a further 10 were sent as reserves. Only 48 tanks were fit for duty on 15 September and a substantial number of these broke down or became stuck during a short approach march and never crossed their start lines. Indeed only 36 seem to have reached their starting positions. About 30 actually started. Others broke down or became ditched before getting within striking distance of the enemy. Perhaps 21 did real fighting.[63]

The attack of 15 September by General Sir Henry Rawlinson's Fourth Army was, in essence, a conventional infantry assault, employing nine infantry divisions, three belonging to each of the three corps: from north to south III, XV and XIV, which were committed. Rawlinson was supported on his left flank by an attack by the 2nd Canadian Division, belonging to the Reserve Army under General Gough, this division also having been allocated a few tanks. The attack was to be on a 7-mile front, preceded by an intensive 3-day preliminary bombardment and supported by a creeping barrage. The tanks were spread out across the front, operating in small groups or (owing to the breakdown of many machines) in some cases individually. The intention was for the tanks to keep ahead of the infantry and this meant that they were advancing virtually *a tempo* with the barrage. In order to avoid hitting the tanks with British shells, "lanes" in the barrage 100 yards wide were left open for them. Given that many tanks failed to cross their start lines these lanes were potentially lethal to the British infantry who were left with no support against German machine gunners within them. The inadequate training of the tank crews, moreover, resulted in some completely losing their sense of direction and firing on their own infantry. For the same reason and because of inept steering some tanks seem to have wandered out of the lanes and into the barrage.[64]

The whole attack achieved very limited gains, only 6 square miles of ground being conquered. The best results were obtained by the 41st Division in the centre of the XV Corps front. This division was exceptionally well endowed with tanks, being allocated 10 of which 7 managed to start. Three tanks managed to reach and attack the village of Flers. Up to this objective (almost 1 mile from the start line) they were accompanied by infantry who secured and held the village. The infantry advance petered out at this point, however, and only one of 41st Division's tanks got as far as the village of Gueudecourt (about 2 miles from the start line) where it was knocked out by a German battery. One tank belonging to another division got into Gueudecourt only to meet with a similar fate.[65]

The tank's debut could not realistically be regarded as a great success (though that was how it was hailed in much of the British press).[66] But neither could it be dismissed as an unmitigated failure. Despite the generally inadequate training of their crews, tanks had managed to advance further than any infantry and in some parts of the front had been of major assistance to the latter in subduing trenches and strongpoints. In a few cases the appearance of tanks had seriously frightened the Germans, inducing flight or surrender. At other points, however, German gunners, even when tanks approached very close to their positions, kept their nerve and engaged them like any other target. Very few tanks were fit for action on 16 September (it seems that only three did any real fighting on that day) but these played a significant part in disrupting a German counter-attack.[67]

After 16 September there was something of a lull. When Fourth Army resumed the offensive on 25 September it appears to have employed only twelve tanks and the performance of those varied greatly. Fewer still were in action the following day. But one distinguished itself on 26 September in an attack by the 21st Division on a major German position known as the Gird Trench. This tank made a contribution (fully attested by the accompanying infantry) to the seizure of the position and the capture of 370 prisoners for small loss to the British. The XV Corps report on the operation stated: "What would have proved a very difficult operation, involving probably very heavy losses, was taken [*sic*] with the greatest ease entirely owing to the assistance of the tank."[68]

Tanks had by no means received universal acclaim from the infantry hitherto and it might be imagined that they badly needed this testimonial. Actually GHQ had already made its decision. Haig had met Swinton at his advanced headquarters at Busquesne on 17 September and pronounced that though tanks had not achieved all that had been hoped of them they had saved many lives and fully justified their existence.[69] The same day Haig's Chief of the General Staff (CGS), Lieutenant-General Kiggell, wrote to Robertson, the CIGS, in the same terms: "Consider that the utility of the tanks has been proved. It has been established that the magnitude [*sic*] of the success on the 15th in certain localities was directly attributable to the employment of Tanks."[70]

A conference on tanks was held at the War Office, 19–20 September 1916. Haig was represented by his Deputy CGS, Major-General Butler, and Swinton was also present. The conference decided that the existing order should be completed (which would mean the delivery of a further 100 of the present type of tank) and placed a further order for 1,000 of a slightly modified type. The French were understood to be producing 800 tanks of their own and the conference expressed the wish to arrange inter-allied co-operation in design, though little appears to have come of this.[71] The most radical decision was to try to establish a total of 5 tank brigades, 1 for each of the British Armies in France. Each brigade was to consist of 144 first-line tanks plus 72 spares. Brigades would be subdivided into "wings" (terminology borrowed, significantly, from the Royal Flying Corps), each of 48 first-line tanks and 24 spares. Wings were to comprise 3 companies of equal size. Companies were to consist of 4 sections, each of 4 first-line and 2 spare tanks. Given that (owing to the interior temperatures of 100 degrees Fahrenheit which were normal in action and the significant amounts of carbon monoxide commonly absorbed) crew fatigue was a major problem, it was decided to supply 2 crews, (each of 8 individuals) for each first-line tank.[72]

Though never completely put into practice all this constituted an extraordinarily generous intended scale of provision for a new engine of war which had yet given only modest evidence of its potential. There were indications at this conference, held only four days after the tanks' first action, that the Heavy Section Machine Gun Corps was expected to develop into something analagous to the Royal Flying Corps and perhaps ultimately to approach the latter organization (already regarded as an elite vital to the operations of the BEF) in size and importance. The conference was informed of Haig's strong recommendation that "the combatant personnel of the Heavy Section should have a distinctive form of dress as is the case with the Royal Flying Corps". It was decided that a depot or depots should be formed in France "on similar lines to Aircraft Parks".[73] On 2 October Haig sent a formal letter to the War Office confirming that: "From the experience of the employment of tanks during recent operations I have the honour to report that this new engine has proved itself to possess certain qualities which warrant further provision on a large scale." He placed in writing the order for 1,000 new tanks and the personnel to go with them.[74] On 9 October 1916 GHQ recommended that the Heavy Section Machine Gun Corps should be redesignated the Tank Corps[75] though the title was not formally conferred until June 1917.

If Haig's order for 1,000 tanks showed remarkable faith, the enthusiasm of Albert Stern knew no bounds. On 1 November 1916 Sir William Robertson felt compelled to write to Haig:

The man Stern who has something to do with the production of tanks has been telling Lloyd George that he can put in hand still another 1,000 tanks for you. Lloyd George is rather in favour of giving out this further order, but it seems to me that the 1,000 you have already asked for is as far as we should think of going at present having regard to the experimental stage of these things and to the large number of personnel they absorb. I therefore told L.G. that I would like to communicate with you first. I should like to know whether you agree with me that we should at present limit our order to one thousand. Besides the men they absorb they also take up a great deal of steel, which is now rather scarce, and in general the tanks should not be ordered unless you think they are really necessary.[76]

This represented the opening shot in a what eventually amounted to a sort of bureaucratic war between Stern's department in the Ministry of Munitions and the War Office. Stern's keenness was, in theory, commendable. But he was a banker with no experience of manufacturing industry and a lack of realism about it. Stern did not in fact secure the immediate doubling of Haig's order. The manpower and raw materials situation made it extremely difficult, in the short run, for Stern to supply even the 1,000 which Haig had actually demanded though he eventually produced rather more.[77]

In late September 1916 Lieutenant-Colonel Hugh Elles DSO was appointed to command the tanks in France.[78] He was a natural choice and a good one. He was, in Swinton's words, *persona gratissima* at GHQ. As already noted he had been one of Haig's observers at the Hatfield Park demonstration and had contributed substantially to GHQ's endorsement of tanks. Born in India in 1880, son of an Army officer, he had gone via Clifton to the Royal Military Academy Woolwich, from which he passed out second, and was commissioned into the Royal Engineers in June 1899. He had passed Staff College before the outbreak of war. Having served on the Western Front from August 1914 he had seen intense fighting and had been wounded near St Julien on 25 April 1915 while serving as a brigade major. He was posted to GHQ as a staff officer the following August. An officer who served as the Tank Corps' historian in 1917–18 described him as:

precociously successful and admirably good looking, reasonably vain of his appearance, but quite modest as to his attainments. He is immensely popular not only in the Tank Corps but in the Army generally. He struck me as one of the paladins of the war, modernised and adjusted to the conditions of the hour. Decisions do not come to him easily, and he is sensitive to influences, taking a good deal of time to make up his mind, but with a great deal of personal charm and power of leadership. He makes no profession of indifference to danger, but probably no-one in the army would lead a forlorn hope as cheerfully.

An original thinker Elles was not and his "reading for the most part was limited to his trade" as a sapper. Apart from his success at Woolwich there is little to suggest that he had more than an average intellectual endowment.[79] But there were others in his headquarters who could supply ideas and imagination in plenty.

But before examining the ideas of the remarkable collection of individuals which was to constitute Elles's staff, it seems appropriate to review GHQ's position on tanks as it stood in the final quarter of 1916. On 5 October Kiggell issued a "Note on the Use of Tanks"[80] which became official doctrine on the subject for several months. It is remarkable for its fairness and balance in assessing tank strengths and weaknesses. It forms a useful corrective to the post-war writings of Swinton and Fuller which sometimes suggest that it was only the obscurantism of higher authority which prevented the tanks winning the war by mid-1917.

Though he argued that in "the present stage of their development they must be regarded as entirely accessory to the ordinary methods of attack, i.e. to the advance of Infantry in close cooperation with Artillery", Kiggell gave tanks full credit for what they had been able to accomplish so far, noting that when they had been able to reach hostile trenches a little ahead of the attacking infantry they had not merely saved lives by drawing a great deal of rifle and machine gun fire on to themselves but had inflicted losses on the enemy in his trenches, knocked out machine guns and, in some cases, "by combined moral and material effect brought about the enemy's surrender or retirement". Even tanks which had only arrived at enemy trenches after the attacking infantry had already got there had been able to deal with barbed wire, machine guns and strongpoints which had been holding the infantry up.

Kiggell by no means exaggerated the vulnerability of tanks. If anything he underplayed it. He made no mention of the problem of bullets shattering the glass vision blocks through which the drivers viewed the outside world, sometimes blinding them, nor of "bullet splash" – fragments of bullets penetrating eye-slits and gaps between armour plates and inflicting extremely painful (though not normally fatal) wounds. Kiggell noted that though, while static, tanks were extremely vulnerable to artillery, they were far less likely to be hit when moving. Once they got close to enemy positions they attained relative safety. The number of tanks knocked out by hostile artillery had proved very small, he noted, compared to the number which had simply broken down.[81]

The difficulties of mounting operations with the Mark I tank were not minimized, however. The ideal was that in an attack the majority of tanks should reach the enemy front-line trench about fifty yards ahead of the infantry. But this was difficult to achieve in practice. The main problem was that tank speed was extremely sensitive to ground:

> Downhill, over easy ground they can move faster than the infantry. Up-hill, or over difficult ground they move slower. If they start . . . any appreciable time before the infantry they will probably bring down the enemy's barrage before the infantry have got away. If they do not start sufficient time ahead of the infantry the latter will soon pass them unless the ground is very favourable to the Tanks. If they are moving any appreciable distance ahead of the infantry there is an immediate complication as regards the barrage which it is essential the infantry should move close up to.

Tanks, in GHQ's analysis, were of most use to infantry in a situation where the start line for the attack was not more than 350 yards from the trench to be assaulted. In these circumstances, if the ground was very favourable, the tanks could start moving at the same time as the infantry and still reach the enemy trench ahead of them. If the ground was less favourable but the distance to be covered no greater, then allowing the tanks to start a minute or two earlier might still be possible without bringing down the enemy's barrage soon enough to prevent the infantry leaving their trenches. Otherwise it might be better, Kiggell implied, to accept that the infantry would arrive at the enemy's first line before the tanks. As tanks were, at their existing stage of development, "merely accessory to the combined action of infantry and artillery", it would not be justifiable "to take any risk of interfering with that combination or of bringing about the risk of failure of the infantry attack through not affording our men the protection of an artillery barrage or by bringing down on them prematurely the enemy's barrage".[82]

Yet despite the long hard look which GHQ had thus taken at the limitations of the new weapon, tanks continued to enjoy a remarkable degree of official sponsorship in the early months of 1917. On 11 February Haig wrote to the War Office giving his views on the priority to be accorded to tank production. (There were heavy demands for petrol engines for various purposes and there had been some discussion on this question at a conference held at the Ministry of Munitions on 5 February at which Haig had been represented by General Butler.) Haig pronounced that:

(a) The essential requirements of the air service in France must have priority.

(b) The requirements of the Light Railways in petrol tractors are urgent and small. An immediate allotment was made at the above conference up to a total of 188 engines. The balance of engines as they become available to take equal place with those required for Tanks.

(c) Except for the above, the prompt and continuous delivery of Tanks at the greatest rate at which they can be turned out and shipped to France should be ensured.

The Commander-in-Chief reaffirmed that he wanted 1,000 fighting tanks as soon as possible, not counting tanks required for training purposes.[83]

The evolution of military thought on tanks in the British Army between June 1915 and November 1916 should not be seen as a dialectic involving radical prophets on the one hand and reactionary authorities on the other. Neither Swinton nor Churchill was proposing a particularly grandiose or dramatic thesis. Both envisaged the use of quite small numbers of machines. Neither expected the operation he was proposing to determine the outcome of the war. Both men doubted that a second armoured operation could meet with any success and thus neither believed the instrument he was advocating had long-term utility. Each came up with remarkable tactical insights but the schemes of attack proposed by both were seriously flawed. If implemented as proposed these would almost certainly have proved dismal failures. GHQ, moreover, did not react in an antithetical manner. Its response to the proposals for the new weapon was generally admirable: interest, followed by endorsement, followed by enthusiastic sponsorship. There was no trace of the hidebound or the Luddite in the attitude of either

French or Haig. Cavalrymen as they both were, each responded positively, though French's response appears to have been less vigorous and persistent than Haig's. (Curiously the only completely negative recorded reaction from GHQ came from a technocrat – Fowke, the chief engineer.) Haig's determined pursuit of the whole concept from Christmas Day 1915 to the order for 1,000 at the conference on 19–20 September illustrates his dominant characteristics in the most favourable light. Undoubtedly he had serious weaknesses as a general, but his optimism, doggedness and educated (if not particularly quick or original) intelligence played a crucial part in giving the British Army a new arm.

The post-war attacks on Haig by Swinton, Churchill and Lloyd George for not waiting till a mass of tanks was available,[84] were grossly unfair. In the case of Swinton, a highly intelligent professional soldier who must, in retrospect, have had a pretty good grasp of what the Mark I tank could and could not do, his vehement criticism of Haig on this point smacks of intellectual dishonesty. Swinton had produced no concept which could have led to a dramatic victory anyway and GHQ's setting aside of his original idea for the employment of tanks came only after failure to deliver machines and trained crews by the date agreed.[85] These failures may not really have been Swinton's (or indeed anyone's) fault. But Haig cannot legitimately be blamed for refusing to halt the war until some ideal number of tanks was available or for taking the view that tanks would, in most respects, have to fit in with what the rest of the army was doing as best they could. Indeed, the most legitimate criticism of Haig's and Rawlinson's conduct with regard to tanks in September 1916 is that recently made by the historians Robin Prior and Trevor Wilson: the generals expected too much of an untried instrument and were too willing to compromise the relatively established and proven technique of the creeping barrage in order to make room for the tanks' advance. Swinton's and Churchill's view that tanks could not be used more than once and that their first employment was all-important turned out to be wrong. The line which GHQ finally took, that the tank was simply another instrument of war, the best tactics for which would have to be worked out by trial and error, was sensible and realistic.

Perhaps the last word on this subject should go to an officer who was to become perhaps Haig's most inveterate and articulate critic in the British Army: J.F.C. Fuller, who served as Elles's senior staff officer. Long after the Armistice Fuller's friend and admirer, the journalist and author Basil Liddell Hart, sent him a manuscript of a book he was writing about the war. Fuller agreed with most of it wholeheartedly. But there was one of Liddell Hart's criticisms of GHQ which Fuller would not endorse. His brief notes summarize the matter adequately: "The use of tanks on 15 September 1916 was not a mistake. Serious mechanical defects manifested. No peace test can equal a war test."[86] During 1917 this opinion apparently became the dominant one in the Heavy Branch/Tank Corps in France.[87]

Notes

1 Swinton to GHQ, "The Necessity for Machine Gun Destroyers", 1 June 1915, Swinton Papers, Tank Museum.
2 *ibid.*, pp. 1 and 2.
3 *ibid.*, p. 3.
4 *ibid.*, pp. 3 and 4.
5 *ibid.*, pp. 4 and 5.
6 M. Farndale, *History of the Royal Regiment of Artillery, Western Front 1914–18* (Royal Artillery Institution) 1986, pp. 82–83.
7 Witness the experience at Neuve Chapelle. R. Prior and T. Wilson, *Command On The Western Front* (Blackwell) 1992, pp. 64–65.
8 Kitchener's failure to give Swinton any encouragement to pursue the tank idea has already been discussed. His real reaction upon seeing the demonstration of Mother at Hatfield Park is not completely clear. Virtually all those to whom he spoke at the time thought it one of complete scepticism. However, Lloyd George, in *War Memoirs of David Lloyd George*, Vol. I (Odhams) undated, pp. 383–384, claims that Kitchener was really a tank enthusiast but wanted to appear otherwise for security reasons. For a strong argument against Lloyd George's interpretation see Liddell Hart, *The Tanks*, Vol. I (Cassell) 1959, pp. 49–50.
9 Document B, undated but obviously June 1915, Swinton Papers, Tank Museum.
10 Document C, June 1915, Swinton Papers, Tank Museum.
11 R. Holmes, *The Little Field-Marshal* (Jonathan Cape) 1981, esp. pp. 195–313. A.D. Harvey, *Collision of Empires* (Hambledon) 1992, 328–334.
12 French to War Office, 22 June 1915, Document F, Swinton Papers, Tank Museum.

13 *ibid.* and Haig to War Office, 9 February 1916, PRO WO 32/5754.
14 A. Stern, *Tanks 1914–18: the Logbook of a Pioneer* (Hodder and Stoughton) 1919, p. 40. E. Swinton, *Eyewitness* (Hodder and Stoughton) 1932, pp. 161–162. Neither Stern nor Swinton is precise about when their first meeting took place. Stern suggests some time in July 1915. But Swinton did not take any action until 26 August and it seems likely that he did not discover the existence of the committee until shortly before that.
15 Swinton to Asquith, 26 August 1915. Photograph of this document included in Swinton, *Eyewitness*, facing p. 169.
16 CID, "The Future Procedure as to the Design and Construction of 'Land Cruisers' or Armoured Motor Cars propelled on the Caterpillar Principle, for the use of the Army, Report and Recommendations of an Interdepartmental Conference held on the 28th August, 1915", PRO ADM 116/1339.
17 CID, "The Question of the Provision of Caterpillar Machine Gun Destroyers or 'Land Cruisers', their Equipment, Manning and Cognate Subjects, Report and Recommendations of an Interdepartmental Conference held on December 24, 1915", PRO ADM 116/1339.
18 Swinton, *Eyewitness*, p. 187.
19 Haig to War Office, 9 February 1916, PRO WO 32/5754.
20 W. Churchill, *The World Crisis, 1915* (Thornton Butterworth) 1923, p. 86.
21 Churchill to GHQ, 3 December 1915, "Variants of the Offensive", PRO WO 158/831.
22 *ibid.*, pp. 1–2.
23 *ibid.*, para. 2, pp. 1 and 2.
24 *ibid.*, para. 3, p. 2.
25 *ibid.*, para. 3, p. 3.
26 D. Fletcher, *Landships* (HMSO) 1984, p. 10.
27 Prior and Wilson, *op. cit.*, pp. 44–56.
28 Churchill, "Variants of the Offensive", para. 5, p. 3, PRO WO 158/831.
29 *ibid.*, para. 5, p. 4.
30 S. Bidwell and D. Graham, *Fire-Power, British Army Weapons and Theories of War 1904–1945* (Allen and Unwin) 1982, pp. 90–92.
31 J. Terraine, *Douglas Haig: the Educated Soldier* (Hutchinson) 1963, pp. 3–65. F. Maurice on Haig in Dictionary of National Biography (DNB) 1922–30, pp. 373–375.
32 Maurice, *op. cit.*, pp. 375–376.
33 On Haig's taciturnity see J. Boraston's article in *The Spectator* 28 November 1952. On his religious convictions see R. Blake (ed.) *The Private Papers of Douglas Haig 1914–1919* (Eyre and Spottiswoode) 1952, pp. 29 and 172. On excessive optimism see Prior and Wilson,

op. cit., pp. 23–35, 52–57, 138–153 and 167–168. On emphasis on airpower see Haig to Robertson, 23 November 1917, BCII/44, Fuller Papers, Liddell Hart Centre for Military Archives, King's College London (henceforth LHCMA). On Geddes and light railways see Haig's diary, 27 October 1916, Blake, *op. cit.*, pp. 173–174. For a general assessment of Haig's personality and achievement see G.J. de Groot, *Douglas Haig, 1861–1928* (Unwin Hyman) 1988, *passim*.

34 B. Liddell Hart, *The Tanks*, Vol. I (Cassell) 1959, p. 48. Terraine, *op. cit.*, p. 220. Churchill has a somewhat different account of how Haig was made aware of the caterpillar landship idea: "In November 1915 when serving in France I wrote a memorandum for Sir John French . . . This memorandum explains the tactical conception of tanks . . . On Sir Douglas Haig being appointed Commander in Chief, I had an interview with him at St. Omer in the early days of January 1916 in which I explained to him these ideas, and informed him that a vehicle was far advanced in construction. I handed in my memorandum of November. He had heard nothing of this. He seemed interested in what I said and two days later I was ordered to tell Major Elles what I knew. Major Elles went to England and got in touch with d'Eyncourt's committee." Churchill to Hankey, paras 9 and 10, 26 January 1938, PRO CAB 45/200. The two accounts are not totally irreconcilable but Churchill's is probably wrong. Churchill did meet Haig at St Omer on 19 January but all he recorded of the event in a letter to his wife was "Quite by chance I met Haig riding on the road . . . He rode up & shook hands and we exchanged a few banalities." M. Gilbert, *Winston S. Churchill*, Vol. III (Heinemann) 1971, p. 643. The present writer has not been able to find the copy of "Variants" with the critical pencil query made by Haig on Christmas Day 1915. The first published account of this incident seems to have been C. Williams-Ellis, *The Tank Corps* (Country Life) 1919, p. 13. It seems unlikely, however, that Liddell Hart would have repeated a story so favourable to Haig (of whom he had a very poor opinion) unless he were fairly certain of its veracity.

35 One of the more recent of several books portraying Haig as a blinkered Blimp is D. Winter, *Haig's Command: a Reassessment* (Viking) 1991, especially pp. 163–167. On Elles's mission to report on the trials of "Mother" see Liddell Hart, *op. cit.*, p. 48, and Haig to War Office, 9 February 1916, PRO WO 32/5754.

36 Haig to War Office, 9 February 1916, PRO WO 32/5754.

37 Stern, *op. cit.*, pp. 64–65.

38 "Recommendations of a Conference held at the War Office on 14 February 1916", PRO WO 32/5754.

39 *ibid.* Swinton, *Eyewitness*, pp. 217–218. Liddell Hart, *op. cit.*, pp. 54–56.

40 Haig to War Office (letter signed by Kiggell on Haig's behalf) 5 April 1916, PRO WO 32/5754.
41 Swinton to GHQ, 26 April 1916, PRO WO 32/5754.
42 Swinton, "Notes on the Employment of Tanks", February 1916, Stern Papers, LHCMA.
43 *ibid.*, para. 21, p. 4.
44 *ibid.*, paras 22–24, pp. 4 and 5.
45 *ibid.*, paras 31–36, pp. 5–6.
46 *ibid.*, paras 37–43, pp. 6–7.
47 *ibid.*, *passim*.
48 *ibid.*, para. 11, p. 3.
49 Swinton, *Eyewitness*, pp. 294–299.
50 A useful summary of the historiography of this topic is provided in A.J. Smithers, *Cambrai: the First Great Tank Battle 1917* (Leo Cooper) 1992, p. 59. See also Swinton, *Eyewitness*, pp. 24–302. Churchill, *The World Crisis, 1915*, p. 89. Lloyd George, *op. cit.*, p. 385, Liddell Hart, *op. cit.*, p. 67. Official History of the Great War (henceforth OH), W. Miles, *Military Operations, France and Belgium, 1916, 2nd July 1916 to the End of the Battles of the Somme* (Macmillan) 1938, pp. 365–367.
51 Swinton, *Eyewitness*, p. 234.
52 "Digest of Decisions Reached at a Conference on the 26th June 1916", PRO WO 32/5754.
53 Swinton to GHQ, 26 April 1916, PRO WO 32/5754. Terraine, *op. cit.*, pp. 221–222.
54 Liddell Hart, *op. cit.*, p. 64 and Swinton, *Eyewitness*, p. 277.
55 Haig to Robertson, 22 August 1916, PRO WO 158/21.
56 Robertson to Haig, 25 August 1916, ROBERTSON 1/22/70, Robertson Papers, LHCMA.
57 Liddell Hart, *op. cit.*, p. 65. Stern, *op. cit.*, pp. 87–90.
58 "Preliminary Notes on Tactical Employment of Tanks", August 1916, PRO WO 158/835.
59 *Ibid.*, para. 4, p. 2.
60 Swinton, "Notes on the Employment of 'Tanks'", p. 2, para. 9, Stern Papers, LHCMA.
61 OH, Miles, *op. cit.*, p. 296. Liddell Hart, *op. cit.*, p. 66.
62 OH, Miles, *op. cit.*, p. 297.
63 Liddell Hart. *op. cit.*, pp. 69–70 and Terraine, *op. cit.*, p. 222.
64 Prior and Wilson, *op. cit.*, pp. 234–239.
65 OH, Miles, *op. cit.*, 327.
66 Williams-Ellis, *op. cit.*, p. 30.
67 Liddell Hart, *op. cit.*, p. 76.
68 *ibid.*, p. 77.
69 Swinton, *Eyewitness*, p. 286.

70   Kiggell to Robertson, ROBERTSON 1/14/40, Robertson Papers, LHCMA.
71   "Recommendations for the Expansion of the Heavy Section (Tanks), Machine Gun Corps, Put Forward by Major-General Butler, Deputy Chief of the General Staff, France, at a Conference Held on 19th and 20th September 1916", paras 1–2, p. 1, PRO WO 158/836.
72   *ibid.*, para. 4, p. 2.
73   *ibid.*, para. 9, p. 3.
74   Haig to War Office, 2 October 1916, PRO WO 158/836.
75   GHQ to AG, QMG etc, September 1916 (exact date not entered on carbon copy held at Kew), PRO WO 158/863.
76   Robertson to Haig, 1 November 1916, ROBERTSON 1/22/86, Robertson Papers, LHCMA.
77   *History of the Ministry of Munitions, Vol. XII, the Supply of Munitions, Part III: Tanks*, 1920, pp. 37–38, SWINTON B2, Swinton Papers, LHCMA.
78   GHQ to the Armies, 29 September 1916, PRO WO 158/863.
79   C.T. Atkinson on Elles in DNB 1941–50, pp. 234–236. "HQ Tanks", pp. 15–16. This unpublished account, apparently by the Tank Corps historian, Captain the Hon. Evan E. Charteris, is held as 355.486.86: (Charteris), in the library of the Tank Museum. Elles is referred to as "the General".
80   "Note on the Use of Tanks", L.E. Kiggell, Advanced HQ, 5 October 1916, PRO WO 158/832.
81   *ibid.*, paras 2–5.
82   *ibid.*, para. 6.
83   Haig to War Office, 11 February 1917, p. 7, PRO WO 158/804.
84   Swinton, *Eyewitness*, pp. 294–299. Churchill, *The World Crisis, 1915.* p. 89. Lloyd George, *op. cit.*, p. 385.
85   Swinton to GHQ, 26 April 1916, PRO WO 32/5754. Terraine, *op. cit.*, p. 222.
86   Fuller to Liddell Hart, 22 September 1926, LH 1/302/100, Liddell Hart Papers, LHCMA.
87   OH, Miles, *op. cit.*, pp. 365–366. Smithers, *op. cit.*, p. 59. Liddell Hart, *op. cit.*, p. 67.

3

The road to Cambrai

In October 1916 a new headquarters was established for the Heavy Branch, Machine Gun Corps at the somewhat delapidated chateau of Bermicourt near St Pol, a mile north of the Hesdin–Arras road.[1] The functions of the Bermicourt HQ were primarily administrative, technical and advisory. Never did Elles's organization exert real command over troops in the field. Even the advanced tank HQs which were established from time to time to supervise preparations for the use of tanks in major battles were largely administrative centres. Though capable of giving tactical advice with regard to the employment of tanks, Elles and his staff did not make decisions on the conduct of operations, and in battle tanks came under the command of the infantry formations to which they were attached. Nor did Bermicourt have a monopoly on the generation of ideas for the employment of tanks. These came from a wide variety of sources.[2] In fact most of the major tank operations of the war arose from concepts generated by the staffs of predominantly infantry formations, i.e. from divisional, corps or Army headquarters. As will be demonstrated later in this chapter, Cambrai was an example of this.

Elles, moreover, did not have control over all aspects of the administration of the Heavy Branch. A superior officer, Brigadier-General F.G. Anley, took over the administrative headquarters in England at the beginning of November 1916, replacing Swinton,[3] who went to work for the War Cabinet. Anley assumed responsibility for recruitment, basic training (most of which was now carried out at Bovington Camp and other sites near Wool in Dorset) and matters of general policy arising out of the expansion of the corps. Formerly the commander of an infantry brigade, Anley was keen to instil discipline and soldierly qualities into the Heavy Branch. Opinions of him varied considerably. Albert Stern thought highly of him:

> It was General Anley who started the famous Tank Camp at Wool. It was splendidly organised, and the Tank Corps, under his command, became a fine well-disciplined force. We who were building the Tanks had every encouragement and help from him, and we were all very sorry when he was appointed to a command in Egypt.[4]

But others thought that Anley's primary goal was to have a quiet life and to avoid, at all costs, antagonizing his superiors.[5] Under both Anley and his successor, Major-General Sir John Capper, who took over in May 1917, relations between Bermicourt and the headquarters at home were sometimes strained.

Capper was an intelligent and technically oriented soldier. Before the war he had captained the Army's first airship, *Nulli Secundus*, in a flight over London in 1907. He had later been commandant of the Army's balloon school and later still of the School of Military Engineering at Chatham. By 1918 he had become a champion of ambitious ideas for the large-scale employment of tanks. But he appears to have been a poor communicator and to have created the impression with much of the Bermicourt staff of being pompous, humourless, reactionary and unreceptive to new ideas. His nick-name at Bermicourt was "The Stone Age".[6]

In addition to its commander, Lieutenant-Colonel Hugh Elles, the key personnel who assembled at Bermicourt in the last months of 1916 included Major J.F.C. Fuller, Elles's senior general staff officer, Captain T.J. Uzielli, the quartermaster, Captain F.E. Hotblack, the intelligence officer, Captain G. le Q. Martel, who assisted Fuller on the operations side, and Captain F. Searle, the technical adviser. Of those mentioned only Fuller and Martel could be described as theorists and in terms of intellectual energy Martel appears to have been dwarfed by Fuller. Yet all contributed to the peculiar ambience of Bermicourt, all helped to make the place work and assisted directly or indirectly with the genesis of ideas about tank use.[7]

Uzielli seems to have produced no ideas himself but contributed to the smooth running of the organization and was important to the well-being of those who did. Small, dark, suave and clever, a brother officer regarded him as "Levantine in method, with much

Figure 11 This Bermicourt group includes Fuller (on the far left), Uzielli (next to him) and Elles (in the middle next to Uzielli).

of the ingratiating technique of an Oriental. Intensely ambitious, he [was] a past master in the art of getting his way with all sorts and conditions of men". A hedonist himself, "disregarding no nuance of good living and comfort"[8] he was ideal in the quarter-master role of fixer and procurer and "never left the Tank Corps in want".[9]

Searle, on the other hand, was an important ideas man and innovator though the ideas and innovations were technical and practical – he was no theoretician. Apparently from lowly social origins, he had worked as a stoker before rising to become a manager in the Wolsely Motor Company. A "tall, rather imposing-looking individual with grey hair and a florid face", he was unpopular at Bermicourt where he was considered to be a rough diamond, ambitious, unscrupulous and hard on his subordinates. His competence, however, was beyond doubt:

Engineers said he was no engineer, business men said he knew nothing of business, soldiers said he had no idea of discipline. In spite of this the mechanical side of tanks seemed to develop under his hands, huge workshops sprang up, remarkable feats of construction and

repair were performed and the complaints about the mechanical efficiency of tanks grew steadily less and less.[10]

Uzielli intermittently tried to assert some sort of control over Searle's
work but the former's technical knowledge was obviously inadequate. An incipient feud between Searle and Uzielli was one of
the constant features of internal politics at HQ. Uzielli's bitterest
foe was Searle's deputy, Captain G.A. Green, a former motor bus
manager with "a good touch of the gutter about him, primitive,
direct and gifted with quite first-rate talents of a practical kind".
Green was a devoted admirer of Searle and these two ran, with
great efficiency, the Central Workshops at Erin about two miles
from Bermicourt.[11]

Fuller was widely regarded as the foremost intellect at Bermicourt.
Born in 1878, the son of an Anglican parson, he went via Malvern
School and Sandhurst, neither of which he liked, into the Oxford-
shire Light Infantry in 1898. He served in the South African War,
part of the time as an intelligence officer in charge of a group of
scouts. During that conflict he began to take his profession (which
he had hitherto regarded as a bore) rather more seriously. In 1906
he began a lasting and apparently happy, though childless, marriage to Sonia, a woman of Polish extraction whose degree of
eccentricity was about equal to his own. He was at Staff College
when war broke out in 1914.[12] But he was largely self-educated
and had a mercurial temperament and an off-beat way of looking
at the world. A brother officer at Bermicourt described him as:

> A little man with a bald head and a sharp face and nose of Napo-
> leonic cast, his general appearance, stature and features earning him
> the title of Boney. He stood out at once as a totally unconventional
> soldier, prolific in ideas, fluent in expression, at daggers drawn with
> received opinion, authority and tradition. In the mess, his attacks on
> the red-tabbed hierarchy were viewed in the spirit of a rat hunt: a
> spirit he responded to with much vivacity and no little wit. But he
> could talk amusingly and paradoxically on any subject. His special-
> ities were Eastern religions about which he could be bewildering,
> spiritualism, occultism, military history and the theory of war ... He
> was an inexhaustible writer and from his office issued reams on
> reams about training, plans of campaign, organization and schemes
> for the use of tanks ... He was neither an administrator nor prob-
> ably a good commander but just what a staff officer ought to be,
> evolving good ideas and leaving their execution to others.[13]

The pen-portrait of Fuller quoted above is very sympathetic. He could certainly be engaging, though he could also be infuriating. The extraordinary vigour and fertility of his mind is apparent in the best of his voluminous published writings, some of which have exerted a considerable influence on military historians writing about the Western Front.[14] But there was a dark side to Fuller's personality and his intellect had a lack of balance about it. It ran to extremes, pushing concepts as far as they would go, often ignoring the inconvenient complexities of the real world.

Before the war he had been a disciple of the charlatan and "magician", Aleister Crowley and had written a book, *The Star in the West*, designed to inaugurate the new religion of "Crowley-anity". He had subsequently dropped Crowley but retained a fascination with the occult which seems to have exerted a continuing influence on his military ideas though this is rather less apparent in his work at Bermicourt than it would be in some of his later writings. (One historian has perceptively written of Fuller's "instinctive leaning towards hocus-pocus".)[15] An incipient Fascism is very evident in certain of Fuller's 1917–18 papers.[16] He was to join Sir Oswald Mosley's British Union of Fascists after his retirement from the Army in late 1933 and to attend Hitler's fiftieth birthday celebrations in April 1939, facts which, like his involvement with Crowley, do not reflect well on his judgement. He continued to produce theoretical work on armoured warfare in the inter-war period, but much of this was misconceived. It was, moreover, typical of Fuller's intellectual waywardness that he lost interest in the subject in the mid-1930s just as it was about to become of supreme practical importance.[17]

It was as Elles's principal staff officer, from autumn 1916 to summer 1918, that Fuller had his greatest impact on the world of action and events. Arguably this was also when he was at his best intellectually. Having a responsible job to do in a major headquarters, and being surrounded by men with qualities of practical leadership and organization to complement his imagination, helped to keep Fuller's mind anchored to reality to a greater extent than before or after his Bermicourt period. Yet, even at Bermicourt, his thinking tended to race far ahead of what was practicable with the means available. He seldom demonstrated an adequate appreciation of the limitations of tanks and many of the "reams and reams" which he produced were of little use as guides to action.

Elles, while well aware of Fuller's intellect, was less sure of his judgement and in a number of cases overrode his advice.[18]

"Boots" Hotblack, the intelligence officer, was an intensely serious and somewhat remote personality: taciturn, unsociable and "a fanatic about the war". Physically imposing, over six feet tall, he was also exceptionally brave. He was awarded the DSO after the Battle of Beaumont-Hamel in November 1916 for guiding a tank on to its objective by personally walking in front of it. A brewer before the war, he had become an intelligence officer because he had good German. But just as important as the intelligence he gathered on the enemy was "ground intelligence" in which he also made himself the HQ's leading expert. Tank routes to the front line had to be chosen with the greatest care, especially as they often had to be negotiated in the dark. Hotblack supervised the marking of these routes with luminous tape and sometimes saw to it that men wearing special jackets with red and green lights attached to the back were provided to guide the tanks on foot. Routes across No Man's Land also had to be checked as far as possible and Hotblack often did this sort of reconnaissance in person. He developed a real dedication to soldiering and stayed on in the Tank Corps in peacetime. Though not a theorist or an original thinker he kept Fuller supplied with information about developments in German defensive methods which were of considerable importance to the evolution of the latter's ideas for tank operations.[19]

Giffard le Quesne Martel, Fuller's assistant on the operations side, was a professional Army officer, and, like Elles, an engineer. Born in 1889 he had attended Wellington College and passed out top on the "modern" side, entering the Royal Military Academy Woolwich in 1908 and being commissioned the following year into the Royal Engineers. Between August 1914 and the summer of 1916 he served with an engineer field company on the Western Front but was then sent home to design a mock battlefield for the tanks at Thetford. His connection with tanks was definitely established when he was picked to serve under Elles early in October. Martel was to have a considerable impact on the development of British armoured forces up to the middle of the Second World War. He had considerable mechanical aptitude and (a great asset to a military career) was a formidable sportsman who had on several occasions been an Army boxing champion. He remained a dedicated pugilist while at Bermicourt where he gained the nickname "Slosher". He was also a literate and literary soldier who was eventually to write two books on armoured forces in addition to his memoirs.[20]

Oddly, the one major theoretical paper that Martel, the practical engineer and sportsman, produced in the First World War was extremely visionary and futuristic – very far removed from present reality. Apparently written in November 1916, it was entitled "A Tank Army". If nothing else it illustrates an atmosphere of extraordinary faith at Bermicourt, perhaps boosted by the small but important victory at Beaumont-Hamel that month, in which tanks gave significant aid to the 63rd (Royal Naval) Division. Martel began with the dubious statement that, "No present-day army could fight against an army consisting of say 2,000 tanks", and he thus concluded that "all large Continental armies will have to make use of tank armies in the future". He speculated that tanks would eventually replace "the present unprotected soldier" except in very wooded or mountainous countries. In any case the tanks would be "of such great importance that future great wars were almost certain to start with a duel between the tank armies of the respective sides".[21]

We have seen that in autumn 1916 GHQ was evolving ideas about a tank corps and the employment of armoured vehicles by analogy with the RFC and air warfare.[22] Martel, on the other hand, proceeded by analogy with maritime warfare and navies. Tanks would operate, Martel imagined, from tank bases, established near national frontiers and protected against attack from the opposing fleet by obstacles such as anti-tank ditches and land mines. These bases would, rather like ports, be defended by permanent garrisons and fixed defences. The whole object of a tank army would be the destruction of the enemy's tanks. In addition to signal tanks and supply tanks there would be three major arms:

1. The Destroyer Tank
2. The Battle Tank
3. The Torpedo Tank[23]

The Destroyer tank (a relatively light and fast machine, firing a small calibre armour-piercing gun capable of dealing with similar enemy tanks) was to be the main arm of the service. It was to do all the work currently done by infantry and cavalry, including reconnaissance, screening and raiding. It would also be responsible for the protection of friendly Battle tanks from enemy Torpedo tanks and play its part in the capture of enemy bases and warlike stores. Battle tanks, of which there were to be no less than three distinct types, were to be virtual battleships on land – juggernauts of almost Hetheringtonian proportions. The main type was to be very slow moving, capable of only 4 or 5 miles an hour, was to have armour 6 to 8 inches thick and was to carry a 6-inch gun. Torpedo tanks would carry a "torpedo tube" – apparently a sort of rocket projector. Its purpose would be to destroy enemy Battle tanks. It would rely on its speed (about 30 mph) and the cover of night or smoke to save it from the fire of the Battle tanks it would attack. The battles Martel envisaged would be decided when one side's Destroyers, supported by the fire of its Battle tanks, managed to disrupt the Destroyer screen of the other, allowing its torpedo tanks to get to close quarters with and put out of action the Battle tanks of the enemy.[24]

This visionary (or perhaps hallucinatory) document could not have been of the slightest immediate use to the BEF and was deeply flawed as long-term prophecy. There was no mention of the impact of airpower and the sole reliance on tanks to take and hold ground, including (presumably) urban areas, seems absurd. Naval warfare was, for several reasons, most notably the absence of terrain factors, a bad analogy, though it was one which influenced Fuller in 1918 and which was greatly developed by him after the war. Apparently conscious of the vast gulf separating his vision from present reality, Martel later attempted, not very successfully, to fill it with a short paper entitled "The Transition from Present Day Warfare to Tank Warfare".[25]

Fuller's first major essay on armoured warfare, the prosaically titled "Tank Training Note No. 16", was completed some time in February 1917.[26] It was less consciously visionary than Martel's "Tank Army" but in some respects it demonstrated a poor grip on reality. Characterizing the tank as a "mobile fortress", Fuller made claims for it which crews would have found little short of absurd and which must raise questions in the reader's mind as to how much time he had actually spent riding in tanks, even behind the lines. There is certainly no indication that he ever went into battle in one.

Tanks, Fuller asserted, had "nothing to fear from shrapnel, shell splinters or bullets" and could move "practically over any ground and through all entanglements". Actually tanks at this period were by no means totally bullet proof. "Bullet splash" continued to be a major problem and led to crews being issued with leather skull caps and leather and mail face-masks, though these were uncomfortable and often not worn. One type of German machine gun bullet, the "K" would penetrate right through the armour. Fuller's suggestion that tanks were insensitive to ground was simply ridiculous. They routinely sank into soft mud, became "bellied" on tree stumps or "ditched" in trenches and big shell holes. Various methods of unditching tanks were being tried, and ditching was much less likely to remove the tank from action for long periods after the introduction of the "unditching beam" which came in with the Mark IV tank in mid-1917. But the process of unditching was to remain tedious and sometimes dangerous (as it obliged at least one crew member to get out of the tank) and the unditching beam was a few months in the future when "Training Note No. 16" was written.[27]

Fuller had been heavily influenced by a paper entitled "MS in Red Ink", written some time in 1916 by a Royal Engineers officer, Captain F.H.E. Townshend, and shown to Fuller before he came to Bermicourt. The premise of this document was that 80 per cent of the German forces on the Western Front were occupying an area some 500 miles long but only 5 miles deep. The Germans had relatively few reserves so, Townshend reasoned, if an advance of of 5 miles could be achieved on a front of 100 the war would be virtually won.[28] There was a serious flaw in Townshend's argument. A mere "advance" of 5 miles on a front of 100 miles would not mean decisive victory if the majority of the German troops in that sector was still at large and was conducting a fighting withdrawal. Townshend, moreover, suggested no method of accomplishing the advance. His "MS" was merely an attempt at the clear statement of a problem in the hope that such clarity would assist its solution. Fuller does not appear to have spotted any flaw in the reasoning and when he first saw tanks he thought he had discovered the method.

In his February 1917 "Training Note", Fuller took up Townshend's basic point, indicating that the "leading characteristic of the present war" was "great extension of front with little depth of reserves". The object of the tanks, therefore, would be "to advance on a broad front of perhaps 20 miles to a depth of 3 or 4 in a few hours". The main objectives of the tanks would be "those lines of trenches and wire which will offer the greatest resistance to the infantry advance, namely the enemy's second and subsequent lines of defence."[29]

Fuller emphasized the importance of surprise, a theme which he was to develop in later papers. Like everyone else on the Western Front he realized that very long preliminary bombardments gave the enemy notice of an offensive and allowed him to draw reserves from his flank to meet the attack. But, again like everyone else, Fuller had no real solution to the problem. The best he could recommend was the reduction of the artillery preparation to 48 hours. Wanting to keep the tanks to deal with the enemy's second- and third-line positions he had to allow time for artillery to subdue the first-line defences and to cut the wire in front of the first line. He reasoned that:

> Experience in past battles has shown that if the artillery is well handled the attacking infantry have no difficulty in carrying most of the enemy's front line system. But when this is captured, what with points hanging out in rear and the general disorganisation resulting from the assault itself, it has been proved by experience that neither will the same troops carry the second line system, nor will time usually be sufficient for new troops to be brought up to do so before the enemy has had time to reorganise his men in order to hold it.[30]

In Fuller's view the mission of the tanks was, while both attacking and defending infantry were still in a state of disorganization after the initial assault, to advance through the attacking infantry and engage the enemy's second line of defence. While the enemy's disorganization was thus accentuated, the attacking infantry would regroup and assault the enemy second line, or fresh infantry would be passed through them to fulfil the same function. In this way Fuller hoped that "the enemy's overthrow [would] be speedy and the ultimate advance from the second system to the third will savour more of a pursuit than an assault". Once the enemy's entire defensive system had been overrun the main duty of the tanks would be to prevent the enemy consolidating further back and thus checking the pursuit.

Tank tactics in such an assault would involve break-ins to each successive enemy position which would in turn result in the creation of internal flanks. Tanks would then be required to make turning or enveloping movements to roll these up. This would mean that each successive line of defence would require its own attack and consequently its own attacking formation. Each echelon of tanks would have some machines designated for mopping up and some assigned to the two "wings" which would move behind the tanks involved in the break-in operation and which would then turn to "work obliquely outward forming the offensive flanks to the infantry advance and broadening the basis of operations by always threatening the enemy in flank".[31]

"Training Note No. 16" is untypical of the kind of writing – full of sweeping generalizations and radical simplifications – which the general reader normally associates with Fuller's name. It is, presumably in an effort to be realistic and of immediate practical use, in some respects extremely conservative, employing phrases which appear odd coming from Fuller:

> The more Tanks are used the more important will the bayonet become because of the opportunity the Tank will create for its use; but it must be remembered that the Creeping Barrage will usually be more effective than the Tank and that the Tank is in no way intended to replace this Barrage but to supplement it when it breaks down or becomes ineffective.[32]

But there are unresolved tensions, even internal contradictions, in Fuller's first major paper on tank tactics. They arise between the grand, decisive military operation which his temperament made him strive to devise and his awareness of limits on the means available to achieve that ideal. Early in the paper he expresses the wishful thought that if the enemy's second defensive system can be broken his third might collapse without a formal assault. Slightly later on, however, he seems to contradict his own wishful thinking, indicating that each defensive system will require a separate echelon of tanks just as "each system requires a separate bombardment and a separate unused force of infantry for its capture".[33]

The source of the tension in this case is Fuller's awareness that tanks were likely to be limited in numbers for the foreseeable future and that, if the attack was mounted on the 20-mile front he was suggesting, the vast majority of them would have to be used against the enemy's second-line system. He was thus left with nothing but a vague hope that a successful assault on the second

line would precipitate a rout. It was presumably the same awareness of a shortage of tanks which led him to allocate none to the
enemy's first-line defensive system (even for mopping up purposes).
In order to cut its wire and soften it up, he recommended a 48-
hour preliminary bombardment of that system,[34] though this would
have very significantly reduced the degree of surprise achievable
and probably given the enemy time to concentrate at least a
modicum of a reserve just outside artillery range.

Even if a complete breakthrough were speedily achieved on a
20-mile front, Fuller knew that this in itself would not decide the
outcome of the war. He was aware that the enemy's resistance
was likely to consolidate further back, outside the range of the
British artillery. A decisive result would not be achieved unless
some effective means of pursuit and exploitation were devised.
Though he made an attempt to find a solution it seems unlikely
that Fuller convinced even himself that he had succeeded. The
traditional answer was cavalry but, given the vulnerability of cavalry to machine guns, he suggested that they work closely with
tanks.[35] As we have already seen, tanks were so slow at this period
that they often could not even keep up with infantry. Their effective range was, moreover, very short. Even if they could be kept
supplied with petrol and did not break down mechanically, crew
fatigue became prohibitive after a few hours in action and the
crews often needed a couple of days rest. Fuller's ideas on exploitation were thus totally unrealistic in the existing state of tank
technology.

One of the strong points of "Training Note No. 16" was the
thought which Fuller gave to the problems of assembly and supply
which would arise in tank operations. Much of the terminology
Fuller employed in this regard was to become standard (though it
is not clear whether it was original to him). Tanks would be
moved, most of the way by rail, to a chosen place of assembly –
the "Tankodrome". From there they would go to "The Position
of Deployment" – the place where they would lie up prior to
moving to their "Starting Points" – the place from which they
would move into battle. (In some circumstances "The Position of
Deployment" and the "Starting Point" could be identical.) He
realized that after an objective had been secured tanks still would
have to return promptly to a pre-arranged "Rallying Point" for
the crew to rest and for vehicles to be replenished and repaired.[36]

Fuller estimated that for 1 day of 10 running hours each tank would require 70 gallons of petrol, 5 gallons of engine oil, 40 gallons of water and 7 pounds of grease. From the railheads to the forward dumps near the tanks' positions of deployment these supplies would be moved by lorry. From the forward dumps to the rallying points they would be moved by a tracked vehicle which Fuller called a "Tank tender". When actually introduced in mid-1917 they were referred to as "Supply tanks".[37]

Fuller had also thought seriously about communications problems, though he had failed to find complete solutions. He recommended tank-to-tank and tank-to-infantry signalling at short range by coloured discs and lights, using simple codes. For communication at somewhat longer ranges he envisaged the use of the Aldis daylight lamp. He also predicted the emergence of specialist signals tanks for sending messages to headquarters in the rear and these did indeed appear by the time of the Battle of Cambrai in November 1917. The coloured disc system of signalling from tanks to infantry was employed with some success to pass simple massages. Communication of any detail and precision between tanks and infantry in battle, however, appears to have been possible only when the former could stop and face-to-face conversation could take place. For sending messages to headquarters carrier pigeons seem to have been as good as anything else.[38]

Despite his undoubted intelligence and dedication, in February 1917 we find Fuller floundering. He greatly underestimated the vulnerability of tanks, overestimated their mobility and, while having some good tactical ideas, had not yet come close to devising the sort of dramatic armoured operation on which he had set his heart.

The best method of using tanks was under consideration, early in 1917, at a level much higher than Fuller's. On 25 January the War Cabinet had addressed the subject.[39] The War Cabinet's proper sphere was grand strategy and that it should be spending time considering the tactics of a new, relatively untried, and so far fairly insignificant weapon may seem surprising. But the Prime Minister, David Lloyd George, was disillusioned with British generals and generalship. As Minister of Munitions he had been in touch with the early development of tanks and had made contact with Albert Stern and Eustace Tennyson d'Eyncourt. Stern was still in charge of the Mechanical Warfare Supply Department which

Lloyd George had established at the Ministry of Munitions and Tennyson d'Eyncourt was still loosely associated with tanks through the Ministry of Munition's Tank Supply Committee on which he served.[40] Stern's and d'Eyncourt's pioneering spirit of assertiveness and self-confidence appears to have been undeterred by their general ignorance of military matters and they, acting through Lloyd George, appear to have been the instigators of the War Cabinet discussion. They pointed out differences between those "responsible for the original conception, the design, the manufacture and the development of tanks" (i.e. themselves) and GHQ in France. Amongst these differences were:

> (a) That in the view of the General Staff, the Tanks should be used as an adjunct to Infantry and should be so constructed as to be able to keep up with Infantry in the attack.
> (b) That in the view of the designers Tanks should not necessarily be used as an adjunct to Infantry but should operate on the flank of the attack, moving over areas which had not been pitted by shell-fire and where they did not draw fire upon our own Infantry.[41]

The War Cabinet decided to hold a conference on the subject involving members of the British and French high commands and those responsible for tank design production and use in the two countries.[42] It is hardly surprising that, when informed of this decision at the end of January 1917, GHQ felt somewhat put out. The questioning of the conduct of military operations by a banker turned munitions procurer and by a naval architect was indeed a novel procedure. Kiggell replied on Haig's behalf that: "On the face of it the idea is somewhat peculiar and it would appear likely to be more useful if the manufacturers concentrated on production and left tactics to the soldiers."[43]

But the conference went ahead anyway, meeting on 4 March. GHQ sent Major-General Butler, Haig's Deputy Chief of the General Staff. It produced a more intelligent discussion than could reasonably have been expected. For this the French delegation, and in particular the principal French tank pioneer, Colonel Jean Baptiste Eugene Estienne, Commandant of the Artillerie d'Assaut (Tank Corps), were primarily responsible. A meeting involving only the British military, on the one hand, and, on the other, Stern and d'Eyncourt – over-assertive of the powers of the tank, lacking in adequate experience of conditions at the front and eager to teach the soldiers their business, would probably have been merely embarrassing. As hosts, however, the British seem to have been content to allow the French to speak first and Estienne appears to have dominated the discussion. He took an interesting line which combined a much greater awareness of the present limitations of tanks than Stern and d'Eyncourt with a preparedness to be more adventurous than any British representative, including Elles, in contemplating their future.[44]

Estienne put forward an idea for "a surprise attack without previous artillery bombardment". Swinton had not thought it possible to dispense entirely with preliminary bombardment and, in "Training Note No. 16", Fuller had merely suggested its limitation to 48 hours or less. Apparently the only British officers who had so far advocated tank attack without preliminary bombardment were Churchill and Haig. Haig had made the proposal only a few weeks earlier, contemplating a major offensive in Flanders. He had wanted the Gheluvelt plateau seized by a surprise attack by massed tanks. The idea was incorporated in a memorandum completed on 14 February by a planning group under Colonel Macmullen which formed the basis of the proposed British Flanders offensive.[45] The offensive was much postponed and at some stage the proposal for the mass tank assault dropped. Very few serviceable tanks existed in the early months of 1917[46] and Haig's proposal for a uphill tank attack, apparently without any artillery support, was in any case asking too much of the Marks I and II, the only types available at this time.

Estienne was aware of the difficulties of concealing preparations for a tank attack and had given the matter considerable thought. A tank detrainment point about 10–12 kilometres behind the front would have to be selected and the arrival of tanks at this point delayed as long as administratively possible. From the detrainment point tanks would move to a point of assembly where stores would have been accumulated for them and a depot established. Prior to the attack the tanks would have to be moved up to the front at night or under the cover of a fog. In a surprise attack of this sort the tanks would actually lead the infantry in the attack.

In deliberate attacks preceded by artillery bombardments, on the other hand, Estienne's view of the role of the tank was very similar to that which Fuller had outlined in February. Tanks would follow the infantry into action, dealing with strongpoints in his first-line defensive system and leading the assault on the second line. For the breakthrough role the French, like the British, favoured heavy tanks but they were also hoping to have medium tanks and light tanks (of which they already had a promising prototype) for a number of roles including exploitation and counter-attack.[47]

Stern and d'Eyncourt wanted to push the claims of the tank further than Estienne, himself much more radical than the British military representatives, was prepared to go at this stage. Stern and d'Eyncourt urged the soldiers to regard the tank as a "fairly reliable arm". The high failure rate of tanks at the Battle of the Somme in September could be largely dismissed, they claimed, as being due to poor crew training and to mechanical teething troubles which had subsequently been resolved to a large extent.

D'Eyncourt asked whether tanks should not now be regarded as "a separate arm". Could not an attack take the form of "Tanks supported by infantry rather than infantry by Tanks"?. To assist the tanks, ought not areas which had not been heavily shelled be avoided altogether? With regard to the light tank, Stern tried to push the argument even further and appeared to be advocating the use of tanks quite separately from infantry. "Should not the light machines be regarded as Cavalry, with this difference, that unlike Cavalry they are immune from wire and machine gun fire? What could a General achieve with such an arm? Would not his object be the German guns?" Estienne sought to moderate Stern's enthusiasm. He considered the notion of a mass light tank cavalry charge "a little premature". The German defences were organized in great depth. Tanks unsupported by infantry would be at the mercy of the enemy's light artillery. Tanks, because of their high profile, tended to be highly visible and to present better targets to artillery than cavalry. Tanks were not sufficiently developed yet for independent use and required infantry support.[48]

When pressed, both the GHQ representative, Butler, and the main War Office delegate, the DCIGS, Major-General Whigham, indicated great scepticism about Estienne's surprise attack concept. The minutes of the conference show significant disagreements and it seems that these were far from fully resolved at its end. Nevertheless the delegates were able to formulate conclusions which were clear, logical and not a mere fudge of the issues. Tanks at their existing stage of development were a supporting arm only. Their main use for the time being was for assisting infantry at points where the artillery had not crushed enemy resistance, which meant that they would not normally lead that attack. Occasions might arise, however, when large numbers of tanks were available and where the ground was suitable for concealment when a large scale surprise attack using tanks might be practicable. Heavy, medium and light tanks all had their uses and the development of all three types was to be pushed ahead.[49]

Thus, by early March 1917, a surprise attack by massed tanks without preliminary bombardment had been officially admitted as a possible future gambit by both GHQ and the War Office, though both organizations clearly had reservations about it. The acceptance of this principle was largely due to Estienne rather than to the British Heavy Branch representatives. (Elles is not recorded as having said anything at all, Fuller was not present and Anley was extremely modest about the potential of the force he administered.) The implanting at GHQ of a concept to be successfully employed at Cambrai in November may thus have been partly attributable to a Frenchman.[50] But months were to elapse before this concept was to be put into practice and in the meantime GHQ was to be prompted from other sources. In fact tanks were no substitute for artillery support to the infantry (though they were a useful supplement) and it would take the virtual revolution in the gunner's art which occurred during the course of 1917 to make a powerful surprise attack truly feasible.

Towards the end of February 1917 it became evident that the Germans intended to evacuate the Gommecourt Salient and to retire to the recently constructed system of fortifications know as the Hindenburg Line. The British found themselves incapable of interfering with this withdrawal to any significant extent. Certainly there was nothing the Heavy Branch could do about it. Production difficulties ensured that there was hardly a serviceable tank in France in the first week of March. The surprise withdrawal, moreover, disrupted British plans for offensive operations in the early part of the year and the first serious British offensive effort of 1917 was not made until the Battle of Arras began on 9 April.[51]

There were still so few tanks available that they could hardly be taken into account as a factor in the planning of the Arras offensive. Only 60 machines of 1st Brigade, under Colonel Baker-Carr, were available, though it was originally intended to employ 2 full battalions of 48 tanks each. (Battalions were supposed to consist of 3 companies, each divided into 3 sections of 4 tanks, plus some reserves.) The tanks were not intended to take part in the attack on the first-line position but would assist by adding weight to the assault at points of anticipated difficulty further back. A high proportion of the tanks involved which were Marks I, II and III (the IIs and IIIs being only minor modifications of the Mark I) failed to arrive at their starting points because of mechanical breakdown, ditching or sinking into mud. Some of those that did cross the British front line performed useful service, but they had a relatively minor influence on the course of the first day of battle, the general pattern of which was that the infantry successfully stormed German first-line positions, which had been thoroughly smashed by the preliminary bombardment, but could make no impression on the second-line position which was outside the range of the ordinary field artillery.[52]

Only the eye of faith could see in the tank of the spring of 1917 an instrument capable of transforming the nature of war on the Western Front. Particularly embarrassing to the Heavy Branch was a hurriedly planned and poorly executed operation directed at the village of Bullecourt on 11 April. Tanks allocated to co-operate with Australian troops failed to turn up on time and the Australians' own planning was thereby upset. The Australians ended up carrying out the attack virtually without tank support and took heavy casualties in the process. The Australians regarded tanks with intense suspicion for the next year and effectively refused any further co-operation with them.[53]

Up to the summer of 1917 the achievement of tanks had been very modest in relation to the expectations of some of their advocates. But if tanks could not be regarded as an unqualified success, little that the BEF had achieved so far could be thus characterized. And there were some causes for renewed optimism. Mark IV tanks had begun to arrive that spring. Though not a major redesign, the Mark IV incorporated many significant modifications. It was more reliable. For one thing, a more efficient system of delivering petrol to the engine, the "autovac", replaced the gravity feed on the Mark I. It was also less vulnerable, being proof against the German "K" machine gun ammunition which had often riddled Mark Is, this level of protection achieved by a better quality and distribution of metal rather than by increased thickness. The petrol tank, inside in the Mark I, was armoured and mounted externally at the rear of the vehicle. A better system of exhaust which emitted less noise and fewer sparks made it somewhat less conspicuous and in some circumstances lessened the amount of fire it was likely to draw.[54] All those who had thought seriously about tank tactics had, moreover, concluded that one of the keys to success was employment *en masse*. Masses had not hitherto been available. In the summer of 1917, however, using hundreds of tanks in the same attack was becoming a real possibility.

Haig, later accused by several writers of a purblind attitude to tanks, resolutely kept his faith in them. He informed the War Office on 5 June 1917 that:

> events have proved the utility of Tanks, both as a means of overcoming hostile resistance . . . and as a means of reducing casualties in the attacking troops and I consider that sufficient experience has now been gained to warrant the adoption of the Tank as a recognised addition to the existing means of conducting offensive operations.[55]

Haig also took a definite interest in the technical development of the new arm. In addition to helping fix the specifications for the next heavy tank, the Mark V, GHQ welcomed the idea of the Medium or "Chaser" tank, to be used for pursuit and exploitation. This type had been conceived by William Tritton not long after tanks were first used in action and he had begun design work upon it in December 1916.[56] By the summer of 1917 development was well underway and GHQ contribution sent its specification for an "ideal" medium which would succeed the first model.[57] Reading between the lines of his statement to the War Office, however, it seems that what Haig was not prepared to do, in the summer of 1917, was to plan operations around tanks. The tank was a useful addition to the armoury of the BEF. But it would have to fit itself in as best it could to operations planned around the capabilities of more battle-tested instruments.

Haig had been contemplating a major push in Flanders since January 1916. The British had come under pressure, however, from their principal ally, the French, to make their main effort of 1916 in a joint operation with the French Army. The BEF's boundary with the French was in Picardy and from mid-summer to late autumn 1916 its resources were devoted to the Battle of the Somme.

A major British effort in Flanders for 1917 appeared to have been definitely decided upon at the Chantilly conference which met under the chairmanship of Joffre, the French Commander-in-Chief, in November. But its start was again delayed, this time by the influence of General Nivelle, whose star had risen in the closing stages of the Verdun battle and now eclipsed that of Joffre in the eyes of the French government. In mid-December Nivelle replaced Joffre.[58]

Nivelle promised that an offensive in Champagne and on the Aisne would give France a swift and decisive victory. He was believed both by the French government and, apparently, by Lloyd George. The acceptance of Nivelle's plan led to another adjustment in British strategy. The Flanders operation was postponed and a British offensive at Arras was organized to assist the French main effort. The Nivelle offensive which commenced on 16 April saw the debut of the French tanks: the Schneiders and St Chamonds. These tanks were employed only in small numbers at the start of the offensive and their designs were much poorer than those of their British equivalents. Their performance was generally disappointing. The campaign itself, though no more catastrophic in terms of loss of life than previous efforts, precipitated a massive loss of faith in the leadership by the French rank and file and a state of mutiny in much of the army.[59]

Belatedly the proposed British campaign in Flanders was reactivated. The first act in this drama was to be the seizure of the Messines–Wytschaete ridge "in order to deprive the enemy of his chief observation areas over the Ypres Salient and as an essential prelude to an advance either eastwards or northeastwards".[60] Preparations for an assault on this ridge had been going on for well over a year. It was one of the most meticulously planned British offensive operations of the war.

The role of the tanks in the plan made by General Plumer's Second Army for the assault on the Messines ridge was less ambitious than the one Haig had suggested they might, in principle, fulfil in his letter to the War Office of 5 June. But it fitted perfectly with the general statement on tank policy which Kiggell had issued the previous October. This reflects the fact that the operation had been in preparation for over a year: for most of that time the tanks available on the Western Front had been so few and of such poor quality that, as at Arras in April, they were hardly worth taking into account. It also reflects the confidence of Second Army that it had found perfectly adequate means of executing the limited operation required without the new arm. Tanks were employed purely as accessories. No reliance was placed on them. The plan was designed to succeed without them and made no concessions to their peculiar characteristics.[61]

The Messines operation of 7 June 1917 was the debut of 2nd Tank Brigade and the first use in action on a substantial scale of the Mark IV tank. The operation was initiated by the explosion under the ridge of 19 gigantic mines containing between them over a million pounds of high explosive. This was followed by an infantry assault behind a creeping barrage, supported by some 68 fighting tanks. Second Army gained all its objectives by nightfall[62] but the part played by the tanks in this was minor and their record mixed. According to the Tank Corps' own statistics only 19 of the 68 fighting tanks rendered any assistance at all to the infantry. The infantry advance was made over ground which had been heavily shelled for many months and was badly cratered. The advance was also predominantly uphill. In most cases the tanks simply could not keep up with the infantry advance. Forty-eight of the tanks taking part became ditched or bellied at some stage. A further 17 broke down mechanically during the course of the day, though some were repaired and returned to action.[63]

These statistics might make the tanks at Messines appear to have been virtually useless. But such an assessment would be wrong. In fact a small number of machines was able to render very valuable assistance. One tank led the successful assault on the heavily fortified village of Wytschaete and the firepower of two disabled machines played some part in breaking up a German counterattack the following morning. It was evident that the proportion of mechanical failures had dropped dramatically since the Somme and the high proportion of ditchings was inevitable given that terrain to be crossed (after months of shelling and the mine explosions) resembled a moonscape.[64] The most pro-tank commentator would have to admit that their achievements were modest, but, as we have seen, this operation had not been planned with them in mind and there was some hope for better results when one was.

In terms of the conduct of tank operations the main innovation at Messines was logistic: the employment of supply tanks similar to the "tank tenders" which Fuller had discussed in "Training

Note No. 16". The Supply tanks used at Messines were not in fact purpose-built machines but obsolescent Mark Is converted for the purpose. Each Supply tank could carry five "fills", a fill being enough fuel, oil, ammunition, grease and water to keep one fighting tank in action for a day. The Heavy Branch's own analysis of the Messines operation commented that:

> The Supply Tanks proved a necessity but they must be just as reliable as the Fighting Tanks.
> The matter of supply is so vital in continuous fighting that it is suggested that Tanks should be specially designed and built for this purpose.
> Sound machines, good crews, and careful Reconnaissance are as essential for the Supply as for the Fighting Tanks.
> Supply Tanks accompanied the Fighting Tanks to just behind the Starting Points, and there remained till required.
> They moved forward to the Rallying Points and established Dumps well forward in captured territory by midday on Z day (June 7th).
> No form of wheeled transport could have got within 1,800 yards of these dumps at the time.[65]

In practice obsolescent fighting tanks rather than purpose-built machines would continue to be used for supply purposes. The commodious Gun-Carrier tanks, which started to arrive in the summer of 1917, were originally designed to provide a self-propelled carriage for guns acting in support of tanks but they were seldom actually employed in that role by the Royal Artillery who seem not to have trusted the concept. Most Gun-Carriers served as Supply tanks.[66]

Another element in the proposed Flanders campaign was an amphibious operation known as the "Hush Plan". The operation was never actually mounted but is worthy of mention here because it was probably the first time that the use of tanks in an amphibious operation was contemplated and because phenomenal ingenuity was devoted to making their employment a success. The landing was planned for the stretch of coast between Nieuport and Ostend. It was intended that the landing parties of all arms should be carried in "pontoons" – primitive unpowered landing craft 600 feet in length, each to be secured between a couple of naval monitors and thus propelled from Dunkirk, which was to be the main base for the operation, and up the beach at selected landing points.[67]

The tanks were given a major role in the proposed landing. One of the main problems was a sea wall which protected the whole of this stretch of coast. It had a smooth, concave face and was topped by a vertical coping with a lip. Fortunately the Belgian architect who had designed the wall was living in France and was able to supply the British with copies of all his drawings. An exact replica of a section of wall was erected at Merlimont where a special tank detachment under Major Bingham was trained for the operation. Special shoes were fitted to tracks to enable the tanks to climb the slope and detachable steel ramps were designed which the tanks could fix against the wall to enable them to climb over the coping. The tanks would then haul up guns and lorries. In practice sessions the tanks repeatedly climbed the wall successfully. The operation was never mounted because the British advance in the main Ypres offensive was judged inadequate to enable a link-up with the proposed landing to be effected before German counter-attacks would destroy it.[68]

The first half of 1917 had been somewhat disappointing for the Heavy Branch. Yet no institutional catastrophe came its way. GHQ collectively continued to show patience and goodwill. On 27 July, some six weeks after Messines and just two days before the start of the main Ypres offensive, the Heavy Branch Machine Gun Corps was, by Royal Warrant, constituted as "The Tank Corps".[69] Its status as an entirely new arm was thus formally recognized and its expansion continued, albeit fitfully. It was the late summer of 1917 which was the nadir of the tank's reputation in the British Army. By August such derogatory remarks were being made about its potential by both Corps and Army headquarters that, in view of the deepening manpower crisis, the continuing expansion of the Corps was jeopardized and major cuts threatened.[70]

General Gough and his Fifth Army staff conceived the Third Battle of Ypres as an artillery/infantry conflict in which tanks would have to take their chances – much the same attitude towards them as had been adopted by Plumer and Second Army before Messines. As at Messines, no concessions were made to the needs of tanks. In that sense tanks were actually getting less consideration from those responsible for planning British operations on the Western Front than they had at their debut on 15 September 1916 when Rawlinson's Fourth Army had left "lanes" in the barrage in order to enable tanks to lead the attack without danger from their own artillery. At Third Ypres there was no intention that tanks should lead the attack and certainly no willingness to deny the infantry the assistance of the crucial creeping barrage on even short sections of the front.[71]

Experience suggested to the planners, correctly as it turned out, that following a very thorough preliminary bombardment and immediately after the enemy had been hit by the creeping barrage, the infantry would be able to overwhelm the German first-line system without the help of tanks. Fifth Army took the view that the tanks would be most profitably employed in sustaining the momentum of the attack. Roughly one-third of the tanks allotted to each corps were to assist in mopping up the zone of strongpoints in front of the main German Second Line position, a third to co-operate in the advance to the Third Line and a third to remain in corps reserve.[72]

The infantry attack began on 31 July at 3.50 a.m. It has been argued that by starting an offensive in this region so late in the year the planners were tempting fate. It was indeed known from meteorological records that heavy rain was normal in Flanders in late summer and autumn though in 1917 it was exceptionally copious unusually early. A summer rather than a spring campaign in Flanders had been made inevitable by General Nivelle. But it is arguable that a start so late in the summer was due to unnecessarily slow staff work and to excessive caution on the part of Gough who ironically was selected to command the operation because he was thought to possess plenty of "cavalry dash".[73] The preliminary bombardment had begun on 16 July and was originally supposed to last only ten days. But plenty of shell was available and Gough eventually secured a six-day extension from Haig. The offensive was supported by 3,091 guns. Four and a quarter million shells were fired up to and including the first day of the infantry assault. All 3 tank brigades then on the Western Front were brought to Flanders to take part – a total of 216 tanks. Only 136 were used on the first day, starting behind the infantry. The ground was so badly cratered that a mere 19 were able to play any part in the assault on the German second line.[74]

Though the first day of this offensive was very much less catastrophic than the first day of the Somme – some gain of ground being made all along the front and heavy losses inflicted on the Germans – its long-term prospects were greatly reduced by the torrential rain which began falling that afternoon. It rained for 4 days continuously and the ground became a quagmire. Thus, early in August, Tank Corps HQ came to the conclusion that the tanks could make virtually no further contribution to the campaign in the Ypres sector. On 2 August Elles suggested to Fifth Army HQ that those tanks still surviving – 42 had been written off on the first day – should be kept for use *en masse* on more suitable terrain.[75] According to the regimental history of the Royal Tank Regiment Fuller then suggested to Elles a stroke with massed armour near Cambrai, a suggestion which Elles passed on to Haig and which "made an impression" on the latter.[76] The evidence for Fuller's suggestion of a Cambrai stroke at this point and of this suggestion being passed on to and debated by GHQ is hard to find. Certainly after inspecting the Ypres battlefield on 2 August Fuller produced a paper for Elles the following day indicating that:

> From a tank point of view the Third Battle of Ypres may be considered dead. To go on using tanks in the present conditions will only lead to good machines and better personnel being thrown away, but also to a loss of good morale in the infantry and tank crews through constant failure.[77]

But this seems to have been no more than Elles had already concluded and told Fifth Army the day before. The concrete suggestion Fuller made for the use of tanks in order "to restore British prestige and strike a theatrical blow against Germany before the winter" was for an Anglo-French operation designed to capture St Quentin.[78] Elles did not think an Anglo-French operation would appeal to GHQ and does not appear to have passed this proposal on. On 8 August Fuller produced a proposal – for "Tank Raids" in 1918. These were to be short, sharp operations designed to inflict loss on the enemy but not to hold ground permanently. Tanks would attack in three echelons supported by low flying aircraft, dismounted cavalry and artillery which would open fire only after the tank advance had begun. One locality he suggested for such a raid was within the area of the Cambrai battle which took place the following November.[79] But it is not clear whether Elles passed on Fuller's "raids" suggestion to GHQ or Third Army. It is usually stated that, while Fuller disagreed with some aspects of the plan actually implemented at Cambrai, the original conception of this offensive was his.[80] In his memoirs Fuller tried hard to give that impression and the regimental history goes to some lengths to reinforce it.[81] In fact there is very little evidence for attributing the Third Army operation mounted on 20 November to Fuller's particular inspiration or influence.

The concept of a surprise attack using a large number of tanks without any preliminary artillery bombardment had been raised a number of times. Probably the first to suggest it was Churchill in his "Variants" paper of November 1915. There is evidence that the notion was present in Haig's mind – possibly as a result of having read Churchill's "Variants" – for many months. Early in 1917 he had, as we have noted, suggested its employment in one part of the offensive then being planned at Ypres.[82] Essentially the same idea had been enthusiastically put forward by Estienne at the War Office conference in early March 1917 and accepted (without enthusiasm) by Butler, the GHQ representative, as a long-term possibility.

Towards the end of August 1917, Haig was reminded of the idea from an unconventional but not totally unfamiliar source. Tennyson d'Eyncourt had already indicated a willingness to prompt GHQ with regard to the proper use of tanks, apparently quite undeterred by his lack of military experience. When writing to Haig on 22 August d'Eyncourt indicated that his tactical suggestions arose from experience on the munitions production side. He suggested that tanks had been asked to operate in virtually impossible conditions in the current Ypres offensive. The Ministry of Munitions had been put under a great deal of pressure to develop systems for unditching tanks which were cumbersome, complex and heavy. Consequently he advocated "selecting more suitable ground which they could comparatively easily negotiate [*sic*]" rather than making constant adaptations, which were ultimately bound to be inadequate, to help them traverse the worst possible ground:[83]

> Of course I am not aware of all the military conditions but I cannot help thinking that if it were possible to use them in large numbers on suitable ground, preferably rather hilly country, where the wet drains off, I believe a Tank attack on a big scale could be made with prospects of success, possibly without much artillery preparation and with comparatively few infantry.

D'Eyncourt did not specifically suggest *no* preliminary bombardment, but was pressing for mass tank employment on suitable ground with a fair degree of surprise. These were themes which Fuller had adopted by this stage and we know that Fuller and d'Eyncourt were in communication.[84] Together with Stern, d'Eyncourt had, however, been thinking about tank use for a long time and it seems likely that the radical suggestions which d'Eyncourt had put forward earlier in the year were quite independent of Fuller's influence. There is thus no reason to believe that he was merely parroting Fuller in August. Fuller's central operational concept in the summer of 1917, that of the "tank raid" is not expounded in d'Eyncourt's memorandum.

Haig must have been irritated by this civilian interference in operational matters but he treated d'Eyncourt with considerable courtesy. Doubtless he was to some extent influenced by knowledge of the d'Eyncourt–Lloyd George connection and by the need, in view of Lloyd George's hostility, not to antagonize others with influence on the Home Front. Nevertheless his reply within a week to a civil servant who was not even in the War Office, with a fairly detailed and carefully argued explanation of his policy, rather than a cursory note, appears the act of a rational and astute individual. Haig indicated that the conditions favourable for the use of tanks were "fully realised" at GHQ and that he realised that the present type of tank could not fulfil its potential in the conditions in which it had been called to operate thus far in the war. He realized that it would be preferable if tanks could operate on firm ground which had not been too heavily shelled but pointed out that:

> the choice of front on which to make an attack has to be made with regard to many considerations, tactical, strategical, political and so forth. In making this choice the tank at any rate in its present state of development can only be regarded as a minor factor. It is still in its infancy as regards design. It is of uncertain reliability. Its true powers are more or less a matter of conjecture. The troops are not yet fully accustomed to it, nor do they place sufficient faith in what it can accomplish to be willing to accept it in lieu of artillery preparation and support. As time goes on and the designs improve the tank will probably become a more important factor in the choice of battlefield, but under present conditions it must be, as I have said, a minor factor.
>
> . . . The question which I have to decide as matters stand is whether to use or not to use the tank under conditions which are unavoidably unfavourable. I have decided that, on the whole, it is advisable to

Figure 12   A Mark IV (male) tank stuck in Flanders mud at "Clapham Junction" near Sanctuary Wood during the Third Battle of Ypres.

> make use of them even under such conditions, and on many occasions they have done valuable service more than sufficient to justify this decision.[85]

Though there were some occasions on which tanks had been of considerable service at Third Ypres it is difficult to pinpoint many.[86] By the beginning of August, Gough, Fifth Army's commander, had become openly dismissive of tanks, reporting to Haig that they were of little use on difficult ground and that the ground on battlefields would always be difficult. His opinion was fully endorsed by at least one of the Corps commanders.[87] One brilliant little feat of arms which had occurred on 19 August, did, however, give Haig a degree of justification for maintaining some tanks in the Flanders sector even once heavy rain had fallen. A small group, operating entirely along a metalled road not yet destroyed by shelling, led infantry in a surprise attack on three concrete pillboxes which had been offering a serious obstacle to further advance. The tanks, more by the moral than the physical effect of their presence, secured the capture of all three positions for minimal casualties.[88]

Haig did not not make specific reference to this operation –

usually known, after the main pill-box attacked, as "The Cockcroft", in his reply to d'Eyncourt. But it is clear that he did not wish to denigrate tanks. Rather he wished to celebrate their still modest achievements, something which he had been doing since their debut on the Somme and would continue to do beyond the Armistice. His argument that the potency of the tank was not such that an entire campaign could be planned around its characteristics was a reasonable one, not really discredited by the November experience at Cambrai, though this is not to argue that a late summer/autumn campaign in Flanders was the most rational of undertakings for the British Army.

Haig concluded his reply to d'Eyncourt by encouraging the work of the tank designers and indicating that he would be delighted to discuss tank matters with him in person when the opportunity arose. Generally, therefore, he dealt with this matter in a tactful manner while giving nothing away about future intentions. As we have seen the possible withdrawal of the bulk of the Tank Corps from the Ypres salient and its use elsewhere had already been discussed and it seems to have been under continuous consideration. Haig sanctioned it little more than a fortnight after despatching this letter.[89]

On 7 September 1917 Elles formally requested GHQ to release 5 of the 8 tank battalions deployed in the Ypres Forward Area on the grounds that:

> The state of the ground on the Ypres Battle Front is such that it will not be possible to use Tanks until the line is advanced 1,000 to 1,500 yards.
>
> When this is done there will still be considerable difficulties, unless the weather is exceptionally good, which will prevent the use of tanks in large masses.

The main argument for withdrawal was the need to conduct training "which [was] impossible to carry out in the Fifth Army Area", but Elles also indicated that there were possibilities for the use of tanks on both the First Army and Third Army fronts, both to the south of the Ypres Salient.[90] GHQ approved Elles's request and did so in terms which suggest that the possibility of a major tank operation later that autumn, probably in the vicinity of Lens in the First Army area, had been under discussion for some time. Elles was told to "earmark and hold available for use in mid-October as many tanks as may be required for that operation".[91]

The proposed attack in the First Army area was ultimately abandoned, but at the same time a Third Army scheme for an attack from the neighbourhood of Albert towards Cambrai gained favour at GHQ. The contemporary record does not support the interpretation that the Cambrai offensive grew out of Fuller's "tank raids" scheme only to be taken over by higher authorities and blown up into a project for a much larger (and ultimately unworkable) offensive. Elles had a commendable preoccupation with secrecy and relatively little was committed to paper at Tank Corps HQ until quite a late date in the planning process. During the battle's course, however, he wrote down his own recollections of its genesis. Elles believed the plan to have come from Third Army and to have been communicated to him for the first time in September. In Elles's words:

> The plan was Sir J. Byng's, the choice of place his too – He also propounded the scheme of attack without bombardment...
>
> The plan was much enlarged subsequently and not perfected till late October.
>
> Only myself and Hardress Lloyd [Commander, 3rd Tank Brigade] knew of the project – Fuller and Searle were not told till mid-October and the rest not till 23 October.[92]

If the basic Cambrai battle plan had been generated within Tank Corps HQ it is difficult to believe that Elles would not have seized the credit for the organization that he commanded. The fact is that Bermicourt had no monopoly on the generation of ideas for tank use. Further, to look at Cambrai as essentially a "tank battle" is misleading. The individual who can most accurately be regarded as the originator of the Cambrai offensive is probably Brigadier-General H.H. Tudor who commanded the artillery of the 9th Division which, in August 1917, was holding a sector of the front of IV Corps in Third Army.[93] The essence of Tudor's idea was a surprise attack on the relatively quiet sector in front of Cambrai. The attainment of a major surprise with regard to the location of an attack as opposed to a slight degree of surprise with regard to its precise timing, had hitherto been practically impossible on the Western Front. The technical change which made it practicable by the end of 1917 was not so much the tank, an instrument which had been available for a year, albeit in small numbers for most of that time, but a series of refinements in the gunner's art. It was now possible to fire reasonably accurately on the basis of what was known at the time as "silent registration" and has been referred to in more recent times as "prediction".[94]

This had come about partly as the result of more accurate maps and survey techniques, which enabled the positions of one's own guns to be precisely fixed, partly as the result of the more systematic collection, analysis and use of meteorological data (wind speed and direction having a major effect on the flight of a shell) and partly as a result of the calibration of individual guns using the equipment of the sound-ranging sections. The muzzle velocity of shells from each gun could be measured and variations from the normal noted. Thus if a gun was becoming slightly worn and tending to drop its shells short, the fact could be taken into account and its elevation adjusted accordingly. Another factor was that by this stage in the war batches of shell from the factories were being sorted by weight, as minor variations, inevitable in mass production, could affect accuracy considerably. Refinements in the arts of taking and using aerial photographs to gain an accurate picture of the layout of enemy defences and the techniques of sound-ranging and flash-spotting for fixing enemy gun positions were also crucial.[95]

Thus, while dispensing with the usual "noisy" method of registration – the practice of making sure a gun was on target by firing a shell at some observed landmark and then adjusting until the target was hit – it was possible to deliver a very effective supporting barrage, together with reasonably accurate counter-battery fire, as soon as the infantry went over the top. Predicted shooting was not expected to be as accurate as one registered in the traditional manner and in the days immediately preceding the offensive some of Third Army's gunners sought permission to do a minimum of registration, disguised within the normal pattern of artillery activity. Byng, concerned with surprise above all, denied this. It was eventually decided not to employ the "creeping" barrage which had become standard in the British Army by this stage in the war. A "creeper" was very useful if the infantry could keep immediately behind it, but at Cambrai it was necessary (as we shall see in the next paragraph) for the tanks to move ahead of the infantry. Instead it was proposed to use a "jumping" barrage,

which would move from one German defensive position to another in a series of fairly big lifts, coupled with a number of
"standing barrages" which would keep some German positions
under continuous bombardment.[96]

It was Tudor's awareness of this possibility of silent registration
which appears to have been the real basis of Third Army's scheme
for an autumn offensive. But there was still one problem that
might have frustrated an infantry assault. Several thick belts of
barbed wire stretched across the German defensive positions – the
Hindenburg and Hindenburg Support Lines – on this sector of the
front. One of the principal functions of preliminary bombardments was to breach wire. If it was intended to dispense with such
a bombardment, using tanks to crush paths through the wire was
an obvious alternative. To carry out this vital role they would
have to be in the van of the offensive, something they had not
done since the Somme more than a year before. Beyond flattening
the wire, however, the scheme which Tudor proposed, and the
modified version which Third Army ultimately adopted, did not
place a very heavy reliance on tanks. The emphasis was on taking
the enemy by surprise with a sudden onslaught by markedly superior forces of artillery and infantry.[97]

Tudor apparently discussed his proposal with Brigadier-General
H. De Pree, the Brigadier-General General Staff at IV Corps who
drew up a plan for a limited offensive designed to last only 48
hours which was accepted by Lieutenant-General Woollcombe,
the IV Corps commander. This was sent to Third Army on 23
August. According to the Official History, Colonel Hardress-Lloyd,
commanding 3rd Tank Brigade, had taken Fuller's tank raids
proposal to Third Army as early as 5 August but if so it must have
been by word of mouth for Fuller's memorandum on the subject
is dated 8 August.[98] Though Fuller specifically suggested that a
raid be mounted in the area Ribecourt–Crevecourt–Banteux, one
section of the eventual Cambrai battlefield, there is little evidence
that he was instrumental in the selection of that battlefield. The
real significance of the Hardress-Lloyd visit of 5 August was probably that Third Army was made aware that the Tank Corps believed its continued employment in the Ypres area fruitless and
was looking for alternative work elsewhere.

Elles's recollection that he was summoned to Third Army HQ
sometime in September and that Byng then put the basic Cambrai

plan to him fits in well with the documentary record of Tank Corps–GHQ correspondence. This indicates that as late as 7 September Elles saw the main possibility for large-scale use of tanks in the near future as existing on the First Army front at Lens. Though Elles regarded "raids" of the type Fuller had outlined as a possibility for the Third Army front, he was not keen on conducting such operations if any more substantial offensive were being contemplated for that front in 1918. Raids would draw the attention of the Germans to that sector and highlight its weaknesses.[99] There is little real evidence, therefore, that Fuller's tank raids concept appealed to anyone – even in his own headquarters – still less that it was the inspiration for Third Army's November operation. According to the Official History, Elles's personal contribution to the genesis of the Cambrai operation was to encourage Byng to expand the Tudor–De Pree–Woollcombe plan into a major breakthrough operation.[100] If so his views on the subject were precisely the opposite of Fuller's.

Some time in the first half of September Byng put before Haig a Third Army proposal for an operation much grander than that originally suggested by Tudor, De Pree and Woollcombe. Haig was definitely interested, but Kiggell was concerned that the operation still in progress in Flanders would deny Byng the reinforcements the latter thought essential. Nevertheless Byng was encouraged to develop his concept into a detailed plan. By 16 September he had done so and brought it to GHQ for personal presentation to Haig.[101] Haig accepted it in principle and sent Brigadier-General Davidson to discuss it with Third Army staff. The only possible obstacle at this stage was the issue of reinforcements. Could sufficient troops be spared to bring up to full strength the Third Army divisions to be employed in the attack? In the middle of October Haig finally decided that they could. Planning conferences were held at Tank Corps HQ on 25 and 26 October and at Third Army HQ on the latter date in which subordinate commanders were let into the secret.

The object of the operation was explained at the Tank Corps conference as: "To carry out a surprise attack against the German lines between the ST. QUENTIN CANAL and the CANAL DU NORD and capture CAMBRAI". The first objective was to be the main Hindenburg line between Bleak House and the Canal Du Nord, the second objective the Hindenburg Support line immediately behind it and the "Third Objective" was exploitation in the direction of Cambrai. Nothing appears to have been said to the Tank Corps conference about the mission of the Cavalry Corps. This was first to cross the St Quentin Canal between Marcoing and Masnières in the wake of the capture of canal bridges by IV Corps and to surround and isolate Cambrai and secondly to secure the crossings of the Sensée river from Paillencourt to Palluel.[102]

In his memoirs, perhaps without conscious dishonesty, Fuller tries to have it both ways. He claims to have originated the idea for the Cambrai offensive but also seeks credit for attacking weaknesses in the Third Army plan which led to ultimate disappointment. It has already been argued that the former claim cannot be substantiated and is probably invalid. Fuller's critique of the Third Army plan, however, was real and, while apparently ignored by Elles, had some merit. Fuller had two main criticisms. First, given that he did not think sufficient reserves of infantry had been made available for exploiting a breakthrough and turning it into a decisive rupture of the enemy's front, he still believed raiding the best policy. (He does not appear to have considered, rightly as it turned out, that the Cavalry Corps was a suitable instrument of exploitation.) Secondly he disliked Third Army's intended distribution of the tanks – placing practically all of them in the van of the attack. He wanted to keep some in reserve to exploit opportunities created on the morning of 20 November that afternoon and the following day. As he put it in a paper to Elles: "To fight without a reserve is similar to playing cards without capital – it is sheer gambling. To trust to the cast of the dice is not generalship".[103]

Fuller had a point but so did the Third Army staff. As far as they were concerned the primary role of the tanks was to flatten wire. They wanted a large number of gaps in the wire right across the front of the attack so that the infantry could get forward quickly without their advance becoming excessively canalised and hence vulnerable, especially to surviving enemy machine gunners.

At the beginning of November 1917 Elles's corps, despite a less than spectacular first year, had survived hostile criticism and was poised on the brink of its biggest ever operation. The Third Battle of Ypres had been very unfortunate for the Tank Corps as it generally was for the BEF as a whole. Yet Haig was one of the tanks' most consistent allies throughout 1917. While not prepared to base his whole strategy around tanks – to have done so would, given their very limited powers, have been ridiculous – Haig continued to insist that they were useful and valuable. GHQ had early been prepared to grant the tanks a status analagous to that of the prestigious RFC and despite many setbacks Haig had taken, and would continue to take, every opportunity of praising their achievements to the maximum extent consistent with reality.[104]

Notes

1   On the establishment of the Bermicourt HQ see B.H. Liddell Hart, *The Tanks*, Vol. I (Cassell) 1959, p. 82. A fascinating, beautifully written and somewhat scurrilous insider's account is to be found in "HQ Tanks", 355.486.86: 92 (Charteris), Tank Museum. It is almost certainly by Captain the Hon. Evan E. Charteris who went to the headquarters in mid-1917 in the office of historian, a request for one having been made to Anley by Elles ("I am very badly in want of a Historian, as my 'G' staff cannot cope with past histroy [*sic*] as well as prepare for the future") on 23 April 1917, PRO WO 158/814.

2   Ideas on the employment of tanks sometimes came from those involved in production and design such as Stern and d'Eyncourt, the latter corresponding with Haig directly on some occasions, e.g. d'Eyncourt to Haig 22 August 1917, BCI/12, Fuller Papers, Liddell Hart Centre for Military Archives, King's College London (henceforth LHCMA). Later in the war the War Office produced some innovative papers such as Stephen Foot's, "A Mobile Army", 24 April 1918, printed in S. Foot, *Three Lives* (Windmill Press) 1934, pp. 345–349.

3   E. Swinton, *Eyewitness* (Hodder and Stoughton) 1932, pp. 308–309.

4   A. Stern, *Tanks 1914–18: the Log-Book of a Pioneer* (Hodder and Stoughton) 1919, pp. 111–112.

5   J.F.C. Fuller, *Memoirs of an Unconventional Soldier* (Nicholson and Watson) 1936, pp. 93 and 112.

6   A.D. Harvey, *Collision of Empires* (Hambledon Press) 1992, pp. 381–382. "HQ Tanks", pp. 38–39. Capper is referred to by the pseudonym "Williams".

7   "HQ Tanks", *passim*. Ranks indicated are those held when the individuals concerned first arrived at Bermicourt.

8   "HQ Tanks", pp. 2–3. Uzielli is called "Edwards".

9   Fuller, *Memoirs*, p. 88.

10   *ibid.*, p. 89 and "HQ Tanks", pp. 18 and 19 in which Searle is "Col. Thomas" and Green is "Walters".

11   "HQ Tanks", pp. 21 and 33.

12   M. Carver in *Dictionary of National Biography* 1961–70, pp. 405–
       408 and A.J. Trythall, *"Boney" Fuller, the Intellectual General*
       (Cassell) 1977, pp. 16–17.

13   "HQ Tanks", pp. 4 and 5.

14   Professor Tim Travers is possibly the modern historian of the West-
       ern Front most heavily influenced by Fuller. See Travers, *How the
       War Was Won* (Routledge) 1992, *passim* and more particularly
       "Could the Tanks of 1918 Have Been War-Winners for the British
       Expeditionary Force?", *Journal of Contemporary History*, Vol. 27
       (1992), *passim*, pp. 389–406.

15   On the Fuller–Crowley connection see A.J. Trythall, *op. cit.*, pp.
       20–27 and on the influence of the occult on Fuller's military thought
       see B.H. Reid, *J.F.C. Fuller, Military Thinker* (Macmillan) 1987,
       pp. 89 and 188. Fuller's book on *The Foundations of the Science
       of War* included "qabalistic" drawings and an obsession with the
       number 3. On "hocus-pocus" see Harvey, *op. cit.*, p. 307.

16   See for example Fuller's paper, "Tank Operations Decisive and
       Preparatory 1918–1919", Part II: "The Preparatory Operations
       1918", iii: "The Political Outlook", undated but apparently late
       1917, TS/40, Fuller Papers, Liddell Hart Centre for Military Ar-
       chives, King's College London (henceforth LHCMA).

17   On Fuller's activities in the British Union of Fascists see Trythall,
       op. cit., pp. 181–184 and 203–206, and on his loss of interest in
       armoured warfare see Reid, *op. cit.*, p. 193.

18   Elles's frequent assertions: "No, Boney, you are wrong; You are
       wrong Boney", are noted in "HQ Tanks", p. 15. On Elles's over-
       riding Fuller's advice, one example is Elles's decision to lead the
       Cambrai attack in a tank. Fuller, *Memoirs*, pp. 200–201.

19   "HQ Tanks", pp. 87–89. D. Fletcher, *Landships* (HMSO) 1984,
       p. 25. Fuller, *Memoirs*, pp. 88–89, 100–101.

20   *ibid.*, pp. 6–7. Liddell Hart in DNB 1951–60, pp. 699–701. G. le
       Q. Martel, *In the Wake of the Tank* (Sifton Praed) 1935, *Our
       Armoured Forces* (Faber) 1945, *An Outspoken Soldier* (Sifton Praed)
       1949.

21   Martel, "A Tank Army", Introduction, undated but late 1916 or
       early 1917, TS/9, Fuller Papers, LHCMA. On the action at Beaumont
       Hamel see A. and C. Williams-Ellis, *The Tank Corps* (Country Life)
       1919, pp. 34–38.

22   "Recommendations for the Expansion of the Heavy Section (tanks),
       Machine Gun Corps, Put Forward by Major-General Butler, Deputy
       Chief of the General Staff, France, at a Conference Held on 19th
       and 20th September 1916", PRO WO 158/836.

23   Martel, "A Tank Army", paras 2–7, TS/9, Fuller Papers, LHCMA.

24 *ibid.*, paras 8 and 9.
25 Martel, TS/10, undated, Fuller Papers, LHCMA.
26 "Training Note No. 16", February 1917, TS/6, Fuller Papers, LHCMA.
27 *ibid.*, Part II: "Tank Operations", Section 1, "Character of Tank". On limitations to the tank's mobility and crew protection at this period see Liddell Hart, *op. cit.*, pp. 89 and 149 and Fletcher, *op. cit.*, pp. 16 and 21.
28 Fuller, *Memoirs*, pp. 78–79.
29 "Training Note No. 16", Part II: "Tank Operations", Section 2, "Principles and Conditions" and Section 3, "Tank Objectives", TS/6, Fuller Papers, LHCMA.
30 *ibid.*, Part II, Section 3.
31 *ibid.*, Part III, "Tank Tactics", Section 1, "Tank Battle Formations".
32 *ibid.*, Part III, "Tank Tactics", Section 2, "Tank Tactics".
33 *ibid.*, Part II, "Tank Operations", Section 3, "Tank Objectives", paras 5 and 8.
34 *ibid.*, para. 4.
35 *ibid.*, Part IV: "Tank Co-operation with Other Arms", Section 3, "Cavalry Co-operation".
36 *ibid.*, "Definitions", p. 1 and Part VI, "System of Supply".
37 *ibid.*, Part VI.
38 *ibid.*, Part VII, "System of Communication". "Summary of Tank Operations 9th–12th April and 23 April 1917", Part III, "Communications", pp. 11–13, PRO WO 95/91. On face-to-face communication between tank and infantry in battle see J.R. Colville, *Man of Valour: the Life of Field Marshal the Viscount Gort, VC, GCB, MVO, MC* (Collins) 1972, p. 47. On the successful employment of specialist signals tanks, equipped with radio, later in the war see "5th Tank Brigade, Report On Operations with the Australian Corps from 8th August to 15th August 1918", Appendix F, TCOIV/5, Fuller Papers, LHCMA.
39 "Extract from the Proceedings of a Meeting Held at 10 Downing Street, on Thursday, January 25th, 1917, at 11.30 A.M.", para. 6, PRO WO 32/5154.
40 On Lloyd George's disillusionment with British generalship see D.R. Woodward, *Lloyd George and the Generals* (University of Delaware) 1983, pp. 116–130. On the connection established between Stern and Lloyd George see Stern, *op. cit.*, pp. 63–66. On Tennyson d'Eyncourt's continuing involvement with the tanks see *History of the Ministry of Munitions, Vol. XII. The Supply of Munitions, Part, III: Tanks*, 1920, p. 31, SWINTON B2, Swinton Papers, LHCMA.
41 "Meeting Held at 10 Downing Street, January 25th, 1917", para.

6, (a) and (b), PRO WO 32/5154. See also Tennyson d'Eyncourt's memorandum to the PM of 26 January 1917, DEY/43, Tennyson d'Eyncourt Papers, National Maritime Museum.

42 War Office to Haig, 31 January 1917, PRO WO 32/5154.

43 Kiggell to War Office, 10 February 1917, PRO WO 32/5154.

44 "Proceedings of a Conference on the Tactical Employment of Tanks, Held, on the 4th March 1917, at the War Office", PRO WO 32/5154.

45 Official History of the War (henceforth OH) J. Edmonds, *Military Operations, France and Belgium 1917, Vol. II, 7th June–10th November, Messines and Third Ypres (Passchendaele)* (HMSO) 1948, pp. 18–19.

46 Historical notes by Captain Charteris, undated, PRO WO 158/837.

47 "Proceedings of Conference, 4th March 1917", pp. 1–6, PRO WO 32/5154.

48 *ibid.*, pp. 8–11.

49 *ibid.*, pp. 9 and 10 and "Report of the Conclusions Reached at a Conference on the Tactical Employment of Tanks, Held on 4th March, 1917, at the War Office", PRO MUN 4/2791.

50 *ibid.*, p. 2, section 2, and "Proceedings of Conference, 4th March 1917", PRO WO 32/5154.

51 Historical notes by Charteris, PRO WO 158/837.

52 "Summary of Tank Operations 9th–12th and 23rd April 1917", Part II, "Operations", pp. 7–11, PRO WO 95/91. OH, C. Falls, *Military Operations, France and Belgium, 1917, the German Retreat to the Hindenburg Line and the Battle of Arras* (HMSO) 1940, pp. 236–240.

53 "Summary of Tank Operations", pp. 10 and 11, PRO WO 95/91. W.H.L. Watson, *A Company of Tanks* (Blackwood) 1920, pp. 50–72. Falls, *op. cit.*, pp. 360–370, and Williams-Ellis, *op. cit.*, 1919, p. 60.

54 Williams-Ellis, *op. cit.*, pp. 64 and 68.

55 Haig to War Office, 5 June 1917, para. 1, PRO MUN 4/2791.

56 Liddell Hart, *op. cit.*, p. 156.

57 Haig to War Office, 5 June 1917 and Appendix B: "Ideal Medium Machine, Specification", PRO MUN 4/2791.

58 OH, Edmonds, *op. cit.*, p. 12.

59 For a relatively recent account see A. Clayton, "Robert Nivelle and the French Spring Offensive", in Brian Bond (ed.) *Fallen Stars* (Brassey's) 1992, pp. 52–63.

60 OH, Edmonds, *op. cit.*, pp. 32–50.

61 *ibid.*, p. 81, and Colonel Courage (commanding 2nd Tank Brigade) to HQ Heavy Branch, "Preliminary Report on Operations of 7 June 1917", 22 June 1917, TCOIV/12, LHCMA.

62 2nd Brigade Report, TCOIV/12, Fuller Papers, LHCMA.
63 *ibid.* and "Messines: Detail of Assistance Rendered by Tanks" (undated) PRO WO 158/858.
64 *ibid.*
65 "Messines", Appendix A, "Supply Arrangements" (undated, apparently notes prepared for the Official History), PRO CAB 45/200.
66 R. Bacon, *The Dover Patrol, 1915–1917*, Vol. I (Hutchinson) undated, pp. 223–260.
67 On the Tank Corps and the "Hush Plan" see *ibid*, pp. 240–242, Williams-Ellis, *op. cit.*, pp. 69–72, and Liddell Hart, *op. cit.*, pp. 109–110.
68 Williams-Ellis, *op. cit.*, pp. 69–72.
69 OH, Edmonds, *op. cit.*, p. 148.
70 Liddell Hart, *op. cit.*, p. 115.
71 OH, Edmonds, *op. cit.*, pp. 148–149.
72 *ibid.* and, pp. 127–139.
73 On Gough and "cavalry dash" see OH, Edmonds, *op. cit.*, pp. 19–20 and pp. 384–385, and on the available rainfall statistics see pp. 133 and 211–212.
74 "Report on Action of Tanks, 31st July 1917", PRO WO 158/839 and Liddell Hart, *op. cit.*, pp. 110–114.
75 Liddell Hart, *op. cit.*, p. 114.
76 *ibid.* Liddell Hart's account seems misleading at this point. Fuller appears not to have mentioned the Third Army area as a possibility for a tank operation in any memorandum until 8 August and then he seems to have been thinking of a raid to be mounted in 1918 rather than something larger as an alternative to Third Ypres. "Tactical Employment of Tanks in 1918, Not Official", 8 August 1918, BCI/2, Fuller Papers, LHCMA.
77 Fuller to Elles, 3 August 1917, BC1/1, Fuller Papers, LHCMA.
78 *ibid.*, BCI/1, Fuller Papers, LHCMA.
79 "Tactical Employment of Tanks in 1918, Not Official", 8 August 1917, BCI/2, Fuller Papers, LHCMA.
80 A.J. Trythall, *"Boney" Fuller, the Intellectual General 1878–1966* (Cassell) 1977, p. 56, and Reid, *op. cit.*, p. 46. More surprisingly the notion that the Cambrai plan originated with Fuller and Tank Corps HQ is accepted by historians with gunner backgrounds. S. Bidwell and D. Graham, *Fire-Power* (Allen and Unwin) 1982, p. 91.
81 Fuller, *Memoirs*, pp. 169–191, and Liddell Hart, *op. cit.*, pp. 129–132.
82 OH, Edmonds, *op. cit.*, pp. 18–19.
83 Tennyson d'Eyncourt to Haig, 22 August 1917, BCI/12, Fuller Papers, LHCMA.

84 Fuller, *Memoirs*, p. 175.
85 Haig to Tennyson d'Eyncourt, 27 August 1917, BCI/13, Fuller Papers, LHCMA.
86 "Report on Action of Tanks, 31st July 1917", PRO WO 158/839, "Summary of Tank Operations 31.7.17–9.10.17.", PRO WO 95/92.
87 Williams-Ellis, *op. cit.*, p. 89.
88 *ibid.*, pp. 91–93.
89 CGS, GHQ to Tank Corps, 11 September 1917, BCI/6, Fuller Papers, LHCMA.
90 Elles to Advanced GHQ, 7 September 1917, BCI/4, Fuller Papers, LHCMA.
91 Lt.-Col. Tandy, GS, Advanced GHQ, to Tank Corps, BCI/5, 11 September 1917, Fuller Papers, LHCMA.
92 Elles's, "Notes on the Battle of Albert" (undated) BCI/3, Fuller Papers, LHCMA. Until recently this document was listed in the index to the Fuller Papers as referring to the Battle of Albert, 21–22 August 1918. From the context in which the document is found in the Fuller Papers, as well as from its content, it is obvious that it refers to Cambrai. Tank Corps Advanced HQ was at Albert and Elles obviously wrote his notes before the battle had formally been named.
93 OH, W. Miles, *Military Operations, France and Belgium 1917, the Battle of Cambrai* (HMSO) pp. 6 and 7.
94 J. Ewing, *The History of the 9th (Scottish) Division* (John Murray) 1921, pp. 222–223. S. Bidwell and D. Graham, *op. cit.*, p. 91.
95 M. Farndale, *History of the Royal Regiment of Artillery* (Royal Artillery Institution) 1986, pp. 216–219 and R. Prior and T. Wilson, *Command on the Western Front: the Military Career of Sir Henry Rawlinson, 1914–18* (Blackwell) 1992, pp. 292–295.
96 OH, Miles, *op. cit.*, p. 47 and Farndale, *op. cit.*, pp. 216–219.
97 Third Army, "Draft Scheme for Operation GY, against Cambrai, Bourlon Wood and Passages over the Sensée River", 25 October 1917, BCI/16, Fuller Papers, LHCMA.
98 "Tactical Employment of Tanks in 1918, Not Official", 8 August 1917, BCI/2. Fuller Papers, LHCMA. Fuller, *Memoirs*, p. 171, indicates that it was an earlier draft of this paper, written on 4 August, which Hardress-Lloyd took to Third Army HQ on 5 August. But no such document exists in the Fuller Papers at the LHCMA or the Tank Museum, the archives which hold his other First World War documents, and Fuller appears to have hoarded everything of significance. Moreover the paper he produced on 8 August was, as its title indicates, recommending raids in 1918, not autumn 1917.

99   Elles to GS, Advanced GHQ, 7 September 1917, BCI/4, Fuller Papers, LHCMA and OH, Miles, *op. cit.*, pp. 7 and 8.

100   OH, Miles, *op. cit.*, p. 8.

101   *ibid.*, p. 9 and "Notes on Conferences Held at HQ Tank Corps on 25–26 October 1917 Regarding the Operations Projected to Take Place on the Third Army Front", 27 October 1917, BCI/15, Fuller Papers, LHCMA.

102   "Notes", Part I, para. 1, BCI/15, Fuller Papers, LHCMA. OH, Miles, *op. cit.*, p. 20.

103   Fuller to Elles, 30 October 1917, BCI/24, Fuller Papers, LHCMA. Fuller, *op. cit.*, pp. 189–191.

104   See, for example, message of congratulations from Haig to Elles, 1 August 1917, TCOIV/11, Fuller Papers, LHCMA.

4

Cambrai to the German spring offensive: November 1917–June 1918

Detailed battle narrative is not the intention here but it is necessary briefly to review the sequence of events in the Albert–Cambrai area in late November 1917 and examine those aspects of the operation which were to lead, in its immediate aftermath, to the most serious debate.

Tank Corps HQ worked at a feverish pace from the last week of October until the battle began on the morning of 20 November (see Map 2). Little time was available for organizing the movement of tanks, for the collection of stores and ammunition and for making arrangements for the tanks to train with Third Army's infantry – tank/infantry training being carried out more thoroughly for Cambrai than for any previous attack. Effective concealment of the tanks until the start of the battle was obviously vital. Havrincourt Wood, immediately behind IV Corps' front and about three miles across, proved an almost ideal assembly area. Other nearby woods were also used, as were some ruined villages. But the tanks has to be entrained, transported and detrained, as close as possible to these positions, by night. From the railheads they had to be driven, also by night, to the assembly areas. To help coordinate this complex work an Advanced Tank Corps HQ was established at Albert.[1]

In addition to the problems of logistics and secrecy there were a number of technical difficulties which the Corps had to solve in time for the attack. The most crucial was that three of the main trenches of the Hindenburg Line position were too wide for tanks to cross. To overcome this problem each tank was to carry a massive, tightly compressed bundle of sticks, weighing about a ton and a half, known as a "fascine". A mechanism was devised for

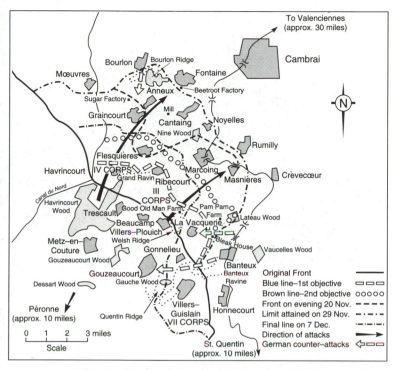

Map 2 Battle of Cambrai, November 1917.

releasing it from inside the tank, into the trench, blocking the trench and allowing the tank to cross. The fascine itself was merely a normal military engineering device for filling inconvenient holes. What took some ingenuity was developing the mechanism for holding and releasing it. The idea of using fascines for the Cambrai operation has been attributed to Fuller[2] but Fuller himself claimed no such credit, ascribing it to Searle and Central Workshops.[3]

The fascines were each composed of about 75 ordinary bundles of brushwood such as were routinely used for road repairs. While preparing for Cambrai, Central Workshops took delivery of 21,000 of these bundles which were bound with chains and then compressed to form the fascines. The initial assembly and binding of the fascines was done by Chinese labour troops, 1,000 of whom were based at Erin. Compression was carried out by a group of eighteen specially fitted up tanks, which

Figure 13 Mark IV tanks of C and D Battalions fitted with fascines at Plateau railhead prior to the Battle of Cambrai.

> acted in pairs pulling in opposite directions at steel chains which had previously been wound round and round the bundles . . . So great was the pressure thus exerted that months afterwards, an infantryman in search of firewood, who found one of these fascines and gaily filed through its binding chain, was killed by the sudden springing open of the bundle.[4]

Each tank however could carry only one fascine and having dropped it had no means of retrieval. Thus Fuller and his operations staff had to devise tactics by which tanks worked together in sections of three (four sections making a company) so that, as they came to successive big trenches, one could drop a fascine on which both it and the rest of the section could cross.[5]

Logistic difficulties were anticipated in keeping the fighting tanks in action. Since Messines old Mark I tanks had often been used as Supply tanks to carry forward stores for use by the Mark IV fighting tanks. The quantity of stores which could be carried inside the 50 to 60 Supply tanks likely to be available for the Cambrai operation was not deemed adequate, however, and, in addition to making the fascines and its other work, the Central Workshops were also asked to construct 110 large sleds to be dragged behind

Supply tanks on which petrol, oil, grease, ammunition and other supplies needed by tanks could be transported. Erin's achievement in preparation for Cambrai was truly prodigious. The Central Workshops operated night and day for 3 weeks.[6]

All three of the Tank Corps' Brigades were used for this operation, a total of 9 battalions, each of 36 fighting tanks plus some spares. A total of 378 fighting tanks were available altogether. In addition, each Brigade had 18 Supply tanks. In preparation for the advance of the cavalry, and to make all movement easier, 32 tanks were fitted with gear to rip up barbed wire and entirely tow it away. There were also a few specialist signals tanks fitted with radio. Only 54 fighting tanks were held in reserve,[7] an aspect of the plan to which, as we have seen, Fuller objected. The Tank Corps Advanced HQ at Albert would thus have little control over the battle once it had started.

Elles decided personally to participate in the attack "leading the attack of the centre division" in a tank called "Hilda". Given that there was no radio in the fighting tanks of this period Elles would have been neutralizing himself as a commander except that, in the absence of a substantial reserve, he was already virtually neutralized. He thus proposed to exercise another traditional function of military leadership – inspiration by example and by the sharing of risks with subordinates. At the time Fuller objected to Elles' action, fearing the consequences for the Tank Corps if the latter were killed or wounded, but in retrospect he admitted that Elles had been right in this matter and he wrong.[8]

Only two German divisions held the 6-mile stretch of front attacked on 20 November 1917. The German artillery in the area was exceptionally weak, there being only thirty-four guns in the sector attacked at zero hour. Surprise was not quite complete. On 16 November General von der Marwitz, commanding the German Second Army, had not the slightest conception that he was about to be attacked. But two British prisoners taken in a trench raid in the IV Corps area on the night of 17 November told their captors that they had seen tanks. A scrap of signals intelligence picked up on the night of 19 November also served to increase the German state of alert. Indeed the German artillery was so active on the night of 19–20 November that some officers of the Tank Corps thought the game had been given away entirely. This was not the case. While the Germans were alert and expecting some sort of attack they were not sure of its precise timing or nature. They were still heavily outnumbered in both men and guns though reinforcements from the now moribund Eastern Front were quite close at hand.[9]

At dawn on 20 November over 300 fighting tanks led five infantry divisions of Third Army's III and IV Corps into the attack. That morning events generally proceeded according to the Third Army plan. Aided by a thick mist, as well as by smoke shell (another crucial artillery innovation of 1917), which formed a significant part of the supporting barrages, the British overran the Hindenburg Line all along the frontage of the attack. The Support Line was attacked in the second half of the morning and that too was captured along most of the frontage attacked. At some points a 4-mile advance had been achieved by the end of the day, a depth of penetration not achieved in four months at Third Ypres. The Royal Flying Corps was more extensively employed in a ground attack role than in any previous battle (though it had also been active in this capacity at Messines) attacking not only German airfields and headquarters but also artillery and in some cases individual machine gun positions. Four thousand German prisoners were taken.[10]

At other points, however, the advance was halted quite early. The most dramatic check occurred at the Flesquières Ridge in the Hindenburg Support Line, an objective of the 51st Division in the IV Corps area, attacked shortly after 9.30 a.m. The main problem there was a number of stubbornly manned German gun batteries behind the ridge. These had not been destroyed by counter-battery fire or by the barrage and the barrage had lifted before the assault on the ridge began. The tanks had also got well ahead of the infantry and ended up advancing towards the batteries unsupported. It seems possible that as many as five tanks may have been knocked out by one gun. It was reported at the time that this gun was served by just one heroic individual and exaggerated rumours suggested that he had accounted for up to sixteen tanks. Fuller claimed in his memoirs that 51st Division's problems were partly the result of its commander, Major-General G.M. Harper, having made a series of minor but cumulatively important alterations in the tactics of tank–infantry co-operation which Fuller had recommended and which other divisions employed. Needless to say the divisional history does not endorse Fuller's version of the reasons for its problems and the issue cannot be resolved without a more minute analysis of the divisions' action on this day than any subsequent historian has yet attempted.[11]

As with so many Western Front offensives, most of the impetus was lost after the first day. It is debatable whether the Cavalry Corps had a fleeting opportunity to penetrate into the German rear areas on the afternoon of 20 November. If so it was certainly not seized.[12] The decision was nevertheless taken to continue the offensive. The tanks took heavy casualties on the first day and, as always happened, their crews were in some instances rendered incapable after the first few hours by the physical effort of operating their vehicles combined with high interior temperatures and carbon monoxide poisoning. Tanks did participate in infantry assaults on subsequent days but these lacked the cohesion and the element of surprise achieved on the 20 November.[13]

By 27 November General Byng had decided that tanks were likely to be of little further use in this battle and that they should be withdrawn from the salient which they had helped to create.[14] This salient inevitably became the target for a major German counter-attack. It was mounted on 30 November. Byng had given no order for transition to the defence. The attack into the IV Corps area in the northern part of the salient had been anticipated by the Corps commander, however, and was largely defeated by artillery defensive fire. But that on the other side of the salient occupied by III and VII Corps completely wrong-footed the British and captured a good deal of ground. German success was partly attributable to the use of highly trained storm troops, who led the attack, and partly to the close co-operation of aircraft which bombed and strafed in support of it. Tanks of 2nd Tank Brigade, already withdrawn from the salient itself but not far removed from the battlefield, were thrown in to check the German advance. Twenty-three took part in a counter-attack from Gouzeaucourt in the direction of Villers Guislain and Guislain Wood which played an important part in stabilizing the situation.[15]

The Battle of Cambrai was effectively a draw. Gains made by the Germans in the counter-attack of 30 November over and above the recapture of terrain lost to the British since 19 November virtually equalled the gains which the British were able to retain. In terms of prisoners and guns taken there was an equivalent result. After a gloriously promising start therefore – church bells were rung in England on 21 November for the first time in the war – the battle ended in disappointment and a considerable amount of recrimination.[16]

For the Tank Corps the first day at Cambrai could be regarded as a vindication of certain ideas: the selection of a battlefield with suitable ground, the use of tanks *en masse* and the attainment of surprise by forgoing a preliminary bombardment. The adoption of this set of ideas by the Tank Corps itself was, however, more belated than is apparent from most accounts. Fuller had argued in February that tanks could traverse "practically any ground" and had not advocated dispensing with a preliminary bombardment until the summer of 1917. He had then recommended only raids with relatively little artillery support.[17] The success of the first day at Cambrai was largely attributable to a great advance in artillery techniques in late 1916 and 1917 without which mounting an effective large-scale surprise attack with no artillery preparation on a well-prepared position (even a rather weakly held one) would have been virtually impossible. Fuller gave little indication in his memoirs of having appreciated this artillery revolution or having grasped that it was the real key to the limited success attained at Cambrai and to the much greater victories of the 1918 counter-offensive.[18]

Whatever Cambrai had demonstrated about the offensive capacity of tanks was of doubtful relevance in the immediate future. It was dawning on the General Staff in the War Office and on GHQ that for the next few months, with the collapse of Russia and the transfer of hundreds of thousands of German troops to the Western Front, the Allies were going to lose the initiative.[19] Though the US Army was beginning to arrive in substantial numbers, it was still being trained in the rear and had yet to enter the line of battle. Because of the British blockade and the limitless manpower resources of the Americans time was not on the Germans' side and the next big offensive would inevitably be theirs.[20]

Nevertheless, in the immediate aftermath of Cambrai the role of the tank in the future British war effort on the Western Front was hotly debated at the highest levels. One of the triggers for this debate was a memorandum by Winston Churchill, the Minister of Munitions, entitled "Munitions Possibilities of 1918", presented on 31 October 1917[21] – too late to influence the planning for the Cambrai operation itself. Churchill made it clear that, whatever his previous views on the subject, he now saw the Western Front as the decisive theatre. In the autumn of 1917 the British infantry were, together with their allies, "slightly superior in numbers, markedly superior in quality". Provided the infantry had adequate support from "six principal forms of machinery" a decisive British offensive ought, he suggested, to be possible in 1918. Churchill listed the mechanical aids to victory in the order of importance in which they appeared to him at the time. It is interesting that tanks merely came fifth on the list – before gas but after artillery, aircraft, railways and trench mortars. Though he was more responsible for their existence than anyone else, Churchill's belief in the tanks' importance was apparently not excessive in the days immediately before Cambrai. He nevertheless had some interesting concepts for tank use which were in some respects prophetic of what was about to happen in the November battle. He argued that:

> We have ... to contemplate the simultaneous or successive fighting of two different types of battle involving in their aggregate all the practicable portions of the front. There is the main battle of Exhaustion and the subsidiary battle of Surprise. They mutually aid each other and it might well be that the results of the Battle of Exhaustion would be reaped on the battle field of Surprise.[22]

In Churchill's view "battles of Exhaustion" were appropriate ground which the enemy could not afford to give up. "Battles of Surprise" on the other hand could be conducted on strategically less vital ground. The battle of Exhaustion appears to have been Churchill's term for the type of battle which the British were currently fighting at Ypres, "proceeding by regular steps from the earliest period of the campaigning season until the culminating period is reached". Churchill proposed that once the enemy's resistance was eroded, a series of "battles of Surprise" should be unleashed. Eventually the whole front would become active. The method of attack for the battle of Surprise would be wholly different from that for the battle of Exhaustion: "Above all the preparations should not reveal the conventional symptoms of an offensive to a hostile aeroplane photograph." Tanks were to be one of the principal means of attack in such battles.[23]

In late 1917 and early 1918 both Fuller and Churchill appear to have been thinking of tanks, in the short term, more as a means by which cost-effective attrition could be inflicted on the Germans than as instruments of decisive breakthrough. Fuller believed that tanks would be able to achieve a big breakthrough only in 1919 after raids and limited offensives in 1918.[24] Churchill believed that victory could be achieved in 1918 (provided technology was adequately exploited) but that the decision would be arrived at by the exercise of overwhelming attritional pressure all along the front rather than by a major breakthrough on any one section of it.[25] This part of Churchill's prescription for Allied success in 1918 has some similarity with what was actually to happen – though the Germans were worn down by their own reckless (and in some respects inept)[26] offensives of March to June rather than by British "battles of Exhaustion". Churchill, however, does not appear to have anticipated in his October paper that there would be a big transfer of German troops from the Russian to the Western Front in the winter of 1917–18 and there is certainly no suggestion that the Allies might lose the initiative at any point in 1918. We have, moreover, drawn attention to some of the sounder parts of Churchill's thesis. Other sections of the paper, proposing the production of a vast numbers of gigantic railway guns and heavy trench mortars, could be (and were)[27] dismissed on the basis of the most elementary tactical analysis.

Churchill's paper on munitions was sent on to Haig by Robertson on 2 November.[28] Haig furnished Robertson with a reply to it on 23 November – the fourth day of Cambrai. Haig's response was cautious and sceptical. He was far from denying the usefulness of technology in the prosecution of the war and provided an account of his own responsiveness to technical innovation as Commander-in-Chief. But he emphasized that the types of hardware which Churchill was pushing were just aids to the infantry; they were not, and in Haig's view could never be, substitutes for it. At the forefront of his mind was the manpower crisis:

> Without sufficient and efficient infantry machinery can never win victory in offence nor save us from defeat in defence. Unfortunately our infantry units have fallen so far below establishment and threaten to fall much further below that it is necessary to examine jealously any proposal which would have the effect of depleting their ranks still further.[29]

Haig believed that Churchill's grandiose plans for prodigious quantities of new equipment might tie up so much manpower as fatally to weaken the infantry. It is noticeable, however, that he was much more dismissive of Churchill's ideas about railway guns and heavy trench mortars than he was about his proposals for tanks.

> Tanks under conditions suitable to their use are of great value and to some extent, for certain purposes are capable of replacing numbers of guns and economizing infantry. But suitable conditions for their employment cannot always or even often be found and our experience shows that methods of defeating tank attacks have already been found.[30]

Though Haig praised the Tank Corps in the fullest terms for its work at Cambrai, it is probable that he was excessively influenced by the Flesquières incident. It was, after all, not really the tanks' fault that the infantry failed to keep up with them and that was the main problem in dealing with the German batteries. To Fuller's intense annoyance the possibly legendary "lone gunner" affair figured prominently in Haig's despatch on the battle – Haig taking the exceptionally chivalrous step of praising the courage of an enemy officer.[31] Generally Haig saw no reason to change the order of priorities for industrial production which he had accorded to the tanks on 20 August 1917 and which placed tanks well below aircraft and artillery and below the light railway locomotives which had become essential to the movement of supplies in the BEF's rear areas.

Driving home the point that he was no Luddite, however, and perhaps trying to counter-attack Churchill, Haig emphasized that: "The importance of air supremacy has been fully recognised by me since I have been in command in France and the supply of aircraft provided has never been nearly equal to my demands."

But (Haig implied, without explicitly saying so) not all new technologies were equal. Airpower had overwhelmingly proved itself, mainly as the indispensable eyes of the BEF's artillery and the means of shielding the BEF from observers for the German guns. It was in constant use. Tanks, however, had been of major importance only on a few days in the last fourteen months. Yet they consumed manpower all the time, not only in the Tank Corps itself but also in the factories at home.

Haig emphasized that his munitions requirements were "calculated with the greatest care after full discussion with officers of experience – now considerable – of use of the various means of warfare concerned and with due regard to the proportion in which all these various means can most usefully be employed". He correctly implied that Churchill's paper demonstrated a certain naivety in tactical matters and that the extent to which the technical means advocated by Churchill could save manpower was limited:

> The full power of an Army certainly cannot be exercised unless the infantry is liberally provided with all the different aids under discussion besides others. But on the other hand an insufficiency of infantry cannot be compensated for by a development of machinery beyond a certain point and the manpower available must be allocated with due regard to this fact.[32]

A more detailed response to Churchill's proposals was provided by a War Office conference held on 5 December. Like Haig the conference was dismissive of Churchill's suggestion for enormous numbers of heavy trench mortars and railway guns but less so of his advocacy of armour. With regard to Churchill's ideas on the mass employment of tanks in "battles of Surprise" it took the view that:

> the advantages and at the same time some of the limitations of such enterprises have recently been exemplified in the action near Cambrai. Favourable weather, that is misty conditions, seem necessary.
> The possibility of again inflicting a similar check on the enemy may, however, result in enforcing caution in regard to the extent to which portions of the hostile line, apparently quiet, may be weakened in order to ensure concentration on other fronts.[33]

The tendency of tanks to absorb manpower could not be ignored, the conference concluded. The tank by itself could not hold ground and the potential threat posed by tanks to apparently quiet sectors of the German front was only credible if there were substantial forces of infantry available to co-operate with them.

> The Tank may at times be used with advantage as an alternative to the heavy gun for the purpose of overcoming the enemy's fixed defences, and its relative mobility combined with the fact that the preparations for its employment can more easily be concealed, endow it with certain advantages.
> On the other hand to exploit the Tank to the prejudice of rifle and man power would be bad policy and would end in exalting the servant above the arm it exists to assist and serve.[34]

While having some (mostly quite reasonable) reservations about tanks and counselling against over-reliance on them, the conference can hardly be accused of adopting a reactionary attitude. It recommended that "provision of Tanks including those for the carriage of supplies and ammunition to the troops should be limited to twenty-seven battalions at about 60 tanks per battalion, or a total establishment of some 22,500 men excluding personnel required as drafts".[35] This represented a very major allocation of resources to an arm which had still not really proved itself a battle-winner and was a very big increase on the nine battalions the Corps then had. The conference was not, however, recommending any increase in the industrial priority given the tank. With the manpower crisis biting in industry as well as on the Western Front and with the Tank Corps already short of tanks, it was very unlikely that these proposals could be implemented in the forseeable future and those attending must have known that.

One voice in the War Office dissented from the conference's report and its dissent centred on tanks. The Master General of the Ordnance, Sir William Furse, a considerable military technologist and innovator[36] did not believe that misty conditions were "necessary" to the success of the tanks. Artificial smoke, of which Furse was a keen advocate, was, he maintained, a perfectly adequate substitute and had been liberally employed by the artillery at Cambrai. The suitable ground at Cambrai and the careful tank/infantry training before the battle were the real keys to the tanks' improved effectiveness, Furse believed.[37] Essentially Furse's difference with the report was one of emphasis. He accepted that tanks without infantry were of little use in either defence or attack. But he did believe that tanks, when employed in conjunction with other forms of relatively new technology, could mean that less infantry was needed for some operations.

> For the last 18 months in all our ... well prepared attacks against a limited objective, it has been the artillery that has captured the position and the infantry that has held it, first by killing or capturing the enemy troops who have been driven underground by the high explosive shells, and then by holding it against counter-attacks. I fear, however, that in a large number of cases our Commanders use just as many and even more infantry in the attack over a given frontage and area as they did at the beginning of the war when the amount of high explosive beating over the area was 1/50th or less

than it is now. A few machine guns well sited and mounted by stout
hearted soldiers will hold up the best of infantry not supported by
accurate artillery. The larger the number of attacking infantry the
better the target for machine gunners. Tanks aided by smoke . . . are
the most effective assistance we can give our infantry to defeat these
machine guns.[38]

Furse believed that for the next eight or nine months the Allies
were going to lose the initiative on the Western Front and would
be compelled to act on the defensive. But even in this period he
thought tanks would be useful. His views on defence were sophisticated. He believed that the British should hold their front line as
thinly as possible "for the enemy will have preponderance in gun
power and is likely to copy our methods of capturing with artillery". Consequently he thought it useless "to sacrifice life and thereafter morale by exposing large numbers of men to be mangled by
high explosive". The British, he believed, ought to depend principally upon wire and machine guns for holding up and disorgan-
izing the German infantry attacks. Most of the troops ought to be
kept outside the range of the enemy's concentrated artillery fire
and trained for counter-attack. British artillery should be kept
further back than it was at present. Tanks might perform useful
service in counter-attacks mounted in conjunction with infantry
specially trained to co-operate with them in this role.

Furse did not think the munitions industry capable of equipping
more than the existing Tank Corps establishment of 18 battalions
in the next 10 to 12 months, though in the long run he recommended that the establishment be doubled, giving the Corps a
total of 36,000 men. In order to find the manpower he proposed
to cut back heavily on the cavalry, apparently virtually to eliminate it ("the transfer would, in my mind, help us greatly towards
victory"), and he was even prepared to see an infantry division
disbanded.[39]

Furse's memorandum demonstrates an intelligent military mind
at work. It represents an inspired synthesis of the debate between
Churchill, on the one hand, and Haig and the General Staff in the
War Office, on the other. In fact Furse's position was rather closer
to Haig's than to Churchill's. Some of the latter's ideas he, like the
rest of the War Office, totally rejected. While being quite critical
of certain aspects of British military practice on the Western Front,
Furse's differences with Haig over immediate policy were minor.

Doubtless Haig would have resisted the total scrapping of the cavalry to man tanks, but such a move would have made little difference in the short run. There were not enough tanks on the Western Front fully to equip the personnel the Tank Corps had.[40] Haig appears to have agreed with most of what Furse said about defensive dispositions. GHQ did attempt to get armies to adopt German methods of defence in depth in time for Ludendorff's spring offensive, though their actual implementation was patchy and inadequate.[41]

Churchill was not the only civilian commentator querying Haig's tank policy in the last months of 1917. In the aftermath of Cambrai, Sir Eustace Tennyson d'Eyncourt (knighted that year) suggested to the War Cabinet that "the best method of using tanks required further consideration". At Cambrai, he suggested, "a complete victory was prevented from developing owing to the breakthrough of the Tanks not having been followed up by the necessary forces backing up the attack". He went on to argue that:

> 3 special Tank Armies should be formed. By the term Tank Armies is not meant merely armies of Tanks but armies with Tanks as their primary offensive weapon, all other items – infantry, artillery, etc. being provided as necessary to help and follow up the Tank attack.

Tank armies, d'Eyncourt thought, should be kept as small and mobile as possible while maintaining a striking power adequate to their function.

> Each army should consist of 500 Tanks with the Tank personnel of about 6,000 or 7,000 men, other units of infantry etc. bringing the total of each army to about 100,000 men . . . had such an additional Tank army been available at Cambrai a really decisive victory would have been gained.

D'Eyncourt, like everyone else, was aware that, by the end of 1917, Great Britain was facing a manpower crisis. Implementing his proposals would have involved roughly doubling tank manufacture and greatly expanding the Tank Corps itself. In order to justify this he argued that tanks were tremendous manpower savers. A tank with a crew of 8 or 9 was, he contended, "probably equal to 400 infantry in the attack".[42]

This was a dubious equation and anyway GHQ and the War Office were well aware that the British Army would not be attacking in the early months of 1918. D'Eyncourt, however, showed no awareness of the change in the balance of forces on the Western Front or of the overall strategic situation. He gave no indication as to how the War Office was going to find 300,000 men for three tank armies in addition to those required for more mundane duties such as holding defensive positions. In one sense D'Eyncourt's paper may be regarded as forward looking and inspired, prophetic of the Panzer Groups and Tank Armies of the Second World War. Had it been written as an academic exercise it might be legitimate so to regard it, even though the tanks of 1916–18 were quite incapable of the rapid operational manoeuvre which was the *raison d'être* of the big mechanized formations of 1939–45. But it was apparently intended as a recommendation for immediate action. Looked at in that way, and considering the context in which it was written and presented, it is better dismissed as amateur strategy of the worst kind. It must have caused intense irritation in the War Office and GHQ when Lloyd George passed it on to them.

Yet the reply which the War Office sent to the Prime Minister on 28 December was a model of coherence, logic and restraint. If irritation can be detected it is only by reading between the lines:

> The value of tanks was demonstrated in the recent fighting near Cambrai, both in the offensive action of the 3rd British Army and also in local counter-offensives when the enemy subsequently atacked the 3rd Army on 30th November/1st December, but the limitation of the success achieved was due to many causes other than those stated.

One of these was the lack of a lighter type of tank designed for the exploitation role, though these were now being produced. The General Staff agreed that the tank could sometimes save manpower but doubted d'Eyncourt's equation of one tank with 400 infantry. Given the strategic situation it was inevitable that they should point out that "the role of tanks on the defensive which he [d'Eyncourt] does not discuss, also merits consideration". The General Staff accepted that:

> The advent of the tank has in reality given us a new arm, and with its aid variety and, therefore, an increased element of surprise can be introduced into the major tactics of an attack . . .
> Sir Eustace rightly visualises the tank acting in co-operation with infantry and not alone, for obviously a breakthrough by tanks must be followed by an adequate force of infantry and other arms to hold

the ground won or exploit the success. It would not be practicable, however, permanently to organize a specialized army around the tank any more than around the artillery. The value of tanks as of guns lies in the assistance they can give to the infantry to overcome the enemy's defences and thereby reach and defeat his troops. What is required is an organization which shall be sufficiently elastic to admit of tanks being successfully employed with other arms in both offensive and defensive warfare. The proportion of infantry, artillery and other units to be employed in conjunction with a given number of tanks is a matter which needs to be investigated most carefully on each successive occasion and with due regard to local considerations before any large offensive scheme is undertaken. Similarly in defensive warfare tanks must be distributed where they are most likely to be able to act effectively in counter-attacks."[43]

In the light of experience gained during the Cambrai fighting the General Staff had decided to reorganize the Tank Corps in France in 3 groups, 2 Heavy and 1 Light. Each Heavy group was to consist of 2 brigades, each of 3 battalions, with 288 tanks altogether. The Light group would have the same structure but more tanks – 410 of the new, more mobile type – the Medium A. It was proposed eventually to have a third Heavy group and to increase both Heavy and Light groups by the addition of a third brigade when the additional tanks and personnel became available to man them. With the manpower currently available, however, even the scale of two Heavy and one Light group was considered unlikely to materialize before August 1918. These Tank Groups were to be self-contained with regard to transport and the necessary accessory units such as signals and engineers. They were to be placed where they could best be used to act counter-offensively in the case of a major German attack.[44]

Presumably because of the shortages of both manpower and tanks which the General Staff here hinted at, the Tank Groups proposal had not been implemented before the great German attack of the spring. The British counter-offensive from 8 August proceeded too rapidly and consumed tanks too fast to allow the establishment here contemplated to be put into effect, though, after Sir Henry Wilson become CIGS in February 1918, the intentions of the General Staff in the War Office for the long-term expansion of the Tank Corps become even more grandiose.[45]

In December 1917 the General Staff was happy to accept

d'Eyncourt's suggestion of close co-operation with the Americans in tank production and believed that such co-operation should also be extended to the French. Tanks could not hold ground by themselves, however, and given the depleted state of the infantry, the manpower crisis and the major German offensive expected, it did not appear to make sense to increase, in the short run, the establishment which had already been approved for the Tank Corps. Nor did current tank output suggest that a greater establishment could be maintained. But it was hoped that: "With American assistance in the production of Tanks . . . it should be possible to provide a combined Tank Force which might have great possibilities in the event of offensive operations by British, French and American forces in the late summer or autumn of 1918."[46]

In fact by this time arrangements were well in hand for the establishment of an Allied Tank Factory at Chateauroux. Set up by Anglo-American agreement, Chateauroux was meant to produce tanks of all types. One of the most far-sighted and enterprising bits of industrial co-operation in the whole war, it had been vigorously promoted by Albert Stern of the Ministry of Munitions.[47] Getting the factory into production was a slow process, however, and the Armistice arrived before its products did.

Even though nothing which had happened in 1917 would have convinced a sceptical observer that tanks were capable of radically changing the conduct of war on the Western Front, that year had been a period of hesitant but impressive expansion for the Tank Corps. There had been only 4 battalions at the beginning of the year though an establishment of 9 had then been authorized. Nine battalions actually fought at Cambrai. Expansion to 18 battalions had been authorized by GHQ in August 1917 and by the War Office on 27 November.[48] By the beginning of December 1917 GHQ had reluctantly accepted that the Germans would have the initiative in the early months of 1918. At a meeting on tank policy at GHQ on the fourth of that month General Butler announced that: "The employment of the British Army in 1918 was to be a defensive one . . . The role it had taken in 1917 was, therefore, to be reversed. The Tank Corps would conform to this policy."

Elles came to the meeting with two possible establishments to be adopted by the Tank Corps in the future: a Lower organization of 18 battalions and a Higher of 27. Given the shortage of manpower a compromise was arrived at whereby: "The C-in-C would adhere to the Lower organization viz: 9 Bns of Heavy and 9 Bns of Light Tanks plus the necessary administrative services. Tanks, however, would be produced on the Higher Organization."

It was considered that men for the extra battalions might eventually be obtained from various sources – the Navy, the USA or the Colonies. But clearly, and probably rightly in view of the impending German offensive, Haig was not prepared to weaken his already depleted infantry. Tank production would obviously depend on the priority GHQ chose to give it. Churchill, attending as Minister of Munitions, wanted it to have priority over everything except aircraft. GHQ, however, was also worried about shell supply. Throughout the discussion Churchill "maintained a sardonic smile contemptuous of the brainpower of the regular soldier". Ultimately he left the meeting "very disappointed" at not having been asked to produce more tanks. But Churchill appears to have shown no appreciation of the enormity of the crisis the Army on the Western Front was facing, of the degree to which its manpower had been depleted, or of the very limited usefulness of heavy tanks in the defensive role.[49]

On 14 December GHQ issued a "Memorandum On Defensive Measures" which formally ordered the BEF to make the transition to a defensive posture.[50] Tank Corps HQ was concerned that this memorandum did not consider the role of tanks at all. In a letter to GHQ on 3 January 1918 Elles accepted that the British defensive stance "must for some time to come depend primarily on Infantry and Artillery action" but he also considered that "a mechanical striking force [should] be built up behind this shield so that offensive power may be added to the defensive imposed on us for the next several months". Elles considered that the twenty divisions which it was hoped to keep as a Western Front reserve should be trained to "co-operate with Tanks and Aeroplanes". If so he thought that: "not only will [the reserve's] potential hitting power be increased many times, but a new method of warfare may be inaugurated against which the enemy is impotent".[51]

Elles's letter of 3 January was accompanied by a memorandum by Fuller on the "Defensive and Offensive Use of Tanks 1918". Fuller was, as always, keen to play up the potential of tanks. But he was forced to admit that the Tank Corps was going to have to fight the German offensive expected in the spring with a tank, the Mark IV, with which it had never been happy, which was already

Figure 14   Mark V tanks moving up with infantry during the "Hundred Days".

considered obsolete and which was not suitable for a very mobile role. The Mark V tank which was expected to be "as superior to the Mark IV as a 1905 motor-car was superior to one of 1895" was, unfortunately, not likely to arrive on the Western Front until August and the Mark VIII, expected to be 100 per cent superior to the Mark V was not until the winter of 1918–19. Fuller's position in January was that:

> As our tactics cannot be radically altered for some time and as the enemy is, or will shortly, face us in superior strength, the defensive has been forced upon us. Consequently the first thing to do is to visualise what this defensive means, the second what should be the main action of the Tank Corps when rearmed with the Mark V Tank.[52]

Fuller recognized that the Germans would be trying "to end the war before the Americans can take the field in large numbers" and would thus be mounting major offensives. This was, of course, no more than GHQ already realized. But whereas Haig predicted that the British Army would be the main target, Fuller assumed that the enemy's initial attack would be focused on the French, "so that he may dislocate his strongest antagonist first, and possibly force his weaker one, the British Army, to weaken itself by reinforcing the French, just as the British Army reinforced the Italian front in November 1917". Fuller expected the German offensive in two phases and anticipated the second (decisive) phase might be aimed at the British.[53] That Fuller should have assumed the French Army stronger than the British (in other than purely numerical terms) at this stage in the war is strange. In terms of fighting power he was certainly wrong – the BEF made most of the running in the "Hundred Days" period of August to November 1918. He was equally incorrect in thinking that the French Army would be the initial German target.

Fuller considered that "a passive defence for Tanks would be under almost all conditions an absurdity". He recommended two basic forms of action – raids to disrupt the enemy's preparations and tie down enemy troops, and counter-attacks. Fuller was still pushing his idea of tank raids very strongly. He argued that:

> Tanks, however, enable us not only to threaten but actually to attack the enemy at small cost. A series of periodical Tank and Infantry raids made at various places down the British front during the late spring and summer of 1918 would probably force the enemy to retain large forces on this front; further, the prisoners alone would more than compensate for the losses resulting. For a one day raid with 3 Divisions, judging from the basis of the Third Army operations of August last, the casualties should not be more than 1,500 killed, wounded and missing.[54]

The fallacies in this are palpable. The premise was that tank raids might force the Germans to retain forces on the British front which they would rather be using on the French. It was completely false. The Germans intended to attack the British first. Fuller had also guessed incorrectly the timing of the German offensive which came in early spring, too early to be disrupted by the operations he proposed. It was absurd of Fuller to base assumptions about casualties in the tank raids he was proposing for 1918 on the Cambrai operation. The latter was mounted immediately after Third Ypres, when the German forces on the Western Front were at a low ebb. The Cambrai sector had been left exceptionally weak, particularly in artillery, the arm to which tanks were most vulnerable. These things would not apply to the heavily reinforced

German armies facing the British in the first half of 1918. Cambrai, moreover, was not a raid. It was an Army attack which had taken weeks of preparation. Whatever success had been achieved was largely owing to massively superior artillery. This crucial factor was one which Fuller tended to play down in his tank raid schemes, in which he placed a good deal of reliance on air support. A further point is that the Mark IV tank was a grossly unsuitable instrument for raiding, having very limited powers of manoeuvre. A significant proportion of these tanks normally broke down mechanically or became ditched or bellied during the course of operations. If the raid were followed by a swift voluntary withdrawal or a determined German counter-attack, broken down machines would have to be abandoned on the battlefield. By making a lot of relatively small-scale attacks in the early months of 1918, moreover, the British would probably have been squandering manpower, energy, morale and resources and thus making themselves unnecessarily vulnerable to the impending German onslaught.

Fuller's idea for a sizeable Allied offensive in 1918 were summarized as follows:

> To strike at the enemy with an army of all arms.
>   The tactics of such an operation to be based on the powers of the Mark V tank.
>   This attack to be carried out either in the British or French front before the enemy's secondary (decisive) attack against either of these fronts can be initiated.

Fuller wanted this offensive mounted on similar principles to Cambrai but employing a much greater number of tanks (between 1,400 and 1,650) allowing the retention of a reserve. But even with such a large armoured force he does not appear to have believed the war could be brought to a successful conclusion in 1918. Even the offensive he advocated for the second half of the year was intended to be little more than a big spoiling attack.[55]

GHQ did not respond positively to Fuller's proposals and came up with somewhat more realistic ideas of its own. On 18 January an instruction was sent to the Tank Corps allocating each of its Brigades to an Army.[56] This was followed by a letter from Lieutenant-General Herbert Lawrence, Haig's new Chief of Staff, outlining the Corps' roles in the expected defensive operations:

1. The use of tanks in the defensive will be restricted to assisting in re-establishing the battle or rear zones by counter-attack should the enemy succeed in penetrating either of these defensive organizations ...

2. In the counter-attack tanks may be used in two ways:-

(a) Without infantry support – within 24 hours of a hostile assault for the purpose either of checking an attacking force which has succeeded in penetrating the battle zone or to disorganize the enemy's next bound.

(b) in co-operation with other arms in the deliberate counterattack.

GHQ was definitely not in favour of "penny-packeting" tanks. Lawrence pronounced that: "It is important that tank units should be kept concentrated as far as possible. If dispersed forward, great damage will be done to signal communications and light railways by lateral movement."[57] It is interesting that GHQ was advocating the concentration of tanks at least as much to minimize the problems they could cause for the defence as to maximize any advantages they might confer.

In a staff paper for GHQ which he signed on 28 January Fuller stated that:

pursuit or field warfare can only be developed from a gap *after* the enemy's reserves have been neutralised. In the present war, as in past ones, reserves include not only the forces behind a battle front but also those on the flanks of the decisive attack. These flanking forces must be held taut otherwise they will pinch inwards. Further, for exploitation to follow penetration the gap created must be no more than half to a quarter of the total battle front.[58]

Fuller visualized the decisive campaign of 1919 as a breakthrough on a front of 100 miles requiring a total force of 12,000 tanks and an allocation to the Allied tank corps of 240,000 men. Even Fuller recognized that the production and manning of such a colossal armoured force was beyond the resources of Great Britain alone by 1919, but he seems to have thought it possible for Britain, France and the USA together. This would appear to indicate how little he understood about industry. The US Army was still largely equipped with British and French weapons at the Armistice and the Americans had barely begun making tanks.[59]

But before the great climactic breakthrough battle of 1919 there would have to be a lot of attrition in 1918. The best way that this could happen would be for the Germans to mount a massive Verdun-style offensive of their own. But, Fuller feared, they might instead adopt a policy of "nibbling away the important points along the British and French fronts". "If we allow him to carry out this nibbling, it will not help to adjust our front to meet next year's requirements; our losses will also be heavy. We dare not do this."[60]

Fuller here demonstrated considerable weaknesses of both strategic and operational/tactical thought. In suggesting that the Germans would be content with "nibbling" at the front he was reversing an earlier and more accurate judgement that they would need to win the war in 1918 to avoid being overwhelmed by American manpower. In suggesting that the Germans would mount an offensive in the Verdun style (by which he presumably meant one designed to implement attrition on favourable terms rather than make a complete breakthrough) it seems that Fuller had failed to appreciate the changes which had taken place in German operational methods since 1916, changes demonstrated not only on the Eastern Front in battles such as that at Riga but in the 30 November counter-attack at Cambrai. With the new-style tactics artillery preparation was brief, surprise sometimes achieved and infiltration methods used by the storm troop infantry who led the attack. The latter by-passed centres of strong resistance and penetrated deep into the British defences as rapidly as possible. Haig has recently been accused, by a leading historian of this war, of failing to appreciate these changes in German offensive methods.[61] The charge may have some validity though there is evidence against it.[62] But Fuller's failure in this respect in late January is quite clear. He obviously had little fear of a major German offensive and no appreciation at this stage of how initially devastating such an onslaught might be.

If, moreover, Haig may fairly be criticized for not ensuring the completion of new-pattern field fortifications in the Fifth Army area by 21 March 1918, he had at least recognized, as early as the beginning of December 1917, the need for a general transition to the defence.[63] At the end of January 1918 Fuller was offering renewed resistance to that policy. He proposed that: "Our policy must be a cautious yet economical one, that is, our activity must be limited to nibbling away his line and strength at the minimum loss in men to ourselves."

As a means of "nibbling" Fuller once again recommended the

"tank raids" policy which he had originally proposed in August 1917. As we have already argued, such "raids" were a dubious concept at the best of times and as a means of disrupting the German spring offensive they were hopeless. If, while preoccupied with raiding, the British had failed to adopt an essentially defensive posture, the disaster they would have suffered that spring might have been even greater than it actually was.

Fuller concluded by examining, in proto-Fascist terms, the political and social background against which the military operations of 1918 would have to be conducted:

> If the politicians and people are to be controlled so that this war may be brought to a victorious conclusion we must show "Profits" – a balance of successes by the autumn of this year. Will "Rifle and Artillery" attacks do this; will passive defence do this? They will not . . . Will mechanical warefare [sic] do so? It may . . .
>
> Unless the mouths of politicians are gagged by military successes, the outcry now beginning to be raised against the Higher Command will grow loud and continuous. Our destiny as a great nation lies in the hands of an ignorant and superstitious proletariat which is swayed by words.[64]

GHQ made no response to the Fuller missive discussed above. Given the numerous military misconceptions it contained (leaving aside the reactionary political and social sentiments) this was just as well. GHQ had already allocated Tank Brigades to Armies and made a general policy statement on how tanks were to be employed in defence. As the German offensive approached, however, GHQ proposed to enter into a more detailed discussion of tank use at a conference of Army commanders to be held early in March 1918.[65] Tank Corps HQ took offence at this, believing that GHQ should decide this issue itself (on the Tank Corps' advice) and simply impose its views on the Armies.[66] But this was not Haig's style. Though he did sometimes interfere unwisely, he was in principle a believer in delegation – in allowing his Army commanders to fight their own battles.[67] Fuller was worried that some Army commanders, particularly General Gough of Fifth Army, wished to use tanks as "pill-boxes or martello towers".[68] In fact the conclusions of the Army Commanders Conference held at Doullens on Saturday 2 March 1918 continued to envisage keeping most tanks concentrated for the counter-attack role. The official record of the conference as circulated to all Army commanders indicated that: "In view of the fact that we now have definite information of an imminent attack on the fronts of the Fifth and Third Armies, it is necessary to consider carefully whether every possible precaution has been taken to ensure success in the battle."[69]

Haig still delegated the detailed conduct of the battle to the Army commanders, indicating that they should "satisfy themselves that their dispositions are those best calculated to meet and defeat the enemy's offensive". With regard to tanks Haig wanted to be pragmatic and not too prescriptive.

> The principle of the employment of Tanks in as great numbers as possible will generally be observed, and in this connection the training of Reserve troops with Tanks is of great importance. In certain special cases, however, where the ground is suitable, it may be advisable to employ a few Tanks from concealed postions on reverse slopes or in valleys as mobile machine gun units. It must be remembered that the Tank is a new weapon . . . it is unwise at this stage to adhere rigidly to any stereotyped rules for its use.[70]

The idea of using "in certain special cases" a proportion of the tanks to lie up in concealed positions and emerge "like Savage Rabbits from their holes" to make immediate counter-attacks against parties of Germans penetrating into the Battle Zone (the main British defensive position) appears to have been accepted by GHQ only on 2 March. The "Savage Rabbits" concept was attributed by Fuller to Lieutenant-General Ivor Maxse, the Commander of XVIII Corps.[71] Though it has become usual to dismiss "Savage Rabbits" as a reactionary idea,[72] historians have generally regarded Maxse as one of the BEF's leading tactical thinkers.[73] In fact this was not a question of GHQ imposing an unwelcome concept on a reluctant Tank Corps. Though disliked by Fuller, the tactic was supported by Elles. But it seems that only a very small proportion of the tanks were used in this way.[74] The great bulk of the Tank Corps was disposed for "deliberate" counter-attacks in conjunction with the infantry reserves of the Armies. It was laid out "in three clusters, some ten miles behind the front, along a forty mile stretch from Lens southward to the Somme near Peronne". The basic fighting strength of the Tank Corps comprised the 1st, 2nd and 4th Tank Brigades, equipped with a total of 324 Mark IV fighting tanks. These were disposed as follows:

Figure 15 A Medium A 'Whippet' tank moves across open country.

- 1st Tank Brigade, which had three battalions, was placed behind Lens in the First Army area.
- 2nd Tank Brigade, at similar strength, was based in the Bapaume area under the command of Third Army.
- 4th Tank Brigade, also three battalions strong, was based in the Peronne area under Fifth Army.

The 3rd and 5th Tank Brigades were largely paper organizations. 3rd Brigade was in the process of being re-equipped with the relatively mobile Medium A "Whippet" tank, which had a top speed of 8 mph and a maximum endurance of 80 miles on one tank of petrol. In fact only about 50 of these had arrived. Most of them were allocated to 3rd Battalion which was detached from the rest of 3rd Brigade and based near Wailly as an additional reserve for the Third Army. Third Brigade's virtually tankless residue was in GHQ Reserve near Bray. Fifth Brigade, which was expecting Mark Vs eventually, was also based at Bray and was at this stage without tanks.[75]

In planning to meet the German offensive, therefore, GHQ did not ignore the Tank Corps' wishes. While rightly rejecting Fuller's tank raids idea, GHQ endorsed the Corps' other preferred role, that of counter-attack. The great bulk of the tanks were not penny-packeted. Neither were they placed so far forward that they were likely to be overrun in the first German rush. There appears to be no evidence that Elles had any serious disagreement with the Corps' dispositions as GHQ had made them immediately before the March offensive. Though Elles had passed on to GHQ Fuller's memoranda advocating "tank raids" it is unclear how far he really believed in this concept. There is no indication of his having thrown his full weight behind it.

There are many published accounts of the German 1918 offensive and here it is necessary to review events only in broad outline and as they affected the Tank Corps (see also Map 3). The first German offensive, codenamed "Michael", fell on the British Fifth and Third Armies on 21 March. The Germans cut their preliminary bombardment to four hours but made it exceptionally intense. The infantry assault was made without the assistance of a creeping barrage. Working in relatively small groups, largely ignoring the activity on their flanks, the storm troops who attacked in the first wave by-passed centres of strong resistance and concentrated on making the maximum possible penetration into the British defences, ultimately aiming to reach the gun-line and silence the British artillery.[76] Subsequent waves used much simpler (indeed often distinctly crude) tactics and tended to suffer heavy casualties as a result.[77]

That these methods worked so well against Fifth Army was largely due to its being much too weak in relation to the stretch of front it was holding, its system of field fortifications, remodelled (on GHQ's instructions) on German defence-in-depth principles, being incomplete, and the system being ill-understood and ill-used by the troops occupying it. A thick mist also helped the Germans by obscuring the signals for artillery support sent up by the British infantry in the Outpost (the furthest forward) Zone of the defence.[78]

The Outpost Zone of the Fifth Army was consequently overrun very quickly indeed. The Outpost Zone was far too thickly held with the result that about 30 per cent of Fifth Army's troops were lost almost immediately. The Germans then made considerable penetration into the Battle Zone. Most of the tanks were much too far back to have any influence on the events of this disastrous first day. Indeed it was only the handful employed in the much derided Savage Rabbit role which were able to intervene at all,

Map 3
Tank Corps
locations map,
corrected to
19 March
1918.

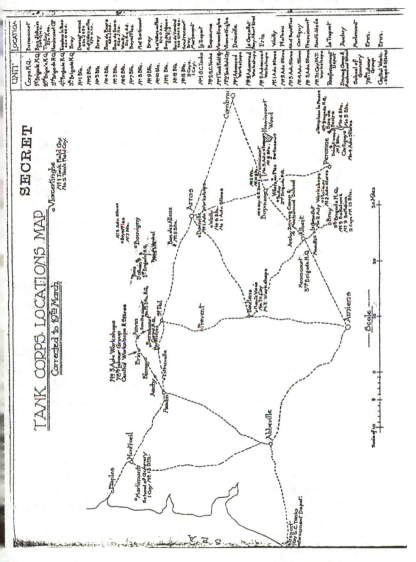

and there were none in the area of the greatest German break-in, on the right wing of the Fifth Army. The first significant tank interventions were on the second day. The most successful was a counter-attack by twenty-five Mark IVs of the 2nd Battalion which managed to plug a gap in the centre of Third Army's front.[79]

The period 21 to 26 March, which was the height of the crisis, saw a virtual collapse of command and control in the Fifth Army sector and considerable disarray in Third Army. The tanks under the command of these armies were either used in rather hurried, disjointed and small-scale counter-attacks or not used at all. The Mark IV tanks were so slow and lacking in manoeuvrability that the German storm troops, seeing tank counter-attacks coming, could sometimes do as they were trained to do with static centres of resistance – by-pass them and continue their advance regardless.[80]

Nevertheless some local counter-attacks by tank units did help slow the German advance and cover the retreat of British infantry units and formations, thus helping the process of reforming a line of resistance. A notable example of this was an attack by 12 Medium A "Whippets" of 3rd Battalion near Colincamps at noon on 26 March which frustrated a German attempt to push through a 4-mile gap which had arisen in the front of the Third Army. The gap was plugged on a more permanent basis by the New Zealand Division later the same day. Between 26 and 30 March the British front in the Somme area stabilized (though only after the Germans had made advances of up to 40 miles) and any opportunity the Germans had created of irreparably breaching the Allied front in this vicinity had passed.[81] By that time, however, 4th Tank Brigade (attached to Fifth Army) had lost all its tanks and 2nd Brigade (attached to Third Army) had only 27 left out of 98.[82]

On 29 March Elles reported to Capper that:

> It has all been very strenuous and particularly difficult. Things have moved as you well know very fast, and the Mark IV Tank is not built or designed for open warfare which is practically what has been going on since the first day.
>
> Supply and mechanical repairs have been extremely difficult on account of the rapid movement. For these reasons we have lost a large number of Tanks which in a slower operation would certainly have been available. The principal losses, however, appear to have been through shell fire.[83]

"Boots" Hotblack, the Tank Corps' intelligence officer, seems to have witnessed much of the fighting personally. Whereas Elles gave Capper the usual anodyne assurance that all ranks had performed splendidly, Hotblack passed a much more acerbic judgement:

All Commanders set far too low a standard of what is required from the fighting units. They were on occasion delighted with small shows in which the Tanks did their bare duty. The Regimental Officers know this and they realize that they need only do a moderate show and get ample praise. These moderate shows are seldom investigated by Battalion or Brigade Commanders, and the result is that the Regimental officer can do a poor show, come back and exaggerate his deeds, and obtain full praise. The result is that there are several young Tank Commanders who are now running down the Infantry and boasting their deeds. This will do the Tank Corps immense harm.

In criticism of the tactics used Hotblack indicated that:

Rear guard actions were urgently required –
   (a)   To steady our Infantry.
   (b)   To gain time.
   (c)   To disorganize the enemy attack and inflict casualties.
What actually happened was –
   (a)   Tanks were withdrawn and unsteadied our Infantry.
   (b)   Counter attacks were made by tanks unsupported by Infantry. (It was evident that infantry support would NOT be forthcoming.)
These counter attacks . . . did delay the enemy and inflict casualties.
As, however, the Tanks advanced in comparatively small numbers *towards* the hostile guns, they offered good targets and suffered heavy losses.

Hotblack considered that reverse slope positions should have been adopted and rear guard actions fought from these. In such positions "enemy guns have to advance and come into action in view of the Tanks instead of the Tanks advancing on stationary and concealed guns".

Hotblack had clearly concluded that Tank Corps HQ's entire policy on defence had been misconceived. A doctrine of "deliberate" counter-attack might have been all very well in theory. But the reserves designated for this purpose had been kept too far back and, by the time counter-attacks could be mounted by slow heavy tanks and unmechanized infantry, the Battle Zone had virtually collapsed. In his brutally frank and rather refreshing style Hotblack admitted that, "Tank Corps Headquarters are to blame for not foreseeing the possibility of rear guard action on the part of the Tanks and not issuing notes on this subject earlier."[84] This was a criticism not only of himself but of Elles and, more particularly, of Fuller, as the senior staff officer. In revised fighting instructions entitled "Notes on the Use of Mark IV Tank in Defence", issued on 9 April, Tank Corps HQ tacitly admitted the validity of Hotblack's main argument and henceforth adopted a policy of rear guard action, tanks "acting as a line of stops to check any forward flow of hostile Infantry and to gain time for own Infantry to reform in the event of a reverse".[85] Perhaps these were not very different from the "Martello tower" tactics to which Fuller had earlier objected so violently. In his memoirs Fuller wrote of the British Army reaping "folly's grim dividend" in spring 1918. The debacle had happened, he stated, because the Army, and especially GHQ, was "crawling with duds". Nowhere in his memoirs is there a hint of how wide of the mark were his own estimates of German intentions and capabilities in the early part of 1918. The memoirs are equally mute about his failure to issue really appropriate fighting instructions to the Tank Corps in time.[86]

The Germans mounted their second spring offensive of 1918 in the Arras area on 28 March. It was easily defeated and the services of the 1st Tank Brigade and the 6th Battalion (newly equipped with Whippets and posted to Second Army) were not required. The third strike was mounted in Flanders, in the First Army area, on 9 April. This attack was much weaker than planned because so many of the German reserves had been used up in the attacks further south. Nevertheless it made remarkably good progress and by 18 April had achieved a maximum advance of 10 miles, creating a salient 30 miles broad at the base. But there were no tanks in this sector and the front was stabilized without them.[87]

A German attempt to renew the offensive in the Somme area at Villers-Bretonneux on 24 April failed miserably despite the use of thirteen of the new German A7V tanks. (Small numbers of these machines had been in use since the opening of the "Michael" offensive on 21 March but so great had been the chaos caused to the British at that time by other means that their presence had hardly been noticed.) The A7Vs were ill-designed. Though possessing powerful engines, which gave them a good road speed of 8 mph, they had very poor cross-country mobility. The first tank-versus-tank clash occurred on 24 April and the outcome was generally favourable to the British. Two British Mark IV female tanks were holed by fire from an A7V and had to turn tail, but fire from a male Mark IV, commanded by Lieutenant Frank Mitchell, caused one A7V to overturn while evading and resulted in another being abandoned by its crew.[88] The effort devoted to tanks by the Germans had been so feeble and belated that captured British tanks outnumbered home-produced German A7Vs in German service right up to the Armistice.[89] Nevertheless the German use of tanks greatly excited the British Tank Corps and, despite their poor design, the A7Vs gained some initial successes against the British infantry on 24 April.[90]

The failure at Villers–Bretonneux did not, however, end the run of German offensive operations that spring. A major attack was made in the Chemin des Dames area on 27 May. British tanks were not involved as this was well to the south of their area of concentration in a sector which was primarily the responsibility of the French Army. Much of the force of the attack fell, however, on the British IX Corps, which, having been very roughly handled on the Somme, was resting on a supposedly quiet stretch of front. The German offensive in Champagne was initially the most successful of the whole series in terms of prisoners taken and ground gained. But it had run out of steam by 6 June, creating a deep but narrow salient vulnerable to counter-attack. The Germans launched another attack on 9 April (the Battle of Matz) to broaden this salient but it was defeated. On 11 June General Mangin's newly organized Tenth Army, which had the support of low-flying aircraft and 144 tanks, counter-attacked. The counter-attack regained some of the lost ground and inflicted significant losses on the Germans. It effectively halted the series of alarming, though Pyrrhic, German victories.[91]

As units lost their tanks during the March fighting the Tank Corps itself had routinely formed them into Lewis Gun detachments.[92] The conversion of whole battalions which had lost their tanks into light machine gun units was agreed within the Tank Corps by a conference held at its Advanced HQ on 2 April.[93] At the same meeting Tank Corps HQ pronounced that, "If a Tank is knocked out, its crew will at once join the first formed Infantry unit it meets with."[94] It was presumably in the same spirit of "all hands to the pump" that, on 12 April, GHQ ordered the Tank Corps to form forthwith a brigade of three Lewis Gun battalions out of its existing (tankless) personnel.[95] The Tank Corps was not quick to comply with this instruction and on 30 April 1918 Haig personally signed a letter to the Corps reiterating GHQ's intention "to ensure the employment to the best advantage of the available trained personnel [and] to form *temporarily* a Brigade of 3 Lewis Gun Battalions out of the existing Tank Corps units in France". Meanwhile "in view of the shortage of Infantry in France" Haig had decided to reduce the Tank Corps' establishment by 1 Brigade leaving 4 brigades with a total of 12 battalions.[96]

This was not a real cut in the Tank Corps' strength. It had possessed only four brigades equipped with tanks on 21 March and it had suffered heavy tank losses since then. With the British Army's "backs to the wall", as Haig had put it in an earlier communication, it was surely not unreasonable to ensure that all men not equipped with tanks be committed to the fighting in some capacity. Policies which the Tank Corps had arrived at of its own volition were driven by that logic. Yet Fuller expressed outrage at Haig's decision which he interpreted as an attack on the Tank Corps' very existence. He was similarly paranoid about a GHQ decision temporarily to delay the despatch of Mark V tanks to France in order to give priority of transportation to other materials. Naturally the proposed cut in its establishment was bitterly resisted by the Tank Corps. Equally naturally GHQ gave way on this issue once the spring crisis was passed and it was once again contemplating offensive operations.[97]

Equilibrium was restored to the front in June. The Germans had drastically depleted their own Army by this series of offensives. They had sustained about a million casualties, not counting lightly wounded likely to return to duty quickly,[98] possibly more than those inflicted on the Allies. The United States Army had, in response to the crisis of the spring, joined in active operations (an event of considerable moral significance) allowing some of its formations to be placed under foreign command. The Germans were now in acute difficulties. Right at the bottom of their own manpower barrel, they were facing the prospect of an apparently limitless injection of fresh American troops into the war on the Western Front.[99] The Germans were weary and serverely stricken with influenza. Having left the Hindenburg Line far in the rear, their field fortifications were now relatively weak and in some cases they seem to have lacked the energy or the will to improve them.[100] The Tank Corps, now being re-equipped with Mark Vs and Medium A Whippets, was about to have its best opportunities of the war.

Notes

1   E. Charteris, "HQ Tanks", pp. 39–41 and 54–70, Tank Museum. On railway moves and the use of the light railways see BCI/21, BCI/34, BCI/35, Fuller Papers, Liddell Hart Centre for Military Archives (LHCMA).

2   B.H. Reid suggests that Fuller's "use of fascines . . . showed a grasp of detail and practical ability of no common order", *J.F.C. Fuller, Military Thinker* (Macmillan) 1987, p. 47.

3   J.F.C. Fuller, *Memoirs of an Unconventional Soldier* (Nicholson and Watson) 1936, p. 180.

4   C. and A. Williams-Ellis, *The Tank Corps* (Country Life) 1919, pp. 102–103.

5   *ibid.*, pp. 103–104, and "Instructions on tanks operating with fascines" (undated) BCI/38, Fuller Papers, LHCMA.

6   Williams-Ellis, *op. cit.*, p. 103.

7   B. H. Liddell Hart, *The Tanks*, Vol. I (Cassell) 1959, p. 134.

8   Fuller, *Memoirs*, pp. 200–201, 211.

9   M. Farndale, *History of the Royal Regiment of Artillery, Western Front 1914–18* (Royal Artillery Institution) 1986, pp. 216–220. "HQ Tanks", pp. 66–67. Hotblack, "Summary of information 27 November 1917, including evidence of information obtained from prisoners about impending use of tanks", BCI/89, Fuller Papers, LHCMA. W. Miles, *Military Operations France and Belgium 1917, The Battle Of Cambrai* (HMSO), pp. 47–49.

10   "Preliminary Report on Tank Corps Operations 20 Nov.–1 Dec. 1917", undated, BCII/12, Fuller Papers, LHCMA. Liddell Hart, *op. cit.*, p. 28. On airpower see Miles, *op. cit.*, p. 287.

11   A version of the "Lone Gunner of Flesquières" story was incorporated, to Fuller's intense annoyance, in Haig's despatch on the battle. See "The Private Journal of Lt. Colonel J.F.C. Fuller Relative to the Expansion and Employment of the Tank Corps December 1917 to July 26 1918" (henceforth Fuller, "Private Journal") p. 11, Fuller Papers, Tank Museum. On the allegedly faulty tactics of 51st Division

see Fuller, *Memoirs*, pp. 198, 209. For 51st Division's own account see F.W. Bewsher, *The History of the 51st Highland Division 1914–18* (Blackwood) 1921, pp. 232–251.

12 Miles, *op. cit.*, pp. 281–283.

13 "Preliminary Report", BCII/12, Fuller Papers, LHCMA.

14 Byng to Elles, 27 November 1917, BCI/90 and Tank Corps Order No. 3. "Withdrawal of Brigades from the Battlefield", 28 November 1917, BCI/92, Fuller Papers, LHCMA.

15 "Action of 2 Bde Tanks on 30 November and 1 December", BCII/15 and "Outline of Tank Operations from 20 November–1 December 1917", undated, BCII/14, Fuller Papers, LHCMA.

16 Miles, *op. cit.*, pp. 273–274.

17 "Tactical Employment of Tanks in 1918, Not Official", 8 August 1917, BCI/2, Fuller Papers, LHCMA.

18 Fuller, *Memoirs*, pp. 169–343.

19 GHQ'S realization of the temporary loss of initiative on the Western Front was certainly complete by the time of its conference of 4 December 1917. See Fuller, "Private Journal", p. 1, Fuller Papers, Tank Museum.

20 J. Terraine, *Douglas Haig: the Educated Soldier* (Hutchinson) 1963, pp. 391, 440–441.

21 Churchill, "Munitions Possibilities in 1918", 21 October 1917, BCII/46, Fuller Papers, LHCMA.

22 *ibid.*, para. 7.

23 *ibid.*, para. 14.

24 "Tank Operations, Decisive in 1919 and Preparatory in 1918", undated but apparently January 1918, TS/40, Fuller Papers, LHCMA.

25 Churchill, "Munitions Possibilities In 1918", 21 October 1917, *passim*, BCII/46 and "Report of a Conference held at the War Office on 5 December 1917", 11 December 1917, section 1, BCII/43, Fuller Papers, LHCMA.

26 T. Travers, *How the War Was Won: Command and Technology in the British Army on the Western Front 1917–1918* (Routledge) 1992, pp. 86–89.

27 "Report of a Conference", sections 2 and 4, BCII/43 and Haig to Robertson (CIGS), 23 November 1917, BCII/44. Even Major-General Furse, the MGO, who had some sympathy with Churchill's approach in general terms, did not accord with his desire for very large numbers of railway guns. Furse to Robertson, 17 December 1917, BCII/42, Fuller Papers, LHCMA.

28 Haig to Robertson, 23 November 1917, para. 1, BCII/44, Fuller Papers, LHCMA.

29 *ibid.*, para. 3.

30 *ibid.*, para. 8.
31 Fuller, "Private Journal", p. 11, Fuller Papers, Tank Museum. Haig's despatch of 20 February 1918, J. H. Boraston (ed.) *Sir Douglas Haig's Despatches* (Dent and Son) 1919, p. 155.
32 Haig to Robertson, 23 November 1917, paras 9–13, BCII/44, Fuller Papers, LHCMA.
33 "Report of a Conference held at the War Office, 5 December 1917", section 3, paras 2 and 3, 11 December 1917, BCII/43, Fuller Papers, LHCMA.
34 *ibid.*, para. 6.
35 *ibid.*, para. 7.
36 On Furse, see S. Bidwell and D. Graham, *Firepower, British Army Weapons and Theories of War 1904–1945* (George Allen and Unwin) 1982, pp. 11, 12, 13, 37, 68, 111, 126.
37 Furse to Robertson, 17 December 1917, para. 2, BCII/42, Fuller Papers, LHCMA.
38 *ibid.*, paras 4–9.
39 *ibid.*, paras 9 and 10.
40 Liddell Hart, *op. cit.*, p. 157.
41 T. Travers, *op. cit.*, pp. 64–65.
42 Tennyson d'Eyncourt [to War Cabinet?], 12 December 1917, BCII/39, Fuller Papers, LHCMA.
43 "Note by the General Staff on E.H.T. d'Eyncourt's Memorandum Proposing the Formation of Tank Armies", paras 3 and 4, 28 December 1917, BCII/40, Fuller Papers, LHCMA.
44 *ibid.*, para. 5.
45 Wilson to Foch, 20 July 1918 enclosing "Memorandum on the Requirements for an Armoured Striking Force for an Offensive in 1919", PRO WO 158/842.
46 "Note by General Staff", para. 6, 28 December 1917, BCII/40, Fuller Papers, LHCMA.
47 Albert Stern, *Tanks 1914–18: the Logbook of a Pioneer* (Hodder and Stoughton) 1919, pp. 190 and 198–201. See also Memorandum by Lt.-Col. Stern to the War Office, 26 April 1918, PRO WO 32/9288.
48 "Organization", undated, pp. 19–20, PRO WO 158/804.
49 Fuller, "Private Journal", Conference GHQ, 4 December 1917, pp. 1–2.
50 Mentioned in Elles to GHQ, 3 January 1918, PRO WO 158/835.
51 *ibid.*, paras 2–4.
52 Fuller, "Defensive and Offensive Use of Tanks, 1918" (undated but attached to Elles's letter of 3 January 1918), para. 2, PRO WO 158/835.
53 *ibid.*, para. 3.

54 *ibid.*, para. 8, (ii).
55 *ibid.*, paras 10–14.
56 Mentioned in Lieutenant-General Lawrence, Chief of the General Staff, GHQ, to the Armies and the Tank Corps, 13 February 1918, PRO WO 158/832.
57 *ibid.*
58 Fuller, "Private Journal", p. 7: "Operations Decisive and Preparatory, 28.1.18. I wrote this paper and intend that Elles sd send it to Genl. Lawrence the CGS". "Tank Operations, Decisive and Preparatory, 1919–1918, Part I: the Decisive Battle 1919: i: General Requirements", TS/40, Fuller Papers, LHCMA.
59 *ibid.*, TS/40, Fuller Papers, LHCMA.
60 *ibid.*, Part II: "Preparatory Operations 1918: Offensive Tactical Plan 1918", TS/40, Fuller Papers, LHCMA.
61 Travers, *op. cit.*, pp. 31–32.
62 On Haig's recognition by the beginning of December 1917 of the need for the BEF to adopt the defensive in the early months of 1918 see Fuller, "Private Journal", p. 1.
63 Haig did know of the use of "Stoss-Truppen" by the Germans at Cambrai though he believed, probably rightly, that the bulk of the German forces had attacked "in great masses" behind them: Haig's diary, Tuesday 4 December 1917, R. Blake, *The Private Papers of Douglas Haig 1914–1919* (Eyre and Spottiswoode) 1952, p. 270. By 17 February the Tank Corps had been issued, probably by GHQ, with a summary of information on "German Methods in the Attack and Indications of an Offensive" which included a reasonably accurate study of "German Offensive Methods in Trench Warfare, Compiled from a Study of Recent German Publications" and "Notes on a Study of the German Orders for the Riga Attack 1st September, 1917", PRO WO 95/93.
64 "Tank Operations, Decisive and Preparatory 1919–1918", Part II: "The Preparatory Operations 1918", iii: "The Political Outlook", TS/40, Fuller Papers, LHCMA.
65 "Notes for GHQ Conference", 2 March 1918, PRO WO 158/864.
66 *ibid.*, para. 1.
67 Bidwell and Graham, *op. cit.*, p. 72.
68 Fuller, *Memoirs*, p. 240.
69 "Record of a Conference of Army Commanders held at DOULLENS on Saturday, 2nd March 1918", para 1, PRO WO 158/864.
70 *ibid.*, para. 2.
71 Fuller, "Private Journal", 5 March 1918, p. 5.
72 See, for example, A.J. Trythall, *"Boney" Fuller, the Intellectual General 1878–1966* (Cassell) 1977, p. 58.
73 On Maxse as a tactical innovator see Bidwell and Graham, *op. cit.*,

pp. 35–36, 84–85 and 125–130, and P. Griffith, *Battle Tactics of the Western Front* (Yale) 1994, pp. 95–100.

74 Liddell Hart, *op. cit.*, p. 162.

75 *ibid.*, pp. 161–162.

76 On the principles of storm troop tactics see P. Griffith, *Forward Into Battle* (Anthony Bird) 1981, pp. 80–82.

77 Travers, *op. cit.*, pp. 86–89.

78 For a more recent account see A.H. Farrar-Hockley, "Sir Hubert Gough and the German Breakthrough, 1918", in Brian Bond, *Fallen Stars* (Brassey's) 1991, pp. 65–85.

79 "Summary Report of Operations of the Tank Corps, March 21st to 27th 1918", B7, Fuller Papers, Tank Museum. Liddell Hart, *op. cit.*, p. 162.

80 Elles to Capper, 29 March 1918 and "Summary Report of the Operations of the Tank Corps March 21st to 27th 1918", B7, Fuller Papers, Tank Museum and Liddell Hart, *op. cit.*, p. 162.

81 "Summary Report of the Operations of the Tank Corps", 27 March 1918, B7, Fuller Papers, Tank Museum and Liddell Hart, *op. cit.*, p. 163.

82 Liddell Hart, *op. cit.*, p. 164.

83 Elles to Capper, 29 March 1918, Fuller Papers, Tank Museum.

84 Various notes on the Tank Corps' performance in March–April 1918. B15, Fuller Papers, Tank Museum. These papers appear to have been collated by Hotblack though some of the material contained therein may have originated with other officers such as Martel and Boyd-Rochefort, another GSO2. All three are mentioned as having commented on the March retreat in Fuller, *Memoirs*, p. 258.

85 "Notes on the Use of the Mark IV Tank in Defence (S.D. 293), 9 April 1918", B25, Fuller Papers, Tank Museum. See also Tanks in Rear Guard Action (S.G. 213), B10, 29 March 1918, Fuller Papers, Tank Museum.

86 Fuller, *Memoirs*, pp. 245–268, esp. p. 259. Some extracts from Hotblack's reports are printed here but nothing which points the finger at Tank Corps HQ or casts any doubt on the performance of the Tank Corps in general.

87 Liddell Hart, *op. cit.*, p. 165.

88 Fourth Army to GHQ, 24 April, B38 and Fourth Army to GHQ, 25 April, B39, and Tank Corps to GHQ "I" 26 April 1918, B40, Fuller Papers, Tank Museum.

89 W. Heinemann, "The Development of German Armoured Forces", in J.P. Harris and F.H. Toase (eds) *Armoured Warfare* (Batsford) 1990, p. 51.

90 Fourth Army to GHQ, 3.0 p.m., 25 April 1918, B39, Fuller Papers, Tank Museum.

91   J. Terraine, *To Win a War: 1918, the Year of Victory* (Sidgwick and Jackson) 1978, pp. 72–74.

92   Elles to Capper, 29 March 1918, para. 6, Fuller Papers, Tank Museum.

93   "Minutes on Conference Held at Adv. H.Q. Tank Corps, April 2nd 1918" (S.G. 175/8), para. 2, B23, Fuller Papers, Tank Museum.

94   *ibid.*, para. 5 (a).

95   GHQ to Tank Corps, 12 April 1918, B34, Fuller Papers, Tank Museum.

96   Haig to Tank Corps, 30 April 1918, B45, Fuller Papers, Tank Museum.

97   For Fuller's extremely one-sided account of the struggle over Tank Corps establishments that spring see Fuller, *Memoirs*, pp. 269–277.

98   Travers, *op. cit.*, p. 108.

99   Terraine, *op. cit.*, pp. 59–74.

100 On the weakness of German field fortification at Hamel and Amiens see R. Prior and T. Wilson, *Command on the Western Front, The Military Career of Sir Henry Rawlinson 1914–18* (Blackwell) 1992, pp. 297–298 and 301.

5

"Mechanical warfare" and victory

In May and June 1918 relative calm descended on those sectors of the Western Front for which Sir Douglas Haig was responsible. While GHQ got its breath back and began to contemplate counter-offensive action for that summer much thought was being devoted elsewhere to the very large-scale use of tanks in 1919.

Recent scholarly writing on the last year of the war on the Western Front has indicated a conflict between the advocates of "Mechanical Warfare" and the defenders of "traditional" methods. The mechanical warfare advocates believed that the conduct of operations could be revolutionized by the application of relatively new technical instruments (notably tanks, but also including trench mortars and gas) which were reckoned capable of making a vast economy of manpower. The traditionalists who predominated at GHQ resisted the mechanical warfare school except for a relatively brief period in July and August 1918. Though they accepted that new technologies could serve as useful auxiliary tools, they insisted on conducting the war using methods based mainly on infantry/artillery co-operation which were necessarily more manpower intensive.[1]

It will be argued in this chapter that the thesis summarized above needs qualification. It derives, however, from a real and important contemporary debate, part of which was described in the last chapter. By the middle of 1918 prominent people based in several different institutions were lobbying vigorously for Western Front operations to be conducted in a more "Mechanical" way and large-scale use of tanks was an idea central to the thinking of all of them. Before examining the explicit suggestions for the development, organization and employment of armoured forces made by what might loosely be termed the mechanical warfare lobby, it seems essential to trace its evolution and examine its composition.

Though it became a major force only in the first half of 1918 such a lobby had been emerging for years. Its roots go back to the formation of the Landships Committee in February 1915 and, even before that, to the RNAS armoured car forces which Churchill had so assiduously fostered in his days at the Admiralty. One of the its key figures was Albert Stern. It was noted in the first chapter of the present work that Stern, an officer of the RNAS armoured cars, became the secretary of the Landships Committee. In February 1916 Lloyd George appointed him head of what became known as the Mechanical Warfare Supply Department (MWSD)[2] which controlled the procurement and supply of tanks. Stern was transferred to the Army in which he ultimately reached the rank of Lieutenant-Colonel. In theory Stern's department was supervised by a Ministry of Munitions Tank Committee. The dividing line between the committee and the department, however, was not clear. Stern headed both. While it included Eustace Tennyson d'Eyncourt and Ernest Swinton, both of whom were already closely associated with Stern, the committee had no one with experience of using tanks in action.[3]

Stern owed his position as virtual dictator of tank production and supply entirely to Lloyd George. As a former businessman and a believer in the application to war production of "business methods" with the minimum interference from professional soldiers, Stern was a natural Lloyd George protégé. Not content to dominate the supply side, Stern and his ally Tennyson d'Eyncourt, attempted, as noted in chapter 3, to use their connection with "The Wizard" to influence the employment of tanks.[4] Neither, however, had a military background and neither had spent a significant amount of time at the front. They were, in fact, tactical ignoramuses and GHQ's irritation with their interference in its affairs[5] is understandable.

GHQ's plea that they should concentrate on organizing supply and not attempt to determine tactics had particular point in that Stern had proved far from ideal as a production supremo. In fact he was rather ignorant technically as well as tactically.[6] Concerned with driving on the production of impressive numbers of tanks and captivated by grandiose visions of their employment, he tended to fail in terms of quality control and the unglamorous business of supplying adequate spares to keep existing vehicles functioning.[7] Stern and Tennyson d'Eyncourt remained, at least up to the end of 1917, the most strident lobbyists on the home front for the mass production and mass employment of tanks.[8] But the ill-feeling between suppliers and users became acute. Not all of this was Stern's fault. Bermicourt was constantly demanding minor changes in tank design many of which were liable to dislocate production to an extent disproportionate to their value.[9] Stern, however, must take a good deal of responsibility.

A series of measures were introduced from the middle of 1917 to exert greater control over his activities, to ensure increased representation of the user in design and production and, above all, to achieve a higher standard of vehicle inspection before shipment to France. A Tank Committee was established at the War Office in May 1917. But those who had to fight in tanks were still not adequately represented – Capper being the sole Heavy Branch member. Stern and d'Eyncourt, who were also members, apparently continued to ignore War Office and Tank Corps pleas. A serious row erupted over this in August 1917, resulting in the break-up of the committee and the establishment of a War Office Tank Directorate with Capper as Director-General. The Ministry of Munitions was made aware of War Office and Tank Corps inability to work smoothly with Stern and he was replaced in October by Admiral Moore with whom those organizations seem to have got on much better. At the same time a more harmonious joint War Office–Ministry of Munitions Tank Committee (sometimes referred to as the "Second Tank Committee") was established.[10]

Stern's activities as a lobbyist for mechanical warfare were not curtailed, however. Before leaving the Mechanical Warfare Supply Department he had been seeking closer relations with the Americans who were in the process of creating their own Tank Corps and wished to play a major role in allied tank production. In June 1917 an Inter-Allied Tank Bureau had been established and upon leaving the Mechanical Warfare Supply Department Stern became the British commissioner. Having lost one empire Stern proceeded rapidly to build another. A Mechanical Warfare (Overseas and Allies) Department of the Ministry of Munitions was created in November and Stern became its head. In January 1918 Stern was instrumental in negotiating the Anglo-American treaty (mentioned in the last chapter) by which an Allied Tank Factory ultimately capable of producing 1,200 tanks a month was to be established in France at Chateauroux.[11] His ambitions did not stop there.

In February 1918 Capper complained to the authorities in the War Office that Stern was trying to extend his powers by gaining a seat on the Tank Committee in London whilst also agitating to become the British representative on the proposed tank commission of the recently created Supreme War Council at Versailles (discussed further below). Capper also alleged that Stern was attacking his old department – the Mechanical Warfare Supply Department at the Ministry of Munitions – for failing to co-operate fully in the joint Anglo-American tank production venture which was intended to produce very large quantities of the Mark VIII or "Liberty" tank for use in 1919. According to Capper, the real situation was that catering for the demands of the Anglo-American venture was absorbing so much of the effort of the Mechanical Warfare Supply Department that it was seriously threatening production of the Mark V tank for issue to the BEF in 1918.[12] Stern's empire-building continued unabated into mid-1918. He seems to have wanted to be a sort of Allied mechanical warfare supremo with a vast influence on the conduct of the war in 1919. Frequently he went outside the normal chain of command. He approached General Pétain and General Sir Henry Wilson directly about the creation of Central Military School and Training Ground for an Inter-Allied Tank Army[13] and he lobbied the Prime Minister through his secretary and mistress, Frances Stevenson.[14] Ultimately Stern received a very severe rebuke from his military superiors for this kind of *ultra vires* action.[15]

The ill-feeling between Stern and the leaders of the Tank Corps probably to some extent delayed the emergence of a really effective mechanical warfare lobby which could speak with one voice and thus negotiate from a position of strength in its dealings with GHQ. Perhaps Elles and Capper would, anyway, have proved too conventionally minded and too bound by the formal chain of command to have played military politics in any such overt and aggressive style. But Fuller was not tied by military etiquette or constrained by feelings of loyalty to superiors. For years he had been striving to build some such coalition of pro-tank interests.

Though the feud between Stern and Tank Corps HQ had been in progress since before Fuller arrived at Bermicourt, Fuller had carefully stayed out of it. He tried to remain on good terms with

Stern and lobbied Stern, Tennyson d'Eyncourt, Churchill, Furse, and anyone else he thought might be sympathetic to his vision of how the Tank Corps should be employed.[16] He was arguing from the early weeks of 1918 that tank forces, after having taking part in some lesser operations and after having been massively expanded in the course of that year, could end the war by acting as spearheads for a colossal breakthrough operation in 1919.[17]

In mid-1918 it must have seemed to Fuller that the chances of bringing enough pressure to bear on GHQ to have the war waged in the style he was advocating were quite good. Developments potentially favourable from Fuller's point of view included the establishment of the Supreme War Council at Versailles in November 1917 with an Allied General Staff of which General Sir Henry Wilson was the first "permanent" British member. The Supreme War Council was to a great extent Lloyd George's creation. His motives in promoting it were to by-pass Robertson and Haig and give higher priority to fronts other than the Western. Though Fuller was a convinced Westerner who had little time for sideshows,[18] a diminution of GHQ's authority was a cheering prospect for him and after the launch of the German spring offensive the diversion of further resources away from the Western Front was unlikely.

The Supreme War Council never acquired much real power but did serve as a forum for the circulation of military ideas. As permanent British military representative at Versailles, Sir Henry Wilson asked Fuller to tell him all about tanks. On 9 January 1918 Generals Weygand, Wilson and Cadorna asked the Supreme War Council to determine Allied tank policy for the future. On 21 January, possibly in response to this expression of interest in tanks at the highest level of Allied policy making, Capper placed before "Wully" Robertson, the CIGS, a detailed paper entitled "Proposals for the use of Tanks in the Campaign of 1919". Capper proposed that Britain and France should raise between them a combined tank force of 8,308 machines and 110,550 officers and men. (This "Plan 1919" apparently had nothing to do with Fuller, who was not even aware of its existence until a good deal later.)[19] As we have already noted, an Allied Tank Committee was established at Versailles under the aegis of the Supreme War Council. Its first meeting was held on 6 May. Capper was the main British representative.[20]

There were also significant developments, favourable from Fuller's point of view, at the War Office. When, in February 1918, Robertson was sacked over the issue of the British component of an Allied General Reserve (which Lloyd George wanted to put under the Supreme War Council and Robertson wanted to control himself),[21] Wilson became CIGS. On 19 March Wilson advised the Cabinet that the fastest way of winning the war would be to achieve a breakthrough on a broad front using around 8,000 tanks in a Cambrai-style attack. The General Staff in the War Office went on to promote a number of grandiose schemes of mechanical warfare for use in 1919.[22]

Equally promising from Fuller's perspective was the appointment, on 26 March 1918, of General Ferdinand Foch, who was reasonably sympathetic to mechanical warfare ideas, as Allied generalissimo. This move (at least in theory) further eroded the authority and independence of GHQ.[23] By the middle of 1918 there was thus a broadly based and powerfully positioned school of opinion in favour of giving the tank forces a very prominent role in a 1919 campaign and a generous allocation of resources in 1918 to enable them to prepare for it.

We have seen that, so far in the war, contrary to the allegations of Fuller and other writers who have followed his lead, GHQ's treatment of its tank forces had generally been enlightened. Haig's broad streak of optimism had allowed him to continue to smile on tanks even in periods when they were giving only the slenderest indication of their potential. If the Tank Corps had not always had everything it asked for as soon as it asked for it which branch of the BEF had? The Tank Corps enjoyed a lower industrial priority than airpower and artillery[24] because those other arms were absolutely indispensable to the conduct of operations right across the front on a daily basis. The Tank Corps' services had generally been of much more marginal value. It had played a central role in the BEF's operations on one day only – 20 November 1917. Even on that day the artillery was no less vital and the artillery could not function adequately without airpower.

GHQ was not hostile to tanks and the Tank Corps in mid-1918 any more than it had been earlier. It was, however, distinctly unimpressed by elaborate schemes for tank use which might become possible only in the long run and when prodigious quantities of scarce resources had been expended on the construction of new and unproven types. The mechanical warfare lobbyists were generally reckoning on a final campaign in 1919 as indeed was the War Cabinet as a whole. (Churchill who, in October 1917, thought the Allies could win in 1918 had now become much more pessimistic and apparently thought the knockout blow would have to wait until 1920.)[25] Haig, on the other hand, was sensing by late summer that the Germans were nearing the end of their endurance.[26] He had falsely come to the same conclusion on several previous occasions but this time he was right. For the war-weary British and French there was much to be said for fighting the war to a finish in 1918 and GHQ wanted to concentrate on making the best use of resources and technologies immediately available.

Major Stephen Foot was one little-known member of the mechanical warfare movement whose ideas gained official approval at this period. In January 1918, while on leave in England, Foot was transferred to a staff post in Capper's Tank Directorate at the War Office. He had served for three years on the Western Front and had been with Courage's 2nd Tank Brigade at Third Ypres and Cambrai, the former battle bringing him (on his own admission) to the verge of a nervous breakdown. A highly educated and intelligent officer, with a background in the oil business, Foot proceeded to write a number of mechanical warfare papers. The most interesting of these, dated 24 April 1918, was entitled "A Mobile Army" and its opening sentences represent a sort of *leitmotif* for the whole mechanical warfare movement:

> The object of this paper is to discuss the question of whether it will be possible for the Allies to obtain a decisive victory in the year 1919 ... I assume that the victory, if obtained, will be by a deep penetration of the enemy's defensive system.[27]

Foot (like Fuller in the later paper usually known as "Plan 1919") was influenced and inspired by the German spring offensive. That effort had ground to a halt, Foot believed, because of logistic failure. The German Army's supplies had simply not been mobile enough to maintain the momentum of its advance. What Foot proposed was to establish a Mobile Army of twelve divisions, in "three Army Corps of four Divisions each" which would take no part in the initial breakthrough operation but which would form a sort of exploitation force or *corps de chasse* of precisely the kind which the Germans had so conspicuously and fatally lacked in the spring of 1918. The actual breakthrough operation, in which the

Mobile Army would take no part, would be an inter-Allied effort and would be conducted on a sort of super-Cambrai basis with heavy use of the newer types of tank. The basis of the mobility of the "Mobile Army" would be what Foot called a "Tank Tractor" – actually just a lorry on tracks. Foot did not envisaged these acting as personnel carriers but merely as transporters of supplies. Given enough of them the Mobile Army could be independent of supply from the rear and would be able, spearheaded by "Light Fighting Tanks" (presumably Whippets or their successors) to advance 60 miles in 6 days, a penetration which might prove decisive.[28]

By April 1918 the War Office was responsive to such ideas. Though the Colonel who was Foot's immediate superior took no interest in Foot's paper, Foot by-passed him and went direct to Capper. Capper put the paper up to the DCIGS, Lieutenant-General "Tim" Harington, who had achieved prominence and general respect as Major-General General Staff to Plumer's Second Army. A few days later a conference was held in the War Office to discuss mechanical warfare. On 18 May a War Office paper entitled "Proposals for the Use of Tanks in 1919" was sent to Haig.[29] Haig commented on this in June, identifying its main hypotheses as:

(a) That the Germans can only be defeated on the Western Front.
(b) That to defeat the Germans a definite "breakthrough" on a broad front is necessary.
(c) That a definite "breakthrough" on a broad front can be made successfully only by the employment of a very large number of Tanks.

Haig was prepared to accept all of these in principle but emphasized that tanks could only succeed as part of a force "of all arms in proper combination". Tanks were "a necessity" but could accomplish little alone and he was not willing to sacrifice everything else to their production.[30]

Fuller's so-called "Plan 1919" has been discussed many times in print. It has usually not been seen in its full context, however, and, perhaps partly for that reason, has often been treated with greater reverence than it really deserves. Since Wells's 1903 short story, visions of the future mechanization of war, some of them very grandiose, had been projected by several people. From 1916, when tanks arrived on the Western Front, such ideas had become almost a commonplace of the *avant-garde* of British military thought.[31] By spring 1918 they were no longer confined to the radical fringe. They had started cropping up, without any direct prompting from Fuller, in official War Office documents. Fuller's May paper was not even particularly good of its kind. A fantastic and somewhat sensationalist "novelette" (as Fuller himself called it)[32] it ignored some of the most important lessons which the war had taught and was less realistic and practical than Foot's proposal of the previous month.

Fuller's original title was "The Tactics of the Attack as Affected by the Speed and Circuit of the Medium D Tank" and the manuscript was dated 24 May 1918. On 30 March Fuller had completed a paper on the "Strategic Outlook 1919".[33] In this he discussed a new type of medium tank, not yet even designed, called the Category D. His main concern was that it should have a high cross-country performance for open fighting. On 28 April a conference was held at HQ Tank Corps at which plans were made to develop a new medium tank with "a possible 20 miles maximum speed and a circuit of 200 miles". Searle produced sketches. The engineer responsible for designing the Medium D was one of Searle's majors, Philip Johnson.[34] But the design work had only just begun and no one expected to see these machines in substantial numbers until mid-1919.

In the spring of 1918 Fuller devoted considerable effort to developing a concept for a colossal 1919 campaign based entirely on the potential of an armoured fighting vehicle for which not even a detailed engineering drawing yet existed. While from one perspective this can be seen as intellectually heroic, it is open to question whether it was the most profitable use of the time of a trained staff officer on the Western Front in the middle of 1918. Though May was a very quiet month for the Tank Corps it is at least arguable that Fuller should have been devoting his time to liaison with Army commanders with a view to planning operations feasible with the resources available to the Tank Corps that summer. Actually the initiative for such operations seems to have come from Army and infantry corps commanders and Tank Corps headquarters appears merely to have responded.

In his May paper on the Medium D Fuller argued that, though it had hitherto not been fulfilled, the tank had the inherent potential to transform war. The basis of this potential was cross-country mobility.

> The network upon which strategy is woven is the system of communication which exists in the theatre of war. Hitherto this system has consisted of roads, railways, rivers and canals. Today the introduction of a cross country petrol driven machine – Tank or Tractor, has expanded this system to include at least 75% of the entire terrain of the theatre of war over & above communications as we at present know them. The possibility today of maintaining supply and moving weapons and munitions over the open irrespective of roads and without the limiting factor of animal endurance introduces an entirely new problem in the history of war. At the present moment he who grasps the full meaning of this change, namely that the earth has become as easily traversable as the sea, multiplies his chances of victory to an almost unlimited degree.[35]

There was, of course, some insight here. Ultimately the introduction of formations whose fighting elements were mounted in tracked vehicles would considerably increase tactical and operational mobility in land warfare. But there was also gross overstatement. Even today the logistics of large armies are heavily dependent on road and rail networks. The extent to which this dependency has diminished is more to do with air mobility and air re-supply than with the use of tracked vehicles. (Logistics was a subject which Fuller, unlike Foot, barely addressed in his paper on 1919.) The notion that tracked vehicles could make the surface of the earth as easily traversable as the surface of the sea was quite wrong. Fuller went on to argue that:

> Up to the present the theory of the tactical employment of Tanks has been based on tying its [*sic*] powers with existing methods of fighting, that is infantry and artillery tactics. In fact the Tank idea which carries with it a revolution in the methods of waging war has been grafted on to a system it is intended to destroy, in place of having been given scope to develope [*sic*] in its own lines.

After a certain amount of platitudinous waffle about immutable principles of war Fuller got to his main point:

> There are two ways of destroying an organization
>   1. By wearing it down (dissipating it)
>   2. By rendering it inoperative (unhinging it)

... In war the first emphasises the killing, wounding capturing and disarming of the enemy soldiers. (Body warfare). The second the rendering inoperative of his powers of command. (Brain warfare) ...

The brains of an army are its staffs – Army, Corps & Divisional Headquarters, could we suddenly remove these from an extensive sector of the German front the total collapse of the fighting personnel which they control would be a matter of hours even if a slight opposition were put against it.[36]

It was from this proposition that the whole argument of the paper was developed. Fuller seems to have arrived at it as a result of his observation of the British Fifth Army's March retreat:

Though of slow development this idea suddenly flashed across my mind during our debacle in March. What did I then see? Tens of thousands of our men being pulled back by their panic-stricken Headquarters. I saw Army Headquarters retiring, then Corps, next Divisional and lastly Brigade. I saw the intimate connection between will and action, and that action without will loses all co-ordination; that without an active and directive brain, an army is reduced to a mob.[37]

It was very much the perception of a staff officer who was used to spending most of his time in headquarters. The British fell back in the Somme sector in March 1918 not so much because of paralysis or panic of their headquarters as because of the over-whelming firepower which the Germans brought to bear and the superior numbers of German infantry who followed in its wake. The temporary collapse of British command and control, which undoubtedly did occur, was a mere side-effect of German fire superiority and of the German penetration right through the sys-tem of field fortification, which superior fire made possible.

Fuller's new theory of tank employment was based on destroy-ing the enemy's system of command and supply "not after the enemy's personnel has been destroyed but before it has been at-tacked". He recommended selecting a 90-mile stretch of front and encouraging the enemy to concentrate as many troops as possible in that sector – a novel approach indeed. An enemy concentration of up to five armies might be achieved, Fuller thought, by making conspicuous preparations for a conventional assault. Such a con-centration would be beneficial because: "The more reserves we can force the enemy to mass and we can disorganize the greater will be the tactical interest on our capital."[38]

Once the conspicuous preparations for a conventional assault were well in hand:

> without any tactical preparation whatever fleets of Medium D Tanks should proceed at top speed, by day or possibly by night, directly onto the various headquarters allotted as their objectives. If by day this objective could be marked by aeroplanes dropping coloured smoke, if by night by dropping coloured lights. As the furthest distance to be covered may be taken at twenty miles the Medium D should attack the German Army Headquarters in about 2 hours.[39]

This was simply preposterous and it is amazing that anyone has ever taken it seriously. Fuller seems to have been adapting German infiltration tactics for medium tanks. But in the spring offensive the tactics of the German storm troop infantry had succeeded only after the most intense preliminary bombardment. How tanks were supposed, without any artillery preparation or support and without the co-operation of infantry, to penetrate right through enemy artillery positions in a sector of the front where the enemy had been deliberately alerted to expect an offensive of some sort Fuller did not even begin to explain. It ran contrary to all operational experience. The stretch of German front which had been attacked at Cambrai was initially very weak in guns. In that operation there was a heavy British artillery barrage supporting the tanks and a good deal of counter-battery fire, yet the setback at Flesquières Ridge had still occurred.

Fuller recommended that, simultaneously with the attack of the Medium Ds on enemy headquarters, aeroplanes should attack supply routes, but: "The signal communications should not be destroyed, for it is important that the confusion resulting from the dual attack carried out by Medium D Tanks and aeroplanes should be made known to all as soon as possible. Bad news confuses, confusion stimulates panic."[40]

Once time had been allowed for the maximum amount of panic to spread, a "carefully mounted Tank, Infantry, and Artillery attack" would be launched, the object of which would be the zone of the enemy guns – a zone some 10,000 yards behind the enemy front. Finally a pursuit would be carried out by more Medium D tanks and by lorry-borne infantry.[41] Fuller estimated that a total of about 2,000 Medium D tanks would be needed for this operation in addition to other types. He was crying for the moon.

Because a 90-mile stretch of front might be too much to be attacked in its entirety, even by the prodigious numbers of tanks which he wanted to use, Fuller proposed what he called a "morcellated front of attack". This was actually a very simple idea. Only some sections of the front would be attacked directly, perhaps 50 miles of it in all, while sections would be enveloped.[42] This scheme had the disadvantage, not pointed out by Fuller, that, from the sections of front not directly assaulted, attacking forces would be bound to suffer enfilading artillery fire.

The official channels through which Fuller's May 1918 memorandum flowed appear to have been obscure even to him. The version held in his papers at the Tank Museum is a pencil manuscript draft which is in need of revision on grounds of spelling and grammar alone. His memoirs do not make it clear to whom (if anyone) subsequent drafts were sent or when they were sent. It appears that at some stage he showed the manuscript to Capper, possibly on one of Capper's frequent trips to Bermicourt. As far as Fuller knew his ideas first surfaced officially, albeit in a modified form, in a memorandum from Capper to the CIGS, Sir Henry Wilson, on 1 July. Two War Office conferences were held on the subject on 3 July and 6 July.[43] Ultimately a War Office paper entitled "Memorandum on the Requirements for an Armoured Striking Force for an Offensive in 1919" was endorsed by Henry Wilson and sent to Foch on 20 July and to Haig a week later.[44]

While Fuller's imprint is still clear even in some of the phrasing used, some of the crazier and more fantastic parts of the argument had been dropped, making the War Office version a very different paper. Gone was the notion of deliberately advertising to the enemy the location of the offensive and gone the unsupported penetration of the enemy's defences by Medium D tanks. The attack on the enemy's system of command and control was apparently to be concurrent with rather than in advance of the assault on his front. The offensive proposed in the War Office paper, while strongly supported by tanks of all available types, was to be very conventional in the first instance. The penetration of medium tanks deep into the enemy's rear was to take place *a tempo* with the assault on his front, not before it.[45] Foch enthused about the scheme but appears to have done little else with it. Haig's reaction was never communicated to Fuller himself and does not appear to have been recorded for posterity.[46]

By the time Haig was sent the War Office's version of Fuller's paper on tank use in 1919, a highly significant little battle had already been fought at Hamel by the Australian Corps and 5th Tank Brigade. Tank Corps HQ appears to have had little to do with its planning. The operation was conceived by Sir Henry Rawlinson, Fourth Army's commander. Rawlinson had become increasingly convinced that the Germans confronting Fourth Army were in poor shape. Their field fortifications were inadequate and they were offering little resistance to the frequent raids mounted by the Australians.[47]

Rawlinson invited both Monash, who had recently taken over command of the Australian Corps, and Courage, the commander of 5th Tank Brigade, to draw up ideas for an attack on the village of Hamel. The two commanders produced similar plans. One of the main features of the scheme adopted was the relatively small amount of infantry (only two brigades) used in relation to the frontage attacked. Such an approach was considered feasible because of the weakness of the German field fortifications in this vicinity, the massive artillery support available for the attack (600 guns), the 60 Mark V tanks which it was intended to employ, and above all because of the surprise which Rawlinson was determined to achieve. The guns were to be silently registered and there was to be no preliminary bombardment.

Originally Monash, Courage and Rawlinson all intended to dispense with a creeping barrage, relying heavily on the tanks. The "creeper", however, was a technique which the BEF's artillery had brought to perfection by this period in the war and British and Dominion infantry had become accustomed to (even psychologically reliant upon) its support in major assaults. The Australians were, moreover, very suspicious of placing much reliance on tanks since their unfortunate experience at Bullecourt in April 1917. Brigadier-General Thomas Blamey, Monash's chief of staff, was unwilling to forego the creeping barrage and eventually persuaded Monash to incorporate one into the plan. In the original scheme of attack the only barrage was to be put down by heavy artillery. It was to be a jumping rather than a creeping barrage and was to keep 300 yards ahead of the attacking infantry. In the final version the heavy artillery concentrated solely on counter-battery fire and on likely centres of resistance deep behind the enemy front. The field artillery offered the customary "creeper" moving just in front of the infantry.[48]

The attack at Hamel was mounted at 3.10 a.m. on 4 July and was a complete success (see Map 4). As with many early morning assaults, it received some help from mist. It lasted only two hours. While the advance achieved was not much over a mile at most, the thousand German prisoners outnumbered total allied casualties and another thousand Germans were thought to have been killed or wounded. A notable feature of the attack was the close support by the RAF which bombed enemy headquarters and parachuted ammunition to the Australian machine gunners. The tanks did not lead the attack. They set off behind the infantry, though in most cases they were able to catch up. (The somewhat higher cross-country speed of the Mark Vs seems to have helped here.) Some tanks did very useful work. But where they failed to appear on time the generally weak opposition offered appears, in most cases, to have been readily subdued without them. The major exception was a position known as the Pear Trench. The tanks supposed to tackle it became lost in the mist. But this probably mattered to the infantry only because the creeping barrage missed the position completely, starting behind it. The Pear Trench thus cost the Australians a large proportion of their total casualties.[49]

In his memoirs Fuller went into ecstasies about the Tank Corps' Hamel success[50] and, like Cambrai, Hamel is often referred to as a "tank battle". But, as already noted, the reliance which the plan actually implemented placed on tanks was not great. Tanks played the familiar role of auxiliaries in an artillery/infantry attack in which, as at Cambrai, the main ingredients of success were artillery superiority and surprise. As at Cambrai, the principal key to surprise was silent registration of the guns. At Cambrai the tanks were indispensable because the Hindenburg position had been covered by massive wire entanglements. At Hamel the German field fortifications were weak and covered by relatively little wire. Thus the tanks did not even need to lead the attack and German positions could be, and in some cases were, successfully assaulted by the infantry without tank support.

The Hamel battle taught little that was new about tanks. Yet such a clear offensive success, after the traumas of the spring, worked wonders for morale, especially at GHQ, and the part which tanks had played gained widespread, perhaps excessive, appreciation. It was increasingly sensed by GHQ, and by Army commanders that, weakened by its exertions and losses of the spring, the German Army was ripe for defeat. The combination of

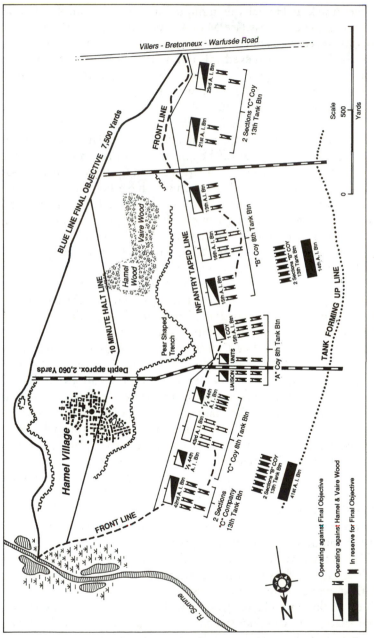

Map 4 Battle of Hamel, 4 July 1918.

techniques used at Hamel was seen to be effective. Surprise attack without preliminary bombardment but with heavy counter-battery fire, tanks and relatively light forces of infantry employed in close conjunction with an intense and slow moving creeping barrage which included high explosive and smoke as well as shrapnel shell: this was a formula which was to prove successful on a larger scale.[51]

Further evidence of the weakened state of the German Army was provided by the success of the French Army's counter-stroke between the Marne and the Aisne on 18–20 July. Like Hamel this attack was launched without preliminary bombardment. A large number of the light French Renault FT tanks were employed and these had some dramatic successes. The first major Allied offensive success of that year, the Battle of Soissons (also known as the Second Battle of the Marne) inaugurated the more sustained effort of the Hundred Days period.[52] As at Hamel the tanks had not been indispensable to French success but had enhanced it while helping to keep French casualties down.

The French victory offered encouragement to GHQ and Rawlinson's Fourth Army staff as they planned their next big venture – an offensive directed at the large bulge in the German front to the east of the important road junction of Amiens. Rawlinson had been thinking about this operation since May and detailed planning began immediately after Hamel. It must be stressed from the start that, like Cambrai and Hamel, Amiens was neither in conception nor in execution primarily a "tank battle". From the start Rawlinson did intend to use a considerable number of tanks. But their importance to his plans has sometimes been exaggerated. Even John Terraine, a historian who is by no means an uncritical admirer of tanks in the First World War, indicates that it was they which allowed Rawlinson to attack with a much lower density of artillery pieces per yard of front than had usually been necessary at Third Ypres the year before.[53] Actually the tanks were a relatively minor factor in Rawlinson's calculations. Far more important was that, as at Hamel, the German field fortifications were so weak that raiding Australian infantry regularly penetrated them with ease.[54] This demonstrated that the normally industrious Germans were exhausted, dispirited or both. It was on weak defences, poor German cohesion, the attainment of a very high degree of surprise, and the delivery of a massive volume of artillery fire by the relatively modest density (by Third Ypres standards) of pieces deployed, on which Rawlinson was primarily relying.

Tanks were to play a useful part in an all-arms ground attack with a great deal of RAF support. But the actions of the other arms were not planned around the tanks, far from it. In the first version of the plan (submitted to Haig on 17 July 1918) Rawlinson wanted only 6 battalions of heavy tanks (196 vehicles, fewer than used at Cambrai) plus 30 Supply tanks and 48 Whippets. The tanks, moreover, were not to lead the attack but merely to accompany the infantry, behind the creeping barrage, to the first objective. Only when that had been seized would the tanks assume the lead. Before Hamel the Australians had been unwilling to forgo the protection of the creeping barrage even if tanks were to be used. Hamel showed that there was no need to make a choice. For getting the infantry to their first objective it was sensible to rely on the "creeper", the infantry moving immediately behind it. Tanks were useful for dealing with any Germans the "creeper" did not neutralize and might also help to assist the infantry to advance beyond the range of the field artillery which provided it.

When Rawlinson approached Tank Corps HQ, the tank role in the battle was expanded at Fuller's suggestion. Instead of the mere 6 battalions of heavy tanks (plus Supply tanks and Whippets) which Rawlinson had originally intended to use, Fuller proposed that Fourth Army employ virtually the entire resources of the Tank Corps. These included 10 heavy and 2 light (Whippet) battalions, a total of 552 vehicles, including Supply tanks and gun-carrier tanks. For the heavy tanks Fuller offered no basic change of role but did indicate that a number of machines be kept in reserve.[55]

Fuller's suggestion for the use of the Whippets – that they cooperate intimately with the cavalry in the exploitation role – was less inspired. Rawlinson's record of planning offensives on the Western Front was one of favouring limited attacks – "bite and hold" operations. Fuller, like Haig, often dreamt of dramatic breakthroughs. In the case of the Amiens operation Rawlinson had recommended, in his original draft of the plan, that the Cavalry Corps be held in readiness to exploit a complete German collapse. But he probably did so only to pre-empt Haig, who had a history of inserting a cavalry role into Rawlinson's plans.[56] Fuller implied in his memoirs that tank/cavalry co-operation was a concept he

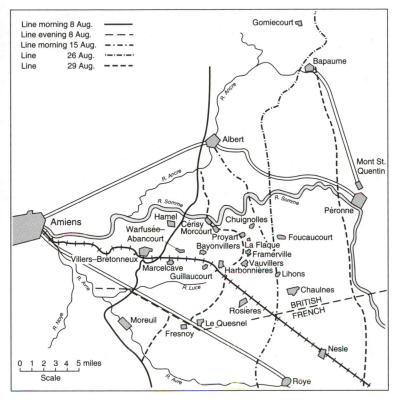

Map 5   Battle of Amiens, August 1918.

never believed in, indicating that it should have been obvious that to tie the Whippets to the cavalry was to cripple them. But he was not being honest about this. The idea of tank/cavalry teamwork for exploitation is to be found in his first essay on tank warfare – "Training Note No. 16" – and there he was advocating co-operation between horsemen and heavy tanks.[57] It is apparent from the surviving documents that, rather than Whippet/cavalry co-operation at Amiens being imposed on the Tank Corps against its better judgement, the idea originated with Fuller.[58]

The opening day of the Battle of Amiens, 8 August 1918, was perhaps the most strikingly successful for the BEF in the entire war (see Map 5). At least temporarily it broke the nerve of General Ludendorff (effectively the German commander-in-chief).[59]

Fourth Army advanced eight miles on a 15,000-yard front, capturing over 400 guns and 12,000 prisoners. About 6 German divisions effectively ceased to exist. The part the tanks played in this
success was primarily to facilitate the advance of the infantry from
the first objective to the second, for which they took the lead. This
moment was the high point of the achievement of tanks in this
war. The infantry were now going beyond the range of their own
field artillery and thus no longer had the help of the creeping
barrage. The mist which had shrouded the battlefield in the early
stages of the advance dispersed at around 8.20 a.m. and the enemy was able to see the approximately 400 tanks in the van of the
attack. Many Germans, overawed by this mass use of tanks, were
thus induced to surrender.[60]

The Whippets and the cavalry did not manage to work closely
together. The vulnerabilities of the two arms were quite different,
as were their cross-country performances. Where opposition was
slight, cavalry outpaced the Whippets. But the cavalry was much
more vulnerable to machine gun and rifle fire and to shrapnel.
That, even without the Whippets, the cavalry did not achieve
more on 8 August may, however, have been primarily due to a
failure of command at Corps level and to a lack of nerve on the
part of subordinate commanders. Having reached the third objective there was a tendency for the cavalry to sit down on it rather
than push on. Though initially most Whippets made slower progress
than the cavalry a handful did advance unaided into the enemy
rear.[61]

One Whippet of the 6th Battalion, commanded by Lieutenant
C.B. Arnold and known as "Musical Box", wrought extraordinary havoc for several hours.[62] Details of the story are narrated in
the regimental history and it seems unnecessary to recount them
here. Two points about "Musical Box" are, however, worthy of
note. One is that after the war its story encouraged those who
believed in "independent" armoured operations. The other is that
"Musical Box" was eventually put out of action. Bullets having
penetrated spare fuel containers on the roof, petrol was leaking
into the tank, giving off noxious fumes and eventually resulting in
fire.[63] The subsequent experience of armoured warfare would indicate that even fast and highly manoeuvrable tanks would always
tend to be vulnerable and would be incapable of achieving much
of lasting value without the support of other arms.

Another disappointing aspect of armoured operations on 8 August was the debut of what modern soldiers call "armoured infantry". The Mark V* – a stretched version of the Mark V – was designed to carry machine gunners. If the tanks themselves could not hold the ground they had captured then perhaps machine gunners carried forward under the protection of armour could. Their failure at Amiens was partly owing to bad luck – they seem to have happened upon determined enemy field gunners with more frequency than other tanks. But there were serious design faults in Mark Vs which made them particularly unsuitable for adaptation as armoured personnel carriers. They were poorly ventilated and even more prone to carbon monoxide contamination than earlier British heavy tanks. Machine gunners carried in these vehicles appear in the great majority of cases to have been incapable of combat upon dismounting.[64]

The difficulty of sustaining tank operations even with the improved tanks available in mid-1918 is well illustrated by figures which the Tank Corps itself compiled. According to these, on 8 August 430 tanks were actually engaged, on 9 August 155, on 10 August 85 and on 11 August only 38.[65] The steepness of the decline was probably only partly due to enemy action. It seems that considerable parts of total tank strength were still being temporarily lost through mechanical breakdown and crew sickness and exhaustion.[66]

It was, moreover, quite noticeable that the fewer the tanks that were engaged the greater the proportion of casualties they were likely to sustain. This was particularly obvious on 10 August at Amiens, when the numbers engaged had dropped by four-fifths since the start of the battle. German resistance having consolidated, tank operations were, by the Tank Corps' own estimate, 75 per cent unsuccessful. The rumps of five tank battalions supporting the Canadian Corps' attack in the Roye–Hally area suffered 50 per cent tank casualties (half of which were caused by direct hits) and failed completely to take their objectives. The Tank Corps' commentary on this event noted that it was due partly to a late issue of orders, which resulted in the attack taking place in broad daylight, without the cover of smoke. But the last point highlights how heavily dependent tanks were on close artillery support and how little they could be expected to accomplish without it.[67]

Fuller's most important contribution to the conduct of the war had been to persuade Rawlinson to commit most of the resources of the Tank Corps to the Amiens offensive. A significant victory would probably have been achieved even if Rawlinson had employed only the 2–300 tanks of his original scheme, but there can be little doubt that the exceptionally large numbers actually used contributed both to the magnitude of the success and to the modesty of its cost. After Amiens, however, events moved too fast for Fuller, most of whose mind appears still to have been focused on the use of improbably prodigious quantities of greatly improved models in 1919. Transferred to the War Office at the end of July to help implement a major reorganization of tank forces, he went on writing ambitious papers.[68] But neither these nor his earlier efforts at Bermicourt had much relevance to the endgame after Amiens.

The reorganization of the Tank Corps which was in progress from July 1918 was based on GHQ's philosophy of "bringing it into the Army". The argument was that when first used, the tanks had been an experimental weapon which, much like military aircraft, had needed an organization with a high degree of autonomy to pioneer them. A lot of experience had now been acquired with tanks and their capabilities were reasonably well understood. Given that their correct use was always in close conjunction with other arms, it was now logical to integrate them more fully with the normal chain of command. Capper's Tank Directorate in the War Office was abolished, something against which the Tank Corps raised no objection. A small branch (SD7) in the Staff Duties branch of the War Office General Staff which was to look after tank affairs was established under Fuller. Colonel Henry Karslake replaced Fuller at Bermicourt. Tank units in France were increasingly integrated into the Armies with whom they operated. Elles, who was given the title of Director General of the Tank Corps, was to be considered henceforth primarily as an adviser on tanks to GHQ rather than the commander of a distinct branch of the Army.[69]

Fuller complained bitterly about GHQ's August 1918 manual – "Tanks and Their Employment in Co-operation with Other Arms", whose author he dismissed as a tank ignoramus.[70] When looked at without prejudice, however, and certainly in comparison with Fuller's wild fantasy about the Medium D, this document appears the literary embodiment of sanity and commonsense. Both the strengths and weaknesses of tanks were outlined with the greatest clarity, with a balance and objectivity which Fuller never managed to attain. Some extracts have recently been quoted to prove that GHQ was rather reactionary in its attitude to tanks.[71] A careful reading may suggest, however, that GHQ was keen to use the existing tank technology to its full potential but anxious not to make claims which would not be legitimate until the next generation arrived.

The booklet did insist that, "infantry is the only arm which can seize and hold a position" and that tanks must be "mainly employed to assist the infantry". Tanks were still not totally reliable mechanically and were vulnerable to artillery. Infantry should be trained to get forward without them if necessary. In the 1918 context all these doctrines were perfectly sound. It was pointed out, on the other hand, that tanks could be a powerful aid to the offensive and could perform useful rear guard service in withdrawals. Very strong emphasis was placed on other arms learning the potential of tanks. It was recommended that officers of other arms should be attached to tank units for definite periods and the whole thrust was that the best results would be obtained from close co-operation between the arms. It was recommended that, in the assault, tanks should lead the infantry through the enemy's wire immediately following the creeping barrage and thus giving the infantry added protection. The importance for reducing tank casualties of employing smoke in the barrage and of accurate counter-battery fire was fully recognized.[72]

Particularly interesting is the passage dealing with tank/aircraft co-operation. While reconnaissance and counter-attack patrols were to keep tanks informed of the movements of the enemy and the positions of his anti-tank guns, contact patrols were to be employed to guide tanks by both day and night, to prevent, as far as possible, enemy aircraft observing tanks, to cover the noise made by tanks when moving to a start position for a surprise attack and to pass messages from tanks to the rear. It was recommended that a simple code of signalling using Very pistols should be employed to transmit messages from tanks to aircraft.[73]

Parts of the Hundred Days campaign would take the form of open warfare in which the BEF would be pressing a retreating enemy not protected by elaborate trench systems. The tactical problems of tank use in this phase of the war were well anticipated in GHQ's August booklet. The main problem would be the necessarily hurried assessment of the enemy's dispositions. Particularly crucial from the tank point of view would be the location of his guns. Careful reconnaissance by tank commanders and aircraft in order to avoid enemy gun concentrations and the close co-operation of friendly artillery to overcome what enemy guns were encountered were thought to be the best solutions. It was not considered a good idea for tanks to form part of the advance guard in a pursuit. They were too vulnerable to direct fire from artillery in the enemy rear guard. Instead:

> tanks should be rallied after the enemy's organized defences have been passed, grouped as may be necessary and should be kept comparatively close behind the advancing troops ready for deployment against strong centres of resistance which may form an obstacle to the ground advance. When such centres of resistance are encountered the co-operation of the several arms should be ensured and . . . the tanks should be used as a concentrated force of such size as may be necessary. Some artillery support will generally be required.[74]

The Corps was busier in this period than at any time in its history and had the greatest difficulty keeping up with the hectic pace of operations. As the entire British Army went over to the offensive so Tank Corps HQ became inundated with demands for tanks. After Amiens the Army as a whole became appreciative of their value to a much greater degree than it had after Cambrai. The reasons are not far to seek. Amiens was a genuine victory as opposed to a drawn battle and even if the difference in the degree of success achieved was only to a small extent due to tanks it was bound to affect the way they were perceived. The Mark Vs and Whippets were, moreover, considerably more flexible and useful machines than the Mark IVs and it was noticed in the August fighting that demoralized Germans sometimes used the mere appearance of tanks as an excuse to surrender.[75]

Some historians have deprecated the failure to employ tanks again on such a scale as at Amiens. In fact they were by no means always used in driblets thereafter. Tank Corps HQ records show 6 days between 11 August and 20 October on which more than 50 and 3 occasions on which over 100 were employed. The biggest post-Amiens tank operation was Third Army's attack between Moyenville and Bucquoy on 21 August, in which 183 took part. This was a major victory and, according to Tank Corps HQ, "Tanks contributed greatly to the small no. of casualties. Many cases occurred of parties of 100–150 surrendering at the first approach of Tanks." On 29 September 181 tanks were in action in support of the Fourth Army offensive against the main position of the Hindenburg Line. The operation as a whole was a great success though the performance of the tanks was mixed.[76]

Though GHQ was finding tanks very useful at this period of the war, their mass employment was not an end in itself but only a means to an end – beating the Germans. For much of the Hundred Days and particularly once the Hindenburg Line was breached in September, the rate of advance, though still slow by the standards of some Second World War campaigns, was too fast to get optimum value from the tanks. Very big tank operations like Cambrai and Amiens, which used most of the Corps on a single axis, were, administratively and logistically, extraordinarily difficult to mount. The Tank Corps as a whole worked flat out for at least three weeks in preparation for Cambrai and, even with greater experience of the work involved, it still took about a fortnight to mount the Amiens operation.[77] After Amiens the victorious Allied advance was sustained by rapidly mounting successive blows in different parts of the front, giving the enemy no respite. To have deliberately reduced the tempo in order to allow most British tanks to be concentrated for action in one place would have been ridiculous. Their concentration would not have conferred sufficient advantage to have offset the loss of momentum. If the pace of operations were maintained, however, by the time a big tank build up had been implemented the front might well have moved away.

All the British heavy tanks of the First World War, even the Mark Vs, were instruments designed mainly to help infantry break into entrenched positions. In open warfare their usefulness declined considerably. Even when operating in a relatively dispersed mode they had great difficulty keeping up with the action. As the report of 4th Tank Brigade on operations between 27 September and 17 October put it:

During a battle of movement it became an interesting problem, and a new experience, moving Tanks forward daily to keep in touch with the battle area in case they were wanted by the Corps to which they were allotted.

Corps and Divisional plans could not be settled till late in the evening for the following day's operations – it was therefore well-nigh impossible to think of getting Tanks up by dawn to precede the Infantry attack.

The only policy under these conditions is for Tanks sparingly used to catch up with the battle after Zero with the advantage of approaching by daylight over unknown ground and help the Infantry when held up in the later stages of their advances.

The daily movement of Tanks tested the endurance of crews, and mechanical troubles had to be dealt with on the spot under conditions which, as far as time available went, were quite different to what the crews had been accustomed to before.

Corps commanders scarcely grasp the fact that though they have Tanks allotted to them, it is not possible to use them 2 days running in battle, nor is it wise to put 12 Tanks in where 4 would do, nor is it sound to use Tanks just because they are allotted – better to keep them till really wanted.[78]

For tank officers to complain that infantry commanders were using too many tanks against an objective was a remarkable change of tune given that the standard complaint of the Tank Corps up to this stage had been about penny-packeting. Indeed complaints about penny-packeting continued to be heard[79] during the Hundred Days so the infantry commanders were virtually bound to be blamed by the Tank Corps on one count or the other when things went wrong for the latter.

GHQ, however, had anticipated many of the points the Tank Brigades were making, both in its August manual on tank operations and in a perceptive memorandum which Haig's Chief of the General Staff, Herbert Lawrence, sent to all five of the BEF's Armies on 1 September. GHQ was well aware from:

captured documents . . . that the enemy has considerably modified his artillery dispositions in order to meet our attacks delivered with tanks.

This fact, combined with the unfamiliarity of many Divisional and Brigade Commanders with the functions and limitations of tanks, has led to losses in this arm which are not compensated for by the results attained.

. . . The following general points in connection with the employment of tanks should be impressed on all concerned: –

. . . (a). Tanks should not be used when they have to make approach marches by day light.

. . . (b). Tanks should not be used without properly organized artillery co-operation, namely, smoke screens or H.E. barrage and counter-battery work.

... (c). In allotting tanks to formations for particular tasks, the time necessary for approach marches, and the establishment of proper liaison between infantry and Tank Corps officers must be taken into account.

Commanders to whom tank units were allocated were advised to consult with Tank Corps officers before committing tanks to battle.[80]

Further evidence of the difficulties tanks were having in the Hundred Days comes from a 5th Tank Brigade report. After an action on 18 September in support of III, Australian and IX Corps of Fourth Army in the assault on the Hindenburg "outpost line": "Exhaustion was again prevalent, and after a hard action there is no doubt that the crews must have at least 48 hours in which to recuperate."[81]

A high tempo of mobile operations by tanks was clearly quite out of the question and this point is reinforced by 5th Tank Brigade's response to a questionnaire put out by Tank Corps HQ. To a query about crew endurance it replied:

This depends entirely on the conditions of weather, ground, state of engine and intensity of fighting.

When a tank is in good condition with a new engine, favourable weather, not exposed to intense hostile shelling or very severe fighting the crew may be counted on for 12 hours in action after leaving the line of deployment.

The average time is, however, about 8 hours, but very hot weather, hard fighting and engines requiring overhaul considerably lessen this period.

In the action of 23 August some crews were physically ill after 2 hours fighting. These Tanks had done a bit of running and it had been impossible to overhaul the engines. Consequently the exhaust had warped and joints became loose, and the Tank was full of petrol fumes. Three men were sent to hospital, one of them in a critical condition.[82]

It is remarkable how different in tone are the statements from those responsible for conducting tank operations in the Hundred Days from the theoretical papers put out by Fuller and others earlier in the year. It is clear that any notion of operational manoeuvre, of dramatic breakouts and pursuits, or of the tank as a major "war winning" weapon is pure fantasy as far as 1918 is concerned. Tanks could barely keep up with the relatively hectic pace of operations in which the infantry and artillery were engaged. It is difficult to believe that 1919 would have seen a complete tactical revolution. Tanks in 1918 were in fact exactly what GHQ said they were: potentially very useful adjuncts to an artillery/infantry assault but "mechanical contrivances"[83] on which it did not make sense for the infantry to rely completely. Indeed the best infantry formations were able to make good progress without them.[84]

As the Allied advance progressed, Rawlinson, moderately pro-Tank Corps for most of 1918,[85] placed a lower value on tanks and did not want infantry strength sacrificed to provide them with manpower.[86] This, however, need not be seen as a reversion to reactionary type. It can be explained as a pragmatic response to current conditions. In open warfare the tanks available in 1918 were, regarded objectively (and as their own Brigade reports tacitly admit), considerably less useful than they had been at Amiens. The declining interest of GHQ in the expansion of the Tank Corps beyond eighteen battalions is similarly explicable on grounds of military expediency, without need for the sort of conspiracy theory in which Fuller tended to indulge.[87]

The Tank Corps paid a high price for the intense activity of the Hundred Days. As Tank Corps HQ reported to GHQ:

> The fighting strength of the Tank Corps on 8 August was approximately 7,200 of all ranks with 500 semi-trained reinforcements.
> Battle casualties to personnel for the period (8 August–20 October) amount to:-
>
> | Officers | Other Ranks |
> |----------|-------------|
> | 561 | 2627 ... |
>
> Casualty figures are high but it should be noted that anti-Tank defence stiffened considerably from August 21st.[88]

The German anti-tank defence referred to here mainly consisted of field guns operating in the direct fire role. But the Germans were also using powerful single shot anti-tank rifles, armour piercing machine gun ammunition and occasionally, when time allowed, were preparing minefields.[89] At around 40 per cent the battle casualties the Tank Corps had sustained were probably proportionally in excess of those of the infantry for the same period of the war.

Much confusion has arisen as to the true extent of British losses in 1918 from the inclusion of influenza cases with other casualties. The Tank Corps makes it clear, however, that in this report it is enumerating battle casualties alone (though these may have included casualties from heat exhaustion and carbon monoxide poisoning). It has been demonstrated that real battle casualties for Fourth Army – the spearhead Army for much of the Hundred Days – were quite low in relation to periods of intense activity earlier in the war.[90] The fact that Tank Corps casualties were so high is indicative of the continuing vulnerability of tanks, as well as of the increased attention the Germans were paying them. The more seriously the Germans took tanks as a threat the less realistic it was for the British to regard them as a panacea, not that many of the BEF's commanders were tempted to do so.

GHQ has been admonished for conducting the last few months of the war in a way which was excessively "traditional" and insufficiently "mechanical". The evidence of the people charged with the conduct of tank operations, however, makes it seem very unlikely that more use could have been made of the Tank Corps without deliberately slowing the tempo of the offensive. To have done this would not appear to have been advisable even in hindsight. Nor is it really appropriate to term traditional the operational style employed by the BEF after Amiens. The tactics employed by the infantry and artillery and the numerous types of military aircraft with whom those arms co-operated would not have been familiar to pre-1914 soldiers. Even if we just consider the period of Haig's command, veritable revolutions had taken place in the tactics of both infantry and artillery.[91]

The firepower of the infantry had improved significantly with increased issuing of the Lewis light machine gun and with the employment on a large scale of rifle grenade launchers. Tactics had kept pace and many formations other than the simple extended lines used on 1 July 1916 were now employed.[92] But it was the British artillery which represented the cutting edge of military technology in three senses: it inflicted more casualties on the enemy than any other arm, it applied mathematics and physics to the conduct of the war in the most sophisticated way, and it was, in the second half of the war, tactically well in advance of the German artillery. The British were ahead in the whole business of artillery survey, in the employment of the creeping barrage, in the application of meteorology, in silent registration and in the development of flash spotting and sound ranging for counter-battery fire.[93] While GHQ was not itself responsible for these innovations it was happy enough to make use of them. It was not hostile to new technology. Haig's decision to give the supply of aircraft (which were vital to the effective use of artillery) the top priority of all the BEF's requirements[94] is far from indicating a Luddite mentality and reinforces this point. Haig had indeed welcomed the concept of the tank when first explained to him, had been largely responsible for the creation of the Tank Corps and had been prepared to allocate it substantial resources. The lavishness of those resources was something to be marvelled at even by Tank Corps officers:

> Taking it all in all, I doubt if there can be anything, even in the exceptional records of this war, to equal in extent and variety the growth of the technical, instructional and supply branches of the Tank Corps during the last two years . . . to visit Erin at any time, to see there the scores of tanks, the acres of vast workshops and store-sheds, the miles of sidings and the tons upon tons of gear and equipment and to reflect that every pound of this material had come from England since the winter of '16, was enough to make one pause and wonder; and looking back now at the whole industry raised in so short a time from nothing at all, it appears with all its obvious shortcomings, a highly remarkable achievement of forethought and energy.[95]

Captain D.G. Browne whose memoirs are quoted above was not describing an orphan organization, half starved by a reactionary high command.

The mechanical warfare enthusiasts had no vision of victory in 1918 to offer from the methods they preferred. At least another year would have had to have elapsed, and possibly more, before their schemes could have been put into effect. The most famous of them, Fuller's paper on the Medium D, could at no time have been implemented with hope of success. It was an ill-thought-out fantasy, the great celebrity of which is largely unmerited.

In war radicals and visionaries are not always right and relative conservatives not always wrong. Intelligent innovation is, of course, commendable and the British in this war were intensely innovative. It is, however, more important both for those developing and for those assessing and applying military ideas in war to be wise in their own generation than prophetic about the next. Suggestions for military operations which might have some validity only after weapons currently available have had years of further refinement and can be used in conjunction with other instruments similarly refined are, while not completely useless, of only limited help to those who must plan the next campaign.

Notes

1   This is the thesis of Professor T. Travers in, *How the War Was Won, Command and Technology in the British Army on the Western Front 1917–18* (Routledge) 1992, *passim* and, "Could the Tanks of 1918 Have Been War-Winners for the British Expeditionary Force?" *Journal of Contemporary History*, Vol. 27 (1992), pp. 389–406.

2   A. Stern, *Tanks 1914–1918: the Log-Book of a Pioneer* (Hodder and Stoughton) 1919, pp. 64–65.

3   *History of the Ministry of Munitions, Vol. XII, the Supply of Munitions, Part III: Tanks*, 1920 (henceforth *Supply of Munitions*), pp. 31–33, SWINTON B2, Swinton Papers, Liddell Hart Centre for Military Archives, King's College London (henceforth LHCMA).

4   On the Stern–Lloyd George connection see R.J. Adams, *Arms and the Wizard: Lloyd George and the Ministry of Munitions 1915–1916* (Cassell) 1978, pp. 155 and 161–162, and "Extract from the Proceedings of a Meeting Held at 10 Downing Street, January 25th, 1917, at 11.30 A.M.", PRO WO 32/5154.

5   Kiggell to War Office, 10 February 1917, PRO WO 32/5154.

6   One example of Stern's technical ignorance causing problems is his initial rejection of the epicyclic drive system advocated by Walter Wilson and eventually incorporated in the Mark V tank. Stern favoured a less satisfactory French system. See D. Fletcher, *Landships* (HMSO) 1984, pp. 22–23.

7   *Supply of Munitions*, pp. 34–36, SWINTON B2, Swinton Papers, LHCMA.

8   See, for example, Tennyson d'Eyncourt [to War Cabinet?], 12 December 1917, BCII/39, Fuller Papers, LHCMA.

9   J.F.C. Fuller, *Memoirs of an Unconventional Soldier* (Nicholson and Watson) 1936, p. 95.

10   *Supply of Munitions*, pp. 52–55, SWINTON B2, Swinton Papers, LHCMA. Williams-Ellis, *The Tank Corps* (Country Life) 1919, pp. 46–47.

11   War Office to Ministry of Munitions, 7 December 1917, PRO WO 158/813. Memorandum by Albert Stern, 26 April 1918, B.44, Fuller

Papers, Tank Museum. Stern, *op. cit.*, pp. 196–201. *Supply of Munitions*, pp. 56–58, SWINTON B2, Swinton Papers, LHCMA.

12 Capper to DCIGS, 25 February 1918, Minute 10, PRO WO 32/9288.

13 Capper to DCIGS, 11 May 1918, Minute 24, PRO WO 32/9288.

14 Stern to Frances Stevenson, 7 May 1918, Stern Papers, LHCMA.

15 "I have seen Colonel Stern on this subject and if he does not now abide by his duties the case will be handed over to the A.G. for action", signature illegible, Minute 26, 18 May 1918, PRO WO 32/9288.

16 On Fuller's lobbying activities see Fuller, *Memoirs*, pp. 95 and 175, Fuller to Churchill, 2 March 1918, A12, and "The Private Journal of Lt. Colonel J.F.C. Fuller Relative to the Expansion and Employment of the Tank Corps, December 1917 to July 26 1918" (henceforth Fuller, "Private Journal") *passim*, Fuller Papers, Tank Museum.

17 "Tank Operations Decisive in 1919 and Preparatory in 1918", undated, TS/40, Fuller Papers, LHCMA.

18 D. Woodward, *Lloyd George and the Generals* (Delaware) 1983, pp. 221–252. On Fuller as a Westerner see J. Terraine, *White Heat: the New Warfare 1914–1918* (Sidgwick and Jackson) 1982, pp. 91–92.

19 Fuller, *Memoirs*, pp. 318–320. Documents produced by the Supreme War Council on Mechanical Warfare in spring 1918 included Sir Henry Rawlinson (succeeding Wilson as "permanent" British military representative) "Notes on Economy of Manpower by Mechanical Means", 15 March 1918, PRO WO 158/25. See also Sackville-West to DCIGS, 23 May 1918, enclosing memoranda by Lieutenant-Colonel A.H. Ollivant and Lieutenant-Colonel C.N. Beresford, PRO WO 158/827.

20 Fuller, "Private Journal", p. 23, Fuller Papers, Tank Museum.

21 D. Woodward, *The Military Correspondence of Field Marshal Sir William Robertson Chief Imperial General Staff December 1915–February 1918* (Army Records Society/Bodley Head) 1989, pp. 245–308.

22 A.J. Trythall, *"Boney" Fuller, the Intellectual General 1878–1966* (Cassell) 1977, pp. 60–61.

23 On Foch's assumption of the position of Generalissimo see Terraine, *To Win a War: 1918, the Year of Victory* (Sidgwick and Jackson) 1978, p. 63. On Foch's sympathy with mechanical warfare ideas see Fuller, *Memoirs*, p. 340.

24 Haig to War Office, 20 August 1917, O.B. 83/G (quoted in "Organization", notes for an official history of the Tank Corps), PRO WO 158/804.

25 J. Terraine, *Douglas Haig: the Educated Soldier* (Hutchinson) 1963, p. 467.

26 *ibid.*, pp. 466–467.
27 S. Foot, *Three Lives* (Heinemann) 1934, pp. 207–218 and 345–349.
28 *ibid.*, pp. 345–349.
29 War Office to Haig, 57/Tanks/18 (S.D.2), 18 May 1918 enclosed "Proposals for the Use of Tanks in 1919". It was responded to in Haig to War Office O.B./83/IV, June 1918 (exact date not recorded on PRO copy) PRO WO 158/830.
30 Note by Haig on War Office memorandum: "Proposals for the Use of Tanks in 1919", June 1918, PRO WO 158/830. Travers treats Haig's comments on this War Office paper as comments on "Fuller's Plan 1919": Travers, *How the War Was Won*, p. 45. But Fuller's pencil manuscript on the Medium D was not finished until 24 May. The War Office paper on which Haig was commenting was sent to him on 18 May.
31 See for example Martel, "A Tank Army", November 1916, TS/9 and Tennyson d'Eyncourt on "Tank Armies" in BCII/39, 12 December 1917, Fuller Papers, LHCMA.
32 Fuller, *Memoirs*, p. 322.
33 "Strategical Outlook 1919", 30 March 1918, B11, Fuller Papers, Tank Museum.
34 "Minutes of 'G' Conference Held at HQ, Tank Corps, April 28th", B46, Fuller Papers, Tank Museum. The clearest account of the origins of the high speed tank concept is to be found in R. Ogorkiewicz, *The Technology of Tanks*, Vol. I (Jane's), 1991, p. 8. Johnson improved the performance of a Whippet in late 1917 by using a form of sprung suspension. In February 1918 he found that speeds of 30 mph were attainable by a Whippet which had both sprung suspension and a powerful Rolls-Royce Eagle aero engine which he substituted for the standard two Tyler engines.
35 Fuller, "The Tactics of the Attack as Affected by the Speed and Circuit of the Medium D Tank" (henceforth Fuller, "Tactics of the Attack"), 24 May 1918, pp. 1–2, B62, Fuller Papers, Tank Museum.
36 *ibid.*, pp. 2–5.
37 Fuller, *Memoirs*, pp. 321–322.
38 Fuller, "Tactics of the Attack", p. 11.
39 *ibid.*, p. 12.
40 *ibid.*, p. 12.
41 *ibid.*, pp. 13–20.
42 Fuller, *Memoirs*, p. 330.
43 *ibid.*, pp. 339–340.
44 Wilson to Foch, 20 July 1981 and War Office to Haig, 27 July 1918 enclosing "Memorandum on the Requirements for an Armoured Striking Force for an Offensive in 1919", PRO WO 158/842.
45 "Memorandum on the Requirements for an Armoured Striking Force

for an Offensive in 1919", Section 3, "Outline of Battle" and Section
4, "Forces Required", PRO WO 158/842.

46 Fuller, *Memoirs*, p. 340.

47 J. Edmonds, Official History of the Great War (henceforth "OH")
    Military Operations: France and Belgium, 1918, Vol. III (Macmillan)
    1937, p. 298.

48 P.A. Pederson, *Monash as Military Commander* (Melbourne Univer-
    sity Press) 1985, p. 227.

49 5th Tank Brigade, "Report on Tank Operations, 4 July 1918",
    TCOIV/3, Fuller Papers, LHCMA. Travers, *How the War Was Won*,
    pp. 113–114 and R. Prior and T. Wilson, *Command on the Western
    Front* (Blackwell) 1992, p. 300.

50 Fuller, *Memoirs*, p. 291.

51 On the "Formula for Success" see Prior and Wilson, *op. cit.*, p. 289–
    300.

52 Terraine, *To Win a War*, pp. 95–101.

53 Terraine, *Haig*, p. 453.

54 Prior and Wilson, *op. cit.*, p. 301.

55 *ibid.*, pp. 306–307.

56 *ibid.*, p. 307.

57 Fuller, *Memoirs*, pp. 314–315. "Training Note No. 16", TS/6, Fuller
    Papers, LHCMA.

58 Fuller to Fourth Army, 23 July 1918, Vol. 49, Fourth Army Papers,
    Imperial War Museum.

59 Terraine, *To Win a War*, pp. 121–122.

60 J. Edmonds, OH, *Military Operations in France and Flanders, 1918,
    Vol. IV, 8th August–26th September, the Franco-British Offensive*
    (HMSO) 1947, p. 48 and Prior and Wilson, *op. cit.*, p. 322.

61 *ibid.*, p. 53.

62 C. and A. Williams-Ellis, *op. cit.*, pp. 201–206.

63 B.H. Liddell Hart, *The Tanks*, Vol. I (Cassell) 1959, pp. 181–182.

64 *ibid.*, pp. 179–180. B. Rawling, *Surviving Trench Warfare: Technol-
    ogy and the Canadian Corps, 1914–1918* (University of Toronto
    Press) 1992, pp. 198–199.

65 Elles to GHQ, 29 October 1918 reporting on tank actions 8 August
    to 20 October 1918, TCOIV/28, Fuller Papers, LHCMA.

66 Rawling, *op. cit.*, p. 196. Stern, *op. cit.*, pp. 227–228. The Mark V
    tank was even more prone to problems of crew poisoning and ex-
    haustion than its predecessors. See Major L.R. Broster RAMC to
    Tank Corps HQ, PRO MUN 4/2802 and 5th Tank Brigade "Report
    on Operations, 18 September 1918", section 12, sub-section ii)
    "Medical", para. (b), TCOIV/7, Fuller Papers, LHCMA.

67 Detailed day-by-day record of Tank Corps actions of 8 August to 20

October attached to Elles to GHQ, 29 October 1918, TCOIV/28, Fuller Papers, LHCMA.

68   Fuller, *Memoirs*, pp. 342–344.
69   On the reorganization of the Tank Corps "to bring the armoured forces into the Army" (Capper's words) see Haig to War Office, O.B./83/IV, para. 3, June 1918 (exact date not indicated on PRO copy) and accompanying "Note", p. 2, PRO WO 158/830; Capper to DCIGS, 1 June 1918, PRO WO 158/127; Capper to Elles, 18 June 1918, PRO WO 158/816; Fuller, *Memoirs*, pp. 348–355.
70   "Tanks and Their Employment in Co-operation with Other Arms", August 1918, PRO WO 158/832.
71   Travers, *How the War Was Won*, p. 143.
72   "Tanks and Their Employment in Co-operation with Other Arms", Introduction and Chapter I, PRO WO 158/832.
73   *ibid.*, Chapter II, Section 8, "Co-operation with Aircraft" and Chapter VI "Communications".
74   *ibid.*, Chapter IV, section 9, "Special Considerations in Open Warfare".
75   Elles to GHQ, 29 October 1918, TCOIV/28, Fuller Papers, LHCMA.
76   "Summary of Tank Operations, 8 August–20 October 1918", TCOIV/28, Fuller Papers, LHCMA.
77   A. and C. Williams-Ellis, *op. cit.*, pp. 192–193.
78   4th Tank Brigade, "Report on Operations, September 27th to October 17th 1918", TCOIV/2, Fuller Papers, LHCMA.
79   In a 5th Tank Brigade "Report on Operations of 18 September", Section 12, "Lessons and Suggestions", sub-section 1: 'Tactical', para. (a), there was a complaint: "That employing tanks in small numbers against Strong Points held by a determined enemy is unsatisfactory and only results in heavy losses to Tanks and Tank Personnel without materially assisting the Infantry." Admittedly the context in this case was rather different: not open warfare but an assault on the outpost line of the Hindenburg position. TCOIV/7, Fuller Papers, LHCMA.
80   Lawrence to the Armies, O.A. 109, 1 September 1918, PRO WO 158/832.
81   Brigadier-General A. Courage, Commander 5th Tank Brigade, "Report on Operations with Australian, III and IX Corps, 18 September 1918", section 12, sub-section ii) "Medical", para. (b), TCOIV/7, Fuller Papers, LHCMA.
82   5th Tank Brigade, "Report on Operations with the Australian Corps, 8 August 1918 to 15 August 1918, Supplementary Report", 1 September 1918, answer to question 1 of a Tank Corps questionnaire, TCOIV/5, Fuller Papers, LHCMA.

83   From the August GHQ booklet, "Tanks and Their Employment in Co-operation with Other Arms", PRO WO 158/832.

84   W.D. Croft, *Three Years with the 9th (Scottish) Division* (Murray) 1919, p. 87.

85   On Rawlinson's support for tanks see Rawlinson, "Notes On Economy of Manpower by Mechanical Means", para. 6, 15 March 1918, PRO WO 158/25 and Capper to Elles, 29 April 1918: "I am very glad to hear that now Sir Henry Rawlinson is converted. Gradually they will all come round." PRO WO 158/816.

86   Rawlinson to Wilson, 29 August 1918, quoted in Travers, *How the War Was Won*, p. 141.

87   Fuller, *Memoirs*, pp. 351–355.

88   Elles to GHQ, 29 October 1918, TCOIV/28, Fuller Papers, LHCMA.

89   On German anti-tank defences at this period see "Organization of Anti-Tank Defence" (translation of captured German order of 23 July 1918) attached to Lawrence to Armies, 1 September 1918, PRO WO 158/832; "Supplementary Report 5th Tank Brigade", 1 September 1918, answers to questions 9 and 10 of a Tank Corps HQ questionnaire, TCOIV/7; translation of captured German document, 21 September 1918, Lt. von Pawelsz for CGS, 17th German Army, "Anti-tank defence", TS/126; "German anti-tank defences, land mines", TS/127, Fuller Papers, LHCMA.

90   Prior and Wilson, *op. cit.*, pp. 390–391.

91   S. Bidwell and D. Graham, *Fire-Power, British Army Weapons and Theories of War 1904–1945* (Allen and Unwin) 1982, pp. 117–146.

92   P. Griffith, *Battle Tactics of the Western Front* (Yale) 1994, pp. 95–100.

93   On the technical excellence of British gunnery by 1918 see Prior and Wilson, *op. cit.*, pp. 292–295 and 311–315 and J. Terraine, *White Heat*, pp. 306–308.

94   On GHQ's top priority for aircraft see Haig to War Office, 20 August 1917, quoted in "Organization" (notes for a Tank Corps history?) p. 16, WO 158/804 and Haig to Robertson, 23 November 1917, BCII/44, Fuller Papers, LHCMA.

95   Captain D.G. Browne, *The Tank in Action* (Blackwood) 1920 quoted in Liddell Hart, *op. cit.*, p. 85.

6

An era of experiment: 1919–31

For the Tank Corps, as for the rest of the British Army, the Armistice brought contraction. At the war's end the Corps comprised, on paper at least, more than twenty battalions. Within months it had been reduced to a mere four battalions.[1] The British Army in the years following the Great War did not, moreover, appear to afford it fertile ground in which to flourish.

The year 1919 was an exceptionally unsettled one. As well as counter-guerrilla action in Ireland and a small war with Afghanistan, the British Army was involved in the Allied intervention in Russia to which it sent three small tank detachments.[2] Though a British Mark V tank played a major role in the capture of Tsaritsin by the forces of General Wrangel in late June and early July 1919, the tanks of 1918 were too slow and cumbersome to be ideal for use in the generally fluid operations in progress in these countries. From his desk in the War Office, Colonel J.F.C. Fuller vaguely suggested that an expeditionary army of Medium D tanks could help stem the tide of Russian Bolshevism. His superiors, aware that only one Medium D tank yet existed and that it had serious faults, rightly rejected the idea.[3]

By 1921 the Army's drastic contraction was being accompanied by a general reversion to the type of soldiering – imperial policing and occasional operations on the frontiers of Empire – which had been its wont before 1914. Imperial defence commitments had in fact substantially increased since then. Not only had the war resulted in the acquisition of new territories, there was also a general increase in nationalist unrest in Asia and the Middle East.[4] The need to maintain garrisons in India and other overseas possessions largely determined the composition of the Army as a

Figure 16
J.F.C. Fuller in pensive mood
circa 1919.

Figure 17   The Medium D.M. experimental tank swimming during trials
at Charlton Park, Woolwich. The driver operates from a cupola on top
of the turret.

whole and established its tone.[5] After a flurry of activity in the war's immediate aftermath the British economy spent the rest of the 1920s in a somewhat sluggish condition and the Army estimates and therefore military manpower were under constant downward pressure.[6]

Some senior officers expressed doubts about the whole future of the tank. In an often-quoted remark, Major-General Sir Louis Jackson (Director of Trench Warfare and Supplies at the Ministry of Munitions 1915–18) told an audience at the Royal United Service Institution on 17 December 1919 that: "The tank proper was a freak, the circumstances which called it into existence were exceptional and not likely to recur. If they do they can be dealt with by other means."[7]

Yet while the United States abolished its Tank Corps at the end of the First World War,[8] the British Tank Corps survived, probably aided by the kudos it had gained in 1918, especially at Amiens, and by its royal association – George V having become Colonel-in-Chief on 7 October 1917.[9] Of at least equal importance was its ability to make itself useful in the post-war world – mainly with armoured cars, on which it gained a short-lived monopoly in the early 1920s, rather than with tanks as such.[10] Armoured cars turned out to be invaluable tools for imperial policing and small wars, and were in constant demand in places as far removed as Ireland,[11] India and Iraq. Iraq was of particular importance to the development of British armoured forces. Three Armoured Car Companies of the Tank Corps, administered as "No. 1 Group Tank Corps", were established there early in 1921. They played a vital role in the policing of the country. Lieutenant-Colonel G.M. Lindsay (of whom more later) who took over command of No. 1 Group in June, developed his concept of an "entirely mechanical force" while in Iraq. This ultimately led to the famous Experimental Mechanical Force on Salisbury Plain in 1927–28. Even more important to the control of Iraq, however, was airpower. The RAF became the senior partner and, after forming its own armoured car units, took sole control of the policing of Iraq towards the end of 1922.[12]

The loss of its role in Iraq, however, was not a crucial matter for the Tank Corps. Not only did it survive, being established as a permanent institution on 1 September 1923, it was granted the prefix "Royal" on 18 October that year, an honour indicative of

Figure 18
A sketch of George Lindsay.
Lindsay was the most
intellectually sophisticated of the
RTC radicals between the wars.

a rather high status for such a young branch of the Army.[13] The Royal Tank Corps (RTC) had an initial establishment of 4 battalions, providing a scale of 1 tank battalion for each infantry division. RTC headquarters were established at Bovington, near Wool, in Dorset. The 4 battalions were based at Farnborough, Catterick, Perham Down and Lydd. The tank battalions were not made integral parts of infantry divisions and the RTC was given a great deal of latitude in the development of doctrine.[14]

It has been suggested that the RTC contained at least as much dross amongst its officers as most other branches of the Army, having become stuck with some who were not wanted in older established regiments and corps at the end of the war.[15] By way of compensation, however, its image of relative mobility and modernity attracted some intellectually lively officers from other arms, most notably George Lindsay, Charles Broad, Percy Hobart and Frederick Pile. It also gained a vociferous and intelligent champion in the world of journalism – Basil Liddell Hart.[16]

The oldest of this band of talented new officers was George Lindsay, who already had a reputation as a military innovator. Born in 1880 he was commissioned originally into the militia but obtained a regular commission in the Rifle Brigade in 1900 and served in the South African War. Later, in the First World War, he was one of the moving spirits behind the formation of the Machine Gun Corps, attaining the rank of colonel. After his period of service in Iraq, mentioned above, he returned to England in 1923, becoming chief instructor at the Royal Tank Corps Centre for two years before becoming Inspector RTC from 1925 to 1929. An inspiring and very likeable officer, he seems to have been the strongest individual influence on the development of British military thought on armoured forces and armoured warfare from the early 1920s up to 1934.[17]

Charles Broad, who was very much in tune with Lindsay intellectually, and who worked closely with the latter on the evolution of RTC doctrine, was slightly his junior, having been born in 1882, in Lahore, India, the son an infantry major. Broad served as a private in the militia in the South African War and was commissioned into the Royal Artillery in 1905. He had a distinguished record as a gunner in the First World World and was appointed as an instructor at the Staff College in 1919 where he taught George Lindsay. When he transferred to the RTC in 1923 he became commandant of the Tank Gunnery School at Lulworth Cove. In 1925 he succeeded Lindsay as Chief Instructor at the corps's Central School. Broad, who, according to Liddell Hart, was known as "The Brain", was mild-mannered and apparently not a very forceful or charismatic leader. His impatience when frustrated led him sometimes to be tactless with superiors, a trait which may have had an adverse impact on the development of his career.[18] His reputation as a "progressive" having been established by the writings of Liddell Hart, his ideas on tank gunnery and on mechanized forces generally (like those of Lindsay and Hobart) have seldom been examined critically enough by military historians.

Percy Hobart, known to his friends as "Patrick", was born in India in 1885, son of a member of the Indian Civil Service. He attended the Royal Military Academy Woolwich and was commissioned into 1st Bengal Sappers and Miners in 1906. After distinguished First World War service on the Western and Mesopotamian fronts, he passed Staff College and transferred to the RTC in 1923. In his early years in the RTC he was essentially a disciple of Lindsay, contributing little that was original. A stronger personality than either Lindsay or Broad, however, he became the most influential officer with an RTC background in the later 1930s.

Figure 19
Percy Hobart. The photograph
is of Second World War
vintage. Between the wars
Hobart was the most radical
and fanatical of the RTC *avant-
garde.*

He had a less subtle and a more dogmatic mind than Lindsay and
seems to have become fixated on a version of the "Armoured
Idea" which Lindsay had advocated in the 1920s but was moving
away from by the mid-1930s.[19] Hobart's opinions on, and role in,
the development of British armoured forces will be examined in
the next two chapters.

Frederick Pile, familiarly known as "Tim", was, like Broad,
originally a gunner. Unlike Broad he reverted to his original arm
before the outbreak of the Second World War. From the most
socially elevated background of any of the RTC radicals, he was
born in Dublin in 1884, son of a baronet, himself succeeding to
the title in 1931. Pile did not have a distinguished academic record
in early life[20] and, though a great favourite of Liddell Hart's,[21]
there seems little reason to regard him as a military intellectual.
Having performed well as a gunner on the Western Front, he took
the usual route via a post-war course at the Staff College at
Camberley, where he fell under Fuller's influence, into the RTC in
1923. Though he did produce some papers on aspects of organization and doctrine, his main contribution to the Corps appears
to have been enthusiasm and dynamic leadership (most notably of
the "Fast Group" of the Experimental Mechanical Force in 1927)
rather than analysis or prophecy. Regarded by critics as a blatant

Figure 20
Sir Basil Liddell Hart in later
life.

careerist,[22] he certainly seized what appeared to be the main chance in 1937. With the possibility of a Continental role for the British Army being pushed into the background, he sought and gained command of 1st Anti-Aircraft Division which had the high profile role of defending London. From this time onward his involvement with armour ceased completely and he commanded the anti-aircraft defences of the United Kingdom throughout the Second World War.[23]

It is of course impossible to examine the development of British military doctrine between the world wars without reference to the journalist and military critic, Basil Liddell Hart. It used to be normal to regard Liddell Hart as the greatest British military thinker of the twentieth century and for many years he was widely believed to be the principal inspiration behind the German "blitzkrieg doctrine". It is now generally realized that both his impact on the Germans and his prescience and insight concerning military developments in his lifetime have been vastly overrated. His once prodigious influence on the writing of military history in the English-speaking world has much declined and it is no longer necessary to take him at his own evaluation.[24]

Born in Paris in 1895, the son of a Cornish clergyman, Liddell Hart was educated at St Paul's and Cambridge, though he only completed the first year of a history degree course at the latter before volunteering for the Army at the outbreak of the First World War. He served in France as an infantry subaltern for a year before being gassed on the Somme in the great offensive of 1916. He remained in the Army until 1924 and would have liked to have made a career as a regular, but was invalided out with a heart condition. He had been involved with infantry training and with the development of new tactical manuals for infantry for most of his period in the Army and was enjoying a growing reputation, under General Sir Ivor Maxse's patronage, as a thinker, writer and lecturer on infantry tactics. He joined the staff of the *Daily Telegraph* in 1925, succeeding Colonel Repington as military correspondent, and quickly became influential.[25]

From the early 1920s Liddell Hart established a correspondence with J.F.C. Fuller, who converted him to the view that the future of war lay with armour rather than with infantry.[26] Liddell Hart was once regarded as a major theorist of armoured warfare. Such a reputation, however, is difficult to justify.[27] Though his support gave much encouragement to the RTC radicals in the 1920s and early 1930s, by the late 1930s he doubted the power of armoured forces to make much impact on the next major European war.[28] Even in the 1920s he seems to have been little more than a very influential media spokesman for tank enthusiasts within the Army rather than a major thinker on this subject in his own right. He was able, sometimes, slightly to modify ideas on armoured forces put to him by radical officers but there is little evidence of substantial original thought.[29]

Despite all the unfavourable external circumstances – financial stringency, a growing anti-military tendency in public opinion, and heavy imperial garrisoning and policing commitments (which needed manpower and traditional methods rather than the latest technology and most radical ideas) there was something of a renaissance of British military thought during the 1920s. Officers from the RTC and the wartime Tank Corps, encouraged by Liddell Hart,[30] were its central figures. Indeed until the early 1930s Great Britain was widely regarded as the world leader in mechanized warfare doctrine, in tank design and in the training and tactical handling of mechanized formations.[31] Considering the disadvantages under which the British laboured this was a creditable performance. On the other hand some of the ideas generated by the tank radicals were distinctly unsound and, gaining the status of dogma within the RTC, seem to have had damaging long-term consequences.

The best known radical British military thinker of the 1920s within the Army was J.F.C. Fuller. In 1919 he won the Royal United Service Institution's Gold Medal essay competition. The subject set for essays that year was, "The application of recent developments in mechanics and other scientific knowledge to preparation and training for future war on land." It was, of course, a natural topic for Fuller to tackle. He held a rather undemanding War Office post and was thus in an ideal position to enter. He also faced little competition. Such was the chaotic state of the Army in 1919 that there were only two other submissions.[32]

Fuller's winning entry contained the essence of much of his thought on mechanized warfare up to the point at which he largely lost interest in the subject in the mid-1930s. Though these ideas would be more fully developed in his 1932 book entitled *Lectures on FSR III*, the 1919 essay is worth examining closely. It exemplified both the best and the worst elements of his published writing. A great sense of the author's enthusiasm, excitement and energy was communicated to the reader. But it had an unbalanced, hyperbolic quality about it. There was a lack of objectivity – little weighing of evidence and little willingness to admit the difficulties inherent in radical courses of action vehemently advocated. Inevitably Fuller saw the tank as the most important 1914–18 development. Indeed, Fuller hardly mentioned the revolution in artillery technique which had taken place in the same period and paid scant regard to significant development in infantry tactics. In 1919 he was even more inclined to ignore inconvenient facts about the vulnerability of tanks and limitations on their mobility and firepower than he had been the previous year.

> From its inception the tank offered the armies which adopted it ... solutions ... to the problem of "how to obtain and maintain offensive superiority". It rendered the soldier immune from the effects of bullets, shrapnel and shell splinters; it provided him with a mobile ammunition dump which could move across trench, mire and field; and it enabled him to dispense with his legs for movement, and by substituting for them mechanical force, to expend the whole of his muscular endurance on the manipulation of his weapons – henceforth he could become a true fighter of weapons by ceasing to be a

human pack mule . . . The change in the art of war effected by the introduction of the petrol engine on the battlefield . . . has opened a new era in the history of war to which we can find no parallel in land fighting, the nearest approach being the replacement of sail by steam as the motive force in naval warfare . . . It has in fact equilibrated movement and fire and by doing so has superimposed naval tactics on land warfare; that is, it now enables the soldier, like the sailor, to discharge his weapons from a moving platform protected by a fixed shield.[33]

Though there was reasonable hope that the worst of them could now be overcome, it was somewhat intellectually dishonest of Fuller to give no indication here of the extreme ergonomic problems from which tank crews had suffered in the First World War and which made their capacity for sustained combat actually much less than that of infantrymen moving on foot.[34] The use of the naval analogy, which he had first employed in his May 1918 paper, was more significant. One of the implications which Fuller drew from it, that the essence of tank tactics was fire on the move, became a dogma in the RTC between the wars and British armoured forces carried it into the Second World War. Especially with regard to tank-to-tank combat it was pernicious, as it made accuracy virtually impossible. The Germans had, by the mid-1930s, adopted the opposite doctrine.[35] How far the adoption of a fire-on-the-move dogma (taught, under Broad's direction, at the gunnery school at Lulworth) by the RTC was directly due to Fuller's influence cannot be definitely determined but the naval warfare analogy certainly does appear to have had an impact on RTC training. In an early tank versus tank exercise tanks even attempted, rather ridiculously but with the approbation of Basil Liddell Hart, to perform the naval manoeuvre of "crossing the T".[36]

Other than armoured vehicles, the developments of the 1914–18 period which appear to have most interested Fuller were military aircraft and gas. Rejecting the idea that "human destinies could be controlled by a 'whiff of phosgene'", he used the threat of gas to underline the importance of armour. A tank, he believed, could be made airtight more easily than a submarine watertight and could be provided with a detector by which its crew could be able to "guarantee the quality of the outer air". Directly the gauge showed the air to be impure the hatches would be battened down "the crew being provided with oxygen or compressed air and its engines if necessary run off accumulators".[37]

Fuller thought it unlikely that future wars would be declared and believed that they would commence with surprise attacks. In frontier defence systems guns would be replaced by "hidden reservoirs containing hundreds of thousands of tons of liquid gas". Centres of resistance defended by "permanent moats, mine fields and gas inundations" would act as "fortified land ports" within which "friendly fleets of landships" could "seek refuge, revictual and refit". They would become "pivots of manoeuvre round and between which naval strategy and tactics will be applied to land operations". Surprise attacks would be made on them. They would be "blockaded by hostile fleets and relieved by friendly ones", and battles would be "won and lost on land as they now are at sea".[38]

For the naval warfare analogy and for much of the subsequent analysis Fuller owed an intellectual debt to Martel's "Tank Army" paper of late 1916.[39] The borrowing, however, was both unacknowledged and ill-advised. In suggesting that tanks would have to operate from ports, Fuller was in fact unduly downplaying their mobility. The means of refuelling, replenishment and repair could follow in their wake, thus relieving them the necessity to return to any fixed base. Though, in the long term, armies would in a sense resemble fleets in which everyone could be carried in some sort of motor transport, they would never consist wholly of tanks or other types of armoured vehicle and their manoeuvres would be influenced by the nature of the ground to a degree which the naval warfare analogy did not allow.

In the final part of his 1919 RUSI essay Fuller argued for the creation of a "New Model Army" which would be utterly different from the armies of of 1914–18. The mass conscript armies which the Great War produced had proved both extremely immobile and very vulnerable, vulnerable presumably in the sense that they took very large casualties. Armies based on tanks would overcome both of these problems, economizing manpower and and also enabling road and rail supply to be dispensed with. Fuller downplayed the importance of arms other than tanks to a dangerous degree. Whilst he seems to have envisaged the need for some infantry to occupy vital ground, their numbers, he believed, could be significantly reduced:

> Tanks, by reducing the resistance offered to infantry in battle, enable a smaller body of unarmoured men to accomplish a given operation more quickly and less dangerously than would be possible for a

larger body of men unaccompanied by these machines. Tanks, therefore, can replace infantry.[40]

Machine gunners and cavalry got even shorter shrift from Fuller.
Cavalry were excessively vulnerable in the face of modern firepower.
Machine guns were most useful when armoured and mobile, i.e.
when deployed as tanks. Whereas artillery could maintain its usefulness by abandoning horse traction and adopting cross-country
mechanical traction this would mean that they would in effect
become big-gunned tanks. As tanks would be less dependent on
fixed lines of communication, Fuller also expected a diminution of
the importance of the traditional sapper role, though mechanical
engineers would become more important. How tanks were to cross
water obstacles without sapper help was not spelt out, but in 1919
Philip Johnson was still trying to develop the Medium D which he
intended to make amphibious. The most perceptive and accurate
element in Fuller's analysis was the stress he placed on armour–
air co-operation. Tanks would have to look on aeroplanes as their
shield and eyes.[41]

Fuller thus envisaged the development of a New Model Army
built up around the capabilities of the tank. He proposed a New
Model Division, tank-heavy but incorporating elements of other
arms. This, however, was to be a short-term measure only. Ultimately the British Army ought to consist, he believed, entirely of
light, medium and heavy tanks, which could between them carry
out all the traditional military functions.

Fuller proposed that India could be controlled entirely by a
combination of a "mechanical police force" and an "independent
striking force" both mounted in types of tank. The Indian Army
would be practically abolished and the British troops in India
reduced from 76,000 to 33,000. At home the Territorial Force
could be abolished as a large manpower reserve was not required
in modern warfare.[42]

All this was radicalism run riot. In arguing that imperial policing could be conducted almost entirely by forces mounted in
armoured vehicles Fuller was leaving much out of account. One of
the essentials of policing is the gathering of intelligence and that
can be done only through the maintenance of the closest links
with the population. This would inevitably have been lost in India
if the numbers of the security forces, never very large in relation

to the total population, had been reduced drastically. Armoured vehicles were of course useful, but they reduced the total need for manpower marginally if at all. Conservative officers were right to be sceptical of the ability of tanks to take over entirely the conduct of military operations on the ground, especially with regard to less developed areas of the world outside Europe.[43]

Yet the RUSI gave Fuller his prize and published his paper. In the immediate post-war period, while Field Marshal Sir Henry Wilson was CIGS (1918–22), there is no evidence of an anti-intellectual atmosphere in which officers had cause to fear the expression of radical views. Fuller was later to feel rather aggrieved when the next CIGS, Lord Cavan (1922–26), a conservative officer, originally from the Brigade of Guards, denied him permission to publish a book based on his Staff College lectures.[44] But even under Cavan, there would appear to be no substantial evidence that Fuller or any of the radical RTC officers were subjected to persecution or adverse discrimination.

Indeed Fuller's ideas, eccentric and unrealistic as they often were, received a remarkably sympathetic hearing from many senior officers in the 1920s. Following his success in the essay prize the previous year, Fuller was asked to lecture to the RUSI in February 1920. He spoke on "The Development of Sea Warfare on Land". Major-General Sir John Capper, the chairman, gave him a glowing introduction based on his work as principal staff officer of the Tank Corps HQ during the war.[45] The quotation of a single paragraph is enough to give the flavour of Fuller's address:

> I saw a fleet operating against a fleet not at sea but on land: cruisers and battleships and destroyers. My astral form follows one side and I notice that it is in difficulty; it cannot see; there appears an aeroplane and gives it sight . . . I see a man in one of the aeroplanes whose head is swollen with the future: he is the Commander-in-Chief of the land fleet I am following . . . I sniff the air; it seems impure. Is it gas? The Tanks submerge; that is to say batten down their hatches. The battle begins.[46]

It was in June 1920 that Liddell Hart first met Fuller. Liddell Hart ultimately decided, in his own words, to "become a disciple". He entered the RUSI essay competition of 1922 on a very Fullerian tack. He did not win but published his entry in the form of two articles, the second of which, appearing in the *Army Quarterly*, was entitled, "The Development of the 'New Model Army: Suggestions on a Progressive but Gradual Mechanization'". Liddell Hart did not significantly differ from Fuller in terms of the ultimate shape of the Army and, like Fuller, he suggested two phases for mechanization. In the second phase:

> The tank is likely to swallow the infantryman, the field artilleryman, the engineer and the signaller, while mechanical cavalry will supersede the horseman . . . The logical sequence points to the land or rather overland forces being composed primarily of tanks and aircraft, with a small force of siege artillery for the reduction and defence of the fortified tank and aircraft bases, and of mechanical borne infantry for use as land marines.[47]

Liddell Hart went into greater detail than Fuller had about the mechanics of converting the Army from its present to its "New Model" form, but in most respects was a rather uncritical disciple at this period. After the Second World War, Liddell Hart exaggerated the differences between himself and Fuller during the interwar period, especially over the issue of mechanized infantry. But it is clear that "land marines" were to be a very minor element in the sort of Army which Liddell Hart was proposing. By the early 1930s Fuller had also accepted the need for some sort of infantry, in the Army of the future, for mopping up and policing conquered areas, roles not greatly differing from those which Liddell Hart appears to have envisaged for his "marines".[48]

But what were the means at the disposal of the British Army for giving some concrete form to these dramatic visions? Since the spring of 1918 a Tank Corps engineer, Philip Johnson, had been attempting to develop the Medium D tank, the hoped for performance of which had been the basis of Fuller's "novelette", now usually known as "Plan 1919".[49] A designer of great originality, Johnson eventually developed two innovative systems of suspension designed to give high speed and good cross-country performance. Though ingenious, both proved initially very unreliable and were taking a long time to perfect. Johnson had, moreover, concentrated on the problem of cross-country performance almost to the exclusion of fighting power. The fighting compartments of both the Medium D and a lighter Johnson prototype, known as the Light Infantry tank, were generally considered badly designed, and whereas Johnson had thought no armament beyond machine

Figure 21 HM King George V and Queen Mary are shown a Medium tank Mark IA at Farnborough in 1923.

guns necessary, opinion amongst senior Tank Corps officers was hardening on the need for all tanks to be equipped with a gun. Becoming impatient with Johnson, the Master General of the Ordnance's Department in the War Office contacted Vickers towards the end of 1921 and asked them to try an alternative approach.[50]

The result was the Vickers Light tank, later redesignated the Medium tank Mark I. The decision to adopt this tank, taken in 1922, was accompanied by the closure of Johnson's small tank design department and by his return to civilian life. Though much simpler and less bold in conception than Johnson's prototypes, the Vickers-designed machine had features completely new to British tanks, including a revolving turret and sprung tracks, and owed little to the trench warfare conditions of the Western Front of 1914–18. The Vickers Medium (as this tank became generally known) was designed to be capable of only 15 mph, significantly slower than either of Johnson's prototypes when they were operating well. But the Vickers tank was much more reliable than Johnson's machines and was faster than intended, achieving a road speed of up to 30 mph on occasion.[51] The armour on the

Vickers Medium Mark I, which entered service in 1923, was very weak, leaving it vulnerable even to close-range small arms fire, but it was equipped with a relatively high-velocity, flat-trajectory 3-pdr gun, obviously adopted with tank-to-tank combat in mind, and indeed suitable for no other purpose as only solid shot ammunition was issued. Apparently the Tank Corps had taken the Villers–Bretonneux incident to heart. A vital feature of the Vickers Medium which gave encouragement to the RTC radicals was the fairly wide radius of action, of up to 130 miles. The Vickers Mediums Mark II, all built between 1924 and 1927, contained several improvements and had armour which could resist all contemporary small arms and machine guns.[52]

In addition to the Vickers Mediums, the RTC had, during the 1920s, several types of armoured car and a small number of "tankettes". The tankette concept was pioneered by Martel, who had gone back to the Royal Engineers after the war rather than remaining with the Tank Corps, but who remained fascinated with mechanization. His initial idea seems to have been to produce a very small, very cheap machine. This could be widely distributed to the infantry. It would be inconspicuous and would support them in the assault by rushing machine guns forward.[53] Martel produced a home-made, one-man machine of this type in a workshop at his house in Camberley in 1925. A two-man version called the Morris-Martel was developed from it. Eight of these and eight of a similar vehicle known as the Carden-Loyd were ordered by the War Office, not as machine gun carriers for the infantry, but as reconnaissance machines for the Experimental Mechanical Force which was established on Salisbury Plain in 1927.[54]

While Fuller's published visions of future war provided publicity and propaganda for the RTC, he seems to have been less important in pointing the way to practical experiment and organizational development than Colonel George Lindsay. From 1924 Lindsay began advocating the setting up of a "properly organized Mechanical Force" which would consist of aircraft, armoured cars, fast tanks, motorized artillery, motorized mortars and motorized machine guns. He believed that "a comparatively small but properly . . . proportioned force of this nature could pin to its ground indefinitely a division of all arms as presently constituted".[55]

The time was not ripe in 1924 to put this vision into effect. Lindsay's post as Chief Instructor did not in itself carry very much

weight outside the RTC and under Cavan the Army had a conservative ethos. The advent of General Sir George Milne as his
successor in February 1926 created a much more favourable atmosphere for experiment. Born in 1866 in Aberdeen, he had entered the Royal Artillery in 1885. He had participated in Kitchener's
Sudan campaign of 1898, and in the South African War. During
the First World War he had served on the Salonika front from
January 1916, commanding the whole British force there for the
last two years of the war. "Uncle George", as he was widely and
affectionately known, was himself by no means a radical and was
constantly aware that he was trying to run an army on a shoe-
string. He was, however, very much open to new ideas and, apparently at the instigation of Liddell Hart, appointed Fuller as his
Military Assistant.[56]

With a tank enthusiast at the right hand of the CIGS, Lindsay,
who took the War Office post of Inspector RTC in 1926, was able
to revive his experimental mechanical force proposal with much
greater hope of practical result. On 15 May that year he submitted
to Milne through Fuller a 62-page memorandum with the rather
pompous title: "Suggestions Regarding the Best Means of Rendering the Tank Corps in Particular and the Army in General More
Suited to the Probable Requirements of Future Warfare". Lindsay,
of course, argued that the future lay with armoured mobility rather
than with "traditional infantry and cavalry formations". Starved
of funds as it was, the Army had to make a choice between man
power and weapon power. Lindsay favoured increased weapon
power to be concentrated in mechanized formations which would
require relatively few troops. He formally recommended that the
General Staff institute a series of experiments with a "Mechanical
Force".[57] Milne commented: "I agree fundamentally with the writer,
but on some points his zeal has outrun his discretion. But Colonel
Lindsay is on the right lines and we have to decide how to trans-
late his ideas into action."[58]

Within the War Office a tussle developed over the precise composition of the force. The officer initially charged with working
this out was the Deputy Director of Staff Duties (DDSD) Colonel
E.O. Lewin. Lewin wanted to include:

1 Tank Battalion
2 Armoured Car Companies
1 Special Reconnaissance Company

1 Field Brigade R.A.
3 Infantry Battalions
1 RE Unit
1 Signal Unit

Lewin had some good ideas. The inclusion of a Special Reconnaissance Company of motor-cyclists made sense since motor-cycles
could be faster and have a better cross-country performance than
any other type of machine, and the notion of equipping part of the
close support artillery brigade with the experimental self-propelled
Birch gun was distinctly progressive. Lewin was also right to want
to include a substantial amount of motorized infantry in the force,
though three infantry battalions to only one tank battalion was
certainly excessive. Lewin was also intending to include a cavalry
regiment which would man both the armoured car companies and
the motor-cycle company.[59] Lewin was clearly concerned that
groups other than the RTC should become involved in the process
of mechanization and wanted to transfer to a cavalry regiment
armoured cars to be taken from an RTC battalion which would
be converted to tanks.

Lindsay, on the other hand, was utterly opposed to the transfer
of any fighting vehicles to the cavalry and wanted no infantry as
such in the Mechanical Force. He did want a battalion of specially
trained machine gunners, but he strongly resisted the inclusion of
any conventionally armed and organized infantry battalions even
if these were to be motorized. "I am very much opposed", Lindsay
commented:

> to the mere rearming of existing units of either Infantry or Cavalry
> with mechanized fighting vehicles or even Machine Guns.
> If we start doing this we shall merely make our future army more
> complicated than ever.
> The real stumbling block in any reform or reorganization is the
> present regimental system by which our army is divided up into
> innumerable small packets each with different traditions and ideas.
> I feel that to perpetuate this in the new arm is only asking for
> trouble.
> We must face this matter now, decide generally the form that the
> the Army of the future is going to take and work towards it gradually.
> . . . experience teaches us that at the beginning of any new move-
> ment it is necessary to concentrate all the effort in one body.
> Therefore I am averse, at any rate for the present, of [*sic*]

complicating Tank Development by the allocation of Mechanical Fighting Machines to any unit outside the RTC. All efforts should be concentrated in the RTC in order that the concentrated experience contained in that corps may be used to the best effect and that dispersion of effort may not lead to waste of money time and brains.[60]

The only exception Lindsay was prepared to make to his rule against armoured fighting vehicles outside the RTC was the artillery. Lindsay expected in the long run to see the development of what he called "Artillery Tanks" (armoured self-propelled guns), to provide close fire support to the RTC's tanks. For the time being Lindsay was prepared to allow the former to be under the control of the Royal Artillery.[61]

Lindsay's approach had two main weaknesses. One was political. Most Army officers were not opposed to mechanization as such, but the ambition of the RTC, which flowed so naked and unabashed from Lindsay's pen, was bound to generate the gravest suspicion. The claims which Lindsay was making appeared designed to give all the best opportunities to his own very young Corps and to offer the older arms little but drastic cuts. The other weakness was tactical. At this stage in the evolution of his military thinking Lindsay, like Fuller, vastly underrated the need for infantry within a mechanized force and was already tending to overestimate what tanks and armoured cars could achieve on their own. This tendency in the thought of RTC radicals became more advanced immediately after the Experimental Mechanical Force trials.

Lindsay, with Fuller's help, to a large extent won the debate on the composition of the Experimental Mechanical Force. Both sides seem to have regarded the Force as being a model for the future of the Army, hence the argument's intensity. Whereas the Director of Staff Duties (DSD's) department saw the Experimental Force as a miniature prototype for an all-arms mechanized division, Lindsay and Fuller saw it primarily as an armoured fighting vehicle force with a minimum of supporting arms and services, the whole tightly under the control of the RTC. Lindsay's victory was confirmed by Milne at the beginning of June 1926. Milne explicitly endorsed the primacy of the RTC in this experiment. He stated that he did not want a prototype mechanized division but a small force consisting primarily of armoured fighting vehicles. He attempted to allay the fears of his colleagues in the War Office by assuring them that he did not "propose that the RTC should swallow the Army". But at the same time he indicated that, "To begin with no infantry will be required in the Experimental Unit." He also excluded the cavalry. "I consider Colonel Lindsay's ideas are very sound", he remarked, "and though at the present moment they are too ambitious I want everything done to put them into practice as soon as possible."[62]

It was decided that the Experimental Mechanical Force should be established at Tidworth in order to take advantage of the relatively wide open space of Salisbury Plain. The Force was to come under the control of 3rd Division commanded by Major-General John Burnett-Stuart. Burnett-Stuart was a complex individual who, as we shall see, did not in practice always help the cause of the development of mechanized forces.[63] He certainly regarded himself as a progressive, however, and argued in a letter to the War Office that:

> It is no use just handing [the Experimental Mechanical Force] over to an ordinary Divisional Commander like myself. You must connect directly with it as many enthusiastic experts and visionaries as you can; it doesn't matter how wild their views are if only they have a touch of the divine fire. I will apply the commonsense of advanced middle age.[64]

Perhaps Burnett-Stuart's advice proved critical. Not only did the tank enthusiasts dictate the form the experimental formation would take, the most famous of them was selected to take charge of it. On 7 March 1927 the Secretary of State for War, Sir Laming Worthington Evans announced to Parliament that the experimental force was to be placed "under the command of an officer who has made a special study of mechanized warfare", a reference to Fuller.[65] By that time the commitment of the War Office to mechanization had been made public in a rather dramatic way. On 13 November 1926 the General Staff held a demonstration of the Army's mechanized vehicles for the benefit of the Cabinet and Dominion Prime Ministers attending an Imperial Conference. According to Liddell Hart the entertainment concluded with:

> the presentation of a future battle compressed into a small space for the benefit of the eminent spectators who in a double sense formed the objective . . . The advance was led by midget reconnaissance tanks and the heavy tanks delivered the assault covered by the fire of the self-propelled guns, while aircraft dived out of the skies in a

synchronized swoop on the defender's position. Infantry machine gunners in armoured carriers followed close by the tanks to take over the conquered ground.[66]

The demonstration of 13 November 1926, followed by the statement to Parliament in March 1927, should have left little doubt of the seriousness of the CIGS's intention to establish a Mechanized Force. Yet in one of the oddest episodes in British military history between the two world wars – usually known as the "Tidworth Affair" – this good faith was dramatically and rather publicly challenged both by Fuller and by Liddell Hart who offered Fuller support in the *Daily Telegraph*.[67]

Fuller's period of service as Milne's Military Assistant may not have been entirely without friction. This may have contributed to Milne's decision to send Fuller on what amounted to a fact-finding mission to India on the applicability of armoured fighting vehicles to Indian conditions in October 1926 while the General Staff was still trying to get Treasury approval for items of expenditure necessary to the establishment of the Experimental Mechanical Force. (Tidworth, for example, lacked sheds to accommodate the vehicles.)[68] Fuller's mission to India, however, was of vital long-term importance. If the Government of India was not persuaded to accept mechanization, the process was bound to be seriously delayed in Britain for, in peacetime, the Army at home was often considered little more than a depot for India. There is, moreover, no solid evidence that Milne's opinion of Fuller had declined and on 18 December, when Fuller was back in Britain, Milne told him that he was to command the Mechanical Force.[69]

On Christmas Eve 1926 Fuller received a letter from the Military Secretary announcing that he had been appointed to command 7th Infantry Brigade. He was apparently surprised by this and enquired what it meant. He was told that the Experimental Force was only a temporary formation and that his posting had to be linked to something more definitely established. He went to Tidworth in February to investigate the position more fully and discovered that he was to be in charge of the Tidworth Garrison as well as 7th Infantry Brigade. The Experimental Mechanical Force was to be composed of units under the command of Major-General Burnett-Stuart as GOC 3rd Division and would be assembled only for exercises in summer and early autumn.[70] All this should have been predictable to an officer of Fuller's experience and should have been quite manageable by him. During the periods when he was required to direct the exercises of the Experimental Force it should have been possible for him to delegate his more routine duties and everyone would have expected him to have done so.

Fuller, however, apparently nervous at the responsibility he was being offered, made demands on Milne for extra help – specifically for an extra staff captain and a short-hand typist. Milne, who clearly believed the resources Fuller had already been allocated were adequate to his task, told him not to be silly.[71] Fuller then wrote to Burnett-Stuart to get the latter's support in procuring more help from Milne. He received a sensible though rather unsympathetic response. Fuller, Burnett-Stuart wrote, was not "being invited to tie a wet towel round [his] head and evolve a new military heaven and new earth". Burnett-Stuart was looking forward to having Fuller under his command but did not think that he should harass the CIGS over details.[72]

Fuller ignored Burnett-Stuart's advice. After renewing his request to Milne for extra help and not receiving a favourable reply, Fuller tendered the resignation of his commission, indicating that "it would be fraudulent on my part to fill an appointment which in no way resembled the one made public by the Secretary of State" (in the announcement of 3 March). He was eventually persuaded to withdraw the resignation and his friend Major-General Edmund Ironside offered him a job as GS01 of 2nd Division, which he accepted.[73] Fuller had, however, thrown away a chance personally to command the Experimental Mechanical Force, still regarded with some justification as a milestone in the history of warfare, and had done his career great damage.

Historians who have examined the Tidworth Affair have generally concluded that it has to be explained at least partly in terms of Fuller's highly strung temperament.[74] Fuller had not been in command of troops for some twenty years, having spent most of his career in staff jobs. He appears to have doubted his own capacity to adjust adequately to a command appointment, particularly one which was in his own eyes so momentous. He had written to Liddell Hart regarding the appointment on 7 January 1927 indicating that, "I am by no means overjoyed as it is a first day of creation show and I am not in a position to emulate the

Almighty." He actually regretted leaving the War Office: "I like this monastery, it is so peaceful and absurd."[75] While Liddell Hart was flattered by pro-mechanization officers, notably Martel, that his journalism had saved the Experimental Force[76] it does not seem likely that the General Staff seriously contemplated dropping it. The experiment had been given a good deal of advance publicity and it would have been ridiculous to have done so had there been no real intention to proceed.

In April 1927 Brigadier R.J. Collins was selected to replace Fuller as both 7th Infantry Brigade and Experimental Mechanical Force commander. Collins was an infantryman with a good service record, reasonable brains and an energetic approach to the task. He had, however, no prior experience of commanding tanks or armoured cars and was not regarded by the RTC officers under his command as an inspirational leader. Indeed, according to Liddell Hart, Collins was so cautious that RTC officers joked that the Force's motto was the same as the banker's, "No advance without security".[77]

The Force was officially formed on 1 May and consisted of a medium tank battalion, a battalion of armoured cars and tankettes, a motorized machine gun battalion mounted in Crossley-Kegresse half-tracks, a field artillery brigade, a light artillery battery and a field engineering company. An RAF Army Co-operation Squadron took part in some exercises and a bomber and fighter squadron also co-operated occasionally. After individual unit training in the earlier part of the summer, the Force's collective training commenced on 19 August. Collins's performance was judged harshly by the RTC radicals but his practical difficulties were immense. The Force comprised numerous distinct types of vehicle, all with somewhat different mobility characteristics. In order to cope with this, Collins divided it into three groups: the Fast Group comprising two armoured car companies, two types of tankette and occasionally some light artillery; the Medium Group included the machine gun battalion and an engineer company; and the Slow Group contained the medium tank battalion and the field artillery brigade. The designations of the three groups were according to their road not their cross-country speeds and early exercises consisted largely of road marches. Inevitably the operational mobility of the Force as a whole would often be determined by its slowest component. Collins calculated that in a day's movement the Fast

Group was capable of 100 miles, the Medium Group 50 miles but the Slow Group only 30 miles.[78]

Milne himself visited the Experimental Force on 8 September and gave an address praising its work in the strongest terms while reassuring the older arms, including the cavalry, that they would still be required for the foreseeable future. Milne pointed out that for the previous thirty or forty years there had been what he called "a gradual stabilization of the battlefield", caused by machine guns, barbed wire and other defensive measures. The Mechanized Force, which Milne rechristened (not altogether accurately) the Armoured Force, had demonstrated the means to overcome this stagnation, to restore the art of generalship and to allow war to be more than indecisive mutual slaughter. Milne went on to predict that in the long run an armoured division would be established in the British Army.[79]

The Force's training for the 1927 season culminated in a major mock battle in September. Known as Eastland for this exercise, the Force was pitted against 3rd Division, an infantry formation, supported by a brigade of horsed cavalry (Westland). Both sides had air support. In order to give plenty of room for manoeuvre the 2 forces started some 35 miles apart: Eastland from Micheldever in Hampshire, Westland from Heytesbury in Wiltshire. Westland's objective was to take the high ground around Andover. Eastland was trying to stop them. The exercise began well for Eastland. The Fast Group, boldly commanded by Frederick Pile, covered nearly 40 miles, evaded enemy cavalry patrols and seized bridges enabling the rest of the Eastland force to cross the major rivers in the area. Though the Eastland forces suffered some losses from enemy bombing, the armoured cars of the Fast Group were able to strike the head of the Westland column on the Chittern road bringing the column to a halt. The Westland column was then attacked by low-flying aircraft and subjected to a flank assault by the tanks.[80]

That night the Eastland force went into laager – a drill which Collins had devised and which the force had frequently rehearsed. Overnight the Westland force stole a march. This was largely owing to a major problem which had influenced all the collective training of the Experimental Mechanical Force – poor communications. Radios suitable for mounting in armoured fighting vehicles had yet to be developed and that night Eastland scouting parties, in armoured cars and tankettes, which had spotted the Westland move, relied on a despatch rider to get the message back and his machine broke down. The result was that by the time Collins was aware of the situation half of the Westland Force was over the River Avon. A part of the Westland force was able to arrive on the objective the following day and in that sense Westland was judged to have won the exercise though the Westland troops on the objective were enveloped and under heavy counter-attack.[81]

The Experimental Mechanical Force exercises of 1927 aroused considerable interest in foreign armies. The Germans observed them and wrote about them but, banned from having tanks by the Treaty of Versailles, were not yet able to copy them. The United States Army flattered the British General Staff in the sincerest way, initiating their own experiments along the same lines.[82] That autumn and the following winter articles appeared in all the main British military journals dealing with various aspects of the experiment and lectures were given on the subject in both military and civilian institutions. Relatively little of what was written or said was revolutionary in its tone. A talk given by Collins himself to the Royal Artillery Institution (a very prestigious military forum) in December 1927 was extremely cautious, emphasizing the unresolved problems of mechanized formations rather than their potential to transform war. He was especially concerned with the vulnerability of armoured fighting vehicles to anti-tank guns and artillery.[83]

Of senior officers, Burnett-Stuart struck the most positive note in the discussions. In a lecture at the University of London, on 8 March 1928, he indicated that tanks should no longer be regarded as an infantry support weapon. They were now "a principal not merely an assistant".[84] The official General Staff evaluation of the exercises in an Army training memorandum of spring 1928, however, criticized a lack of co-ordination between the arms within the Experimental Mechanized Force and especially a failure to secure proper fire support before assaulting positions. This criticism was an intelligent and probably a valid one. The training memorandum was, however, at least as concerned to reassure the older arms as it was to stress the potency of the mechanized force:

We must not allow the threat of action by a mechanized enemy to upset all our preconceived notions of war. Given an infantry anti-tank weapon and provided we have a proper conception of how to handle our artillery and provided, futher, that we [know how] to use our reconnaissance units, aeroplanes, armoured cars, etc, there is no reason why the presence of a mechanized force should strike terror into formations and commanders.[85]

The training of the "Armoured Force", as it was now known, recommenced in the spring of 1928. But despite demonstrations laid on for students of the Army Staff College, for visitors from the Indian Army and for MPs,[86] the Force aroused much less interest in 1928 than it had done the previous year. The RTC radicals themselves were becoming bored and frustrated with the experiments – irritated with attempts to make the motley collection of vehicles (15 different types in a force totalling 280) work together effectively and continuing to lack confidence in Collins. To make matters worse many of the exercises that year were designed, perhaps not unreasonably, to test the Force's limits and put it on its mettle.[87]

At the end of the 1928 training season the Armoured Force was effectively closed down, a decision announced to Parliament on 27 November. Liddell Hart portrayed this as a triumph for reactionary interests within the Army.[88] Certainly one conservative officer, General Sir Archibald Amar Montgomery-Massingberd, the General Officer Commanding (GOC) Southern Command, had attempted to use influence with Milne to have the experiment terminated. Though he adopted a much more positive attitude to armoured forces in the mid-1930s, Montgomery-Massingberd still defended the stance he took in 1928 in his unpublished memoirs:

When I took over the Southern Command I found the "Armoured Force" already in existence under Brigadier R.J. Collins and doing good work as an experimental organization . . . After watching it at training . . . against . . . the other arms I came to the conclusion that, although invaluable for experimental purposes, it was definitely affecting adversely the Cavalry and Infantry. What should have been done was to gradually mechanize the Cavalry Division and the Infantry Division and not to introduce an entirely new formation based on the medium Tank. Nor was it sound to pit the new formation, with its modern armament, against the older formations, in order to prove its superiority. What was wanted was to use the newest weapons to improve the mobility and firepower of the old formations . . . What I wanted in brief was evolution and not revolution.[89]

Montgomery-Massingberd communicated to Milne his opinion that "as it appears likely that at any rate during the first six months of the next war we shall have to fight with Cavalry and Infantry, it is important that we should continue to study the problem of supporting these two arms with tanks".[90] This line was endorsed by other senior officers.[91] But the feeling appears to have been fairly general that the Armoured Force experiment had run its course and that little more could be learned from further trials with a force of essentially the same composition and equipment. There was little opposition even from the RTC radicals to a shift in the nature of experiment for the next training season.

Milne was not in fact ending radical experimentation but merely ordering a one-year pause. For 1929 he intended to establish an experimental brigade composed of a battalion of light tanks and tankettes and three battalions of infantry. Because light tanks and tankettes were in such short supply he proposed "to disperse the Experimental Armoured Force for one year. During the year 1930/ 31 I hope to be in a position to form the 1st Armoured Brigade as a permanent formation of the Army".[92] An experimental Tank Brigade did in fact undergo trials in 1931 though it was not formally established as a permanent formation until November 1933.[93] A pause for thought to absorb the lessons of the trials of 1927–28 was probably no bad thing. What was ultimately more serious was that both the RTC radicals and Liddell Hart, their principal spokesman in the media, tended to learn the wrong lessons, moving towards the idea of all-tank rather than balanced all-arms formations.

In an article published in the Journal of the Royal United Service Institute in November 1928 Liddell Hart suggested that while the 1927–28 experiments had provided useful experience in driving and maintaining vehicles, they had demonstrated something which should have been obvious all along, that armoured and unarmoured vehicles could not work together in the same formation. He believed that a future armoured force should consist very largely "of light tanks such as the new Carden Loyd, with a proportion of 'gun tanks' for its extra fire support, and perhaps a sprinkling of six-wheeled armoured cars as its long-range feelers". A "true armoured force", Liddell Hart believed, would be able to avoid the obstacles which would require infantry co-operation. Liddell Hart was completely opposed to the inclusion of an infantry battalion and did not even consider including a battalion of specialized machine gun troops as in Lindsay's original conception of the Experimental Mechanical Force. The most he was prepared to allow was the inclusion of a company-sized force of "land marines" in a brigade-sized armoured formation.[94] Liddell Hart's post-Second World War claims to have been superior to Fuller in seeing the need for close co-operation between tanks and mechanized infantry were, as already indicated, largely, if not wholly, spurious.[95]

The job of formulating the lessons of the 1927–28 experiment in a more official format was given to Lieutenant-Colonel Charles Broad. In 1927–31 Broad was serving as Deputy Director of Staff Duties at the War Office. During this period Broad was responsible for producing two handbooks: *Mechanized and Armoured Formations* which appeared in 1929 and an updated version: *Modern Formations*, published in 1931. The 1929 booklet, written in consultation with George Lindsay, was known in the Army as the "Purple Book", "Purple Primer" or "Mauve Manual" because of the colour of its binding.[96] Though they were official General Staff booklets and were apparently disseminated fairly widely in the Army, these works were essentially embodiments of the thought of the RTC *avant-garde*. Liddell Hart's writings after the Second World War made much of their progressive nature. The modern reader is just as likely to be struck, however, by their neglect of some critical areas of mechanized warfare and by their propagation of false dogma on a number of important issues.

Broad envisaged the Army being divided into "Mobile Troops" on the one hand and "Combat Troops" on the other (a false dichotomy in itself). The "Mobile Troops" would consist of cavalry divisions or brigades and light armoured divisions or brigades. The "Combat Troops" would include infantry divisions and "medium armoured brigades". The light armoured brigade which Broad envisaged comprised:

> Headquarters and signal section
> Two or three battalions of light tanks
> One close support tank battery
> One anti-aircraft armoured battery

The medium armoured brigade was to be made up as follows:

> Headquarters and signal section
> One medium tank battalion

Two light tank battalions
Two close support tank batteries
One anti-aircraft armoured battery[97]

Though Broad mentioned the possibility of having light armoured divisions, he discussed neither the roles nor the composition of such formations. Medium and light armoured brigades were the largest formations he dealt with. Weaknesses are apparent in the structure of both which would have severely limited their effectiveness in sustained independent operations. No infantry was to be included in either. Broad did not even make the concession which Lindsay had earlier accepted of including machine gunners. He also intended to leave out field artillery as such. Fire support would be provided by "close support tanks" – tanks equipped with a relatively large calibre, low velocity gun for firing high explosive shell instead of the normal medium tank armament of a low calibre, relatively high velocity armour piercing gun for firing solid shot. Broad believed that armoured brigades would not normally require the support of conventional field artillery unless required to attack a prepared position and he seems to have regarded such missions as the exception rather than the rule. In the "Purple Primer" the RTC was moving away from the concept of the all-arms mechanized formation. Broad saw future armoured brigades consisting entirely of tanks, albeit tanks of a number of different types.[98]

The discussion of the missions of armoured formations in Broad's 1929 booklet was far from profound. The functions of light armoured brigades, as Broad described them, were essentially those of late nineteenth-century cavalry: reconnaissance, screening, flank protection and occasional flank attacks. Medium armoured brigades were expected to carry out armoured raids and to work closely with infantry divisions in the offensive. The concept of the deep, decisive penetration by armoured formations into the enemy's rear was absent from this booklet and there was no discussion of the employment of armour for counter-penetration or counter-stoke. The whole subject of the clash between armoured forces was dismissed in a mere two sentences:

The presence of considerable bodies of tanks on both sides in a suitable theatre of war is likely to cause considerable modification in operations generally.

Such formations do not, however, exist at the moment, and as the subject is therefore purely theoretical it will not be discussed further in these pages.[99]

In fairness to the British General Staff of the late 1920s it must be pointed out that no one thought of this booklet as definitive. It was an account of a process of doctrinal development still in progress and a basis for further thought and discussion. The 1931 up-date did represent something of an advance. It briefly discussed the possibility of having a "Mobile Division of say one embussed infantry brigade, two tank brigades and a due proportion of divisional troops". But despite suggesting that it have a significant infantry component, Broad appears to have seen the Mobile Division's roles as similar to those of the horsed cavalry division of the BEF in 1914: acting as a covering force for the infantry divisions and possibly to make strikes against the enemy's flanks or rear if they became exposed. The penetration of the enemy's front was not contemplated. There was an encouraging passage in which Broad indicated an important role for arms other than the RTC in mechanized operations:

Owing to the limited manpower available armoured fighting units cannot carry out all the tasks required from a mobile army.
Riflemen and machine-gunners in buses, mechanized artillery etc. are also required and these must be able to travel at the same pace as the armoured fighting vehicles.[100]

The point is not developed, however, and it might well have been thrown in as an all-arms sop to the infantry and artillery while the main thrust of the argument was in an all-tank direction. Again Broad did not discuss in detail any formation larger than a brigade and the armoured brigades were all-tank, all-RTC affairs. Even in the 1931 booklet there is no concept of a deep, decisive penetration through the enemy's front by a large mechanized force. The use of mechanized formations as an operational or strategic reserve was still not discussed and combat between armoured formations was totally omitted.

Broad provided some justification for not examining operations by mechanized forces larger than a brigade by indicating that a general reduction in the size of armies was to be expected. In *Modern Formations* he asserted, without producing any evidence and without detailed supporting argument, that airpower had "accelerated the decay of the conception known as the 'nation in arms'" and that for "reasons economic, industrial and military, armies will be small".[101] This wishful thinking was an important part of the mindset of the British tank radicals. Fuller, while not being certain that conscription would entirely disappear on the Continent, believed that the outcome of future wars would be determined by small, all-professional, all-mechanized forces.[102] Hobart also doubted whether it would be possible for mass armies to manoeuvre in the face of airpower and thus seems to have expected that small, agile armoured forces could have a determining influence.[103]

A Tank Brigade was established as an experimental formation for the training season of 1931, under Charles Broad's command. The Brigade consisted of three mixed battalions of medium and light tanks and a single battalion equipped with Carden Loyd machine gun carriers which served as light tanks and were used in the reconnaissance role. It was an all-RTC formation, devoid of other arms. The main challenge which Broad set himself was to find effective means of command and control. The Brigade was still dependent to a considerable extent on signalling using flags. Only a small minority of tanks had radio. Within a fortnight of its assembly, however, the brigade was able to put on for the Army Council a convincing display of movement in formation under the control of Broad's voice on the radio as received in battalion and company commanders' vehicles. The Brigade managed to stay in formation even when passing through a dense fog.[104]

The most complete embodiment of the radical trends in British thought on mechanized warfare in the period immediately after the first Tank Brigade experiment was Fuller's *Lectures On FSR III*, published in 1932. FSR stood for Field Service Regulations, the Army's general tactical manual. Volume II of the Field Service Regulations dealt with operations and in 1931 Fuller had published a collection of lectures he had given the previous year on this part of the current manual.[105] In 1932 he published a set of "lectures" on a manual (yet to be written) dealing with operations between mechanized formations. Assessing *Lectures on FSR III* fairly is difficult because Fuller does not always define his terms clearly. For example in 1932 Fuller claimed that: "To combine tanks and infantry is tantamount to yoking a tractor to a draft horse. To ask them to operate together under fire is equally absurd." But in a footnote in the 1943 edition Fuller explained, "When I wrote this I had in mind infantry as commonly understood - namely as footsoldiers whose *raison d'être* is to fight their like. Motorized infantry equipped with anti-tank weapons are not infantry, they are anti-tank mounted foot".[106] If, however, we decide to ignore this sort of retrospective casuistry, the basic elements in the argument can be summarized simply enough. The petrol engine had produced a complete revolution in warfare. Skill and mobility were going to replace the immobile bulk of the armies of 1914–18.

> Whereas in the World War millions of infantry were mobilized, in the next war it is highly improbable that any nation will be able to put into the field more than a few thousand tanks and as these machines can move far more rapidly than infantry, in order to be in a position to seize the initiative on the outbreak of war, mechanized forces will have to be kept fully mobilized during peace time ... for fighting purposes highly trained professional armies will replace the present-day short service conscript masses. This does not necessarily mean that conscription will disappear, but that the conscripted man will become what may be called a soldier of the "second degree" – that is, a second grade fighter; one who will occupy, organize and hold the areas conquered by the mechanized forces. From this it may be predicted that in the main, those soldiers will be a combination of pioneer and gendarme.[107]

Future war would be determined by the "power of aircraft to strike at the civil will, the power of mechanized forces to strike at the military will, and the power of motorized guerrillas to broadcast dismay and confusion". The concept of the motorized guerrilla was a very odd one. Because civilian society was becoming motorized, Fuller argued, a motorized irregular soldier would replace the light infantry irregular of the past. But Fuller did not manage either to produce a very convincing picture of the operations of motor guerrillas or show clearly how these would relate to tank operations.[108]

Operations in the open field would, in Fuller's opinion, be totally dominated by tanks. "To combine tanks and infantry is tantamount to yoking a tractor to a draught horse. To ask them to operate together under fire is equally absurd ... In battles between armoured machines infantry can play no part worth their risk".[109]

Infantry would be confined to actions in mountainous or thickly wooded country, in which Fuller thought tanks could not operate effectively, and to police and pioneer work, and the protection of lines of communication. He appears to have given little consideration to the problem of fighting in built up areas.

Fuller did not believe that indirect fire artillery could play much of a role in armoured battles:

> In present day fighting the eighteen pounder and 4.5 in howitzer cover the infantry attack from a distance, and depend upon indirect laying. In the tank battle, except when smoke shells are used, such support is not practical; for it is out of the question to attempt to render assistance by firing into a melay [*sic*] of tanks, some of which may be moving at between 20 and 40 miles the hour.[110]

For the provision of smoke in front of advancing tanks and for fire support in attacking fortified positions Fuller recommended a "howitzer tank" firing a heavier round than the 3-pdr anti-tank weapon fitted in current British tanks.[111] Whether or not the "howitzer tank" itself would employ indirect fire is not completely clear from Fuller's wording but it seems that it would not. While Fuller did see a role for anti-tank guns in protecting a movable base of operations for the tanks, he does not seem to have visualized close co-operation in mobile battles between tanks and anti-tank guns of the sort which became an essential feature of German tactics in the Western Desert in the Second World War.

But while tanks would dominate in mobile operations in open country, Fuller was worried about carefully constructed anti-tank defences, laid out in depth. He was not sure how they ought to be tackled but thought that "either they will have to be demolished by artillery or rendered untenable by gas attack. Of these the second will, in all probability, prove the more speedy." In fact Fuller was not sure that a really well organized anti-tank defence could be broken through. He was willing to concede that if both sides constructed such defences complete stalemate on land might result. In that case offensive operations would be "translated to the air, every effort being made to demoralize the enemy by attacking his cities, industrial centres and civil population. Whereas mobile warfare means attack on armed forces, static warfare can lead to but one end – attack on the civil will".[112] These remarks cast doubt on the validity of much of the rest of the book and the profound doubts which they display provide an important clue to Fuller's loss of interest in armoured warfare in the mid-1930s.[113]

Fuller's *Lectures on FSR III* was his last major theoretical treatment of armoured warfare. It has been presented as a very individual, highly original work.[114] In fact Fuller shared several basic assumptions with other radical tank advocates: armies would get smaller; all-armoured formations were necessary for mobile operations in the open field; the integration of conventional infantry into a mobile, armoured battle and therefore into mechanized formations was extremely problematic, perhaps impossible; conventional artillery had little place in the armoured battle. While *Lectures* does not appear to have been widely read, the influence of these basic assumptions was more considerable and the last three still seem to have exerted a baneful influence on the tactics of British armoured forces in the desert campaigns of 1941 and 1942.[115]

Up to the early 1930s the British believed themselves to be leading the world both in tank design and in the training and tactical handling of armoured formations.[116] This self-congratulation was by no means baseless. The Germans still had only a few prototype tanks and these had to be kept hidden away while the disarmament clauses of the Versailles Treaty were still in force. They had yet produced very little literature of any degree of sophistication on tank use. The Americans had only recently started to imitate British experiments. The Soviets appeared the most serious competitors but at this stage some of their better tanks were developments of Vickers models.[117] Though their leading military thinkers were beginning to develop sophisticated concepts it was very questionable whether their army had the requisite skills to put these into practice.[118] That the British had maintained a lead in this field was particularly creditable in that their army was both small by Continental standards and committed to the garrisoning of a vast Empire which required much soldiering of a routine and pedestrian nature, largely unrelated to the latest technical and doctrinal developments.

But the picture was beginning to darken. A financial crisis was about to strike the British Army which would threaten to paralyse it for several years. A vigorous German rearmament programme would quickly follow the accession of Adolf Hitler to the German chancellorship in January 1933 and this would not be matched in

Britain. These events were beyond the control of the British Army. But another disturbing development cannot be blamed on external circumstances. The views of some of the group of British officers most strongly advocating the development of armoured forces were becoming wayward. They were tending to regard mass armies as things of the past. They favoured small, virtually all-tank formations and they were contemplating independent tank operations without close co-operation with other arms. These were heresies pregnant with danger for the long term.

Notes

1   B.H. Liddell Hart, *The Tanks*, Vol. I (Cassell) 1959, p. 205.
2   On British military intervention in Russia see Michael Kettle, *The Road to Intervention, March to November 1918* (Routledge) 1988, *passim* and *Churchill and the Archangel Fiasco, November 1918–July 1919* (Routledge) 1992, *passim*. On the role of British tanks see Liddell Hart, *op. cit.*, pp. 210–213.
3   On Fuller's proposal see Fuller (DDSD) to Lynden-Bell (DSD) 25 March 1919, Minute 1, and "Proposals towards the formation of a Tank Expeditionary Force", Appendix 9A, PRO WO 32/5685. On the proposal's rejection see same file, minutes 13 and 14.
4   "The Present Distribution and Strength of the British Army in Relation to Its Duties", memorandum by the General Staff, March 1928, PRO WO 32/2823.
5   S. Bidwell and D. Graham, *Fire-Power: British Army Weapons and Theories of War 1904–1945* (Allen and Unwin) 1982, pp. 150–151.
6   J.A.R. Marriot, *Modern England 1885–1945* (Methuen) 1948, pp. 507–509, 538. H. Gordon, *The War Office* (Putnam) 1935, p. 331.
7   "Possibilities of the Next War", Lecture to the RUSI by Major-General Sir Louis C. Jackson, Wednesday 17 December 1919, *RUSI Journal*, Vol. 65, February to November 1920, p. 74.
8   On the post-war fate of the US Tank Corps see D.E. Wilson, *Treat 'em Rough: the Birth of American Armor, 1917–20* (Presidio) 1989, pp. 291–231.
9   On Tank Corps kudos see Haig's extremely laudatory final despatch in J.H. Boraston (ed.) *Sir Douglas Haig's Despatches* (J.M. Dent) 1919, 302. George V became Colonel-in-Chief of the Tank Corps on 17 October 1918. See Stephen Foot, *Three Lives* (Heinemann) 1934, pp. 228–229.
10 During the First World War armoured cars had initially been run

by the RNAS. They were transferred to the Army in the middle of the war, the majority being run by the Machine Gun Corps in "Armoured Motor Batteries", though the Tank Corps also had one battalion equipped with armoured cars on the Western Front in 1918. D. Fletcher, *War Cars, British Armoured Cars in the First World War* (HMSO) 1987, *passim*. After the war not only did the RAF take over the cars in Iraq, but two cavalry regiments, 11th Hussars and 12th Lancers, were issued with armoured cars in 1928–29. D. Crow, *British and Commonwealth Armoured Formations* (1919–46) (Profile) 1971, pp. 2–3. From that time onward the RTC was gradually squeezed out of the armoured car business to make room for the cavalry.

11 On the use of armoured cars in Ireland in the 1919–21 period see PRO WO 32/9539 and PRO WO 32/9541.

12 Liddell Hart, *op. cit.*, pp. 206–209.

13 Army Order No. 369, given at St James's, 18 October 1923. Quoted in Anon, *A Short History of the Royal Tank Corps* (Aldershot) 1938.

14 Liddell Hart, *op. cit.*, p. 226

15 R. Lewin, *Man of Armour, a Study of Lieutenant General Vyvyan Pope CBE, DSO, MC* (Leo Cooper) 1976, pp. 58–59.

16 On Liddell Hart's career the standard works are B. Bond, *Liddell Hart: a Study of His Military Thought* (Cassell) 1977 and J. Mearsheimer, *Liddell Hart and the Weight of History* (Cornell) 1988, *passim*. Neither is uncritical but Bond was handicapped by a close relationship with his subject. Mearsheimer gives the full exposé treatment, undoubtedly necessary in view of the scale of historical deception and distortion for which Liddell Hart was responsible.

17 On Lindsay's role in the development of the Machine Gun Corps see P. Griffith, *Battle Tactics of the Western Front: the British Army's Art of Attack 1916–18* (Yale) 1994, pp. 120–129. On his career as a whole see the obituary in *The Tank*, No. 453, January 1957 and Liddell Hart's assessment in *Dictionary of National Biography* (DNB) 1951–60.

18 For Broad's view of his own career see Broad to Rickard, 23 June 1970, II/3, Broad Papers, LHCMA. See also B. Bond on Broad in DNB 1971–80, pp. 86–87.

19 The Present writer's views on Hobart are presented at somewhat greater length in J.P. Harris, "Sir Percy Hobart: Eclipse and Revival of an Armoured Commander", in B. Bond (ed.) *Fallen Stars* (Brassey's) 1991, pp. 86–106. For a much more favourable treatment see K. Macksey, *Armoured Crusader: a Biography of Major-General Sir Percy Hobart* (Hutchinson) 1968, *passim*. For Hobart's

view of his own contribution see LH 9/28/77, Liddell Hart Papers, LHCMA.

20 K. Macksey on Pile, DNB 1971–80, p. 670.

21 On Liddell Hart's sponsorship of Pile's career see diaries of Lieutenant General Sir Henry Pownall, 30 May, B.J. Bond (ed.) *Chief of Staff*, Vol. I (Leo Cooper) 1972, p. 148.

22 Pownall described Pile as a "creature" (presumably of Liddell Hart and Hore-Belisha): Pownall's diaries, 2 February 1938, Bond, *op. cit.*, p. 131.

23 F.A. Pile, *Ack-Ack* (Harrap) 1949, p. 72 and *passim*.

24 The dangers for historians in not accepting Liddell Hart at his own valuation in works published during his lifetime are discussed in Mearsheimer, *op. cit.*, pp. 208–226.

25 Fuller told Liddell Hart that, "when I make a criticism the Army Council is perturbed. When you make one it is shaken to its roots". "Engagements and Notes", 2 October 1929, LH 11/1929/1b, Liddell Hart Papers, LHCMA.

26 Fuller to Liddell Hart, 25 August 1920, LH 1/302/7 and Liddell Hart to Fuller, 31 January 1922, LH 1/302/13. Liddell Hart to Fuller, 11 March 1928, LH 1/302/128, Liddell Hart Papers, LHCMA.

27 The paucity of Liddell Hart's pre-1939 writings on the employment of armoured forces in relation to the later claims he made for his influence is indicated in Mearsheimer, *op. cit.*, p. 35, n. 8. Books such as *Paris or the Future of War* (Kegan Paul, Trench, Trubner) 1925 and *The Remaking of Modern Armies* (John Murray) 1927, in which Liddell Hart is sometimes thought to have set out a prophetic vision of the future of armoured warfare, contain no more than a few suggestive passages.

28 On Liddell Hart's doubting the offensive power of armoured forces in the later 1930s see, for example, "Talk with Deverell", 29 June 1937, LH 11/1937/56, Liddell Hart Papers, LHCMA.

29 See Broad's comments to K. Macksey quoted in Macksey, *The Tank Pioneers* (Jane's) 1981, pp. 82–83.

30 A summary of Liddell Hart's pro-mechanization journalism is to be found in, "Suggestions and Forecasts: Salient Points from Captain Liddell Hart's Articles in the *Daily Telegraph*, 1925–1934", LH/13/3, Liddell Hart Papers, LHCMA.

31 Sir Laming Worthington-Evans, Secretary of State for War, told the House of Commons on 28 February 1929 that, "We have carried out experiments on a large scale and with such success that we can confidently claim to lead the world not only in our equipment of tanks but also in our ideas as to their use in War", *House of Commons Debates*, 225, 2214–2215.

32 Liddell Hart, *The Tanks*, Vol. I, p. 221.

33 Fuller, "The Application of Recent Developments in Mechanics and other Scientific Knowledge to Preparations and Training for Future War on Land", Gold Medal (Military) Prize Essay for 1919, *RUSI Journal*, Vol. 65, February–November 1920, p. 249.

34 On the effects of crew exhaustion in First World War British tanks see "Supplementary Report, 5th Tank Brigade, 1 September 1918, answer to question 1 of a Tank Corps questionnaire", TCOIV/7, Fuller Papers, LHCMA.

35 On German doctrine on tank gunnery see H. Guderian, *Achtung Panzer!* (English translation by C. Duffy of a German text originally published in 1937, Arms and Armour) 1992, p. 183.

36 On tanks "crossing the T" on manoeuvre in 1930, see Liddell Hart, *The Tanks*, Vol. I, p. 281.

37 J.F.C. Fuller, Gold Medal Prize Essay 1919, *RUSI Journal*, Vol. 65, February to November 1920, p. 250.

38 *ibid.*, p. 254.

39 Martel, "A Tank Army", undated but claimed by Martel to be November 1916, TS/9, Fuller Papers, LHCMA.

40 J.F.C. Fuller, Gold Medal Prize Essay 1919, *RUSI Journal*, February to November 1920, p. 261.

41 *ibid.*, p. 262.

42 *ibid.*, pp. 264–265.

43 See, for example, the General Staff's comments on "the advocates in the country of an extreme degree of mechanization who would like to see the infantry abolished and replaced by men in fighting machines", DRC 14, paras 93–96, 28 February 1934, PRO CAB 16/109.

44 J.F.C. Fuller, *Memoirs of an Unconventional Soldier* (Nicholson and Watson) 1936, pp. 371–372 and 420.

45 Fuller, "The Development of Sea Warfare on Land and its Influence on Future Naval Operations", Wednesday 11 February 1920, *RUSI Journal*, Vol. 65, p. 281.

46 *ibid.*, p. 291.

47 On Liddell Hart's "becoming a disciple" of Fuller see J. Luvaas, *The Education of an Army: British Military Thought 1815–1940* (Chicago) 1964, p. 382. Liddell Hart, "The Development of the 'New Model' Army: Suggestions on a Progressive but Gradual Mechanicalisation", *Army Quarterly*, Vol. 9, pp. 37–50. Extract quoted in H. Winton, *To Change an Army, General Sir John Burnett-Stuart and British Armoured Doctrine 1927–1938* (Brassey's) 1988, p. 21.

48 The largely spurious nature of Liddell Hart's claim to have been more prescient than Fuller about the need for mechanized infantry

in armoured formations is indicated in B.H. Reid, *J.F.C. Fuller: Military Thinker* (Macmillan) 1987, p. 164.

49 "The Tactics of the Attack as Affected by the Speed and Circuit of the Medium D Tank", 24 May 1918, B62, Fuller Papers, Tank Museum.

50 D. Fletcher, *Mechanised Force* (HMSO) 1991, pp. 2–7.

51 *ibid.*, pp. 7–8.

52 *ibid.*, p. 5.

53 See Martel, "Small Tanks and Cavalry", written for the *Cavalry Journal* in June 1927, LH 1/492/1925–48 and "Design of Tankettes", LH 9/28/74, Liddell Hart Papers, LHCMA.

54 Martel, "One and Two-Man Tanks" from *Royal Tank Corps Journal* (1992), LH 9/28/74, Liddell Hart Papers, LHCMA.

55 "The Organization and Employment of a Mechanical Force, a memorandum from Lieutenant Colonel Lindsay", 25 April 1924, LH 15/12/1/2, Liddell Hart Papers, LHCMA. Lindsay's concept was endorsed by Fuller in a lecture to the RUSI on "Progress in the Mechanicalisation of Modern Armies", 19 November 1924, *RUSI Journal*, February 1925. But Fuller does not appear to have originated the idea as suggested in Winton, *op. cit.*, p. 74.

56 A.J. Trythall, *"Boney" Fuller: the Intellectual General* (Cassell) 1977, p. 120.

57 "Suggestions Regarding the Best Means of Rendering the Royal Tank Corps in Particular and the Army in General More Suited to the Probable Requirements of Future Warfare", Branch Memorandum No. 796, 15 May 1926, LH 15/12/4, Liddell Hart Papers, LHCMA.

58 *ibid.*, undated covering note by Milne.

59 "Scheme for Experimental Work with a Mechanical Force", Minute 1A, undated, PRO WO 32/2820.

60 Lindsay's, "Remarks on 'Scheme for Mechanical Force", dated 14 May 1926 (but the date is possibly incorrect as the document contains a reference to an earlier Lindsay paper dated 15 May), para. 5 (a), PRO WO 32/2820.

61 *ibid.*, paras 5 and 6.

62 CIGS to DSD, Minute 2, 1 June 1926, PRO WO 32/2820.

63 A very detailed account of Burnett-Stuart's military career between the wars is to be found in Winton, *op. cit.*, *passim*.

64 Liddell Hart, *The Tanks*, Vol. I, p. 244.

65 *ibid.*, p. 245.

66 *ibid.*, p. 242.

67 Liddell Hart, "An Army Mystery, Is there a Mechanized Force?" *Daily Telegraph*, 22 April 1927, p. 9.

68 Colonel A.F. Thullies (Director of Fortifications and Works) to

Lieutenant General N. Birch (Master General of the Ordnance), 30 June 1926, WO 32/2820.

69 Fuller, *Memoirs*, pp. 431–441.

70 This had been decided the previous summer. Minute 10, 11 June 1926, PRO WO 32/2820.

71 Fuller to Liddell Hart, 7 January 1927, LH 1/302/103, Liddell Hart diary notes, 1 April and 25 April 1927, LH 11/1927/1b, Liddell Hart Papers, LHCMA.

72 Burnett-Stuart to Fuller, 18 February 1927, quoted in Winton, *op. cit.*, p. 77.

73 Liddell Hart's diary notes, 1 April and 25 April 1927, LH 11/1927/ 1b, LHCMA.

74 See for example R. Larson, *The British Army and the Theory of Armoured Warfare, 1918–1940* (University of Delaware), pp. 134– 137 and Trythall, *op. cit.*, pp. 138–144.

75 Fuller to Liddell Hart, 7 January 1927, LH 1/302/103, Liddell Hart Papers, LHCMA.

76 Martel to Liddell Hart, 11 October 1927, LH 1/492, Liddell Hart Papers, LHCMA.

77 Liddell Hart, *The Tanks*, Vol. I, p. 249.

78 *ibid.*, p. 248–249.

79 "Address to the Officers of the Experimental Mechanized Force by the CIGS at Tidworth", 8 September 1927, LH 11/1927/7, Liddell Hart Papers, LHCMA.

80 Fletcher, *Mechanised Force*, p. 62.

81 *ibid.* and Martel, *In the Wake of the Tank: the First Fifteen Years of Mechanization in the British Army* (Sifton Praed) 1931, pp. 159– 163.

82 S. Badsey, "The American Experience of Armour 1919–1953", in J.P. Harris and F.H. Toase, *Armoured Warfare* (Batsford) 1990, pp. 128–130. Liddell Hart, *The Tanks*, Vol. I, p. 255.

83 R.J. Collins, "The Experimental Mechanical Force", *Journal of the Royal Artillery*, Vol. 55, April 1928, pp. 12–26.

84 J. Burnett-Stuart, "The Progress of Mechanization", *Army Quarterly*, No. 16, April 1928, pp. 30–51.

85 "Extracts from Memorandum on Army Training: Collective Training Period, 1927", Section 9, "A Sense of Proportion regarding New Arms and New Weapons", LH 15/3/23, Liddell Hart Papers, LHCMA.

86 See Liddell Hart's articles in *Daily Telegraph*, 6 and 13 July 1928, LH 10/1928/70 and LH 10/1928/72–73, Liddell Hart Papers, LHCMA.

87 Minutes 16 and 5A, "Experimental Armoured Force Report 1928", PRO WO 32/2828.

88 Liddell Hart, *The Tanks*, Vol. I, pp. 260–261.

89 A.A. Montgomery-Massingberd, "The Autobiography of a Gunner", p. 53, M-M 159, Montgomery-Massingberd Papers, LHCMA. Quoted in Winton, *op. cit.*, p. 197.

90 "Experimental Armoured Force Report", 1928, GOC Southern Command to Under Secretary of State, the War Office, 24 November 1928, RH87, RTC:MH.4 (41), Tank Museum.

91 General Sir Walter Braithwaite (Adjutant General) to Milne, 18 December 1928, PRO WO 32/2828.

92 Milne to Secretary of State, 12 November 1928, "Experimental Formations for 1929", PRO WO 32/2825.

93 "Third Report of the Mechanical Warfare Board, covering the Period 1st January, 1931, to 31st December, 1932", p. 8, PRO WO 33/1283.

94 Liddell Hart, "Armoured Forces in 1928", *RUSI Journal*, Vol. 73, November 1928, p. 723.

95 This point is made in Reid, *op. cit.*, pp. 160–161.

96 Liddell Hart, *The Tanks*, Vol. I, p. 268.

97 *Mechanized and Armoured Formations*, 1929, pp. 1–18, 623.438 (41), Tank Museum.

98 *ibid., passim.*

99 *ibid.*, p. 27, section 25, para. 5, iv.

100 *Modern Formations*, 1931, pp. 1–12, 623.438 (41), Tank Museum.

101 *ibid.*, section 8, para. 1 (v), p. 14.

102 J.F.C. Fuller, *Armoured Warfare* (Eyre and Spottiswoode) 1943, p. 11. (The retitled 1943 edition of *Lectures on FSR III* is identical to the original 1932 edition, published by Sifton Praed (of which copies are now quite rare), except for the addition of a new preface and footnotes indicating the relevance of Fuller's ideas to the war then current.)

103 Hobart to Lindsay, 10 November 1933, LH 1/376/5, Liddell Hart Papers, LHCMA.

104 Liddell Hart, *op. cit.*, pp. 286–287 and "Third Report of the Mechanical Warfare Board", p. 8, PRO WO 33/1288.

105 Fuller, *Lectures on FSR II* (Sifton Praed) 1931.

106 Fuller, *Armoured Warfare*, p. 19.

107 *ibid.*, p. 11.

108 Actions by motor guerrillas are discussed in several parts of *Armoured Warfare* but especially in pp. 66–68.

109 *ibid.*, p. 19, 95 and *passim.*

110 *ibid.*, pp. 3–24.

111 *ibid.*, pp. 24–25.

112 *ibid.*, p. 118.

113 This loss of interest is noted in Reid, *op. cit.*, p. 193.

114   *ibid.*, p. 154: "The thinking behind *Lectures on FSR III* was almost entirely Fuller's own. There are no major important influences on his thinking." Surely this is to rate Fuller's individual genius too highly and not to take sufficiently into account an intellectual environment which included Lindsay, Broad and Hobart amongst others.

115   For a German point of view on the influence of British all-tank ideas in the campaign in the Western Desert see Major-General F.W. von Mellenthin, *Panzer Battles* (Oklahoma) 1956, Introduction, p. xv.

116   Worthington-Evans's comments to the House of Commons, 28 February 1929, *House of Commons Debates*, 225, 2214–2215.

117   R. Ogorkiewicz, *Armour* (Stevens and Sons) 1960, pp. 224–225. The Soviet T26 series of tanks was based on the Vickers Six Ton Tank.

118   On the development of Soviet ideas on the employment of armoured forces in the inter-war period see J. Kipp, K. Schulz *et al.*, *Historical Analysis of the Use of Mobile Forces by Russia and the USSR* (Centre for Strategic Technology, Texas A and M University) 1985, pp. 115–157 and C. Dick, "The Operational Employment of Soviet Armour in the Great Patriotic War", in J.P. Harris and F.H. Toase, *op. cit.*, pp. 88–91.

7

Losing the lead: 1931–36

In order to comprehend the development of British thought on armoured forces in the critical period of 1931 to 1936 it is necessary to review some of the objective realities which formed its context and helped to shape it. The year 1931 was one of both economic and political crisis in Great Britain as the effects of the Wall Street crash began to resonate on the eastern side of the Atlantic. Ramsay MacDonald's Labour Government (1929–31) disintegrated as a result of the crisis. One Labour Party faction, led by MacDonald himself, accepted the need for deep public expenditure cuts (some of which were rejected by the rest of the party) and in August 1931 went into coalition with the Conservatives and an element of the Liberal Party, forming a "National Government".[1] Drastic cuts were duly implemented and the Army was hard hit.

The Estimates were cut from £40 to £36.5 million for the financial year 1932/33 and it was not until 1934/35 that they returned to the 1931/32 level. In 1932/33 the sum devoted to tracked vehicles fell to £301,000 from £357,000 the previous year and, as in the case of expenditure on the Army generally, the 1931/32 level was exceeded only in 1934/35. A serious rearmament effort for the Army began significantly later than that for the other two services, being sanctioned by the Cabinet only in February 1936. Thus expenditure on tracked vehicles climbed only slowly in the mid-1930s. In 1934/35 the figure was £501,000 and though this had risen to £842,000 by 1936/37 it was not until 1937/38 that expenditure on these items reached an entirely new (rearmament) level at £3,625,000.[2] The financial treatment of the British Army during the 1930s, especially when constrasted with the open-handed policy towards the German Army of the National Socialist regime,[3] itself goes a long way to explain the British loss of the lead in the development of armoured forces. The impact of financial cuts on the development of British tanks in the early 1930s was dramatic and very damaging and the disruption of technical development at this period was to have a pernicious and lasting influence on the development of British military thought on armoured warfare.

The Vickers Medium tanks Marks I and II (which equipped a substantial part of the experimental Tank Brigade for the exercise of 1931) had been quite useful machines for the 1920s. In the early 1930s, however, the RTC already considered them obsolescent. By the mid-1930s their 18 mph road speed was considered inadequate for the far-ranging manoeuvres envisaged and the muzzle velocity of their 3-pdr guns was regarded as insufficient to penetrate the armour of the heavier foreign tanks that they might encounter. Most were, moreover, showing serious signs of wear and tear,[4] an indication perhaps of the pace of activity over this period in relation to the small number of machines in service.

As a replacement for the Vickers Mediums the RTC and the authorities in the War Office had high hopes of a new medium tank known as the "Sixteen Tonner". Designed by Vickers–Armstrong in 1928 the Sixteen Tonner was believed to be the best medium tank in the world at that time. It was recognized to be somewhat under-armoured and the authorities were not totally satisfied with the Armstrong-Siddeley 180 b.h.p. V-8 air-cooled engine,[5] even though this was a type specifically designed for tanks. But its 100-mile range and 30 mph top speed were considered impressive. In addition to a 3-pdr gun and machine gun in its main turret, it had two forward-mounted subsidiary turrets each containing a pair of machine guns. It was hoped that once this vehicle was in service, the British lead, both in tank design and in the tactics of armoured warfare, could be maintained well into the 1930s. The Sixteen Tonner was, however, never built beyond six prototypes, falling victim to the expenditure cuts of the early 1930s.[6] Major-General Brough, who became Director of Mechanization in 1932, despaired of being able to purchase such an expensive and sophisticated machine (unit cost approximately £16,000) in substantial numbers and all work on it was stopped.

Work continued into the mid-1930s on a parallel medium tank

Figure 22 A Medium Mark III (Sixteen Tonner) serving as a command tank during the 1st Tank Brigade exercises of 1934.

project, the A7 programme, run by the Superintendent of Design and his staff at the Royal Ordnance Factories. Three prototypes were produced by this project but all proved failures and were ultimately abandoned, though some of their design features were incorporated into the later A12, Infantry tank Mark II.[7] In Brough's period as Director of Mechanization the War Office gradually slackened its efforts to develop medium tanks based on powerful purpose-built engines and sought cheaper options.

In the late 1920s the War Office received the unsolicited offer of a light, inexpensive machine produced by Vickers in 1928 as a commercial project. This was the Six Ton tank which was successfully exported to the Soviet Union and other countries. One variant of this machine had a single turret capable of mounting both a 3-pdr gun and a co-axial machine gun – the same armament as the main turret of the Sixteen Tonner. It also had the same thickness of armour as the Sixteen Tonner and used a variant of the Armstrong–Siddeley V-8 engine. While not quite so fast, being capable of only 22 mph as opposed to 30 mph, it had the same operating range of approximately 100 miles. A good design, easy to manufacture and a major improvement on the Vickers Mediums

Marks I and II, the Six Ton tank could have proved a very useful stop-gap machine for the early and mid-1930s until rearmament allowed the production of something a little more costly. Indeed the Panzer 35t, a tank similar to the Vickers Six Ton tank built in Czechoslovakia, was found quite useful by the Germans and was employed in the western campaign of May 1940.[8] The Six Ton tank, however, was never seriously considered for adoption by the British Army, being contemptuously dismissed by the RTC as shoddy goods.[9]

In the mid-1930s the War Office went on trying to procure medium tanks but, to save money, these were generally based on commercially produced engines. Sir John Carden, regarded by the War Office as the leading tank designer of the inter-war period, was asked by Major-General Brough to produce a machine of this type. By the time of his death in an aeroplane crash in 1935[10] Carden had done the basic design work on what became known as the A9 and by 1936 a more heavily armoured variant, the A10, was also under development. But neither machine was regarded as satisfactory by the RTC or by the Directorate of Mechanization in the War Office. The fundamental problem was one of power-weight ratio. The 14 mm armour basis of the A9 was seen as inadequate for a medium tank and its top speed of 23 mph as barely adequate. When the vehicle was up-armoured to a 30 mm basis to produce the A10 (at the same time losing two subsidiary turrets mounting machine guns) the speed was reduced to a mere 16 mph, regarded as completely unsatisfactory for work with the Tank Brigade.[11] It is arguable that, as with the Six Ton tank, the RTC and the War Office authorities were being too perfectionist. The 14 mm armour on the A9 was of the same thickness as that on the Panzer II, the most numerous German tank of the 1940 campaign, and while the A9 was somewhat slower (23 mph maximum compared with 30 mph) the 2-pdr gun with which it was equipped had a better penetration against armour than the 37 mm main armament of the Panzer II. But given that there were some mechanical teething troubles to be eradicated there appeared to be no prospect of either the A9 or the A10 entering production, even as a stop-gap, before 1938 at the earliest.[12]

In May 1934 Lieutenant-General Sir Hugh Elles, the former commander of the Tank Corps in France during the First World War, took up office as Master General of the Ordnance. By this date the General Staff, considering existing British tanks rather too lightly armoured for lending support to unmechanized infantry in the assault, had already issued a specification for a specialist "Infantry" tank. Elles, who appears to have been heavily influenced by his First World War experience, strongly supported this measure. He asked Vickers, the only substantial private armaments firm, to design a tank for close co-operation with the infantry, capable of withstanding any existing anti-tank weapon and cheap enough to produce in substantial numbers even in peacetime. By 1935 a Vickers team led by Sir John Carden had achieved this. A small tank with a crew of only two, armed only with a machine gun and powered by a commercially produced Ford V8 engine of only 70 hp, it was capable of a mere 8 mph. Its virtues were armour 60–65 mm thick and a high degree of mechanical reliability.[13] Designated A11 or Infantry Tank Mark I it became the first in a series of Infantry or "I" tanks which the British were to go on producing for the rest of the inter-war period and throughout the Second World War. It marked the beginning of a split in the development of British medium tanks. As will be discussed in more detail in the next chapter, such development was, from the mid-1930s, to go off down two diverging routes marked "Infantry" and "Cruiser" tank. The two different types of fighting tank were to be provided to different types of unit and formation with quite different functions, doctrines and tactics.[14]

Financial constraints, the lack of clarity about the Army's role, the very limited capacity of the specialist armaments industry, the low industrial priority accorded by the government to tank production even once rearmament had begun and the consequent design and production difficulties all had a negative influence on the way in which British armour developed in the 1930s. It has also been suggested, however, that a sort of reaction against mechanization set in amongst senior officers from the early years of the decade.[15] Field Marshal Sir George Milne, it has sometimes been argued, stayed on too long as CIGS, serving for an unprecedented seven years altogether and resigning only in February 1933 by which time he was worn out. There were indications that as early as 1929 Milne had become tired and depressed, "an old man – mentally and physically".[16] The General Staff Directors who served under Milne in his last years were regarded by many observers as a rather conservative and uninspired group. The severe financial constraints of the early 1930s denied Milne the opportunity to do very much but, it has been argued, he lost the will to do anything.[17] Such a judgement seems rather harsh. Between 1931 and 1933 the British Army was, in terms of funding, at its nadir for the whole of the inter-war period and it is difficult to imagine any CIGS being able to give its armoured forces much impetus at that time. Up to 1931 the most radical advocates of tanks and mechanization had obtained from the War Office, in terms of both practical experiment and the development of doctrine, as much of their own way as it was realistically possible to let them have. Indeed not all of the RTC radicals believed that they were being badly treated, even in the financially desperate period of 1931–33. In September 1931 Pile told Liddell Hart that the CIGS was trying to consolidate the gains that had been made with mechanization even though the "awful" financial stringency would not permit further advance.[18]

If Milne's performance in his latter years was judged harshly by some contemporaries and later by some historians, the next CIGS, Field Marshal Sir Archibald Amar Montgomery-Massingberd (February 1933–April 1936) has had a still worse press. Montgomery-Massingberd had the misfortune to end up on extremely poor terms with the two most influential British military writers of the twentieth century – Fuller and Liddell Hart.[19] For Liddell Hart in particular Montgomery-Massingberd became a *bête noire*, being presented as the worst military reactionary of the inter-war period in the journalist's influential *Memoirs*.[20] While there is no doubt that Montgomery-Massingberd's outlook was fundamentally conservative, this assessment, sometimes uncritically echoed by subsequent historians, is unbalanced and unfair.

Born in 1871 into an Anglo-Irish landed gentry family, Montgomery-Massingberd had entered the Army through the Royal Military Academy Woolwich and was commissioned into the Royal Artillery. During the South African War of 1899–1902 he had served with horse artillery operating in close conjunction with cavalry. He had developed a lasting affection for the cavalry which seems to have been allied to his social conservatism.[21] In the First World War he had been chief of staff to Rawlinson's Fourth Army, ultimately the most successful of the BEF's armies, playing the leading role in the Hundred Days campaign in 1918. While Rawlinson's part in the conduct of the war on the Western Front has been the subject of intense study, Montgomery-Massingberd's has remained relatively obscure. There is, however, evidence to suggest that he was an advocate of the cautious, artillery-based, "bite and hold" approach to operations, which Rawlinson himself tended to prefer, rather than the rather reckless efforts at complete rupture of the enemy front on which Haig sometimes insisted.[22]

Serving in 1926 as chairman of the War Office Cavalry Committee (which investigated the efficiency of and made recommendations for the future of that arm) Montgomery-Massingberd had shown himself sympathetic to the view that horse-mounted soldiers had continuing roles in war, while at the same time indicating that, as presently equipped and organized, they could not perform these roles adequately.[23] This might seem an extraordinarily conservative position until it is remembered that virtually all European powers, even those without overseas empires, maintained a horsed cavalry arm at this period and that the Soviet and German armies went on using horsed cavalry in the Second World War itself.[24] Montgomery-Massingberd went on to arouse the ire of Liddell Hart by rebuking the latter over his support for Fuller and criticism of the War Office during the Tidworth affair in 1927. Montgomery-Massingberd's stance at this time was indicative of a very strong sense of hierarchy, a reluctance openly to criticize or to tolerate criticism of higher authority and a rather rigid and narrow sense of loyalty. (These traits, apparently fundamental to his psychology,[25] do not appeal to the liberal minds of most modern historians and this partly accounts for the unsympathetic treatment he has received at the hands of some of them.) In 1928 he had, as indicated in the last chapter, played a considerable role in the decision to close down the Experimental Mechanical Force and had done so using arguments which certainly appear, with hindsight, somewhat reactionary.[26]

As CIGS Montgomery-Massingberd's basic outlook was to remain conservative but he was fairly progressive on mechanization issues and he demonstrated a clear strategic vision. A Francophile, he believed Britain's fate was linked to that of Continental Europe and that German aggression on the Continent could be contained only by the preparation of a British Field Force to assist France in wartime.[27] By 1935 he wanted to include a very substantial proportion of armour in such a Field Force.[28] A significant change in his attitudes to armoured and mechanized forces seems to have occurred between 1928 and 1933, though it is not possible to trace this in detail or to discern its causes. If Montgomery-Massingberd is judged on the decisions he made as CIGS he appears, on balance, an enlightened officer.

In the autumn of 1933 Montgomery-Massingberd decided to establish a Tank Brigade as a permanent formation. Its command was given to Percy Hobart, the most ardent and radical member of the RTC *avant-garde*. Hobart and Montgomery-Massingberd appear to have established a warm mutual regard and Hobart, not known for sycophancy to superior officers, lavished praise on the CIGS for the support he gave to the Brigade's work.[29] It is typical of the element of personal bias in Liddell Hart's writings that while in *The Tanks* Montgomery-Massingberd is blamed for Fuller's being retired from the Army in December 1933, he is not given real credit for either the establishment of the Tank Brigade as a permanent formation or for Hobart's selection to command it. In 1934 Montgomery-Massingberd was offered and accepted the honorary position of Colonel Commandant of the RTC, something which hardly indicates a spirit of antagonism between the CIGS and the RTC's leading lights.[30]

In February 1934, at the time of the report of the Defence Requirements Committee (a body consisting of the Chiefs of Staff and Treasury and Foreign Office representatives which advised the government on its defence policy response to the growing military menace of Japan, Germany and Italy), Montgomery-Massingberd wanted to include both a Tank Brigade and a horsed cavalry division in the Field Force to be prepared for the Continent. The horsed cavalry division was to have its first line transport mechanized and was to be supplied with some light motor vehicles for reconnaissance but the bulk of the division was to remain horsed.[31] By October 1934, however, Montgomery-Massingberd had decided, apparently at Lindsay's instigation, that a fully mechanized "Mobile Division" should be substituted for the horsed cavalry division.[32]

Before exploring in detail the General Staff's plans for the formation of this Mobile Division, however, it seems essential to review the work of the Tank Brigade under Hobart's direction in the training season of 1934. Hobart made an early start to thinking and planning for that season. On 10 November 1933 he wrote to George Lindsay, then commanding the experimental motorized 7th Infantry Brigade at Tidworth:

I enclose a few notes I've jotted down about possible use of a Tank force *early* in a European campaign. One's main difficulty is forming any sort of picture of what these opening stages will be like.

My own feeling is that Air and Gas will play so large a part that concentration of troops or any plans involving deployments à la von Schlieffen will be quite impossible . . .

All this implies that large armies and mass movements are out of date. That only forces which can work dispersed and be controlled dispersed will have much effect.[33]

It is easy to see with hindsight that Hobart's assumptions about the early stages of the next major European war were quite erroneous. Mass armies were not made redundant. Airpower did not negate the importance of the concentration of ground forces. The Germans won the 1940 campaign against France by a very concentrated thrust involving no less than seven Panzer and three motorized infantry divisions through the rather restricted road network of the Ardennes. This move was protected from interference by Allied air forces by the high degree of surprise it achieved, by rapidity of movement, and, even more significantly, by the high degree of local air superiority which the German air force was in a position to guarantee.[34] This operation, moreover, culminated in the envelopment of a large part of the Anglo-French forces in a manner which was very much "à la von Schlieffen". In fact, for the purposes of the 1934 training season, while devising for the Tank Brigade what he regarded as the most modern tactics, based on speed and dispersal, Hobart ultimately decided to assume that the enemy would be attempting to advance much as in 1914.[35]

In his letter to Lindsay of 10 November 1933 Hobart went on to discuss possible co-operation in the 1934 training season between Lindsay's brigade and his own. Like both Fuller and Liddell Hart, Hobart thought infantry had only very subordinate roles to play in the operations of mechanized formations. He believed, however, that the Tank Brigade "must have a Secure Base of operations and this must be mobile". Motorized infantry could help form and protect such a base. An attached infantry unit (not an integral part of the Tank Brigade) might also be useful to the Brigade, Hobart believed, for tasks such as: "Collection of prisoners etc. Holding a defile by which Tank Brigade require [*sic*] to return. Securing a town or other centre."[36] Hobart was hardly

offering starring roles to the motorized infantry which Lindsay
commanded in the Tank Brigade exercises for the coming year.

While expressing agreement with much of Hobart's analysis,
Lindsay suggested in reply that "having gone as far as we have
in the development of the Tank Brigade and the Motorized Infantry Brigade, we must now take a step forward and organize and
experiment with a Mobile Division". He wanted this to include a
mechanized cavalry brigade, a tank brigade and a motorized infantry brigade, with supporting arms and aircraft. The motorized
cavalry brigade, consisting of armoured cars and troops with rifles
and machine guns mounted in light motor vehicles, would locate
the enemy and help fix him for assaults by the tank brigade. The
motorized infantry brigade, consisting of four relatively small infantry battalions with a large number of automatic weapons and
anti-tank guns, would form bases, occupy vital ground and secure
lines of retreat for the rest of the division. The division's supporting troops would include motorized field artillery, signals, engineers and anti-aircraft units. Attached aircraft would be specially
trained to co-operate with the division, offering it reconnaissance,
close support and air re-supply. In order to test his Mobile Division concept Lindsay wanted the Tank Brigade and his motorized
infantry brigade to be combined for an exercise towards the end
of the 1934 training season.[37]

Though Hobart's and Lindsay's ideas on mechanized warfare
still had much in common, they were diverging. Hobart saw the
Tank Brigade as an ideal formation in itself, in concept if not in
its current equipment. He wanted it encumbered as little as possible
with non-RTC, non-tracked, non-armoured elements. As one of
Hobart's closest disciples in the RTC remarked of his and Hobart's
views in the 1930s:

> We didn't want an all tank army . . . but what could we do? The
> infantry were in buses, they couldn't come with us. The artillery were
> obstructive. They never put the rounds where you needed them, and
> when you called it always came too late.[38]

In effect, therefore, Hobart *did* want mechanized formations which
were practically all tanks – an inadequate and ultimately dangerous concept. Lindsay's ideas, on the other hand, had become much
more sophisticated since he had advised Broad on the writing
of the "Purple Primer" at the end of the 1920s. In proposing an

all-arms mechanized division including an air element, Lindsay was on the right lines even if, for the actual fighting, he was expecting the Tank Brigade to do too much and suggesting for the division's other elements roles which were too minor.

Hobart invited Lindsay and Broad to dinner on 12 December 1933 in order to discuss the outline of a "charter" for the Tank Brigade which he had recently sent them. Further discussions relating to the co-operation of Hobart's and Lindsay's Brigades in the coming training season were held at Lindsay's HQ a week later. Hobart's aim at this stage was to get Montgomery-Massingberd to issue a directive which would serve as the basis for the Brigade's work in the coming training season.[39] Montgomery-Massingberd obliged and on 25 January 1934 the directive was issued. It rather deprecated the use of the Tank Brigade in support of infantry assaults and emphasized "independent" missions such as raids and flank attacks. It was also indicated that: "A Tank Brigade may be employed on a strategic or semi-independent mission against some important objective in the enemy's rearward organization . . . The Tank Brigade should avoid strength and attack weakness."

The directive laid down that the main objective of the training season of 1934 was "to test the manoeuvrability of the Brigade as a whole, to practise co-operation with the RAF, to try out methods of supply and maintenance and to aim at moving seventy miles a day or 150 miles in three days including an action in each case".

In spring 1934 Hobart's Brigade comprising 2nd, 3rd and 5th Battalions RTC was gradually assembled on Salisbury Plain. These battalions were equipped with a mixture of Vickers Medium tanks and tankettes. On 8–12 May at Cambridge an RTC staff exercise was held to develop the techniques to be used in deep operations behind enemy lines. The general situation was envisaged as being: "Similar to Sept. 1914. An enemy advance into invaded territory has been checked, a great counter-offensive is about to start, and includes a hundred mile move wide round a flank by a Tank Brigade directed on rear organizations forty miles behind the main battle front."[40]

The Cambridge staff exercises seem to have confirmed Hobart's existing view that his Brigade should advance on a broad front and in a very dispersed manner in order to keep the enemy confused and minimize the targets offered for air attack. RAF co-operation with the Tank Brigade was thought necessary for reconnaissance, defence against enemy air attack, logistic support and the flying artillery role – friendly field artillery not being expected to be able to keep up. Hobart's report on these exercises recognized that the Brigade's existing equipment – largely Vickers Mediums and Carden Loyds – was in reality inadequate for the sort of task proposed, but he deemed it appropriate to think and train beyond these limitations, especially as a small number of new Vickers light tanks were becoming available and these were believed more appropriate tools for the job. Hobart was aware that the Achilles' heel of the Brigade for the type of operation he was contemplating was logistics. He was thinking of eventually attaching to the brigade trucks with cross-country mobility for carrying petrol and a perhaps a type of large petrol tanker. But suitable vehicles were not yet available and for the exercises of 1934 it would be necessary to proceed without them, taking some logistic risks in the process.[41]

In July 1934, as the period of the collective training of his Brigade was about to begin, Hobart was in a mood of cautious optimism. He conveyed this in a letter to Liddell Hart whom he encouraged to observe and report on the exercises. He was particularly encouraged by the attitude of Montgomery-Massingberd: "Most of the Great Ones scoff of course but we are lucky indeed in at least having so far-seeing, resolute and open-minded a CIGS who is giving us a chance to try and is so remarkably understanding."[42]

By the start of the collective training period Hobart's Brigade consisted of 4 battalions, 3 of mixed medium tanks and tankettes and 1 of light tanks. The 3 mixed battalions consisted of a headquarters section of 4 medium tanks, and of 3 mixed companies composed of a command tank, a section of 7 tankettes or light tanks, a section of 5 medium tanks and a section of 2 tanks which were intended to act in the close support role and which should have been fitted with small howitzers to fire high explosive shell. Real close support tanks were not available, however, and for exercise purposes the part was played by ordinary Vickers Medium tanks for whose 3-pdr guns high explosive shell was not manufactured. The light tank battalion consisted solely of light tanks and tankettes organized into 3 companies. The whole was a virtually undiluted force of tracked armoured fighting vehicles, devoid of infantry and artillery – in that respect the natural result of the main trend in British thought on mechanized formations in the period 1929–33.[43]

In manoeuvring his Brigade Hobart normally employed a formation 10 miles broad by 10 miles deep. In daylight it was possible to move at about 8 mph thus covering some 60 miles or more per day. Movement sometimes continued at night though at a rather slower pace. Generally the performance of the Tank Brigade against the unmechanized units against which it was pitted was deemed so convincing that the umpires received complaints that the unmechanized troops of the Aldershot Command "were being put up as a cockshy . . . and being made fools of".[44]

In September 1934 the Tank Brigade was, as Lindsay had suggested the previous autumn, combined with 7th Infantry Brigade, a motorized field artillery brigade and other supporting units, to form a small mechanized division known as the Mobile Force. It was put under Lindsay's command and pitted against a more conventional force consisting of an unmechanized infantry division, a horsed cavalry brigade and two armoured car units, this force being commanded by Major-General J.C. Kennedy. A great deal of controversy has surrounded this exercise, more ink having been expended on it than on many small battles.[45] Though the exercise probably did have a negative impact on the way British armour developed, the extent of this has sometimes been overplayed and the reasons for it misinterpreted.

The exercise director, Major-General Burnett-Stuart, GOC Southern Command, considered himself generally a friend to the cause of mechanization. But in the autumn of 1934 he felt that the older arms' morale needed a boost and that the mechanized forces had had rather too much of their own way recently. He thought they had paid insufficient attention to logistic problems and needed to be given more demanding tasks.[46] He designed the exercise in such a way as to make Lindsay's job exceptionally difficult. The Mobile Force was given the mission of raiding a set of objectives, all quite close together, near the town of Amesbury, behind the enemy's lines. The Mobile Force was told to be ready to participate in a major battle immediately after completing the raids. The Force had to make a very long approach march from its assembly area west of the River Severn and then had to cross the defended obstacle of the Kent and Avon Canal. The start time for the Force's movement was set by Burnett-Stuart at 2.00 a.m. on 19 September, leaving only four hours of darkness and meaning that the move would probably have to be completed in daylight.[47]

Lindsay was not in the right frame of mind to be tackling a task as demanding as this while managing a subordinate as temperamental and potentially wayward as Hobart. Lindsay's wife was apparently suffering from a form of mental illness and had been behaving eccentrically for some years. This situation worried Lindsay and left him "unable to concentrate on or take real interest in anything" and feeling that he was "not pulling [his] weight . . . or doing really good work". He had the further problems that there was no real Mobile Force staff, only two separate brigade staffs, and that his Brigade Major, the Honourable Robert Bridgeman, did not enjoy a good working relationship with Hobart or with Hobart's Brigade Major, the taciturn John Crocker.[48]

Lindsay's initial plan for the exercise was to advance on a broad front with mixed columns of armoured cars, light tanks, motorized infantry and the slower-moving Vickers Medium tanks. Crossings over the canal would be seized by the faster moving vehicles, the medium tanks following in their wake. The raids would be mounted at dawn on the second day. Hobart effectively vetoed this suggestion, largely because he did not like the idea of splitting up the Tank Brigade amongst mixed columns. This plan, therefore, was not presented to Burnett-Stuart in his capacity as exercise director. Lindsay's second plan, which he did present to Burnett-Stuart, envisaged a wide outflanking sweep around the enemy rather than an attempt to penetrate his front. Movement would take place at night. In the daytime the force was intended to lie up to undertake the maintenance work which such an ambitious movement would undoubtedly have necessitated for the Brigade's vehicles. The raids would take place on the third day. Burnett-Stuart warned against the adoption of this plan which he thought (apparently for logistical reasons) might result in a spectacular failure. Lindsay's third plan, the one finally adopted, involved the seizure of a canal crossing site by the 7th Infantry Brigade on the first day. The Tank Brigade would follow, moving as a complete formation, the next night. Details of the attacks would be worked out later.[49]

In the event, 7th Infantry Brigade seized crossings at Hungerford without great difficulty but was subject to heavy air attack while awaiting Hobart's Tank Brigade. By the time the latter had caught up the element of surprise had been lost and the Mobile Force found its advance strongly opposed. On the afternoon of 20 September the necessity for the Mobile Force's withdrawal was pointed out by Burnett-Stuart and recognized by Lindsay. It was made difficult however by the initiative of the opposing force commander, Major-General Kennedy, who used motorized elements of 1st Division to establish roadblocks in the Mobile Force's rear. Despite suffering from umpiring which throughout the exercise was markedly biased against them, Lindsay and Hobart managed to withdraw their forces by splitting them up and by-passing the main obstacles.[50]

Liddell Hart believed that the Mobile Force's repulse was the result of (in Hobart's words) "a frame-up". In his history of the Royal Tank Regiment he portrayed it as a disaster which severely set back the development of armoured and mechanized forces in the British Army.[51] In fact it had no discernible effect on the policy of the General Staff. Hobart, the most fanatical of the RTC radicals, did not himself take the episode very seriously. While he agreed with Liddell Hart that the Mobile Force's life had deliberately been made difficult to raise the morale of the non-mechanized troops, he accepted that such a revival was badly needed and defended the exercise authorities on the grounds that: ". . . the Powers were confident that the morale of the Tank Brigade would be unbroken whatever they did. And I think they were justified in that confidence."[52]

If the Mobile Force exercise had a negative effect on the development of British armoured forces this was entirely due to its impact on the career of George Lindsay, the most sophisticated of the Army's tank enthusiasts. Lindsay had little role in the making of mechanization policy beyond this point. He was deemed to have failed as a commander, his performance being subjected to severe criticism by Burnett-Stuart, in front of other officers, in the debrief at the end of the exercise – an experience he found deeply humiliating.[53] Despite Montgomery-Massingberd's continued belief in Lindsay, his reputation in the Army as a whole was irretrievably damaged. Hobart's lack of co-operation during parts of the Mobile Force trial had contributed significantly to Lindsay's problems. Indeed at one stage Hobart virtually withdrew his co-operation on the grounds that the whole exercise had become a farce. But Hobart's performance was, by contrast, regarded quite favourably by Burnett-Stuart.[54] In the aftermath of the 1934 training season Hobart's star appeared to be rising as Lindsay's waned.

Lindsay's performance in September 1934 does appear to have been characterized by a lack of "grip". His wife's illness was a significant problem to which there was no obvious solution. But while there were thus good reasons for regarding Lindsay as henceforth unsuitable for command on active service, this did not negate his value as a military thinker and organizer. His ideas on armoured forces had, by the autumn of 1933, become much more sophisticated than those of Hobart. Of the Army's tank advocates it was Lindsay who had the clearest perception of the need to integrate the Tank Brigade within an all-arms mechanized division and it was Lindsay who had produced the best concept for the organization of such a force. Lindsay appears to have been the inspiration behind Montgomery-Massingberd's decision of October 1934 to form a Mobile Division[55] and the CIGS seems to have continued to have believed, despite Lindsay's disappointing performance on exercise that year, that the latter was the strongest candidate to command it.[56] By October 1937, when sufficient equipment had materialized for the Mobile Division to be established, Montgomery-Massingberd had, however, long since retired and Lindsay lost his chance. In 1935 Lindsay was sent to India to serve as a District Commander. He was to retire from the Army in 1939 and though he was recalled to service during the Second World War and was promoted, he neither commanded in battle nor, apparently, had any impact on doctrine.[57]

As Lindsay's career went into decline the process of materially preparing the British Army to face the growing threat of war with Germany was just beginning. In February 1934 the Chiefs of Staff, meeting as the Defence Requirements Committee (DRC), proposed that the government spend £40 million on the re-equipment of the Army over a five-year period. The DRC recommended that a large part of this sum should be devoted to the preparation of a Field Force for a Continental campaign.[58] On the advice of the Chancellor of the Exchequer, Mr Neville Chamberlain, who indicated that the government was faced with proposals financially "impossible to carry out",[59] the Army's proposed allocation of funds was halved, although the Navy's was unaffected and the RAF's significantly increased.[60] While the Cabinet accepted that the British

Army might have to go to the Continent to fight alongside the French against the Germans, its refusal to sanction the financial allocation proposed by the DRC left the Army as the "Cinderella of the services"[61] and delayed the start of a serious rearmament programme for the Army for about two years. In the sequence of events which brought about a real rearmament programme for the British Army the Abyssinian Crisis of 1935 was prominent. Italy had not hitherto been regarded as a likely enemy and British opposition to that state over its efforts to conquer Abyssinia, when combined with accelerating German rearmament, forced a reappraisal of defence problems. In July 1935 the DRC prepared another report.[62] After considering this, the Cabinet authorized the DRC to draw up proposals for a more thoroughgoing programme of rearmament.[63]

It was against this background that the General Staff drew up its most comprehensive policy paper of the 1930s, a paper which contained rather ambitious plans for the development of armoured forces. Entitled "The Future Reorganization of the British Army" it was signed by Montgomery-Massingberd on 9 September 1935. A bulky document of some thirty-eight typescript pages, it was sweeping in scope, penetrating in many of its insights and remarkably prescient in some of its predictions.[64] Yet it has been largely neglected by historians, being mentioned neither in the official history of British rearmament policy nor in the standard work on British military policy between the wars.[65]

It is not possible to trace the evolution of this document. A paper of its magnitude would probably have been drafted by a number of different hands, although such drafts do not appear to have survived. A staff officer of Montgomery-Massingberd's experience would not, however, have put his signature to a document of this importance, embracing as it did all aspects of British military policy, unless he had studied and approved it in its entirety. In the final analysis it was his paper, putting forward his policies.

In Part I the paper entered into an analysis of the lessons of the First World War, gave an account of developments in weapons, tactics and organization since 1918, offered a lengthy scenario of the probable course of a future war with Germany and then drew conclusions as to how a British Field Force should be organized, equipped and trained for a Continental role. In Part II the peace commitments of the Army and secondary (non-Continental) war commitments were examined as was Territorial Army organization. In Part III, the final part, general conclusions were drawn.

In its account of the lessons of the First World War, which drew heavily on the report of the Kirke Committee,[66] the General Staff argued that the primary cause of the static, positional warfare which had predominated on the Western Front was:

> the relative superiority of defensive weapons and methods over those of the attack. This outstanding feature of the campaign was the outcome of the development in the defensive power of the machine gun, artillery and field fortification. Of these the machine gun perhaps exerted the greatest influence ... whereas in August 1914 we had one machine gun to 300 infantry, we had at the Armistice, one automatic weapon to 20 infantry.[67]

The British General Staff did not, however, assume in the mid-1930s that the defensive was still completely dominant. A clear appreciation was shown of the role played by tanks and aircraft in breaking the stalemate in the closing stages of the war and these were seen as important weapons for the future:

> The tank provided the most effective means yet produced of dealing with wire obstacles and with rifle and machine gun fire. The employment of tanks when available in numbers, greatly assisted the infantry in the attack ...
>
> The use of aircraft enabled the offensive to be carried beyond the battle zone and into the enemy's country. The effect of their development on the armies was, at first, chiefly felt in the increased facilities offered for observation and reconnaissance, in the restrictions consequently imposed on movement by daylight, and in the more efficient direction of artillery fire. There was, towards the end of the war, however, an increasing tendency to use aircraft for offensive operations against the enemy's rearward organisation. It can hardly be claimed that the potentialities of an air striking force acting in conjunction with land operations were ever fully developed, although there were significant instances of offensive action against lines of communication and retreating troops.[68]

The main operational problem of the 1918 campaign in Montgomery-Massingberd's assessment had been "the difficulty of exploiting a breakthrough. Cavalry which carried out this role in other theatres were never able to perform it on the Western Front". But means to overcome this problem were now in sight. "It seems reasonable to assume that suitable mechanized and armoured formations, acting in conjunction with light aircraft could have achieved it."[69]

By the mid-1930s the British General Staff had recognized the futility of sending a horsed cavalry division to the Continent and understood that armoured and mechanized formations were potentially of the greatest importance. Montgomery-Massingberd regarded the "introduction of a self-contained armoured formation into our field army" as one of the most significant developments since 1918. He recognized that, by 1935, armoured vehicles were "capable of operations widely differing from the close support of infantry for which tanks were originally produced".[70] The paper went on to show, in the scenario which it presented of the opening stages of the next war, that the combined use of mechanized ground forces and tactical airpower would give the Germans the best chance of the early victory they would inevitably seek.

In its "Forecast of the Opening Stages of a War with Germany" the General Staff pointed out that, "The Great War has left a firm conviction amongst European nations that long drawn out struggle is disastrous even for the victor." There were indications that Germany would make "strenuous endeavours" to secure an "early decision" and that the German Army was training for mobile operations to this end.[71] The attitude of the French at the outbreak of war was expected to be defensive and in the circumstances it was thought that the Germans would have three possible strategies for securing a quick victory. They could launch a sudden attack with a "small, highly trained, highly mobile force" on a selected portion of the French defences on the Franco-German border (the "Maginot Line"), or by-pass these defences in an outflanking sweep either through Switzerland or through Holland and Belgium. The British General Staff in 1935 was of the opinion that a direct German assault on the Maginot Line offered poor prospects of success: "Although an advance on this front may became more practicable in the future if and when new methods of overcoming fortifications may have been devised, it would appear most unlikely that Germany's main effort would be made here and especially as long as the demilitarized zone exists."

Switzerland was, for a number of reasons, not thought a very likely option, and the Germans were consequently expected to seek victory through the Low Countries. The British General Staff

wanted to get the first contingent of their Field Force, which was
to include four infantry divisions and one mechanized mobile division, to the Continent in time to prevent the whole of Holland
and Belgium falling into German hands. If this were accomplished
it would provide depth for the air defence of Great Britain and
offer protection to British air bases on the Continent from which
an air counter-offensive against Germany could be mounted. The
initial role of the British Army would be "to provide sufficient
moral and material support to our Allies" to prevent western
Holland and Belgium being overrun by the Germans. Montgomery-
Massingberd envisaged the role of the British Field Force as being
strategically defensive though it might be possible to adopt the
tactical offensive at times.[72]

It is evident that by the mid-1930s the British General Staff had
devoted considerable thought to the use of airpower in the next
war and to the relationship between airpower and ground forces,
especially armoured and mechanized forces. Conclusions had been
reached which were very much at variance with the philosophy of
the Air Staff. The British General Staff did not share the prevailing
fears of some politicians and some airmen that Germany would
open any war in which Great Britain was involved with a knockout blow from the air against London. Montgomery-Massingberd
had earlier stated his belief that Germany would not use more
than a small part of its air force against targets in Great Britain
until it had secured decisive victory on the Continent and that the
intensity of air attack on London would inevitably be very limited
unless the German Army overran Holland and Belgium.[73] In September 1935 the CIGS stated his agreement with the French and
Belgian General Staffs that the targets the Germans would select
for air attack in the early stages of the war would "conform to the
objectives of the Field Armies air action being directed against
enemy air bases . . . railway nodal points and concentration areas".
In fact the object of air attack would be to "paralyze the enemy's
movements and make possible a breakthrough by highly mobile
land forces".[74]

In view of its assessment of the way the Germans would use
their airpower the British General Staff believed it essential to
establish, "at the outset of a war and in conjunction with Allied
armies, an effective system of air defence on the Continent", considering it important to ensure that "demands for local defence at

home are not given undue weight". The General Staff was very concerned about the attitude of the RAF and regarded the existing state of Army–RAF co-operation as completely unsatisfactory. In a sentence which would no doubt have horrified the Air Staff and confirmed its worst fears about the attitude of the other services it was remarked that "it may be necessary to examine the question of whether a system analagous to that of the Fleet Air Arm would not give better results".[75]

The first contingent of the Field Force was intended to contain a high proportion of armoured and mechanized troops. The Mobile Division was supposed to have 2 Armoured Car Regiments, 1 or 2 Mechanized Cavalry Brigades, probably 2, 1 Tank Brigade, 2 mechanized Royal Horse Artillery Brigades and other supporting units. The roles of the Mobile Division were provisionally defined as reconnaissance before the main forces made contact, the protection of the Field Force's flanks, the seizure and tenure of important positions and co-operation with the rest of the Field Force in battle either by outflanking manoeuvre or by exploitation of success if the enemy's resistance appeared to be breaking down.[76]

In addition to the armour included in the Mobile Division Montgomery-Massingberd was planning to have a total of 4 Army Tank Battalions, 1 per infantry division, in the First Contingent. These battalions, manned by the RTC and equipped with heavily armoured, slow moving infantry tanks were, as already indicated, intended for close co-operation with the infantry divisions, particularly in assaults. As Army troops they could be massed on a single axis for a major attack. It was anticipated that: "the provision of infantry tanks will undoubtedly increase the offensive power of the divisions for the main battle whilst the provision of armoured MG [machine gun] carriers should also strengthen the offensive power of infantry brigades in loose fighting".[77]

Mechanization was the key-note of Montgomery-Massingberd's whole Field Force policy. The Mobile Division and the Army Tank Battalions were not intended to be the only armoured forces in the first contingent. Traditionally horsed cavalry regiments had been attached to infantry divisions for reconnaisance and screening. General Staff policy was now to mechanize the transport of the infantry division and to provide enough motor transport with the first contingent of the Field Force to lift a complete infantry division if required. The problem had arisen of providing a suitable substitute for horsed cavalry to work with infantry columns carried in motor transport. The General Staff was experimenting with various forms of mechanized cavalry and hoped that this would provide the answer.[78]

Like other senior officers of this period, Montgomery-Massingberd had earlier exhibited a degree of attachment to the horse which perhaps has to be explained more in terms of social background and a sense of tradition than strict military logic. He continued to regard equestrian activities as useful for the training of officers and did not discount the possibility of horsed cavalry finding significant military roles outside Europe in the short run. But by 1935 he had accepted the "gradual disappearance" of the horse from both civil and military life.[79] From this time onward the General Staff moved gradually but steadily towards the complete mechanization of the cavalry of the line. In this respect British General Staff thinking seems to have been somewhat ahead of the General Staffs of the other major military powers. Montgomery-Massingberd's 1935 proposals seem to have been intended to establish the British Army as the most highly mechanized in the world and the one with the highest proportion of armour.

The General Staff's policy of mechanizing the cavalry was fraught with difficulty. Not only was it hard to obtain the necessary funds from the Treasury, the process also involved complicated negotiations with the Government of India. There were five regiments of British cavalry stationed in India and the Indian Government was for some time undecided as to its policy on their mechanization. But as the Adjutant-General, General Sir Cecil Romer, pointed out in November 1934, as cavalry units at home were progressively mechanized it was going to become increasingly difficult to find drafts for India.[80]

There was, moreover, a natural tendency for RTC officers to believe that any increase in the British Army's armoured forces should be accomplished entirely by the expansion of their own Corps. There was certainly something to be said for such a course. Though the 3rd (King's Own) Hussars volunteered for experimental mechanization in the 1935 training season, they did so only on the understanding that this would not affect their chances of remaining horsed if it were ultimately decided to retain some horsed regiments. While most cavalry officers were prepared to accept mechanization rather than face the abolition of their regiments,[81] they had little enthusiasm for it. In his history of the Royal Tank Regiment Liddell Hart commented that:

> the official mind rolled itself up like a hedgehog on the advance of any suggestion that the one corps already experienced in mechanized mobility was the medium through which mechanization should be extended. That defensive posture was prompted not only by care for old established interests but by fear that if the Tank Corps was allowed its head the pace of progress might become too fast to be controllable.[82]

But the above criticism is partisan and crude. Liddell Hart, both as journalist in the inter-war period and as a historian after the Second World War, was a blatant propagandist for particular interest groups within the Army, notably the RTC and (especially in the late 1930s) the anti-aircraft troops. He seldom made the attempt to see the whole picture as it appeared from the War Office. Later historians have concluded that the abolition of the cavalry was simply not a practical proposition.[83] The Army had felt itself almost squeezed to death by hostile external forces in the early 1930s and it is quite understandable that the General Staff had no stomach during rearmament for creating serious internal rifts. In the late 1920s Liddell Hart had been an advocate of cavalry mechanization, arguing that cavalry officers had precisely the instincts for manoeuvre and rapid decision required in mechanized warfare.[84] He changed his mind in the mid-1930s just as some prospect was emerging of gaining the money to bring this about.[85] In the passage quoted above Liddell Hart also ignored the fact that the RTC to a large extent *was* the medium through which mechanization was extended, in the sense that RTC personnel gave training and advice to the cavalry on all aspects of the maintenance and employment of armoured fighting vehicles.[86] Liddell Hart's identification of the RTC with "progress" was itself an over-simplification. Some of the tactical ideas of the RTC radicals were, as already commented, dangerously wrong. By the mid-1930s, Lindsay was beginning to correct his own earlier errors. But Hobart, the dominant tank enthusiast of the later 1930s, remained fixated on dubious concepts, desiring small all-armoured, all-tracked formations, containing little infantry or artillery, moving excessively dispersed. To the extent that cavalry regiments in the Western Desert in the Second World War made tactical mistakes in dealing with the Germans these may well have been the product of an education in bad habits by the RTC rather than errors peculiar to themselves.[87]

The General Staff's ideas on the future of the cavalry were tightly bound up with its plans to create a Mobile Division. These had been evolving since the autumn of 1934, if not earlier. On 15 October that year Montgomery-Massingberd announced to his colleagues on the Army Council that:

> I have recently been considering the suitability of the present mobile element in the Field Force in the light of conditions likely to obtain in the Western Plan [for the despatch of a Field Force to the Continent] and I have reached the provisional conclusion that instead of having an independent Tank Brigade and a Cavalry Division, a more suitable organization would be a Mobile Division consisting of the Tank Brigade and one *mechanized* cavalry brigade together with an adequate proportion of reconnaissance troops.[88]

This decision may have had its origins in a letter which Lindsay sent to Montgomery-Massingberd the previous February which proposed the formation of a mechanized Mobile Division and (in an appendix) suggested its composition. While the detailed plans for a Mobile Division which the General Staff drew up that December were significantly different from those that Lindsay had proposed the previous February, the fact that the same name was used for the division and some similarities in the proposed structure do indicate that the one was derived from the other. The type of division which Lindsay had been contemplating in February has already been described in broad outline. Its most notable features were a motorized cavalry brigade, the Tank Brigade, a motorized infantry brigade of three or four small infantry battalions, supporting units of artillery, engineers, signals and air defence and some integral aviation. Lindsay's motorized cavalry brigade was to include, in addition to a regiment of armoured cars, three motorized cavalry regiments mounted in light motor cars. These were apparently intended to operate in a sort of light infantry role, engaging in reconnaissance and harassment of the enemy (perhaps rather like the "motor guerrillas" of Fuller's *Lectures on FSR III*) and helping to "fix" him, ahead of the rest of the division. The General Staff's proposal of December 1934 differed mainly in that it incorporated an extra two armoured car regiments in addition

to the motorized cavalry brigade (thus offering even more employment for cavalry), that it dispensed with the motorized infantry
brigade and that it did not include integral aviation, probably
because there was no prospect of the Army having aviation assets
under its own control in the near future.[89]

Whereas Lindsay's original concept is open to criticism on the
grounds that it included too many rifle units (a total of at least six)
making the division excessively bulky, the General Staff's first
detailed proposal included just three, and these all converted cavalry regiments whose eventual role, equipment and tactics were at
this stage matters of conjecture and debate. The General Staff's
proposal of December 1934 did, however, include two brigades of
motorized artillery so the division would have had no shortage of
firepower. Perhaps suspecting that its initial proposal would leave
the division with an inadequate rifle strength, the General Staff
contemplated the inclusion of another, similarly organized, motorized cavalry brigade by September 1935. By December the same
year this step had definitely been decided upon, the intended composition of the Brigade being at the same time reduced to three
regiments, two motorized and one of light tanks. At the same time
the decision was taken to mechanize the cavalry brigade in Egypt.
The transport of all infantry battalions and of divisional artillery
was also to be motorized.[90]

Montgomery-Massingberd must be given credit for the decisions to replace the horsed cavalry division with a mechanized
Mobile Division and to mechanize a substantial part of the cavalry
of the line. The fact that he wanted such a high proportion of
armoured forces in the Field Force, coupled with his high professional regard for both Lindsay and Hobart, tends to give the lie
to Liddell Hart's portrayal of him as a blinkered reactionary. Yet
there were undoubtedly conceptual weaknesses in the approach of
the General Staff under his leadership to the development of armoured forces. The Mobile Division was seen too much as a direct
replacement for the old horsed cavalry division. Most of its proposed functions: reconnaissance, the seizing of vital ground ahead
of the rest of the Field Force, the protection of an exposed flank
and manoeuvre against an enemy flank were old cavalry division
roles. Although one paper on the subject did suggest that the
Mobile Division could sometimes be used for the breakthrough
role,[91] such a role appears to have been given relatively little

attention. The British General Staff was aware that the Germans were contemplating the use of mechanized formations in conjunction with air forces for breakthrough operations.[92] Counter-penetration and counter-stroke were not, however, suggested in 1934–35 as roles for the British Mobile Division. The General Staff was not proposing to include any infantry as such in the division and the concept of the mechanized cavalry regiment was less than half-baked. Indeed the division's composition as provisionally laid out in papers of 1934 and 1935 seems to have been designed more to find roles for otherwise redundant cavalry regiments than to create the most potent possible fighting force.

The General Staff's proposal to use cavalry in motor cars and light trucks as part of the Mobile Division led to the trial conversion of one squadron of the 3rd (King's Own) Hussars for the training season of 1935. The regiment's commanding officer, Lieutenant-Colonel Grubb, set a rather narrow objective for the trial. He decided to test only whether cavalry soldiers in light motor vehicles could perform the roles traditionally allocated to horsed cavalry in the early twentieth century – reconnaissance, screening and pursuit. He did not attempt to work out from first principles the roles which motorized riflemen and machine gunners could perform within a new mechanized, partially armoured division. Clearly Grubb should have been given more guidance by the General Staff. It would have been appropriate to have asked an officer with experience of working with mechanized forces but appreciative of their need to have an all-arms composition – Lindsay being the obvious candidate – to have supervised the experiments closely. Grubb reported that troops mounted in cars and light trucks could actually perform the traditional cavalry roles better, under modern conditions, than could horsemen.[93] But Wend-Fenton, Grubb's successor as CO of the 3rd Hussars, and Brigadier Heydeman, Wend-Fenton's immediate superior, protested that to mount cavalry in cars or trucks would inevitably mean turning them into a kind of motorized infantry. In this role cavalry would, they maintained, be inferior to true infantry and anyway it was not a role they wanted. Brigadier Heydeman argued that:

> motorized cavalry as presently equipped are only inferior mobile infantry but if cavalry are mechanized in Light Tanks they can continue all their old roles and maintain their cavalry dash in reconnaissance, fire, with outflanking movement and shock action.[94]

These cavalry officers wanted their regiments to be preserved by mechanization from an otherwise inevitable extinction. But they were trying to insist that this should be done in the way most congenial to them, not necessarily that most useful to the Army. Ultimately the General Staff indulged them and by 1938 was trying to put a total of twelve cavalry regiments marked for mechanization into light tanks.[95] This was both an expensive decision and one of very dubious wisdom. Throughout the inter-war period the British Army was short of infantry, the arm most in demand for overseas garrison duty. The balance of the Cardwell System which required an equal number of infantry battalions of the line at home and abroad was never perfectly maintained.[96] Thus it was virtually impossible to spare infantry battalions in peacetime to concentrate for long periods on the infantry role within an armoured division. To have converted some cavalry regiments into troops specializing in what the Germans were later to call the "panzer grenadier" role could have made sense, provided an officer with sufficient vision and determination had been put in charge of the process. The British light tanks of this period were primarily reconnaissance machines and had little fighting power. By the outbreak of the Second World War even the latest model was regarded as obsolescent.[97] The conversion of the majority of cavalry regiments to light tanks made sense only in as much as it would make their subsequent conversion to cruiser or medium tanks easier and that was an argument which never appears to have been offered in support of the policy.

As a result of the decision not to put cavalry into cars and trucks the proposed composition of the mechanized cavalry brigade of the Mobile Division had been changed by January 1937 to include two cavalry light tank regiments and one motorized infantry battalion in each.[98] The intention to introduce motorized infantry battalions into the Mobile Division was a step forward but their proposed numbers were still inadequate – four infantry battalions in an armoured division became standard in the Second World War[99] – and it made little sense to brigade them with light tanks. The proportion of armoured car and light tank units proposed for the Mobile Division was now absurdly high in relation to more battleworthy elements.

The beginning of a major rearmament effort for the British Army virtually coincided with Montgomery-Massingberd's retirement as CIGS. His health was failing and he decided to go somewhat early, in April 1936.[100] He was generally agreed to have fought the Army's case in committee vigorously, persuasively and as effectively as possible under the circumstances.[101] He had a coherent and systematic approach to the Army's preparation for war which, in detailed "Handing Over Notes", he tried to pass on to his successor.[102] Hobart, a stringent critic of many senior officers, saw Montgomery-Massingberd as definitely progressive on mechanization issues.[103] Montgomery-Massingberd was not, however, an expert (and knew that he was not) on mechanized forces. The official suggestions put forward by the General Staff under his leadership for the composition of the Mobile Division had serious weaknesses and seem to have been unduly influenced by a desire to find congenial employment for cavalry regiments. But Montgomery-Massingberd was very serious about establishing a Mobile Division and there is some evidence to suggest that he knew its composition as suggested by the General Staff in 1935 might require revision. After visiting France in the summer of that year, and having seen one of the new Divisions Légères Mécaniques, the organization of which was quite similar to that of German Panzer divisions,[104] Montgomery-Massingberd wrote to the Secretary of State for War, Lord Halifax:

> I do feel that we should be getting on with our Mobile Division as quickly as we can, and the sooner we can appoint a commander to supervise its instruction and necessary changes in organization the better. That such a formation is a powerful engine of war I have not the slightest doubt after what I have seen and it would be quite invaluable at the beginning of a campaign.[105]

Under Montgomery-Massingberd the General Staff had tried to establish too many distinct types of armoured and mechanized units and formations. As well as the armour included in the Mobile Division there were to be Army Tank Battalions equipped with "Infantry" tanks and mechanized divisional cavalry whom it was decided to put into light tanks. It would have been better to have concentrated resources on establishing armoured divisions and on producing a single type of fighting tank. Montgomery-Massingberd must be given credit, however, for having a clear vision of the Western Front in the next European war and the role which the British Army ought to play on it. He had understood quite well how the Germans would want to fight such a campaign, had placed a great deal of stress on the development of British armoured and mechanized forces and had given support and patronage to both Lindsay and Hobart.

During Montgomery-Massingberd's regime the Germans had rearmed much more rapidly than the British and had stolen a lead in the development of armoured forces with the establishment of the first three Panzer divisions in October 1935. The very sluggish start to the rearmament of the British Army must, however, be blamed largely on the overruling of General Staff advice by the Cabinet and the Treasury. Montgomery-Massingberd had been wanting to establish a British Mobile Division since October 1934 but the British Army lacked the equipment to give substance to the concept. Montgomery-Massingberd's ideas on the structure of mechanized divisions remained somewhat muddled but there was still time after he retired for their organization to evolve before the outbreak of war. The technical development of British tanks had been massively disrupted by the financial stringency of the early 1930s, however, and Cabinet and Treasury dislike of any clear military commitment to the Continent resulted in tanks receiving a very low priority during rearmament. The rate of production of fighting (as opposed to light) tanks was depressingly slow and this was scarcely outpaced by the development of the General Staff's thinking on how they should be organized and used.

Notes

1 A.J.P. Taylor, *English History 1914–45* (Oxford) 1965, pp. 262–297.
2 B.H. Liddell Hart, *The Tanks*, Vol. I (Cassell) 1959, pp. 272 and 298.
3 W. Deist, *The Wehrmacht and German Rearmament* (Macmillan) 1981, pp. 36–53.
4 B.H. Liddell Hart, *The Tanks*, Vol. I (Cassell) 1959, p. 318. In "The Tank Situation, Memorandum by the Secretary of State for War", 15 October 1936, para. 4(b), PRO WO 32/4441, the Vickers Mediums Marks I and II were described as "obsolete and unfit for war".
5 Milne to Worthington-Evans, 12 November 1928, para. 1 (2), Minute 1, PRO WO 32/2825. "Evolution of Armoured Brigades", 14 May 1929, section 4 (a) (i), LH 15/12/3, Lindsay Papers,

LHCMA. Martel, "Notes on Fighting Vehicles I", February 1937, LH 9/28/69, Liddell Hart Papers, LHCMA.

6 Martel, "Notes on Fighting Vehicles I", and R. Ogorkiewicz, *Armour* (Stevens and Sons) 1960, pp. 153 and 349–350.

7 D. Fletcher, *Mechanised Force* (HMSO), pp. 18–20 and "Report on Experimental Tank A7E3", 18 May 1937, PRO WO 32/3349.

8 "Vickers-Armstrong 6-ton Tank Trials in U.S.A. – June–July 1931", LH 9/28/70 Liddell Hart Papers, LHCMA and Ogorkiewicz, *op. cit.*, p. 154.

9 Ogorkiewicz, *op. cit.*, p. 154.

10 "The Tank Situation, Memorandum by the Secretary of State for War", 15 October 1936, PRO WO 32/4441.

11 Martel, "Notes on Tank Rearmament", para. 5, "Notes on Fighting Vehicles II", March 1937 and "Notes on Fighting Vehicles V", May 1938, para. 3, LH 9/28/69, Liddell Hart Papers, LHCMA. Ogorkiewicz, *op. cit.*, pp. 155–160.

12 "The Tank Situation, Memorandum by the Secretary of State for War", 15 October 1936, para. 13, PRO WO 32/4441. B.H. Liddell Hart, *The Tanks*, Vol. I (Cassell) 1959, p. 370.

13 Col. Macready, "Agenda for meeting of CIGS's Research Committee, 25 April 1934, circulated 23 April, enclosing General Staff Specification for an Infantry Tank", LH 15/12/3, Lindsay Papers, LHCMA. "History of the Infantry Tank and the Anti-tank Gun", 1937, PRO WO 32/4444. "Design and Production of British Tanks, 1936–June 1940", para. 39, PRO CAB 102/851. Martel, "Notes on Fighting Vehicles II", March 1937, para. 4, LH 9/28/69, Liddell Hart Papers, LHCMA. Ogorkiewicz, *op. cit.*, p. 156. Liddell Hart, *op. cit.*, pp. 372–373.

14 Martel, "Notes on Fighting Vehicles II", March 1937, para. 4, "Notes on Fighting Vehicles IV", March 1938, para. 4, LH 9/28/69, Liddell Hart Papers, LHCMA. Ogorkiewicz, *op. cit.*, pp. 156–165.

15 Liddell Hart, *Memoirs*, Vol. I (Cassell) 1965, pp. 227–228.

16 "Talk with Sir Sam Hoare", 31 October 1929, LH 11/1929/18, Liddell Hart Papers, LHCMA, quoted in B. Bond, *British Military Policy Between the Two World Wars* (Clarendon Press) 1980, p. 159.

17 Liddell Hart, "Seven Years: the Regime of Field Marshal Lord Milne", *English Review*, Vol. 56, April 1933, pp. 376–386 and "Field Marshal Lord Milne", *Daily Telegraph*, 20 February 1933. Even more critical of Milne are S. Bidwell and D. Graham, *Firepower: British Army Weapons and Theories of War, 1904–1945* (Allen and Unwin) 1982, p. 155.

18 Pile to Liddell Hart, 16 September 1931 and "Talk with Pile", 24 September 1931, LH 11/1931/5, Liddell Hart Papers, LHCMA.

19 On the antagonism between Fuller and Montgomery-Massingberd,

see Montgomery-Massingberd to Liddell Hart, 3 May 1926, LH 1/520, Liddell Hart Papers, LHCMA, in which Montgomery-Massingberd dismisses Fuller's *Foundations of the Science of War* (Hutchinson) 1926 as pretentious and obscurantist. See also B.H. Reid, *J.F.C. Fuller: Military Thinker* (Macmillan) 1987, pp. 87, 89, 127.

20 B.H. Liddell Hart, *Memoirs*, Vol. I (Cassell) 1965, pp. 70–71, 102–103, 300–301.

21 "The Autobiography of a Gunner" (unpublished memoirs), M-M 159, Montgomery-Massingberd Papers, LHCMA.

22 This inference is taken from R. Prior and T. Wilson, *Command on the Western Front* (Blackwell) 1992, especially pp. 141 and 148–149.

23 "Interim Report of the Cavalry Committee", 23 November 1926, and "Final Report of the Cavalry Committee", 4 January 1927, M-M 157(a), Montgomery-Massingberd Papers, LHCMA.

24 J. Piekalkiewicz, *The Cavalry of World War II* (Jane's) 1979, *passim*.

25 On Montgomery-Massingberd's loyalty complex see "Talk with Duff Cooper", 18 January 1936, LH 11/1936/28, Liddell Hart Papers, LHCMA.

26 "The Autobiography of a Gunner", p. 53, M-M 159, Montgomery-Massingberd Papers, LHCMA.

27 On Montgomery-Massingberd's Francophilia see "Handing Over Notes for My Successor", Section VII, M-M 158/9, which details his contacts with and respect for senior French officers. On Montgomery-Massingberd's support for the principle of a Continental commitment for the British Army see, "Statement by the Chief of the General Staff" (DRC 7), 9 January 1934, PRO CAB 16/109.

28 "The Future Reorganization of the British Army", Part 1, Section 6, PRO WO 32/4612.

29 Hobart to Liddell Hart, 24 July 1934, LH 1/376/8, Liddell Hart Papers, LHCMA.

30 Liddell Hart, *The Tanks*, Vol. I (Cassell) 1959, pp. 302–303, 305 and 344.

31 Committee of Imperial Defence, Defence Requirements Sub-Committee Report, 28 February 1934 (DRC 14), para. 84, PRO CAB 16/109.

32 Minute 1, 15 October 1934, PRO WO 32/2847.

33 Hobart to Lindsay, 10 November 1933, LH 1/376/5, Liddell Hart Papers, LHCMA.

34 A. Horne, *To Lose a Battle* (Macmillan) 1969, pp. 245–281, esp. pp. 276–277.

35 "Report on Royal Tank Corps Staff Exercise", quoted in Robert H.

Larson, *The British Army and the Theory of Armoured Warfare 1918–1940* (Delaware) 1984, p. 164 and Liddell Hart, *op. cit.*, p. 306.

36 Hobart to Lindsay, 10 November 1933, LH 1/376/5, Liddell Hart Papers, LHCMA.

37 Lindsay to Hobart, 17 November 1933, BRIDGEMAN 5/3/2, Bridgeman Papers, LHCMA.

38 Colonel Eric Offord in an interview with the American historian Harold Winton, 27 September 1972, quoted in Winton, *To Change an Army* (Brassey's) 1988, p. 210, n. 23.

39 Liddell Hart, *The Tanks,* Vol. I, p. 306. "Notes of a discussion held at HQ 7th Inf. Bde. on 19 Dec. 33", LH 15/12/8, Lindsay Papers, LHCMA.

40 "Army Training Memorandum No. 10": "The Collective Training Period, 1933", Addendum dated 24 January 1934 and "Report on Royal Tank Corps Staff Exercise" (8–12 May 1934), referred to in Larson, *op. cit.*, pp. 163–164, 170 and quoted in Liddell Hart, *The Tanks*, Vol. I, pp. 306–307.

41 Larson, *op. cit*, p. 264.

42 Hobart to Liddell Hart, 24 July 1934, LH 1/376/8, Liddell Hart Papers, LHCMA.

43 Liddell Hart, *The Tanks*, Vol. I, pp. 317–318.

44 Wavell to Liddell Hart, 27 May 1948, LH 1/733, Liddell Hart Papers, LHCMA.

45 That this exercise has become such a focus of so much historical interest is largely owing to the emphasis placed upon it by Liddell Hart in *The Tanks*, Vol. I, pp. 332–337. All subsequent writers dealing with British armour between the wars have felt it necessary to give it considerable attention. See for example Bond, *op. cit.*, pp. 166–170. Larson, *op. cit.*, pp. 165–167. Winton, *op. cit.*, pp. 178–183.

46 Winton, *op. cit.*, p. 179.

47 Liddell Hart, *The Tanks*, Vol. I, pp. 332–333.

48 K. Macksey, *The Tank Pioneers* (Jane's) 1981, p. 131.

49 Winton, *op. cit.*, pp. 179–180.

50 Liddell Hart, *Memoirs*, Vol. I, p. 254. J.R. Kennedy, *This Our Army* (Hutchinson) 1935, pp. 222–234.

51 Liddell Hart, *The Tanks*, Vol. I, pp. 335–337.

52 Hobart to Liddell Hart, 7 October 1934, LH 1/376/9, Liddell Hart Papers, LHCMA.

53 Lindsay's diary, quoted in Macksey, *op. cit.*, p. 133.

54 Viscount R.C. Bridgeman, Interview 000991/03, Department of Sound Records, Imperial War Museum and Winton, *op. cit.*, p. 181.

55 Lindsay to Montgomery-Massingberd, 5 February 1934, enclosing

proposal for Mobile Division drawn up by Lindsay and Bridgeman (Lindsay's Brigade Major), LH 15/12/8, Lindsay Papers, LHCMA. The proposed Mobile Division organization which was enclosed with this letter was not transferred to the LHCMA with the rest of the Lindsay papers (the Lindsay papers are treated as a sub-section of the Liddell Hart papers) but can be found as BRIDGEMAN 5/3/2, Bridgeman Papers, LHCMA.

56   Hobart to Lindsay, 18 October 1934, mentioned in Larson, *op. cit.*, p. 193, n. 2. The present writer has been unable to find his letter in the now relocated and reorganized Liddell Hart archive, but the same point is made in Liddell Hart, *The Tanks*, Vol. I, p. 337.

57   Lindsay Obituary in *The Tank* No. 453, January 1957, 06902 (41) LINDSAY/AC6, Lindsay Papers, Tank Museum. Liddell Hart on Lindsay in Dictionary of National Biography, 1951–1960, pp. 644–645.

58   CID Defence Requirements Sub-Committee Report, 28 February 1934, DRC 14, para. 28, PRO CAB 16/109.

59   Ministerial Committee, Defence Requirements Report, 31 July 1934, para. 47, PRO CAB 16/110.

60   Ministerial Committee Report, *passim*, PRO CAB 16/110.

61   Pownall's diary, 17 July 1934, Bond (ed.), *Chief of Staff*, Vol. I (Leo Cooper) 1972, p. 48.

62   Defence Requirements Committee, Interim Report (DRC 25) July 1935, PRO CAB 16/112.

63   Defence Requirements Committee, Third Report (DRC 37) Vol. I, "Introduction", para. 5, PRO CAB 16/112.

64   "The Future Reorganization of the British Army", 9 September 1935, PRO WO 32/4612.

65   N.H. Gibbs, *Grand Strategy*, Vol. I (HMSO) 1976, *passim* and B. Bond, *op. cit.*, *passim*.

66   The Kirke Committee on the Lessons of the Great War, Report, PRO WO 32/1297 and PRO WO 32/1305.

67   "Future Reorganization", Part I, "The Main Characteristics of the War 1914–18", pp. 3–6, paras 3 and 4, PRO WO 32/4612.

68   *ibid.*, para. 5.

69   *ibid.*, para. 6.

70   *ibid.*, "Tendencies between 1918 and 1935", pp. 8–11, para. 3.

71   *ibid.*, "Forecast of the Opening Stages of a War with Germany", pp. 11–14.

72   *ibid.*, "Probable Conditions of Our Entry into a European War and Forecast of the Type of Force required", pp. 14–19.

73   Montgomery-Massingberd had made this point in an earlier paper: "Statement by the Chief of the General Staff", 9 January 1934 (DRC 7), para. 8, PRO CAB 16/109.

74 "Future Reorganization", Part I, "Probable Condition of Our Entry into a European War and Forecast of the Type of Force Required", pp. 19–28, para. 5, PRO WO 32/4612.

75 *ibid.*, para. 8 and "Considerations Governing the Organization and Equipment of the Field Force".

76 *ibid.*, "Considerations Governing the Organization and Equipment of the Field Force: Mobile Troops", p. 24.

77 *ibid.*: "The Infantry Division and Its Supporting Units", pp. 20–21.

78 *ibid.*, War Office Letter 20/Cavalry/831, 8 December 1934 and acompanying memorandum on "Organization of Mobile Troops", PRO WO 32/2847.

79 On Montgomery-Massingberd's earlier pro-horse stand see Cavalry Committee reports M-M 157(a), Montgomery-Massingberd Papers, LHCMA. On his continuing enthusiasm for equestrian pursuits for officers see Minute 7, 14 October 1935, PRO WO 32/4005. On his reluctant acceptance of the "gradual disappearance of the horse" from the mainstream of British civil and military life see "Future Reorganization", Part I, "Tendencies between 1918 and 1935", para. 4, 9 September 1935, PRO WO 32/4612.

80 Minute 3, 7 November 1934 and Minute 4, 12 November 1934, PRO WO 32/2847.

81 WO Letter 20/Cavalry/831, 8 December 1934 and "3rd Hussars Experiment in Mechanization", 26 September 1935, pp. 13–14, PRO WO 32/2847.

82 Liddell Hart, *The Tanks*, Vol. I, p. 342.

83 Bond, *op. cit.*, pp. 175–176. Larson, *op. cit.*, pp. 172–176.

84 Liddell Hart, "Armoured Forces in 1928", *RUSI Journal*, Vol. 73, November 1928.

85 Liddell Hart, *The Tanks*, Vol. I, p. 357.

86 As Liddell Hart himself noted in *ibid.*, Vol. II, p. 7.

87 On Hobart's thinking on armoured formations in the later 1930s see "Organization of Higher Mobile Formations", 3 February 1937 and "Organization of Units and Formations in the Regular Field Force Using Armoured Fighting Vehicles", September 1937, LH 15/11/6, Liddell Hart Papers, LHCMA. For evidence that armoured regiments formed from the cavalry used tactics in the desert little different from those of armoured regiments formed from the RTR see P.G. Griffith, "British Armoured Warfare in the Western Desert 1940–43", in J.P. Harris and F.H. Toase, *Armoured Warfare* (Batsford) 1990, pp. 72–73 and 77–78.

88 Minute 1, 15 October 1934, PRO WO 32/2847.

89 Lindsay to Montgomery-Massingberd, 5 February 1934, LH 15/12/8, Lindsay Papers, LHCMA. WO Letter 20/Cavalry/831, 8 December

1934 and accompanying memorandum on "Organization of Mobile Troops", PRO WO 32/2847.

90   Liddell Hart, *The Tanks*, Vol. I, p. 356.

91   "3rd Hussars Experiment in Mechanization, April–September 1935", Section 1 (d), 26 September 1935, PRO WO 32/2847.

92   "Appreciation by the Military Attaché, Berlin, of the Views of the German General Staff on Future War, Together with a Summary of Information Regarding recent Developments in Germany", 26 November 1934, section 1: "General doctrine as to the form of a future war in which Germany will be engaged", PRO WO 190/283. "The Future Reorganization of the British Army, Part I, Forecast of the Opening Stages of a War with Germany", 9 September 1935, PRO WO 32/4612.

93   "3rd Hussars Experiment in Mechanization, April–September 1935", Section 1, General, 26 September 1935, PRO WO 32/2847.

94   "Mechanisation Report – 3rd King's Own Hussars", G.A. Heydeman, Commander 2nd Cavalry Brigade, 13 October 1936, PRO WO 32/2847.

95   Treasury Inter-Service Committee, War Office Memorandum No. 242, 18 January 1938, PRO WO 32/4445.

96   "Report of the Committee on the Cardwell System", para. 61 (c), 8 August 1937, PRO WO 32/4614.

97   DCIGS (Ronald Adam) to DGMP (Sir Harold Brown) 27 March 1939, and "Meeting on the Tank Programme", 15 March 1939, para. 4, PRO WO 32/4445.

98   Army Training Memorandum No. 17, January 1937, p. 30, LH 15/3/23, Liddell Hart Papers, LHCMA.

99   Ogorkiewicz, *op. cit.*, pp. 59–60 and 73–74.

100 "The Autobiography of a Gunner", M-M 159, Montgomery-Massingberd Papers, LHCMA.

101 General Sir Charles Bonham-Carter expressed this view in conversation with Liddell Hart on 12 December 1935, LH 11/1935/114, Liddell Hart Papers, LHCMA. And at the 170th Meeting of the Chiefs of Staff Committee, on 31 March 1936, Admiral Sir Ernle Chatfield, the chairman, said that, "on the last occasion on which Sir Archibald Montgomery-Massingberd would attend a COS meeting, he wished to express his gratitude to him for the valuable co-operation which he had rendered during the past three years. The various problems which had confronted the COS had been solved in the most amicable way and he felt that was largely due to the geniality and goodwill of Sir Archibald Montgomery-Massingberd." (PRO CAB 35/5) Such fulsome valedictions were not normal practice.

102 "Handing over Notes for my Successor", undated but presumably

March or April 1936, M-M 158/9, Montgomery-Massingberd Papers, LHCMA.

103   Hobart to Liddell Hart, 24 July 1934, LH 1/376/8 and Hobart to Liddell Hart, 21 September 1936, LH 1/376/35b. In the former letter, already quoted, Hobart called Montgomery-Massingberd "far-seeing, resolute and open-minded". In the latter, written after Montgomery-Massingberd had retired Hobart claimed that "Jock [Burnett-] Stuart . . . is absolutely defeatist and despairing . . . I can't help feeling he could have done more than he has to stop this reversal of the very modest bid for mobility that Archie Montgomery started."

104   Ogorkiewicz, *op. cit.*, pp. 65–66.

105   Montgomery-Massingberd to Lord Halifax, 17 August 1935, M-M 158/5, Montgomery-Massingberd Papers, LHCMA.

8

The approach of war: 1936–39

In the later 1930s the development of both British armoured forces and British military thought on their employment was painfully slow. The extent to which the General Staff itself may be held responsible for this retarded development will be explored in this chapter. In order to arrive at a balanced assessment, however, it is necessary constantly to bear in mind the practical constraints within which the General Staff was operating at this time. A serious rearmament programme for the British Army was approved by the Cabinet only in February 1936.[1] This left little time before the outbreak of war for the development and production of tanks, perhaps the most technically complex weapons the Army required. The chances of their being produced in the quantity and quality needed for a Continental campaign were further diminished by the disarray into which the technical development of British tanks had fallen by the mid-1930s, largely as a result of the financial squeeze of 1931–34.[2] The problems thus caused were compounded by severe financial and industrial restrictions imposed on British rearmament as a whole and by the much lower priority accorded to the Army compared with the RAF and the Royal Navy.[3] Moreover, while Hitler's Germany was obviously a growing menace to the European balance of power, and while it seemed increasingly likely that there would be a major European war sooner or later, the role the British Army would play in such a conflict was, at least until February 1939, left completely undecided by the Cabinet.[4]

Neville Chamberlain, Chancellor of the Exchequer and Stanley Baldwin's heir-apparent as leader of the Conservative Party, was a powerful figure in the National Government formed in November 1931. From the first discussion of the question of rearmament in the period 1933–34 he had forcefully expressed his doubts (on both political and financial grounds) about preparing a British Field Force for the Continent.[5] Chamberlain became Prime Minister in May 1937 and his attitude ensured that the Army remained the "Cinderella of the Services" throughout the 1930s. During the rearmament period of 1936–39, moreover, the Cabinet pressed the War Office to spend ever increasing amounts on the anti-aircraft defence of Great Britain, thus further diminishing the funds available to be spent on Field Force requirements like tanks.[6]

In October 1936 the War Office admitted to the Committee of Imperial Defence that the tank situation was extremely unsatisfactory. The main cause of the problem was presented as the financial stringency of previous years. In the years 1927–36 the sum available annually for experimenting with tanks had varied from £22,500 to £93,750, whereas the cost of designing and producing a single experimental medium tank could be as much £29,000. The shortage of money had resulted in the confinement of research and development to two organizations only – Vickers and the Royal Ordnance Factories – and even these could afford to maintain only very small design staffs. The money available annually for expenditure on tanks had barely sufficed to keep these two contractors occupied. It was impossible to interest other firms in tank design and development without giving a definite guarantee of orders later and this had not been practicable until the beginning of a serious rearmament effort in 1936. There had consequently been a dearth of ideas and "a very narrow field of research and experiment". The situation had been made even worse by the untimely deaths of some of the most experienced tank designers, especially by the loss of Vickers's Sir John Carden in an aeroplane crash in 1935.[7]

In October 1936 the Army had 209 light and 166 medium tanks in service. The vast majority, including all the medium tanks, were regarded by the General Staff as obsolete. Two-thirds of the light tanks were of Vickers patterns produced in the early 1930s which carried only 2 men. The 2-man light tank had gone out of favour by 1936 as it was no longer believed possible to drive, fight and navigate a fast tank effectively with such a small crew. The armour on these early types was regarded as grossly inadequate. They were liable to be penetrated even by rifle bullets at close ranges. There were also, however, about 70 of the 3-man Light

Figure 23 A Light tank Mark VIB of the Westminster Dragoons early in the Second World War. The Light tank Mark VI was the only type of tank ready for production when rearmament began in 1936. By the outbreak of war it was obsolescent.

tank Mark VI, armed with 2 machine guns, capable of 35 mph on roads and proof against normal rifle fire. At this stage the General Staff regarded the Mark VI as "superior to any light tank produced by other nations" and well adapted to its reconnaissance, screening and colonial warfare roles. The War Office was expecting to have procured a total of 608 of these machines by April 1938.[8]

But the Light Tank Mark VI was the only tank with which the War Office was ready to proceed with manufacture when rearmament began. Medium tank development had, as indicated in the last chapter, hit severe problems after the cancellation of the Sixteen Tonner project in 1932. The cheaper A7, A9 and A10 mediums tanks existed, in 1936, only as prototypes undergoing trials, and all were considered rather unsatisfactory. In addition to a host of minor technical problems which had not yet been ironed out, the relatively low power generated by their commercially produced engines ensured that they were either very slow for the medium role or very poorly armoured. Anyway it was considered

Figure 24 An A9 of the 1st Armoured Division. This is the "close support" version with a 3-pdr howitzer firing high explosive instead of the more usual 2-pdr firing solid shot.

unlikely that any of them would be ready for production before 1938. As mentioned in the last chapter, dissatisfaction with the armour protection on the medium tank prototypes then under development had led to the development of a heavily armoured "Infantry" tank which it was accepted would be slow. A pilot model of the cheap and very crude two-man "I" tank known as the A11 or Infantry tank Mark I existed by October 1936, but it needed some modifications before it would be ready for production.[9] The "cruiser" tank, a concept initiated by Martel, complementary to that of the Infantry tank, was at this stage no more than a notion.

Martel was appointed as Assistant Director of Mechanization early in 1936, after having spent the previous year as a student at the Imperial Defence College. In September 1936 he visited the Soviet Union and attended the Red Army's manoeuvres in the company of Major-General A.P. Wavell. The sheer number of tanks on display was impressive (on one occasion he saw 1,000 tanks in a single march-past) and the mechanical performance of most Soviet vehicles was excellent. The Soviet B.T. "light medium" tank proved itself capable of speeds up to 30 mph, could traverse rough country at 20 mph with ease and had remarkable obstacle-crossing ability. The B.T. employed a suspension system of a type invented by the American designer J.W. Christie. Martel began to think seriously about the adoption of Christie's suspension system for British tanks. Initially he seems to have envisaged a British Christie tank as a replacement for the existing types of light tank for work with the Tank Brigade. But he also commented that, "Unless we can improve the A9 to a considerable extent I cannot help feeling dismay at the idea of our building any large number of these tanks which will be inferior to existing Soviet tanks." So he may also have been thinking of British Christie tanks, "cruiser" tanks as they were designated, performing the role hitherto allotted to medium tanks and thus forming virtually the whole equipment of the Tank Brigade.[10]

Immediately after his return from Russia Martel set about obtaining a Christie tank for development in Britain. The purchase of a Soviet machine did not prove possible and so Martel arranged for contact to be made with Christie himself. Christie had not done well from his invention. Though it was ingenious in principle he had never succeeded in eliminating all the mechanical snags. He had built three prototypes. One had been bought by the American military who had not succeeded in developing it. Another had been purchased by the Russians with the better results which Martel had noted. By the time the British War Office became interested in Christie's idea he had only one tank left and that was mortgaged. Christie agreed over the telephone to sell this remaining model for £8,000 but Martel had to persuade War Office Finance not only to find the £8,000 but also to pay off the mortgage. Nor did Martel's troubles end there. The American government tried to prevent the deal on the grounds that the export of war material was forbidden and eventually the tank had to be smuggled out of the United States in crates labelled "tractor" and "grapefruit". As, owing to pressure of other work, no existing armaments firm was in a position to take on the development of Cruiser tanks, Martel and his superior, Major-General A.E. Davidson, the Director of Mechanization, made contact with Lord Nuffield's industrial organization. Lord Nuffield agreed to form a new company, Nuffield Mechanization, expressly for this purpose.[11] Martel had certainly demonstrated remarkable initiative and had acted with great speed and determination. He had returned from Russia on 26 September. By 17 November Christie's tank had arrived in England.[12] But the wisdom of initiating the development of a rather technically complex form of tank through a newly formed firm, lacking personnel experienced in this kind of work, was somewhat more questionable.

A general dissatisfaction with the underpowered medium tank prototypes of the mid-1930s led to the bifurcation of British medium tank development. Ultimately all British fighting tanks (as opposed to the light tanks mainly intended for reconnaissance and screening) became classified as either infantry tanks or cruisers, the medium classification being abandoned by the outbreak of war. Unhappy with all their attempts to produce a standard, all-purpose medium tank, the British military authorities made efforts, during rearmament, to develop, on the one hand, fast cruiser tanks which they accepted would be lightly armoured, and, on the other, heavily armoured but slow moving infantry tanks.

The bifurcation of the development of British medium tanks down the infantry and cruiser routes was a historical accident. Though there were elements in British military thought which could be and were used to justify it, it was not the result of any preconceived doctrine.[13] Had the Sixteen Tonner been allowed to go into production and been succeeded, in the mid-1930s, by further medium tanks designed and built without severe financial constraints, it is likely that the RTC would have continued to use a single type of medium tank both for the close support of attacking infantry and for more mobile roles. Indeed the perceived failure of medium tank development and the bifurcation which derived from it seem to have driven organization and doctrine rather than vice versa. At the outbreak of the Second World War the two distinct classifications of tank were allocated to distinct types of unit and formation. Infantry tanks were allocated to "Army Tank

Figure 25
Giffard le Quesne Martel.

Battalions" which could be grouped under an administrative head-quarters known as an "Army Tank Brigade". All of these were manned by the Royal Tank Regiment (RTR), as the RTC was by then known. Cruiser tanks were allotted to "Armoured Regiments" which were normally components of armoured divisions. Some of the armoured regiments were formed from the RTR but as the war went on an increasing number were manned by the cavalry, most cavalry regiments of the line having been mechanized by September 1939. Distinct doctrines and operating procedures were, inevitably, devised for the specific types of armour: infantry tank doctrine being essentially derived from the experience gained in 1916–18 with the Marks I–V heavy tanks, while armoured divisions were intended primarily for flank protection, movement against the enemy's flanks and rear, pursuit and counter-attack.[14]

Giffard le Quesne Martel, the father of the cruiser tank, served in the War Office as Assistant Director of Mechanization until January 1938 when he became Deputy Director, a post he held until the outbreak of war. During the late 1930s he appears to have been regarded as the serving officer with most expertise on the technical side of armoured fighting vehicles and he continued to be an important figure in the first half of the Second World War, serving as Commander of the Royal Armoured Corps between

December 1940 and September 1942. It thus seems appropriate
here to explore the evolution of his personal ideas on the organization and employment of armoured forces. As noted in chapter
3, Martel's involvement with tanks went back to October 1916
when he became one of the first officers employed at Hugh Elles's
headquarters at Bermicourt. He had produced a visionary paper
on future armoured warfare as early as November 1916.[15] Having
reverted to the Royal Engineers after the war he had served in the
War Office between 1923 and 1926 as deputy Assistant Director
of Fortifications and Works, a post unrelated to tanks. But his
involvement with armour did not cease during this period. From
1925 he had, by unofficial efforts in his spare time, pioneered the
"tankette" concept, which had ultimately led to the development
of both light tanks and armoured machine gun carriers. He went
on to command the first RE company to be fully mechanized and
served with it when it formed part of the Experimental Mechanized Force in 1927–28, after which he taught at the Indian Staff
College at Quetta between 1930 and 1934. He had published
extensively on armoured forces. His book *In The Wake Of The
Tank* appeared in 1931 and, by the mid-1930s, he had established
a reputation as an expert in this field both in the British Army and
abroad.[16] His ideas, however, were not always in tune with those
of the RTC radicals. Though most of the time he was on reasonably good terms with them,[17] they tended to look askance at his
desertion of the Tank Corps at the end of the First World War
and did not regard him as one of themselves.[18]

   In the mid-1930s Lindsay, Broad and Hobart all saw the Tank
Brigade as the essential armoured force. They regarded the medium tank as the basic equipment of such a force and wanted to
keep the development of British armoured strength firmly under
the control of the RTC. At least up to 1935 Martel had his doubts
on all these counts. He considering medium tanks complex, expensive and, when used as part of an independent Tank Brigade
without the close support of infantry, rather vulnerable to anti-
tank guns. He also, quite rightly, refused to believe the RTC claim
that medium tanks could deliver fire with reasonable accuracy on
the move.[19] Martel was inclined to favour the employment of
"large numbers of comparatively small and simple fighting vehicles". He reasoned that the enemy would find these more difficult
to deal with than a small number of expensive medium tanks. He

had in mind a sort of crude Infantry Fighting Vehicle (IFV), as it would today be called, with an armoured cab containing the driver and a light machine gun, and an unarmoured body behind it containing a small rifle section. The riflemen would dismount when the vehicle came under fire but would be able to advance against light opposition with the support of armoured, tracked light machine guns:

> The men working forward on the ground would belong to the same unit as the men advancing in the machines to cover them and co-operation would be automatic, whereas with tanks and men in different units co-operation is far more difficult to arrange.[20]

Martel had some valid points here. He had perhaps found a reasonable solution to the problem of maintaining the advance of infantry against light opposition in open warfare. If, however, British tank development had been neglected in favour of IFVs, how would the British Army have coped with enemy formations containing substantial numbers of tanks? In any case, once he had moved to the Directorate of Mechanization in 1936 and a serious rearmament programme had begun, Martel seems to have largely dropped his IFV fixation. (A smaller type of machine gun carrier based on a design by Sir John Carden was in any case already being provided for the infantry.)[21] Martel's views, however, still differed from those of the RTC radicals in some respects. He was, for example, much more sympathetic than they to the infantry tank concept. He had not consciously sought the infantry tank/cruiser tank split and, in the period between 1936 and 1939, still favoured efforts to design a general-purpose medium tank as a long-term measure. But he seems to have regarded the bifurcation of medium tank development as having a certain intrinsic logic behind it. While Commander of the Royal Armoured Corps in 1940–42 he came to accept it as a permanent feature of British tank policy and continued to argue in its favour after the Second World War.[22] He believed that armies had always consisted of two types of troops:

> There were the lighter and more mobile troops, whose duties were to push out, gain touch with the enemy and then work around his flanks or rear. This had always been the role of the cavalry. Then there had been the slower moving, harder hitting troops whose duty it was to close with the enemy, fix him, and if necessary assault his

defences. This had always been infantry role. We realized that tanks
would be needed to assist in both of these roles: the faster tanks for
the Cavalry role as light cavalry, and heavier tanks for the slower
role to be used in much the same way as heavy cavalry had assisted
infantry in the past.[23]

There was thus no essential disagreement on this issue between
Elles as Master General of the Ordnance and Martel as Assistant
Director of Mechanization. Each officer accepted that tanks were
needed both for mobile operations within armoured formations
and for close support to unmechanized infantry in the assault of
strong positions. Given that no machine which could do both jobs
adequately had yet been designed in Great Britain, it was generally
accepted that two complementary types would have to be produced. Martel praised Elles's efforts to develop infantry tanks.
Martel's own work to develop cruiser tanks was going on within
the Master General of the Ordnance's department in the War
Office and though, as Liddell Hart indicates, Elles might have had
little initial enthusiasm for it,[24] it could not have proceeded as it
did without his approval.

Deciding on the types of tank the Army ought to try to procure
was difficult enough. Actually procuring them was even more so.
The first step was for War Office officials to go cap-in-hand to the
Treasury in the form of the Treasury Inter-Service Committee.
This body, which controlled the purse strings, in effect ran the
rearmament programme.[25] The elaborate hierarchy of defence com-
mittees which the influential Cabinet secretary, Maurice Hankey,
had constructed[26] still in theory formulated defence policy but
could only approve rearmament measures "in principle". The
Treasury controlled the practice. By November 1936 the War Office
was seeking approval for a programme which included:

No.	Unit	Unit Establishment
6	Light Tank Cavalry Regiments	58 Light Tanks
4	Divisional Cavalry Regiments	58 Light Tanks
1	Light Tank Battalion RTC	59 Cruiser Tanks
3	Mixed Tank Battalions RTC	23 Cruiser Tanks and 27 Medium Tanks
4	Army Tank Battalions	4 Light, 15 Medium and 60 Infantry Tanks
1	Tank Brigade H.Q.	4 Cruiser and 5 Medium Tanks[27]

The Treasury did not give financial approval for any part of this programme until March 1937[28] and then only for the light tank element. It is evident that the Treasury regarded Field Force requirements as a low priority and was particularly reluctant to spend money on preparing the British Army to fight the Germans on the Continent.[29] Nevertheless persistent and skilful argument by War Office officials had secured the clearance of the great bulk of the programme by July 1937.[30] By that time, however, a new Prime Minister was in office and the tank programme was to come under renewed financial pressure from the end of 1937 as a result of a change in strategic policy which Chamberlain's government introduced. In the meantime, however, the General Staff pressed ahead with its plans for the development of armoured forces and in particular for the creation of a fully mechanized Mobile Division.

Though Montgomery-Massingberd had announced the General Staff's intention to establish a Mobile Division as long ago as October 1934,[31] the acute shortage of tanks had imposed a long delay. It was not until September 1937 that Montgomery-Massingberd's successor, Field Marshal Sir Cyril Deverell, considered it worthwhile to appoint a commander. This appointment became the source of an acrimonious dispute between Deverell and Leslie Hore-Belisha whom Neville Chamberlain had appointed as Secretary of State for War upon the formation of his Cabinet the previous May.

Hore-Belisha, who was forty-three when he came to the War Office, liked to regard himself as a great reforming war minister in the tradition of Cardwell and Haldane. This self-image was regarded as completely phoney by certain officers on the General Staff who served under him, but has been accepted by some historians of standing and ability. Educated at Clifton and St John's College, Oxford, he served as an officer in the Army Service Corps from 1914 to 1918. After a short career at the bar he entered Parliament as a Liberal in 1923. He adhered to the "National" Liberal branch of his party in the split of 1931 and gained his first Cabinet post as Minister of Transport in 1936. In this job he had displayed a willingness to innovate and a flair for publicity. His selection for the War Office may also have owed something to the fact that he was totally dependent on Chamberlain for his political future and consequently likely to prove a ready tool in Chamberlain's hands. He lacked any firm political base. His own party was minute and, after 1935, completely dependent for its future on the goodwill of the Conservatives. He was not popular with other ministers. He made some useful reforms in Army personnel policy but (at least until events in the aftermath of the Munich agreement of September 1938 caused him doubts) he was essentially Chamberlain's instrument at the War Office, implementing Chamberlain's wishes. Amongst these, cutting down the scale of expenditure proposed by the General Staff and driving away the spectre of the British Army fighting again on Continental battlefields were at least as important as mechanization or reform. While the fact that Hore-Belisha was of Jewish descent may not have helped in his dealings with some senior officers, their distrust of him seems to have owed more to their (not wholly unwarranted) perception that he was shallow, fickle, vain and self-serving.[32] The career of Benjamin Disraeli argues against the idea that Jewish origins are a fatal obstacle to the leadership of even the more right-wing elements of the British establishment.

In September 1937 Deverell nominated Major-General Blakiston-Houston, the Inspector of Cavalry, as commander of the Mobile Division.[33] In this he was merely following a course of action proposed as long ago as October 1935 that the Inspector of Cavalry and his staff should form the nucleus of the Mobile Division headquarters.[34] When sending Hore-Belisha to the War Office Chamberlain had apparently intimated that drastic changes were needed. Hore-Belisha quickly made contact with Liddell Hart, whom he used as unofficial adviser on virtually every aspect of military policy. This relationship, which both men referred to as the "Partnership", lasted until the middle of 1938.[35] Hore-Belisha consulted Liddell Hart over the Mobile Division appointment and found the latter keen that the division should be commanded by one of three officers from the RTC: Pile, Broad and Hobart. (It is not clear why Liddell Hart did not suggest the recall of Lindsay from India. Perhaps he felt that Lindsay's credibility had been too badly damaged by the Mobile Force fiasco of 1934.) Pile and Broad had both recently been promoted to Major-General and were seeking appropriate employment. Pile, however, was becoming increasingly interested in anti-aircraft defence and was about to return to his original calling as a gunner, taking charge of the 1st AA Division which covered London. Broad was regarded in the War Office as quarrelsome and Liddell Hart himself noted that

Broad lacked both humour and tact – qualities which would probably have been needed in a commander attempting to adjust the
cavalry to the demands of modern war.[36]

Liddell Hart's real preference was clearly for Hobart. But the
latter would probably not have been a very good choice. Like
Broad, Hobart was distinctly humourless and tactless and, more
importantly, did not believe in the idea of a large all-arms mechanized division.[37] According to Liddell Hart, one of the main War
Office objections to Hobart's appointment was that he might be
unacceptable to the cavalry because he had had an affair with the
wife of a student when teaching at the Indian Staff College at
Quetta in the mid-1920s and had thus been cited as the co-
respondent in a brother officer's divorce. This affair, however,
which eventually resulted in Hobart's marriage, appears to have
had remarkably little impact on his career up to this point. There
is no reason to think that it would have made him any more
socially unacceptable to the cavalry (who were not known for
prudishness) than to the rest of the Army.[38] The real reason for
Deverell's opposition to Hobart as commander of the Mobile
Division cannot now be known with certainty. Probably Deverell
viewed him (not without reason) as a tank fanatic and RTC chau-
vinist who would have found it difficult to weld the different
arms within the division into a cohesive team. The matter was
ultimately resolved, at the suggestion of Hore-Belisha's Military
Secretary, Lieutenant-General Gort, by the appointment of Major-
General Alan Brooke (an officer from the Royal Artillery who was
then serving as Director of Military Training), as a compromise
candidate. In discussion with Deverell on 3 November 1937 Hore-
Belisha finally agreed that Brooke should command the Mobile
Division provided that Brooke's old job as Director of Military
Training should go to an officer from the RTC. Deverell suggested
Hobart and Hore-Belisha accepted.[39]

While there is some evidence that he was less favourable to the
RTC than Montgomery-Massingberd had been in his period as
CIGS, Deverell's motives in this affair were probably more com-
plex than Liddell Hart (who portrayed him merely as an obstinate
reactionary) was prepared to allow. The policy of the General
Staff seems to have been fully to reconcile the cavalry to mechan-
ization. It was probably to that end, in itself commendable, that
Deverell wanted a cavalry general to command the division. It is

also likely that the constant attempts of Liddell Hart to interfere in the making of military appointments were both recognized and resented by the General Staff.[40] Thus Liddell Hart's sponsorship of particular officers from the RTC for this job may actually have damaged their chances of getting it. Brooke, though lacking experience of mechanized units, was a highly competent and dedicated officer and probably not a bad choice. The real pity perhaps was that Brooke's command of the division was so brief, lasting only until July 1938.[41]

Another, ultimately more important, controversy concerning the Mobile Division was going on concurrently with the dispute over its command. As part of the General Staff's programme to train mechanized cavalry units for their roles in the Mobile Division, 2nd Cavalry Brigade held a series of exercises, under the supervision of Major-General Burnett-Stuart, in summer 1936. Following these Burnett-Stuart told his officers that:

> for lack of official guidance he had had to make up his own mind as to the proper role of the Mobile Division before he could start the study at all. He had taken it to be exactly the same role which the old Cavalry Division had been intended to perform for the pre-war Expeditionary Force. Only the instrument was being remodelled, not the purpose for which it was wanted. It was to provide the same kind of protection and reconnaissance for the force, to clear away the enemy's mobile troops and minor centres of resistance and to follow up the enemy if he retired. When a battlefront was formed it would slip aside to cover the flank or lie up in readiness.
>
> He had made up his mind that the Mobile Division was not to be regarded as a force to be sent on independent strategic missions, nor as an armoured mass of manoeuvre on the Continental model. Hence there was no need of heavy assaulting power, and for that reason he thought that the Tank Brigade should be left out. The Tank Brigade would be held back for great occasions, and it had no part in the normal day's work of armoured light cavalry. It was because he had formed this view that he kept the Tank Brigade out of the picture in this year's trials.[42]

Liddell Hart had a high regard for Burnett-Stuart's abilities but correctly pointed out that the concept of the Mobile Division having exactly the same roles (basically reconnaissance, screening, flanking manoeuvre and pursuit) as the old horsed cavalry division was a dangerous one. Any move towards the exclusion of the

Tank Brigade was likely to produce a formation lacking in offensive and even counter-offensive power.[43] It is odd that Burnett-Stuart should have complained of lack of official guidance on this issue. The Tank Brigade had been specifically included in the Mobile Division in General Staff papers written in Montgomery-Massingberd's period.[44] But it seemed for a while that Deverell might adopt Burnett-Stuart's conception of the Mobile Division rather than Montgomery-Massingberd's. Deverell even used the possible exclusion of the Tank Brigade as a reason for not appointing an RTC officer to command the formation.[45] At some point Deverell must have changed his mind, however, and when the composition of the division was officially announced in November 1937 it included 1st Tank Brigade. The inclusion of the Tank Brigade was confirmed in the Army List of March 1938.[46]

But, as listed, the division was still something of a monstrosity. All six of the cavalry regiments included in its two cavalry brigades were now intended to be converted to light tanks. When these were added to the tanks of the 1st Brigade RTC (then a mixture of lights and mediums but ultimately intended to be cruisers) there would be far too many tanks in the division – apparently over 500 altogether.[47] The vast majority of them, being light tanks and armed only with machine guns, could have been of little use in engaging enemy armour unless that too was very light. Liddell Hart was thus correct to advise that the Mobile Division's bulk was tending to become disproportionate to its fighting power.[48] His own views on the structure of armoured formations (which appear to have been derived from Hobart's and which will be discussed below) were, however, distinctly faulty.

The units which made up the Mobile Division were scattered over much of Southern England. When Alan Brooke took command in November 1937 he established his headquarters at Andover and appears to have worked hard, until he left the division in July 1938 to weld them together as a team. His comments in his unpublished memoirs are in some ways illuminating:

> I was thrilled with my new job as Commander of Mobile Division, new ground to cover, new doctrines to evolve, and all concerned with the arm destined to play a major part in future war.
>
> Command of this division entailed tackling two definite problems, the one a tactical and strategical one, the other mainly a psychological one.

There was on the one hand the necessity to evolve correct doctrine for the employment of armoured forces in the field of battle, and on the other hand some bridge must be found to span the large gap that existed in the relations between the extremists of the Tank Corps and of the Cavalry. There was no love lost between the two. The Cavalry naturally resented deeply losing their horses, giving up their mounted role and becoming dungaree mechanics!

The Tank Corps, suffering perhaps from a slight inferiority complex, due to their youth as a Corps and lack of tradition, were apt to look on the cavalry as amateur soldiers who only thought of polo hunting and racing, and never took their profession seriously.

Amongst all the best on either side their feelings were suppressed, and only one desire prevailed, namely, to weld together the best armoured force in the minimum of time. There always exist, however, some men who fail to rise to the occasion, and being unable to absorb the bitterness that faces them, endeavour to embitter the lives of those that surround them.

While Brooke indicates that he did not approve of Hobart's excessively tank-centred views on mechanized warfare, it is not clear that he had a very definite vision of his own. He appears to have accurately identified most of the problems:

> The role of the close support Rifle battalions had to be worked out from bedrock, the question of Artillery support for armoured forces on the move presented many new problems, whilst medical and administrative requirements had to be readjusted to meet the peculiar requirements of armoured forces. Added to the above, the whole technique of wireless control, so essential to armoured forces, required expanding and improving.[49]

But there is little evidence that, by the time he left the division to become the corps commander for the home anti-aircraft defences in July 1938, he had found solutions. He was succeeded by Major-General Roger Evans, a cavalryman who, like Brooke, had no previous knowledge of mechanized forces and who appears to have had no definite ideas of his own on how the division should be organized and handled.[50]

After the departure of Lindsay to India in 1935, moreover, there appears to have been no one in Great Britain who could provide clear, authoritative advice on these critical issues. Liddell Hart seems never to have been an original thinker on armoured forces. He seems to have acted as little more than a sounding-board for the opinions of other tank enthusiasts with whom he was associated. Fuller had been out of the Army since 1933, had become involved with Moseley's British Union of Fascists and had, by the late 1930s, largely lost interest in armoured warfare. Martel's expertise was technical rather than tactical.[51] Broad appears not to have been in the same league as Lindsay intellectually and certainly never had the ear of a CIGS to the degree that, in the Milne and Montgomery-Massingberd eras, Lindsay once did. Pile had moved into anti-aircraft defence[52] which was also supplanting armour as the focus of Liddell Hart's military interests. Amongst senior officers from the RTC, Hobart, as DMT, should have been the most influential, but did not achieve harmonious relationships with colleagues in the War Office and anyway his views on the subject of armoured formations were seriously flawed.

Hobart's pride and joy was the Tank Brigade which he had commanded for three-and-a-half years. Writing about the Brigade in a letter to Liddell Hart, Hobart had quoted Cromwell: "I have a lovely company. If you could see it you would love it too."[53] He was uncomfortable with the concept of a large mechanized division of all-arms and thought the Tank Brigade, a virtually all-tank formation, should form the basis of a slimmed down, easily manoeuvrable armoured division or "Tank Striking Force", as he preferred to call it. "I am convinced", he wrote in February 1937, "that the faster a formation moves, the smaller it must be if control is to be properly exercised." He thought it necessary to "avoid adding anything to the Force beyond the minimum necessary to its protection at rest, temporarily holding the enemy's attention and forming a point for manoeuvre and for holding an obstacle for a short time". He wanted only one infantry battalion and a very small amount of artillery in his Tank Striking Force, together with the Tank Brigade and a reconnaissance element consisting of armoured cars and light tanks.[54]

In a slightly later paper on the same subject Hobart explained that the artillery of the type of "Tank Striking Force" or "Tank Division" which he advocated "must be reduced to a minimum in view of the weight of ammunition and numbers of vehicles". He recommended only eight 75-pdr gun/howitzers. Similarly, he did not wish to encumber tank formations with any large numbers of engineers. Their integral engineer component needed to be just sufficient to conduct "hasty, improvised repairs of a minor character" and to carry out minor demolitions. While he recognized that river and canal crossings might occasionally be necessary, Hobart insisted that *ad hoc* attachments of engineering personnel and bridging equipment would have to suffice for that purpose.[55]

Liddell Hart reckoned that the armoured division which Hobart was proposing in 1937 comprised about 400 tanks and only about 4,000 men.[56] The experience of the Second World War would indicate that this was vastly too tank-heavy. A total of 2–300 tanks per division would suffice. At least 3 infantry battalions were needed, 4 were desirable.[57] The 1 battalion Hobart recommended was quite inadequate. A mere 8 guns could not have provided sufficient firepower to suppress a serious enemy anti-tank defence. That Hobart should have intended a division with so many tanks to have no integral bridging capability is truly amazing, and mine clearance was a problem he does not appear to have considered at all. Yet he retained this basic conception of the armoured division until at least 1941 and Liddell Hart appears to have endorsed it over the whole 1937–41 period.[58]

Liddell Hart thus had little to offer the War Office in terms of useful advice on the organization and training of armoured forces. Nor were his pronouncements on strategic issues conducive to the development of British armoured strength. From 1937 he became increasingly obsessed with three ideas: the great power of the defence in modern land warfare, the excessive offensive mindedness of armies in general and the British Army in particular (an outlook which entailed the risk of repetitions of the Somme and Passchendaele), and the urgent need for defence against the acute threat to the British homeland presented by the German air force.[59]

Liddell Hart's conviction that the defence was supreme on land emerged very clearly from a series of articles written for *The Times* entitled "Defence or Attack". Emphasizing the tremendous effectiveness of modern defensive firepower, Liddell Hart gave the false impression that the British General Staff was devoted to ill-thought-out doctrine of offensive *à l'outrance*.

> Attack is so deeply rooted in the military tradition that its power to succeed as a natural result of the offensive spirit properly directed is the first article of the soldier's creed. Thus despite the memory of a century of machine warfare, culminating in 1914–18, it is still a

normal tendency, indeed a habit, to assume that an attack will succeed so long as the executant has a numerical advantage which would
have sufficed when men fought with hand weapons, mainly at short
ranges.[60]

By 1937 Liddell Hart appears to have been losing his faith in the
ability of armoured and mechanized forces to transform war.
Gradually, during the late 1930s, he seems, like Fuller, to have
lost interest in, or at any rate enthusiasm for, the whole subject of
armoured warfare. Commenting on a staff exercise involving a
Mobile Division, in September 1937, Liddell Hart noted that "the
lot of a commander who is charged with an offensive role under
modern conditions is not an enviable one. It requires almost a
superman to make a good show". The German Panzer force commanders of the Second World War were, generally speaking, thoroughly competent professionals but by no means supermen. Liddell
Hart was a long way from foreseeing the sorts of operation which
they were to conduct.[61]

Because of his belief that the British Army was obsessed with
the offensive yet ill-advised to adopt it in the face of the defensive
firepower of modern weapons, Liddell Hart became increasingly
opposed to the whole idea of sending a Field Force to the Continent. In June 1937 he submitted a memorandum to Hore-Belisha
which indicated that participation in a campaign on the Continent
should be considered the "least likely" role of the Army[62] and his
distaste for the Continental commitment became more pronounced
as the decade drew to its close. The General Staff insisted that a
German breakthrough in France or the Low Countries was a definite
possibility in the event of war and that a British Field Force might
be required to protect the Channel Ports while the French Army
regrouped.[63] Liddell Hart's response to this suggestion shows that
his conviction of the supremacy of the defensive was unshakeable
and that he was not far from believing in dramatic breakthroughs
by armoured forces. He argued that the possibility of even a temporary collapse of the French Army's front was so remote as not
to be worth preparing for:

In preparing defensive measures it is wiser to base them on the balance of probabilities rather than attempt the impossibility of being
equally prepared for any possibility . . .
There is no sign at present of any development in military technique

so potent as to promise an attacking army a reasonable prospect of breaking through the front of a defending army of more or less equal strength ... Even if a particular part of the front should be penetrated by a suprise onslaught before the defender had mobilized, experience provides little grounds for believing that the thrust could be pushed far enough to produce a general collapse.[64]

In his history of the Royal Tank Regiment Liddell Hart makes it seem by selective quotation that he was arguing against sending an old-fashioned infantry force to the Continent but in favour of sending armoured divisions.[65] Actually he was arguing against sending any kind of Field Force at all. Though he believed that the French would "undoubtedly welcome the promise of any mechanized divisions we could send", he emphasized that in his view by the time they arrived on the Continent any German thrust mounted in the initial phase of a war would have been brought to a halt and equilibrium restored. If the British sent armoured forces the French would only waste them in suicidal offensives:

> The only serious chance of French resistance collapsing completely is as sequel to a rash offensive on their part, and the crippling of their forces in it as in 1914. Nothing could be more likely to encourage them to repeat this folly than the pre-war promise of a force from us.[66]

Liddell Hart's growing doubts about the power of armour to restore mobility to warfare appear to have been fed by the Spanish Civil War, which had broken out in July 1936, and upon the course of which armoured forces had little effect. In conversation with Liddell Hart on 29 June 1937, however, Deverell rightly insisted that tanks had been too badly handled in Spain for any lessons to be drawn.[67] To its credit the British General Staff consistently refused to accept that a German breakthrough in the west in a future war was an impossibility and continued its efforts to prepare a Field Force, including a substantial amount of armour, for service on the Continent.

Liddell Hart's position became increasingly contradictory. On the one hand he advocated the establishment of up to six Mobile Divisions[68] (though tank production was not proceeding rapidly enough adequately to equip one). On the other he attacked the General Staff's arguments for sending a Field Force to France and thus to a great extent undermined the General Staff's rationale for the development of armoured forces and for adequate access to the limited funds and industrial capacity made available for rearmament. (Until 1939 rearmament was conducted on a "business as usual" basis by which the Service departments were not supposed to supplant normal commercial production. The Treasury's grip on the purse strings was exerted partly to prevent this.)[69] Liddell Hart's journalism, moreover, encouraged the National Government to insist that the General Staff should devote an increasing proportion of the very meagre resources at its disposal to home anti-aircraft defence.[70]

In December 1937 Hore-Belisha, with the encouragement of Liddell Hart, sacked Deverell and most of the other military members of the Army Council. Hore-Belisha thus made way for a change in the orientation of strategic policy to which the Army Council had been fundamentally opposed.[71] From January 1938 he began to formulate the so-called "New Army Policy" by which emphasis was to be given to home and imperial defence.[72] Preparing to send a Field Force to the Continent was henceforth regarded as the lowest priority. The motive for the new policy was to a large extent financial and the tank programme was a particular area in which the Treasury and the Prime Minister (who was the real driving force behind the policy) expected to make cuts.[73] Indeed Hore-Belisha, when considering the reorientation of military policy in November 1937, had contemplated the abolition of the RTC,[74] though Liddell Hart seems to have talked him out of that.

The General Staff attempted to retain as much as possible of the War Office programme for tank production by emphasizing the potential threat to Egypt from Italian forces based in Libya.[75] Though Sir Warren Fisher, the Permanent Under Secretary at the Treasury, privately dismissed the whole idea of a desert war as "merely silly"[76] and though the British General Staff was itself contemptuous of the Italian Army,[77] this ploy had some degree of success. Hore-Belisha nevertheless forecast to Chamberlain on 31 January 1938 that the New Army Policy would save the government about £14,000,000 out of a total rearmament programme for the Army estimated at £100,000,000 for the 1936–39 period. More than half of the intended saving, £7,150,000, was to be on armoured fighting vehicles and a further £300,000 was cut from the budget for petrol, oil and lubricants, of which tanks were obviously a major consumer. One of the most significant cuts immediately agreed to by the General Staff was to scale down the provision of Army Tank Battalions (59 infantry tanks each) from four to three.[78]

General the Viscount John Standish Gort, the CIGS who replaced Deverell in December 1937, was fifty-one years old, considered young for a CIGS at this period. From Anglo-Irish gentry roots, he was a peer, an Etonian, a former Grenadier Guards officer and a winner of the Victoria Cross on the Western Front in 1918.[79] Gort had a poor opinion of Deverell (though it is not completely clear why) and, as Military Secretary, had encouraged Hore-Belisha to dismiss him.[80] On the central strategic issue over which Deverell was sacked, however – the priority to be given to preparing a Field Force for the Continent – Gort's views were really no different from Deverell's. After Gort became CIGS his relationship with Hore-Belisha deteriorated drastically. Gort became worried both by the low priority Hore-Belisha accorded to the Field Force and by the extraordinary influence of Liddell Hart on War Office policy, an influence which often seemed to outweigh that of the General Staff. He and Hore-Belisha were soon scarcely on speaking terms. The conduct of War Office business was made possible largely by the good-humoured diplomacy of Lieutenant-General Sir Ronald Adam who had been appointed Deputy CIGS at the same time as Gort became CIGS.[81]

Gort's face, as revealed in contemporary photographs, is that of the caricature upper-class Army officer – expressive of determination and pugnacity but not of intellect. The appearance was to some degree deceptive. While he was essentially a fighting soldier, the post of CIGS not being a natural one for him,[82] he was more studious and reflective than he looked. This emerges clearly from his comments on Liddell Hart's 1937 "Defence or Attack" articles in *The Times*. Denying that a successful German offensive against France in the early stages of a war was an impossibility, and doubting the wisdom of the purely defensive policy which Liddell Hart by then seemed to be advocating, he wrote:

the French today are most surely on the defensive but whether a troglodyte existence in the Maginot Line is going to maintain the fighting spirit of the nation remains to be seen. As years pass will these defences be maintained at their proper level or will they follow the usual fate of all French fortifications in the past? May it not be possible for panzer divisions and concentrated air forces to effect a breach and this attack can take place with little previous warning. If by rapidity, deception and surprise it is possible to make a bridge-head then the war will pass into open country once more. I feel novelty lies in some direction such as this, as Belgium is hackneyed.[83]

Gort had a particularly large, ferocious and, as events would prove, thoroughly justified bee in his bonnet about the importance of airpower in a future land campaign on the Continent. He resented the unreasonable fixation of the RAF on strategic bombing – the same complaint which Montgomery-Massingberd had made in September 1935. He commented to Liddell Hart:

> I am inclined to think that you do not stress enough the part that aircraft will play in the opening moves. It is largely the fault of the Air Staff who are so obsessed with the independent role of the RAF that they forget that their real task is that of long range artillery. The result is that we do not have nearly enough air with the Field Force organization ... In the winter of 1917/18 Lloyd George etc. were wrangling about the formation of a general reserve to meet the coming offensive and Trenchard was busy with his Independent Air Force bombing industrial targets in Germany ... From all the records Trenchard did not postpone Ludendorff's March attack by 10 minutes and yet had we formed a general reserve of aircraft to interfere with the concentration would the attack ever have been launched? I think this is a conception which needs development. We need close support aircraft for the nearer targets, medium aircraft for the attack of [more rearward] troops and longer range air for the checking of strategic movements. You will see I use the artillery nomenclature as being the terminology which expresses most clearly what I have in mind.[84]

As CIGS, Gort took a keen interest in the reports of MI3, the intelligence branch of the General Staff which dealt with the German armed forces. He was especially interested in German armour and its possible co-operation with airpower. Commenting to the Deputy CIGS, Lieutenant-General Sir Ronald Adam, on an MI3 appreciation of German armoured forces which he examined early in 1938: "I am rather surprised that [this] paper makes no reference to air and mechanized forces working together ... I will hope for more guidance on German thought on the use of all natures of air in operations by mechanized forces."[85]

In fact MI3 officers had frequently referred to air/ground co-operation in previous reports on German mechanized forces[86] and they were unlucky to incur Gort's displeasure by neglecting the topic in this one appreciation.

In November 1938 Gort minuted to Hore-Belisha, using material from MI3 reports, that:

> there is no doubt that the German General Staff have great expectations from armoured forces. There are a number of interesting publications by responsible military authorities on the strategy and tactics of armoured formations.
>
> German principles of employment of such formations are based on three requirements:-
>
> (a)   suitable ground
> (b)   surprise
> (c)   large masses
>
> A tank attack is envisaged in successive waves, biting deep into the enemy defences. Speed is the essence of such an attack. The Germans insist, however, that the role of the armoured formations is to clear the way for the other arms and that only by co-operation with them can decisive results be achieved. The armoured units punch holes through which the other arms can penetrate.[87]

Gort's statement, quoted above, contained some weaknesses of interpretation and some ambiguity. His idea of an attack by German armoured formations was somewhat stereotyped and did not give sufficient credit to German tactical flexibility. The tanks would not necessarily lead the attack. In the Meuse crossing operation of 12–13 May 1940 engineers and infantry inevitably led and tanks followed later.[88] Gort, moreover, uses the terms "unit", "formation" and "arm" carelessly. In the last sentence it is not completely clear whether he is discussing co-operation between Panzer divisions and infantry divisions or between tanks and the non-armoured elements within Panzer divisions. With these qualifications, however, it must be recognized that Gort was presenting his Secretary of State with a reasonably accurate picture of the approach to operations which the German Army would be likely to adopt.

Gort's awareness of the potential of armoured and mechanized forces is clear. Yet his relationship with Hobart, his Director of Military Training, was far from cordial. Gort asked Hore-Belisha several times to remove Hobart from his post. It is not possible to say precisely why this was. Clash of personalities may have been as important as doctrinal differences and Gort disliked having officers in the War Office who, like Hobart, had a close relationship with Liddell Hart. Doctrinal differences did probably exist, however. Gort's apparent belief in close co-operation between tanks and other arms and between armoured divisions and infantry divisions probably did not sit well with Hobart's notion of independent action by small, very tank-heavy armoured formations. Towards the end of 1938 the General Staff took the decision to form, around the nucleus of a mechanized cavalry brigade already stationed in Egypt, a second Mobile Division and, perhaps largely to get him out of the War Office, Hobart was selected to command it.[89]

Early the following year it was decided to reduce the bulk of the Mobile Division based in England, which was renamed 1st Armoured Division. The process by which the restructuring of the division was decided upon is not possible to trace in detail. (Whereas many documents on the early development of the division are available in the War Office papers in the Public Record Office, for the late 1930s this primary source material most frustratingly dries up. The historian is forced to rely on memoirs and secondary sources which are somewhat vague on the issue.) The outcome, however, was that the division's infantry battalions were reduced from two to one and one of the two armoured cavalry brigades was removed. This left one armoured cavalry brigade equipped with light tanks – which was renamed the Light Armoured Brigade – the Tank Brigade – renamed the Heavy Armoured Brigade – which was eventually supposed to be equipped with cruisers – and a Support Group consisting of a motorized rifle battalion and a motorized artillery regiment plus engineer and logistic support. The tank strength of the division was set at 213 cruiser and 108 light tanks. The removal of one of the cavalry brigades made sense. The number of light tanks had undoubtedly been excessive. Leaving the division with only a single infantry battalion, however, was a serious mistake. The experience of the Second World War would indicate that four battalions was the ideal.[90]

In February 1939 the Cabinet tacitly recognized that a British Field Force would have to be sent to fight alongside the French Army on the Continent in the event of war with Germany. The

War Office was authorized to put in hand measures to bring the
Field Force up to Continental standards and financial and industrial restrictions were significantly relaxed.[91] The problems created
by constraints enforced earlier could not quickly be solved, however. Believing (especially after the British government guaranteed
Poland against German aggression in March 1939) that a Continental campaign might be imminent, the General Staff regarded
the tank issue with mounting dismay.

The situation with medium and cruiser tanks was especially
worrying. Though most of the mechanical teething troubles with
A9 and A10 had been eliminated, the fundamental problem of
power/weight ratio remained. The 14 mm armour basis which had
been specified in A9's original design was regarded as inadequate
by 1938 but the armour could only be substantially increased at
the cost of drastically reducing the 25 mph maximum speed. A10,
which was basically a simplified and better protected version of
A9, had an armour basis of 30 mm but a top speed of only 12–
14 mph, considered inadequate for the operations of the Mobile
Division. Nevertheless, because Martel's pet project, the Nuffield
Christie cruiser tank, was still not fully developed, the decision
had been taken to go to production on both A9 and A10. A batch
of 50 A9s was ordered in August 1937. By May 1938 orders had
been placed for a further 50 with an increased armour basis of 30
mm and for 100 A10s, but very few A9s had materialized by the
spring of 1939. During 1938 the classification of A9 and A10 was
rather confusingly changed to "heavy cruiser". But these machines
were merely stop-gaps until a real Christie cruiser was ready for
mass production.[92]

The A13, the first of the British Christie tanks, appeared in
November 1937, a remarkably short time after Martel had initiated its development following his return from Russia in September 1936. Martel had initially specified, however, a 14 mm armour
basis only. This was considered inadequate for a fighting tank by
the late 1930s and steps were taken to increase the armour to 30
mm in later models. There were also problems of mechanical
unreliability. Martel pointed to the "very rapid rate at which this
tank has been developed and produced" and hoped that the initial
mechanical difficulties would prove to be merely "teething troubles". Some of these problems were indeed eliminated later, but all
the British Christie tanks of the late 1930s and the Second World

Figure 26 A13 Cruiser tanks of the 1st Armoured Division on a training exercise in the Aldershot area.

War developed a reputation for being somewhat unreliable and difficult to maintain. This to a great extent detracted from their advantages of speed (30 mph maximum in the case of A13 Mark I) and cross country performance. The A13 Mark I, with an armour basis of 14 mm, began to be delivered in January 1939. But A13 Mark II, with a 30 mm basis, did not come into service until after the outbreak of war, though it eventually saw action with 1st Armoured Division in France in May–June 1940 and with 7th Armoured Division in the Western Desert in 1940–41.[93]

The situation with infantry tanks was only marginally better. The crude A11 (Infantry Tank Mark I) was in production but was obviously a product of haste and the financial stringency of the mid-1930s. It was armed only with a machine gun, and having a crew of only two and a turret too small to accommodate radio, could be of no use in combating enemy armour, a job it was not really designed to do. A superior infantry tank, A12 (Infantry Tank Mark II), had been under development since 1936. This machine turned out to be one of the more successful British tanks of the first years of the Second World War. Though slow (top speed only 15 mph) it had a 60 mm armour basis and 70 mm of

Figure 27   An A11, the original infantry tank. The one pictured is serving with the BEF in France.

Figure 28   An A12 Infantry tank Mark II. This one is serving with the Canadian Army in Britain during the Second World War.

frontal armour. This made it virtually impenetrable by the guns carried by any of the German tanks of the first two years of the Second World War and by the standard 3.7 cm gun issued to the German infantry. Its crew of four and turret capable of fitting a radio allowed it much greater tactical responsiveness and flexibility. It also mounted a 2-pdr gun – standard in cruiser tanks and issued to infantry as an anti-tank gun, but not fitted in light tanks or the A11 – a high velocity weapon firing solid shot. (This gun was one of the better features of British tanks in the early years of the Second World War, being capable of penetrating all German tanks of 1939–40 at normal ranges.) But because both Vickers and the Royal Ordnance Factory at Woolwich were, in 1936, "full up with work for the Navy and Air Force which had priority over Army requirements"[94] the A12's development, like that of Christie tanks, had to be carried out by a firm inexperienced in tank work – in this case Vulcan Foundry of Newton-le-Willows, Lancashire. Vulcan's lack of experience had been a significant problem, however, and it was aggravated by a general shortage of designers and draftsmen. The firm was not ready to go to production with the "Matilda", as the A12 became generally known, until early in 1939 and it was still not in service when war broke out.[95]

The General Staff's alarm at the tank situation in the spring of 1939 was stated with admirable clarity in a memorandum from the Deputy CIGS, Adam, to the Director General of Munitions Production, Sir Harold Brown:

(1) . . . two horns of the dilemma are:-

(a) If orders of known and tried equipments are not placed we may be caught short of tanks in the near future.

(b) Immense progress is being made in both anti-tank weapons and tanks in other countries, particularly in Germany, with the result that if we do not press ahead with new designs we shall find ourselves with tanks which are quite incapable of coping with German standards and which instead of being assets are death traps.

(2) We have ordered, purely as insurance, tanks of the type of A9 and we are faced with the fact that although the first of these orders was placed in early August 1937, hardly any of these machines have been delivered up to last week, some twenty months later . . .

(3) In order to cope with the problems with which we are faced the factor which is of paramount importance is to speed up the time

between acceptance of the specifications and delivery of the tanks. This is not a temporary difficulty but the whole future of our successful employment of tanks depends on this; if Germany can carry out this process far more quickly than we can the prospect of our successful employment of tanks is indeed dismal.[96]

In addition to the suspected obsolescence of A9 and A10 for the purposes of a European war, the A13 Mark I was thought to be desperately vulnerable:

> Recent trials of the German 20 mm gun, which is being fitted even in the light tanks and into some of the armoured cars, show that its projectile can not only pass through the armour carried on the A13 Mark I but that it can burst effectively after penetration of the armour.[97]

But the most serious problems were faced by the light tank units. Thin-skinned and armed only with machine guns, British light tanks were acutely vulnerable to hostile armour. Adam pointed out that, at the very least, light tank units would need "a stiffening of 2-pdr guns". The General Staff's ultimate intention was to provide each light tank unit with a squadron of cruiser tanks and to fit the high velocity 15 mm Besa machine gun to all light tanks. But these measures were obviously going to take a long time, especially as there was already an acute shortage of cruisers. As a stop-gap measure it was decided to order a batch of 2-pdr guns on light tank chassis, but these vehicles lacked overhead protection and were thus at a grave disadvantage. The General Staff had thus recognized the unsuitablity of the light tank for the purposes of a European war and in March 1939, shortly after a Continental commitment for the British Army was finally accepted, it was decided not to reserve any industrial capacity for their production in wartime.[98]

The availability of industrial capacity for tank manufacture, for so long constrained by the Cabinet and the Treasury, could not be expanded rapidly enough to meet the demands for tanks which they were now prepared to approve. In March 1939 orders for 211 financially sanctioned cruiser tanks had not even been placed because no firm was in a position to accept them. There was now no capacity at all for tank production available in the Royal Ordnance Factories which were full up with work for the other armed services. Of 1,277 light tanks which had been financially

sanctioned by June 1939, 1,050 were scheduled to arrive by the
end of September. But, as already noted, the General Staff no
longer regarded the light tank as really suitable for warfare on the
Continent. Of 1,062 cruiser tanks approved by June 1939 only
125 were expected by the end of September and only 115 of 369
infantry tanks.[99] The Army was thus acutely short of tanks capable of meeting the requirements of a Continental campaign. At
the outbreak of war only 1,002 Light Tanks Mark VI, 79 Cruiser
Tanks Marks I and II and 67 Infantry Tanks Mark I appear
actually to have been manufactured.[100] According to the Official
History, at the outbreak of war the British Army had at this time
only 196 light tanks, 50 infantry tanks and 38 armoured cars in
the hands of operational units.[101]

On 4 April 1939 Hore-Belisha announced a major administrative reform affecting British armoured forces. The details had been
worked out by a committee chaired by Lieutenant-General Sir
Bertram Sergison-Brooke. A Royal Armoured Corps (RAC) was to
be established which was to include both the old Royal Tank
Corps (now renamed the Royal Tank Regiment), which was in the
process of expansion to 8 regular battalions and 7 territorial battalions, the 18 already mechanized regiments of cavalry and 8
yeomanry regiments. The driving force behind the reform appears
to have been the need to solve cavalry manpower problems. Because the cavalry was perceived, in the popular mind, to be obsolete, most regiments were having severe recruitment difficulties.
The RTC on the other hand had, by the late 1930s, a surplus of
good quality recruits. The reform put all recruits to armoured
units in a common pool with centralized depot and training schools
– effectively those of the old RTC, located in Dorset and now
significantly expanded. Officers of the individual cavalry regiments
and of the Royal Tank Regiment continued to be listed separately,
however, so that the cavalry could maintain its distinctive regimental traditions and, in peace time at any rate, its socially exclu-
sive messes.[102]

By the middle of 1939 the General Staff's plans for the long-
term future of British armoured forces had, despite the disappointing tank production figures, become quite ambitious. They included
3 armoured divisions, 5 Army Tank Brigades and 11 armoured
divisional cavalry regiments.[103] The General Staff's concept of the
different types of mechanized forces it would require – divisional

cavalry regiments and Army Tank Battalions, as well as armoured (or Mobile) divisions – had not changed very much since Montgomery-Massingberd's paper on "The Future Organization of the British Army", completed in September 1935. This is perhaps indicative of a lack of flexibility and fresh thinking in the meantime.

The concept that every infantry division needed a mechanized cavalry regiment equipped with light tanks for reconnaissance was, as Hobart pointed out before his departure for Egypt, a very dubious one.[104] Infantry divisions were still intended to move on foot most of the time and thus the discrepancy between the mobility of the bulk of the division and its reconnaissance element was extreme – quite unparalleled in the German Army which did not incorporate any tank unit within its infantry divisions. Far more important in the long term, however, were the Army Tank Brigade/armoured division and infantry tank/cruiser tank dichotomies which, most authorities agree, proved to be pernicious, dissipating design effort and making British armoured forces less versatile and flexible than those of the Germans.[105] Though the Germans did keep a proportion of their tanks out of the Panzer divisions for close co-operation with unmechanized infantry, they did not, to the surprise of the British, design specialist tanks for that purpose.[106]

The General Staff's perception of the imminence of crisis in the period 1936–39, when coupled with the extreme shortage of modern equipment and the lack of a definite government decision about the Army's wartime role, may to some extent have acted as a break on the development of its military thought. Much of the effort of the senior General Staff personnel seems to have gone into battles with the Cabinet and the Treasury to secure recognition of the necessity for a well-equipped Field Force and to procure adequate funding for it.[107] In the face of burgeoning German military power, mere theorizing about mechanized warfare in the absence of the funding to put theory into effect must have seemed rather fruitless. The departure of Lindsay to India in 1935 and the assumption by Hobart of the intellectual leadership of the RTC was most unfortunate in terms of the development of doctrine. Hobart had a rather narrowly tank-centred outlook and an inadequate concept of how armoured divisions should be organized and handled. His RTC chauvinism and acerbic personality did not do his Corps' cause any good and made it impossible for him to play adequately the leading role in the development of British armoured forces in the late 1930s.

While the British General Staff certainly had a high opinion of the importance of armour in modern war, it is doubtful whether the War Office's rearmament programme had made the best use of the very limited funds and industrial capacity available. The armoured divisional cavalry idea and the initially excessive allocation of light tanks to the Mobile Division, coupled with the fact that the Light Tank Mark VI was the only tank ready for production when rearmament began, had contributed to gross overproduction of light tanks. While these were of some use in adjusting cavalry regiments to an age of mechanization (functioning as a relatively inexpensive training machine) their combat value was very limited. The latest British infantry tank, the Mark II (A12), the intended equipment of the Army Tank Battalions and Brigades, proved useful in some of the earlier campaigns of the war, especially those fought against the Italians, but it could not keep up with the high tempo of operations of which German armoured forces were capable.[108] The General Staff's plans in 1939 to create five Army Tank Brigades but only three armoured divisions, would appear to indicate an insufficient emphasis on truly mobile armour. Planning, however, may have been influenced by the fact that whereas a fairly successful infantry tank design was available, no truly satisfactory cruiser was yet in prospect. The critical mistake, perhaps, was the dissipation of the effort of the grossly inadequate numbers of designers available for tank work over so many different types of tank – the cruiser tank/infantry tank split complicating matters considerably in this regard. It would probably have been better to have concentrated most effort on developing a really good medium tank while being prepared to go to mass production on the far-from-ideal A9s and A10s in the short run. All the medium tanks thus produced could have been concentrated in armoured divisions.

In the second half of the 1930s, however, the British General Staff had shown itself uncertain as to how armoured divisions should be composed, trained and employed. At least until 1937 the General Staff appears to have been excessively influenced by analogies with the old horsed cavalry division. By the outbreak of war the cavalry division analogy appears to have been declining in influence and the British armoured division was becoming more the sort of slimmed down, cruiser-tank centred formation for which Hobart had long been striving. But Hobart's ideas on the structure and handling of armoured divisions were themselves wide of the mark. The 7th Armoured Division, based in Egypt, which Hobart himself trained from September 1938 to November 1939, was to prove effective in outflanking manoeuvre against and intercepting the flight of predominantly unmechanized Italian forces and Hobart has been given considerable credit for this. Hobart, however, appears not to have had much understanding of the German approach to mechanized warfare and this division did not, to put it mildly, enjoy comparable success against Rommel's Afrika Korps.[109]

When analysing the development of British armour between the world wars two quite distinct questions suggest themselves: (1) Why were British armoured forces so desperately weak up to the period of the disaster in the west in May-June 1940? (2) Why, even when British armour was numerically much stronger than and qualitatively equivalent to that of the Axis (as it was in the Western Desert for most of 1941 and 1942) did it often perform so dismally?

Though the War Office's conduct of the rearmament programme is not above reproach, the responsibility for the weakness of British armour at the outbreak of war and for the first year thereafter must lie primarily with Cabinet policy. The late start to the Army's rearmament, its inadequate funding, the restrictive policy on access to industrial capacity and the lack of clarity about the Army's strategic role were the most important factors. With regard to the performance of British armoured forces in the desert campaigns, however, the Army itself must assume responsibility. While part of the problem may have been that British standards of generalship were on the whole inferior to those of Rommel, this will not do as a complete explanation. Even when British generals successfully concentrated at the decisive point armoured forces equal or even superior to those of the enemy, they frequently met with frustration and defeat. The flawed tactics of British armoured divisions – excessive reliance on tanks *per se*, poor co-ordination between the arms, the wasteful and ineffective practice of firing on the move[110] and the tendency to mount inadequately supported tank charges at what often turned out to be German anti-tank screens – must take much of the blame.[111] These dangerous tactical practices were in accordance with many of the ideas developed by the RTC radicals of the inter-war period.[112] Official British doctrinal pamphlets of the Second World War never altogether lost sight of the need for all-arms co-operation and the poor performance of British armoured divisions may sometimes have been due to their component units having been given inadequate time to train together. Yet it is clear that the influence within the Royal Armoured Corps of radicals like Hobart was long-lasting. Hobart's precepts were being quoted in 7th Armoured Division long after he was dismissed from command of that division (partly over of his superiors' perception of the inadequacy of his tactical ideas) in November 1939.[113] Liddell Hart blamed the weaknesses of British armour in the first half of the Second World War on the resistance to the tank radicals by conservative senior officers. Many historians have wholly or partially accepted this interpretation. In reality many of the worst faults of British armour in the desert campaigns appear to have stemmed not from excessive resistance to the ideas of the RTC *avant-garde* but from their excessive adoption.

Notes

1 Henry Pownall's diary, 24 February 1936. Pownall, originally a gunner, served on the secretariat of the Committee of Imperial Defence and later as Director of Military Operations and Intellingence at the War Office in 1938–39. B. Bond (ed.) *Chief of Staff*, Vol. I (Leo Cooper) 1972, p. 103.

2 "The Tank Situation, Memorandum by the Secretary of State for War" (DPR 128), 15 October 1936, paras 1–6, PRO WO 32/4441.

3 Pownall's diary, 1–13 January 1938, Bond, *op. cit.*, pp. 123–129

4 It was only in February 1939 that the Army was given a clear authorization to prepare a Field Force with equipment adequate for fighting on the Continent. Pownall's diary, 20 February 1939, Bond, *op. cit.*, pp. 188–189 and Bond, *British Military Policy Between the Two World Wars* (Clarendon Press) 1980, pp. 300–301.

5 Ministerial Committee on Defence Requirements, Minutes, 3, 10, 15 May 1934, PRO CAB 27/507. Ministerial Committee, Defence Requirements Report, 31 July 1934, para. 47, PRO CAB 16/110.

6 On 17 March 1938, the Secretary of State for War argued at the Committee of Imperial Defence that, "the question now at issue was whether the priority of home defence was so absolute that the extension of the air defences of Great Britain was to be pressed

forward without any regard whatsoever for every other commitment of the Army". CID 313th Meeting, PRO CAB 2/7.

7   "The Tank Situation, Memorandum by the Secretary of State for War" (DPR 128), 15 October 1936, paras 1–6, PRO WO 32/4441.

8   *ibid.*, para. 4 (a).

9   *ibid.*, paras 4 (b) and (c).

10 Martel to Major-General Davidson (Director of Mechanization) 15 September 1936, LH 9/28/69, Liddell Hart Papers, LHCMA. R. Ogorkiewicz, *Armour* (Stevens and Sons) 1960, pp. 225–228.

11 G. Martel, *An Outspoken Soldier* (Sifton Praed) 1949, p. 128.

12 Martel's "Notes on Fighting Vehicles I", February 1937 and "Notes on Fighting Vehicles III", January 1938, LH 9/28/69, Liddell Hart Papers, LHCMA.

13 See for example the classification of forces as either "Mobile Troops" or "Combat Troops" in Broad's *Mechanized and Armoured Formations*, 1929, p. 16, Tank Museum.

14 On doctrine for Army Tank Battalions see "Army Training Memorandum No. 20", April 1938, Appendix I, "Lessons of War Office Skeleton Exercise, 1937", pp. 41–42, LH 15/3/23, Liddell Hart Papers, LHCMA. For "mobile" or "armoured" divisions the main roles stated in the mid-1930s were flank protection, turning enemy flanks, screening and pursuit: "Future Organization of the British Army", Part I, Section 6, sub-section 2 (iii) "Mobile Troops", 9 September 1935, PRO WO 32/4612. By 1939 a counter-attack role was being given more emphasis: "The Employment of Armour in the BEF 1939–40", September 1939, PRO WO 197/13.

15 Martel, "A Tank Army", TS/9, Fuller Papers, LHCMA.

16 G. Martel, *In the Wake of the Tank: the First Fifteen Years of Mechanization in the British Army* (Sifton Praed) 1931. On Martel's international reputation see H. Guderian, *Achtung Panzer!* (Arms and Armour) 1991 (C. Duffy's English translation of a German text originally published in 1937), pp. 141 and 213.

17 For example Hobart expressed his admiration for Martel's work on the technical side of tanks in a letter to Liddell Hart dated 3 December 1936: "Martel . . . has done marvels already. We have a very promising pattern of 'cruiser' . . . under trial." LH 1/376/40b, Liddell Hart Papers, LHCMA.

18 Liddell Hart on Martel in *Dictionary of National Biography* 1951–56, pp. 699–701.

19 "Ground on a battle field is apt to be fairly rough; does anyone who has ever travelled over rough ground in any sort of Tank imagine that accurate fire is possible?" Martel, "Two Questions on

Mechanization" (undated but probably 1935) p. 5, LH 1/492/1925–48, Liddell Hart Papers, LHCMA.

20 Martel, "Mobile Forces Equipped with Small Fighting Vehicles" (undated but probably 1935) para. 9, p. 6, LH 1/492/1925–48, Liddell Hart Papers, LHCMA.

21 Liddell Hart, *The Tanks*, Vol. I, p. 337.

22 G. Martel, *Our Armoured Forces* (Faber and Faber) 1945, p. 161.

23 Martel, *Outspoken Soldier*, p. 142.

24 Liddell Hart, *The Tanks*, Vol. I (Cassell) 1959, pp. 371–372.

25 G.C. Peden, *British Rearmament and the Treasury 1932–39* (Scottish Academic Press) 1979, pp. 36–38 and the papers of the Treasury Inter-Service Committee (TISC), PRO T161/1315 – T161/1335.

26 S. Roskill, *Hankey, Man of Secrets*, Vols. II and III (Collins) 1974, *passim*. For a clear diagram of the defence committee system as it existed in the 1930s see the endpiece in Bond (ed.), *Chief of Staff*, Vol. I.

27 TISC War Office Memorandum No. 57, 10 November 1936 and TISC 45th Meeting, 13 November 1936, PRO WO 32/4441.

28 TISC War Office Memorandum No. 95, para. 5, 19 March 1937, TISC 69th Meeting, 23 March 1937, PRO WO 32/4441.

29 TISC 45th Meeting, 13 November 1936, PRO WO 32/4441.

30 TISC War Office Memorandum No. 145, 26 July 1937 and TISC 92nd Meeting, item 4, 27 July 1937, PRO WO 32/4441.

31 Minute 1, 15 October 1934, PRO WO 32/2847.

32 A hagiography of the Hore-Belisha years at the War Office is available in R.J. Minney, *The Private Papers of Hore-Belisha* (Collins) 1960, *passim*. For a much more critical view see J.P. Harris, "Two War Ministers: a Reassessment of Duff Cooper and Hore-Belisha", in *War and Society*, Vol. 6, No. 1, May 1988, pp. 65–68. On Hore-Belisha's general unpopularity with other ministers see Liddell Hart, *Memoirs*, Vol. II, p. 82. On his troubled relations with the General Staff see Pownall's diary, Bond (ed.), *Chief of Staff*, Vol. I, pp. 136, 140, 151–153, 163, 165 and J.R. Colville, *Man of Valour: the Life Of Field Marshal Lord Gort, VC GCB, DSO, MVO, MC* (Collins) 1972, pp. 73–75.

33 "Talk with Hore-Belisha", 12 September 1937, LH 11/HB 1937/43b, Liddell Hart Papers, LHCMA.

34 "The Mobile Division and Cavalry Mechanization", para. 6 (a), 14 October 1935, PRO WO 32/2826.

35 Liddell Hart, *Memoirs*, Vol. II (Cassell) 1965, pp. 1–125.

36 "Talk with Hore-Belisha", 5 October 1937, LH 11/HB 1937/50b and Liddell Hart's notes on senior Army officers, LH 11/HB 1937/29, August 1937, Liddell Hart Papers, LHCMA.

37 Hobart, "Organization of Units and Formations in the Regular Field Force using Armoured Fighting Vehicles", para. 1, sent to Liddell Hart on 22 September 1937, LH 1/376/55b, Liddell Hart Papers, LHCMA.

38 "Talk with Hore-Belisha", 1 October 1937, LH 11/HB 1937/47b, Liddell Hart Papers, LHCMA. K. Macksey, *Armoured Crusader* (Hutchinson) 1967, pp. 87–89.

39 "Talk with Hore-Belisha", 3 November 1937, LH 11/HB 1937/76–77b, Liddell Hart Papers, LHCMA.

40 This was certainly true by February 1938. See Pownall's diary, 2 February, Bond (ed.) *Chief of Staff*, Vol. I, pp. 130–131.

41 "Notes On My Life", p. 88, ALANBROOKE 3/A/2, Alanbrooke Papers, LHCMA.

42 Liddell Hart, *Memoirs*, Vol. II, pp. 45–46.

43 *ibid.*, p. 47

44 "The Future Reorganization of the British Army", Part I, Section 6, Sub-section 2 (iii) "Mobile Troops", PRO WO 32/4612.

45 "Talk with Hore-Belisha", 2 October 1937, LH 11/HB 1937/48b, Liddell Hart Papers, LHCMA.

46 Liddell Hart, *Memoirs*, Vol. II, p. 59.

47 "Army Training Memorandum No. 20", April 1938, Appendix I: "Lessons of War Office Skeleton Exercise 1937", para. 1: "Mobile Division – the Mobile Division has in it some 600 tanks and carriers and some 600 to 700 other motor vehicles." LH 15/3/23, Liddell Hart Papers, LHCMA.

48 Liddell Hart, *Memoirs*, Vol. II, pp. 47–48.

49 "Notes on My Life", pp. 86–88, ALANBROOKE 3/A/2, Alanbrooke Papers, LHCMA.

50 R. Larson, *The British Army and the Theory of Armored Warfare, 1918–1940* (Delaware) 1984, 219.

51 B.H. Reid, *J.F.C. Fuller: Military Thinker* (Macmillan) 1987, p. 193.

52 F. Pile, *Ack-Ack* (Harrap) 1949, p. 39.

53 Hobart to Liddell Hart, 21 September 1936, p. 2, LH 1/376/35(a) b, Liddell Hart Papers, LHCMA.

54 "Organization of Higher Mobile Formations", 3 February 1937, LH 15/11/6, Liddell Hart Papers, LHCMA.

55 Hobart to DSD and DMT, 28 September 1937, accompanying memorandum on "Organization of Units and Formations in the Regular Field Force using Armoured Fighting Vehicles", especially pp. 16–19, LH 15/11/6, Liddell Hart Papers, LHCMA.

56 Liddell Hart to Hobart, 2 January 1941, LH 1/376/121. Hobart himself had estimated 300 tanks, 100 armoured carriers and scout cars and 4,500 men: Hobart to Liddell Hart, 23 November 1937, LH 1/376/61, Liddell Hart Papers, LHCMA.

57 R. Ogorkiewicz, *op. cit.*, pp. 72–81.

58 Liddell Hart to Hobart, 2 January 1941, LH 1/376/121 and Hobart to Liddell Hart, 12 January 1941, LH 1/376/122, Liddell Hart Papers, LHCMA.

59 On Liddell Hart's concerns about air defence see his notes on various talks with Pile: LH 11/1937/107, 30 December 1937, LH 11/1938/11, 14 January 1938, LH 11/1938/40, 26 March 1938 and "Outline of the Opposition to the Development of the Anti-Aircraft Defence of Great Britain", LH 11/1938/89, 30 July 1938, Liddell Hart Papers, LHCMA.

60 Quoted in Liddell Hart, *Memoirs*, Vol. II, p. 24.

61 *ibid.*, p. 92 and B. Bond, *Liddell Hart: a Study of His Military Thought* (Cassell) 1977, p. 98.

62 "Suggestions on the Reorganization of the Army", Part C, "The Infantry Division", para. 5, PRO WO 32/4614.

63 This had been a long-standing General Staff argument. See Neville Chamberlain's diary, 25 October 1936, Chamberlain Papers, Library of the University of Birmingham.

64 "Note on the Question of the Channel Ports and the need of a British Field Force", 26 August 1937, LH 11/HB 1937/23, Liddell Hart Papers, LHCMA.

65 Liddell Hart, *The Tanks*, Vol. I, p. 387.

66 "Note on the Question of the Channel Ports", 26 August 1937, LH 1/HB 1937/23, Liddell Hart Papers, LHCMA.

67 "Talk with Deverell", 29 June 1937, LH 11/HB 1937/56, Liddell Hart Papers, LHCMA.

68 Liddell Hart, *The Tanks*, Vol. I, p. 394.

69 On the origins of the "business as usual" policy see Defence Policy and Requirements Committee, Minutes of 1st Meeting, 30 December 1935, WEIR 17/1 and Weir to Duff Cooper 2 June 1936, WEIR 17/8, Weir Papers, Churchill College Cambridge. Lord Weir, a Scottish industrialist and adviser to the National Government, was one of the architects of the policy.

70 B. Bond, *Liddell Hart*, pp. 108–111 and Pownall's diary, 20 June 1938, Bond, *Chief of Staff*, Vol. I, p. 151.

71 Minney, *op. cit.*, pp. 71–76. B. Bond, *British Military Policy between the Two World Wars* (Clarendon Press) 1980, p. 255.

72 Pownall's diaries, 31 January to 14 February 1938, Bond, *Chief of Staff*, Vol. I, pp. 130–133.

73 Hore-Belisha to Chamberlain, 31 January 1938, and reply from Chamberlain's office to Hore-Belisha's private secretary in the War Office, 2 February 1938, PRO PREM 1/241.

74 "Talk with Hore-Belisha", 11/HB 1937/57b, 19 October 1937, Liddell Hart Papers, LHCMA.

75 "Proceedings of a meeting held in CIGS's room", 23 December 1937, PRO WO 32/4441.

76 Peden, *op. cit.*, p. 143.

77 See J.P. Harris, "Egypt: Defence Plans", in M. Cohen and M. Kolinsky (eds.) *Britain and the Middle East in the 1930s: Security Problems, 1935–39* (Macmillan) 1992, pp. 61–79.

78 Hore-Belisha to Chamberlain, 31 January 1938, PRO PREM 1/241 and TISC WO Memorandum No. 343, 2 May 1938, PRO WO 32/4445.

79 J.R. Colville, *Man of Valour: the Life of Field-Marshal the Viscount Gort, VC, GCB, DSO, MVO, MC* (Collins) 1972, pp. 1–49.

80 "Talk with H-B", 26 October 1937, LH 11/HB 1937/67(a). Gort's hostility to Deverell may have arisen as the result of a quarrel over Gort's income tax. "Lunch with Gort (Athenaeum)", 21 January 1938, LH 11/HB 1938/12, Liddell Hart Papers, LHCMA.

81 Pownall's diary, 2 February 1938, Bond (ed.) *Chief of Staff*, Vol. I, pp. 130–131. Conversation between the present writer and General Sir Ronald Adam, 18 November 1979, at his home in Faygate, Sussex.

82 Sir Ronald Adam told the present writer that, "CIGS was not really Jack Gort's thing". Gort seems not to have sought the appointment and it may have been a surprise to him. "Dinner with Gort", 22 November 1937, LH 11/HB 1937/96, Liddell Hart Papers, LHCMA. Bond, *British Military Policy*, p. 255.

83 Gort to Liddell Hart, 31 October 1937, LH 1/322/52(a), Liddell Hart Papers, LHCMA.

84 *ibid.*

85 Gort to Adam, 2 March 1938, PRO WO 216/189.

86 "Note on the Trend of German Rearmament", paras 3 and 4, 20 November 1934, PRO WO 190/281. "Appreciation by the Military Attaché, Berlin, of the Views of the German General Staff on Future War, together with a Summary of Information regarding Recent Developments in Germany", section 4, PRO WO 190/283.

87 Gort to Hore-Belisha, 21 November 1938, PRO WO 190/723.

88 A. Horne, *To Lose a Battle, France 1940* (Macmillan) 1969, pp. 308–360.

89 Liddell Hart, *The Tanks*, Vol. I, p. 398.

90 Martel, *Our Armoured Forces*, p. 378. R. Ogorkiewicz, *Armour*, pp. 59–60 and 81.

91 Bond, *British Military Policy*, pp. 300–301.

92 Martel's "Notes on Fighting Vehicles III", para. 3, January 1938, "Notes on Fighting Vehicles IV", para. 3, March 1938, "Notes on Tank Rearmament", para. 5, April 1938 and "Notes on Fighting Vehicles V", May 1938, LH 9/28/69, Liddell Hart Papers, LHCMA.

Adam to Sir Harold Brown (Director General of Munitions Production), 27 March 1939, PRO WO 32/4445.

93 Martel's "Notes on Fighting Vehicles V", para. 9, May 1938, LH 9/28/69, Liddell Hart Papers, LHCMA. Liddell Hart, *The Tanks*, Vol. I, pp. 377–379.

94 Quoted from Martel, *Outspoken Soldier*, p. 130.

95 "A Chronology and Description of Progress in the Design and Production of Infantry Tank A12E1", November 1937, PRO WO 32/4441.

96 Adam to Brown, 27 March 1939, PRO WO 32/4445.

97 *ibid.*, Section 4 (f). Adam had probably received reports of what was in fact a 20 mm gun which the Germans mounted in the Panzer II, the most numerous type of tank employed in the 1940 campaign against France.

98 *ibid.* Section 6 and "Meeting on the Tank Programme", para. 4, 15 March 1939, PRO WO 32/4445.

99 "28th Progress Report by the War Office" (DPR 314), 15 June 1939, Appendix 1, Annex A PRO CAB 16/230.

100 "Design and Production of British Tanks 1936 – June 1940", p. 76, PRO CAB 102/851.

101 L. Ellis, *The War in France and Flanders 1939–40* (HMSO) 1953, pp. 369–370.

102 "Report of the Committee on the Mechanized Cavalry and Royal Tank Corps", April 1938, PRO WO 33/1512. Liddell Hart, *The Tanks*, Vol. I, p. 401.

103 Martel, *Outspoken Soldier*, p. 131.

104 Hobart, "Organization of Units and Formations in the Regular Field Force Using Armoured Fighting Vehicles", September 1937, p. 2, LH 1/376/55b, Liddell Hart Papers, LHCMA.

105 See, for example, Ogorkiewicz's comments in Ogorkiewicz, *op. cit.*, pp. 158–160.

106 On the British expectation that the Germans would design specialist infantry tanks see "German Tank Design", para. 11, 7 April 1937, PRO WO 190/534.

107 The extent to which this issue preoccupied the General Staff is obvious from Pownall's diary, especially entries for 1 and 3 January 1938, 7 November 1938 and 20 February 1939. Bond (ed.) *Chief of Staff*, Vol. I, pp. 123–124, 169 and 188–190.

108 Ogorkiewicz, *op. cit.*, pp. 158–160.

109 P.G. Griffith, "British Armoured Warfare in the Western Desert", in J.P. Harris and F.H. Toase (eds) *Armoured Warfare* (Batsford) 1990, pp. 70–87.

110 On the pre-war obsession with firing on the move and false ideas on gunnery generally see E.F. Offord, transcript pp. 62–75, interview

000867/06 for Department of Sound Records, Imperial War Museum. On the ineffectiveness of firing armour piercing ammunition on the move as recognized by the British Army in the latter half of the Second World War see "Minutes of Gunnery Conference Held At RAC School North Africa, 17–20 January 1944", PRO WO 32/ 10390. Even Liddell Hart eventually admitted that the emphasis placed by people like Hobart and Broad on this tactic had been excessive. Liddell Hart, *The Tanks*, Vol. I, p. 229.

111   On British "Balaclava" tactics in the desert see J. Wardrop, *Tanks Across the Desert* (Kimber) 1981, p. 61 and R. Crisp, *Brazen Chariots* (Muller) 1959, pp. 15 and 39 and P. Griffith, *op. cit.*, pp. 72–73 and 78.

112   On the very tank-heavy formations recommended by Hobart in the late 1930s see "Organization of Higher Mobile Formations", 3 February 1937, LH 15/11/6. On his emphasis on the tactical dispersal of armour see "Use of Armoured and Mechanized Formations in the Early Stages of a European War", November 1933, LH 1/ 376/5. His addiction to the dogma of firing on the move was rigid. He wrote to Liddell Hart: "I hear the new DMT [Director of Military Training] thinks tanks ought to halt to shoot! God! I thought we had killed and disproved that heresy ten years ago." Hobart to Liddell Hart, 21 September 1936, LH 1/376/35(a)b. See also Hobart's December 1936 memorandum on "Tank Gunnery", LH 15/ 11/4. All these documents are in the Liddell Hart Papers, LHCMA. For the thoughts of an eminent soldier, then a junior officer in the RTC, on the false dogmas being taught within the corps in the late 1930s, particularly by Hobart, hear Lord R.M.P. Carver, interview (000877/03) recorded for Department of Sound Records, Imperial War Museum. Hobart, Carver states, believed quite falsely that "tanks could do everything". Carver adds that the criticisms made of Hobart by his superiors were largely justified and that in his opinion Hobart would not have made a successful commander in the field.

113   On the continuing influence of Hobart's ideas in 7th Armoured Division after his dismissal see R. Neillands, *The Desert Rats: 7th Armoured Division 1940–1945* (Weidenfeld and Nicolson) 1991, p. 37. On the reasons for Hobart's dismissal see J.P. Harris, "Sir Percy Hobart: Eclipse and Revival of an Armoured Commander", in B. Bond (ed.) *Fallen Stars* (Brassey's) 1991, pp. 98–99.

Conclusion

Many widely held beliefs about the history of British armoured forces have been challenged in the course of the last eight chapters. Swinton should not be regarded (as he is still often portrayed) as the prime mover in the British genesis of the tank. Haig cannot really be blamed for using tanks in relatively small numbers on 15 September 1916 and it is probably wrong to think in terms of a great lost opportunity with regard to the first use of tanks. An overworked War Office undoubtedly failed to take up the tank idea as enthusiastically as it should have done in 1915. But it is generally wrong to think of a reactionary British military establishment in the First World War, blind to the opportunities afforded by such new technologies. Both of the successive British commanders-in-chief in France responded positively to the tank idea as soon as it was put to them. Sir Douglas Haig's attitude to tanks, throughout the period of his command, was as positive as could reasonably have been expected given their limited combat power.

Before Cambrai Fuller had no real solutions to offer to the problem of an entrenched stalemate on the Western Front. His thinking failed adequately to come to terms with the tank's limitations and he overestimated its potential in the short term. Nor was he really the architect of the Cambrai offensive. What success was achieved on 20 November 1917, moreover, owed as much to improved artillery tactics as it did to the concentrated use of tanks. Fuller's military ideas between Cambrai and the German March offensive were far from helpful. Indeed in some cases they were so dangerously wrong that had they been implemented they might have led to a much greater disaster than was suffered in the event.

Fuller was only one of several people who, by the middle of 1918, had grandiose ideas for the large-scale use of tanks in 1919. Fuller's "Plan 1919" has become a sort of icon for historians of military thought. It was, however, grossly unrealistic. Any attempt to implement it would have involved making exorbitant demands on already overstretched industrial capacity and placing excessive reliance on technology only just emerging. Fuller, moreover, was advocating tactics, including the penetration the enemy's front with tanks unsupported by other arms, which experience had already shown to be unworkable. Though the War Office did adopt a version of Fuller's concept, a lot of the tactical nonsense was cut out before it was presented to Foch and Haig.

The notion of a lost opportunity for the BEF to have waged war in a more "mechanical" way during the Hundred Days is a counter-factual illusion. Tanks were still characterized by low mobility and severe ergonomic problems. Their acute vulnerability, especially to artillery, is clearly demonstrated by the Tank Corps' very high casualty rate for this period of the war.

Though it can be applauded for offering inspiration and intellectual stimulation, Fuller's military thought of the 1920s continued to lack realism. His superiors were, however, generally quite tolerant of his eccentric ideas. There is really no solid evidence that the expression of radical ideas on the future of war was bad for an officer's career at that time. Indeed, despite Fuller's strictures on the obstructive and obscurantist character of the War Office, the most advanced experiment in the field of military mechanization in the late 1920s occurred under the auspices of the British General Staff, the first in the world to establish a permanent tank corps. The officer primarily responsible for translating radical thought into radical experiment was not Fuller but George Lindsay, though Fuller supported him. The "Tidworth affair" and the damage to Fuller's career which resulted from it were (as some historians have already indicated) largely Fuller's own fault.

Liddell Hart's role with regard to the development of British armour in the inter-war period was essentially that of a commentator on the military ideas of others and a publicist for those ideas. On the subject of armoured forces he was not really a significant thinker in his own right. After the Second World War, Liddell Hart falsified (as J. Mearsheimer has clearly shown) his own pre-war position on several military matters. One such issue was (as

B.H. Reid has indicated) the composition of armoured forces. Liddell Hart exaggerated the difference between his own views and those of Fuller. The latter was widely recognized to have placed excessive emphasis on tanks *per se* and to have underplayed the need for all-arms co-operation.

In fact the officers who formed the intellectual leadership of the RTC in the inter-war period all had military ideas which were excessively tank-centred to varying degrees. The most intelligent and broad-minded of them was George Lindsay. He was beginning to place renewed emphasis on the need for all-arms co-operation in 1933–34, but his career fell under a cloud as a result of the Mobile Force exercise of 1934. Lindsay's ineffectiveness during this exercise was probably partly due to a problem in his personal life. But the exercise organizer, Burnett-Stuart, must take a great deal of responsibility for the collapse of Lindsay's influence in the Army. So must Lindsay's unco-operative subordinate, P.C.S. Hobart. Lindsay's loss of face in 1934 cleared the way for Hobart to become the dominant RTC personality of the second half of the 1930s, a development which was most unfortunate. Though a man of the highest integrity who was intensely serious about his profession, Hobart was rude, overbearing and something of a bully. He had a narrow, intolerant mind, was a poor ambassador for the RTC and held tactical ideas which were dangerously misconceived.

The extent to which the intellectual leaders of the RTC were in conflict with higher military authority during the inter-war period has (largely as a result of the influence of Sir Basil Liddell Hart) often been exaggerated by historians. Of course, like all who see themselves as reformers, the RTC *avant-garde* had the sense of being engaged in an uphill struggle. But the more reasonable of them sometimes recognized that they were being allowed as much of their own way as, given the general scarcity of resources, their superiors could reasonably let them have. The loss of the British lead in mechanization came in the first half of the 1930s when the Army was almost paralysed by financial stringency.

Fuller's and Liddell Hart's extreme dislike of Montgomery-Massingberd has tended to obscure the fact that the latter enjoyed good relations with both Lindsay and Hobart. As CIGS he encouraged the work of both of them and gave a considerable boost to mechanization. Many in the RTC looked askance at the extensive programmes of cavalry mechanization initiated under Montgomery-

Massingberd and Deverell and these programmes were severely criticized by Liddell Hart. But in reality the General Staff had little option. The wisdom of the introduction of the infantry tank concept at the same period may legitimately be queried, but must be seen in the context of the failure of medium tank development in the early 1930s.

The weakness of British armoured forces in 1939 was largely due to the extreme financial stringency of the early 1930s, the late start to the Army's rearmament and the low priority accorded by the Cabinet and Treasury to Field Force requirements even once rearmament had begun. Though the General Staff made some mistakes with regard to the development of armoured forces, generally its attitude was positive. In the late 1930s Lord Gort was much more perceptive about the place of armoured and air forces in the early stages of the next European war than were Liddell Hart and Fuller. These last doubted the ability of armoured forces to overcome the factors making for stalemate on land. Both Fuller and Liddell Hart were tending to regard air attack on cities as a more likely means for a future war to be decided. While becoming increasingly obsessed with the anti-aircraft defence of the British homeland in the late 1930s, Liddell Hart campaigned against the commitment of a British Field Force to the Continent. His role as an adviser to Hore-Belisha in the introduction of the so-called New Army Policy was negative in its impact on the development of British armoured strength.

The somewhat indifferent performance of British armoured forces for much of the Second World War, and especially during most of the desert campaigns, cannot really be attributed to neglect of armour by the General Staff. British armour outnumbered that employed by the Axis against it in many of these campaigns. It was also, generally speaking, of comparable technical quality (as a result of the inclusion of American Grants and Shermans), at least up to and including the Second Battle of El Alamein (though by that time only by the inclusion of American-built Grant and Sherman tanks). After the introduction of the Tiger and the Panther by the Germans (tanks which the British could not qualitatively equal until the very end of the war) the numerical superiority of British tanks over German tanks ranged against them was usually very great and was normally combined with superior airpower. Some of the more perceptive of the British tank officers of the

Second World War have long recognized that many of the setbacks and defeats of British armoured forces must be explained in other ways.

This book has examined developments only up to the outbreak of war. But it seems likely that many of the failings of British armour in the war itself can be attributed to faulty tactical ideas which had become prevalent in the RTC in the inter-war period, ideas of which Hobart in particular was a militant proponent. An excessive conception of the potency of tanks *per se*, and an inadequate grasp of the need for inter-arm co-operation were amongst these. Exaggerated emphasis on tactical dispersal and incorrect ideas on gunnery were also important. Errors in the thinking of RTC officers were particularly crucial because the rest of the Royal Armoured Corps learned armoured tactics largely from them.

The writings of Fuller and Liddell Hart present the history of British armoured forces in the period covered by this book in terms of struggle between prescient innovators on the one hand and a very conservative, sometimes reactionary, military establishment on the other. This is misleading. The British were world leaders in the field for much of the period. Such leadership was possible only because the authorities were, for the most part, remarkably open to innovation. Fuller and Liddell Hart, moreover, failed (for obvious reasons) in their post-Second World War writings adequately to indicate the importance of mistaken thinking by the radical tank advocates themselves. Such has been the influence of these two writers on subsequent historians that our understanding of an important topic in twentieth-century military history has been seriously distorted.

Bibliography

ARCHIVAL SOURCES

Birmingham University
Neville Chamberlain Papers

Churchill College Cambridge
Sir Maurice Hankey Papers
Lord Weir Papers

Imperial War Museum
Fourth Army Papers

Tapes of interviews, conducted by the Department of Sound Records, with the following individuals:

Viscount Robert Clive Bridgeman 000991/03
Lord Richard Michael Power Carver 000877/03
Eric Francis Offord 000867/06

Liddell Hart Centre for Military Archives, King's College London
Field Marshal the Viscount Alan Alanbrooke Papers
Lieutenant-General Sir Charles Noel Frank Broad Papers
Major-General Robert Clive, 2nd Viscount Bridgeman Papers
General Sir John Burnett-Stuart Papers
Major-General John Frederick Charles Fuller Papers
Lieutenant-General Sir Launcelot Edward Kiggell Papers
Captain Sir Basil Liddell Hart Papers (this collection includes substantial bodies of papers originated by Hobart, Lindsay and Martel)
Field Marshal George Francis, 1st Baron Milne Papers
Field Marshal Sir Archibald Montgomery-Massingberd Papers
Field Marshal Sir William Robertson Papers
Lieutenant-Colonel Sir Albert Gerald Stern Papers

Major-General Sir Ernest Dunlop Swinton Papers
Admiral Sir Frederick Charles Tudor Tudor Papers
Quotations from documents in the Liddell Hart Centre for Military Archives are included in this book by kind permission of the Trustees of the centre.

National Maritime Museum, Greenwich
Sir Eustace Tennyson d'Eyncourt Papers

National Army Museum, Chelsea
General Lord Rawlinson's Papers

Public Record Office, Kew
ADM 116/1339 Origins of the tank in the RNAS and Admiralty
CAB 2 Committee of Imperial Defence, Minutes
CAB 4 Committee of Imperial Defence, Memoranda
CAB 16 Committee of Imperial Defence, Sub-Committees
CAB 23 Cabinet Minutes
CAB 45 Papers relating to the Official History of the Great War
CAB 53 Chiefs of Staff Sub-Committee papers
MUN 4 Ministry of Munitions papers
MUN 5 Ministry of Munitions papers
PREM 1 Prime Minister's papers
WO 32 War Office general files
WO 33 War Office printed documents
WO 95 Tank Corps war diaries and HQ papers
WO 106 Directorate of Military Operations and Intelligence papers
WO 158 Papers relating to military operations on the Western Front
WO 161 Master General of the Ordnance's papers
WO 163 Minutes and Precis of Army Council meetings
WO 190 Intelligence appreciation files
T 161 Treasury Supply files
T 173 Treasury files on awards to inventors

Tank Museum, Bovington
Hon Evan E. Charteris Papers
Major-General J.F.C. Fuller Papers
Major-General G.M. Lindsay Papers
Major-General Sir Ernest Swinton Papers
Royal Commission on Awards to Inventors, 1919. Proceedings and Report on the invention of the tank
Sir Murray Sueter Papers
General Staff doctrinal manuals
Walter Wilson Papers

Army Staff College, Camberley
Proceedings Of General Staff Conferences
General Staff doctrinal manuals

SELECT BIBLIOGRAPHY OF PUBLISHED SOURCES

Collections of contemporary documents published in book form
B.J. Bond (ed.), *Chief of Staff: the Diaries of Lieutenant-General Sir Henry Pownall, Volume One, 1933–1940* (Leo Cooper, London) 1972.
J.H. Boraston (ed.), *Sir Douglas Haig's Desptaches (December 1915–April 1919* (J.M. Dent, London and Toronto) 1919.
R. Blake (ed.), *The Private Papers of Douglas Haig 1914–1919* (Eyre and Spottiswoode, London) 1952.
K. Jeffrey (ed.), *The Military Correspondence of Field Marshal Sir Henry Wilson 1918–1922* (Army Records Society/Bodley Head, London) 1985.
D.R. Woodward (ed.), *The Military Correspondence of Field-Marshal Sir William Robertson, Chief Imperial General Staff December 1915–February 1918* (Army Records Society/Bodley Head, London) 1989.

British Official History of the First World War
J.E. Edmonds, *Military Operations France and Belgium 1918: the German March Offensive and Its Preliminaries* (Macmillan, London) 1935.
Military Operations, France and Belgium, 1918, May–July: the German Diversion Offensives and the First Allied Counter-Offensive (Macmillan, London) 1939.
Military Operations, France and Flanders, 1918, 8th August–26th September: the Franco-British Offensive (HMSO, London) 1947.
Military Operations, France and Belgium, 1918, 26th September–11th November: the Advance to Victory (HMSO, London) 1947.
Military Operations, France and Belgium, 1917, Vol. II, 7 June–10 November: Messines and Third Ypres (Passchendaele) (HMSO, London) 1948.
C. Falls, *Military Operations, France and Belgium, 1917: the German Retreat to the Hindenburg Line and the Battles of Arras* (HMSO, London) 1948.
W. Miles, *Military Operations, France and Belgium, 1916, 2nd July to the End of the Battles of the Somme* (Macmillan, London) 1938.
Military Operations France and Belgium, 1917: the Battle of Cambrai (HMSO, London) 1948.

British Official History of the Second World War
L. Ellis, *The War in France and Flanders 1939–40* (HMSO, London) 1953.

N.H. Gibbs, *Grand Strategy*, Vol. I (HMSO, London) 1976.

M.M. Postan, *British War Production* (HMSO, London) 1952.

M.M. Postan, D. Hay and J.D. Scott, *Design and Development of Weapons* (HMSO, London) 1964.

Standard works of reference
Army List
British Imperial Calendar
Dictionary Of National Biography
War Office List

Other books
R.J.Q. Adams, *Arms and the Wizard: Lloyd George and the Ministry of Munitions, 1915–1916* (Cassell, London) 1978.

R. Bacon, *The Dover Patrol, 1915–1917, 2 Vols* (Hutchinson, London) n.d.

F.W. Bewsher, *The History of the 51st Highland Division 1914–18* (Blackwood, London) 1921.

S. Bidwell and D. Graham, *Fire-Power: British Army Weapons and Theories of War 1904–1945* (Allen and Unwin, London) 1982.

I.S. Bloch, *Is War Now Impossible? Being an Abridgement of the War of the Future in Its Technical, Economic and Political Relations* (Gregg Revivals, London) 1991.

B.J. Bond, *Liddell Hart, a Study of his Military Thought* (Cassell, London) 1977.

B.J. Bond, *British Military Policy between the Two World Wars* (Clarendon Press, Oxford) 1980.

B.J. Bond (ed.), *Fallen Stars: Eleven Studies of Twentieth Century Military Disasters* (Brassey's, London) 1991.

D.G. Browne, *The Tank in Action* (Blackwood, London) 1920.

M. Carver, *The Apostles of Mobility: the Theory and Practice of Armoured Warfare* (Weidenfeld and Nicolson, London) 1979.

M. Carver, *Out of Step, Memoirs of a Field Marshal* (Hutchinson, London) 1989.

R. Churchill, *Winston S. Churchill, Youth, 1874–1900* (Heinemann, London) 1966.

W.S. Churchill, *The World Crisis, 1915* (Thornton Butterworth, London) 1923.

W.S. Churchill, *The World Crisis, 1916–1918, Part I* (Thornton Butterworth, London) 1927.

M.J. Cohen and M. Kolinsky, *Britain and the Middle East in The 1930s: Security Problems, 1935–39* (Macmillan, London) 1992.

J.R. Colville, *Man Of Valour: the Life of Field Marshal Lord Gort* (Collins, London) 1972.

B. Cooper, *The Ironclads of Cambrai* (Souvenir, London) 1967.

W.D. Croft, *Three Years with the 9th Scottish Division* (John Murray, London) 1919.

D. Crow, *British and Commonwealth Armoured Formations (1919–46)* (Profile, Windsor) 1971.

G. De Groot, *Douglas Haig 1861–1928* (Unwin Hyman, London) 1988.

W. Deist, *The Wehrmacht and German Rearmament* (Macmillan, London) 1981.

J. Ewing, *The History of the 9th (Scottish) Division 1914–1919* (John Murray, London) 1921.

M. Farndale, *History of the Royal Regiment of Artillery: Western Front 1914–18* (Royal Artillery Institution, London) 1986.

D. Fletcher, *Landships: British Tanks in the First World War* (HMSO, London) 1984.

D. Fletcher, *War Cars: British Armoured Cars in the First World War* (HMSO, London) 1987.

D. Fletcher, *The Great Tank Scandal: British Armour in the Second World War, Part I* (HMSO, London) 1989.

D. Fletcher, *Mechanised Force: British Tanks between the Wars* (HMSO, London) 1991.

S. Foot, *Three Lives* (Heinemann, London) 1934.

D. French, *British Economic and Strategic Planning 1905–1915* (Allen and Unwin, London) 1982.

D. French, *British Strategy And War Aims 1914–1916* (Allen and Unwin, London) 1986.

J.F.C. Fuller, *Tanks in the Great War, 1914–1918* (John Murray, London) 1920.

J.F.C. Fuller, *Memoirs of an Unconventional Soldier* (Ivor Nicholson and Watson, London) 1936.

J.F.C. Fuller, *Armoured Warfare, an Annotated Edition of Fifteen Lectures on Operations between Mechanized Forces* (Spottiswoode, London) 1943.

M. Gilbert, *Winston S. Churchill, Vol. III, 1914–1916* (Heinemann, London) 1971.

H. Gordon, *The War Office* (Putnam, London) 1935.

K. Grieves, *Sir Eric Geddes: Business and Government in War and Peace* (Manchester University Press, Manchester and New York) 1989.

P. Griffith, *Forward into Battle: Battle Tactics from Waterloo To Vietnam* (Antony Bird, Chichester) 1981.

P. Griffith, *Battle Tactics of the Western Front: the British Army's Art of Attack 1916–18* (Yale University Press, New Haven and London) 1994.

H. Guderian, *Achtung Panzer!* (Arms and Armour, London) 1992.

J.P. Harris and F.H. Toase (eds), *Armoured Warfare* (Batsford, London) 1990.

A.D. Harvey, *Collision Of Empires* (Hambledon, London) 1992.

R. Holmes, *The Little Field-Marshal: Sir John French* (Jonathan Cape, London) 1981.

A. Horne, *To Lose A Battle: France 1940* (Macmillan, London) 1969.

H.C. Johnson, *Breakthrough!: Tactics, Technology and the Search for Victory on the Western Front in World War I* (Presidio, Novato, California) 1994.

J.R. Kennedy, *This Our Army* (Hutchinson, London) 1935.

M. Kettle, *The Road to Intervention, March to November 1918* (Routledge, London) 1988.

M. Kettle, *Churchill And The Archangel Fiasco, November 1918–July 1919* (Routledge, London) 1992.

J. Kipp, K. Schulz *et al.*, *Historical Analysis of the Use of Mobile Forces by Russia and the USSR* (Centre For Strategic Technology, Texas A and M University, Texas) 1985.

R.H. Larson, *The British Army and the Theory of Armoured Warfare, 1918–1940* (University of Delaware, Newark) 1984.

R. Lewin, *Man of Armour, a Study of Lieutenant General Vyvyan Pope CBE, DSO, MC* (Leo Cooper, London) 1976.

B.H. Liddell Hart, *Paris or the Future of War* (Kegan Paul, Trench, Trubner, London) 1925.

B.H. Liddell Hart, *The Remaking of Modern Armies* (John Murray, London) 1927.

B.H. Liddell Hart, *When Britain Goes to War: Adaptability and Mobility* (Faber, London) 1935.

B.H. Liddell Hart, *Europe in Arms* (Faber and Faber, London) 1937.

B.H. Liddell Hart, *The Tanks* (2 Vols) (Cassell, London) 1959.

B.H. Liddell Hart, *Memoirs* (2 Vols) (Cassell, London) 1965.

D. Lloyd George, *The War Memoirs of David Lloyd George* (Odhams, London) n.d.

J. Luvaas, *The Education of an Army: British Military Thought 1815–1940* (Chicago University Press, Chicago) 1964.

K. Macksey, *Armoured Crusader: a Biography Of Major-General Sir Percy Hobart* (Hutchinson, London) 1968.

K. Macksey, *The Tank Pioneers* (Jane's, London) 1981.

J.A.R. Marriot, *Modern England 1885–1945* (Methuen, London) 1948.

G. Martel, *In the Wake of the Tank: the First Fifteen Years of Mechanization in the British Army* (Sifton Praed, London) 1931.

G. Martel, *Our Armoured Forces* (Faber and Faber, London) 1945.

G. Martel, *An Outspoken Soldier: His Views and Memoirs* (Sifton Praed, London) 1949.

F. Maurice, *The Last Four Months: How the War Was Won* (Little Brown, Boston) 1919.

J. Mearsheimer, *Liddell Hart and the Weight Of History* (Cornell, Ithaca) 1988.

F.W. von Mellenthin, *Panzer Battles* (Oklahoma, London) 1955.

F. Mitchell, *Tank Warfare: the Story of the Tanks in the Great War* (Thomas Nelson, London) n.d.

R. Neillands, *The Desert Rats: 7th Armoured Division 1940–1945* (Weidenfeld and Nicolson, London) 1991.

R.M. Ogorkiewicz, *Armour* (Stevens and Sons, London) 1960.

R.M. Ogorkiewicz, *The Technology of Tanks* (2 Vols) (Jane's, London) 1991.

G.C. Peden, *British Rearmament and the Treasury 1932–39* (Scottish Academic Press, Edinburgh) 1979.

J. Piekalkiewicz, *The Cavalry of World War II* (Jane's, London) 1979.

F. Pile, *Ack-Ack: Britain's Defence against Air Attack during the Second World War* (Harrap, London) 1949.

R. Prior and T. Wilson, *Command on the Western Front: the Military Career of Sir Henry Rawlinson 1914–18* (Blackwell, Oxford) 1992.

B. Rawling, *Surviving Trench Warfare: Technology and the Canadian Corps, 1914–1918* (University of Toronto, Toronto) 1992.

B.H. Reid, *J.F.C. Fuller, Military Thinker* (Macmillan, London) 1987.

G. Ridley, *Bend'Or, Duke of Westminster* (Robin Clark, London) 1985.

S. Roskill, *Hankey, Man of Secrets* (3 Vols) (Collins, London) 1974.

G.M. Ross, *The Business of Tanks 1933 to 1945* (Arthur H. Stockwell, Ilfracombe) 1976.

C.R. Samson, *Fights and Flights* (Ernest Benn, London) 1930.

D. Smith, *H.G. Wells: Desperately Mortal* (Yale University Press, New Haven) 1986.

A.J. Smithers, *Cambrai: the First Great Tank Battle 1917* (Leo Cooper, London) 1992.

A. Stern, *Tanks 1914–1918: the Logbook of a Pioneer* (Hodder and Stoughton, London) 1919.

H. Strachan, *European Armies and the Conduct Of War* (Allen and Unwin, London) 1983.

M. Sueter, *The Evolution of the Tank* (Hutchinson, London) 1937.

E. Swinton, *Eyewitness* (Hodder and Stoughton, London) 1932.

E. Swinton, *Over My Shoulder* (George Ronald, Oxford) 1951.

A.J.P. Taylor, *English History 1914–1945* (Clarendon Press, Oxford) 1965.

E. Tennyson D'Eyncourt, *A Shipbuilder's Yarn* (Hutchinson, London) 1948.

J. Terraine, *Douglas Haig: the Educated Soldier* (Hutchinson, London) 1963.

J. Terraine, *To Win a War: 1918, the Year of Victory* (Sidgwick and Jackson, London) 1978.

J. Terraine, *White Heat: the New Warfare* (Sidgwick and Jackson, London) 1982.

T. Travers, *How the War Was Won: Command and Technology in the British Army on the Western Front 1917–1918* (Routledge, London) 1992.

A.J. Trythall, *"Boney" Fuller, the Intellectual General 1878–1966* (Cassell, London) 1977.

W.W. Wagar, *H.G. Wells: Journalism and Prophecy 1893–1940* (Bodley Head, London) 1964.

J. Wardrop, *Tanks Across the Desert* (Kimber, London) 1981.

W.H.L. Watson, *A Company of Tanks* (Blackwood, Edinburgh) 1920.

H.G. Wells, *The Complete Short Stories of H.G. Wells* (Ernest Benn, London) 1966.

N. and J. Wells, *The Time Traveller, the Life of H.G. Wells* (Weidenfeld and Nicolson, London) 1973.

C. and A. Williams-Ellis, *The Tank Corps* (Country Life, London) 1919.

D.E. Wilson, *Treat Em Rough: the Birth of American Armor, 1917–20* (Presidio, Novato, California) 1989.

D. Winter, *Haig's Command: a Reassessment* (Viking, London) 1991.

H. Winton, *To Change an Army: General Sir John Burnett-Stuart and British Armoured Doctrine, 1927–1938* (Brassey's, London) 1988.

D.R. Woodward, *Lloyd George and the Generals* (University of Delaware Press, Newark) 1983.

Articles in periodicals

D.J. Childs, "Were the Tank Problems of 1918 'as Much Mental as Mechanical'?", *The Bulletin of the Military History Society*, Vol. 44 (1994).

R.J. Collins, "The Experimental Mechanical Force", *Journal of the Royal Artillery*, Vol. 55 (1928).

D. Fletcher, "'A New System of Heavy Goods Transport', the Extraordinary Story of B.J. Diplock", *The Vintage Commercial Vehicle Magazine*, Vol. 5 (1989).

J.F.C. Fuller, "The Application of Recent Developments in Mechanics and other Scientific Knowledge to Preparations and training for Future War on Land", Gold Medal (Military) Prize Essay for 1919, *RUSI Journal*, Vol. 65.

J.F.C. Fuller, "The Development of Sea Warfare on Land and Its Influence on Future Naval Operations", lecture to the RUSI, Wednesday 11 February 1920, *RUSI Journal*, Vol. 65.

J.P. Harris, "The British General Staff and the Coming of War 1933–39", *Bulletin Of The Institute Of Historical Research*, Vol. 59 (1986).

J.P. Harris, "Two War Ministers: a Reassessment of Duff Cooper and Hore-Belisha", *War and Society*, Vol. 6 (1988).

J.P. Harris, "British Armour and Rearmament in the 1930s", *Journal of Strategic Studies*, Vol. 11 (1988).

J.P. Harris, "British Military Intelligence and the Rise of the German Mechanized Forces 1927–1940", *Intelligence and National Security*, Vol. 6 (1991).

L.C. Jackson, "Possibilities of the Next War", lecture to the RUSI, Wednesday 17 December 1919, *RUSI Journal*, Vol. 65.

B.H. Liddell Hart, "The Development of the New Model Army: Suggestions on a Progressive but Gradual Mechanicalisation", *Army Quarterly*, Vol. 9 (1924).

B.H. Liddell Hart, "Armoured Forces in 1928", *RUSI Journal*, Vol. 73.

B.H. Liddell Hart, "Seven Years: the Regime of Field Marshal Lord Milne", *The English Review*, Vol. 56 (1933).

B.H. Reid, "J.F.C. Fuller's Theory of Mechanized Warfare", *Journal Of Strategic Studies*, Vol. 1 (1978).

B.H. Reid, "The Attack by Illumination: the Strange Case of Canal Defence Lights", *RUSI Journal*, Vol. 128 (1983).

B.H. Reid, "The Tank and Visions of Future War", *History Today*, Vol. 31, December 1987.

T. Travers, "Technology, Tactics and Morale", *Journal of Modern History*, Vol. 51 (1979).

T. Travers, "Could the Tanks of 1918 Have Been War-Winners for the British Expeditionary Force?", *Journal Of Contemporary History*, Vol. 27 (1992).

Index